HARUKI MURAKAMI AND THE MUSIC OF WORDS

Jay Rubin is emeritus professor of Japanese Literature at Harvard University. He is the author of *Injurious to Public Morals: Writers and the Meiji State* and *Making Sense of Japanese*, and he edited *Modern Japanese Writers* for the Scribner Writers Series. He has translated into English two novels by the Japanese writer Sōseki Natsume, and also Haruki Murakami's *Norwegian Wood*, *The Wind-up Bird Chronicle*, *after the quake*, *After Dark* and Books 1 and 2 of *1Q84*.

JAY RUBIN

Haruki Murakami and the Music of Words

VINTAGE BOOKS
London

by Vintage 2012

10 9

Copyright © Jay Rubin 2002

asserted his right under the Copyright, Designs
Act 1988 to be identified as the author of this work

piece photograph of Haruki Murakami © Marion Ettlinger.
pts from Raymond Carver's poem 'The Projectile' reprinted by
mission of Tess Gallagher. © Raymond Carver 1986, 1987, 1988;
Tess Gallagher 1989, 2002. Chapter 1 of Haruki Murakami's novel
Hear the Wind Sing, translated by Alfred Birnbaum, reprinted by
permission of Kodansha International Ltd. English translation ©
Kodansha International Ltd, 1987. Drawings of Notebook with pen
and of Haruki Murakami, by Mizumaru Anzai, reproduced from *Sō
da, Murakami-san ni kiite miyō* by permission of Asahi Shinbun sha.
© Mizumaru Anzai 2000.

First published in Great Britain by The Harvill Press in 2002

First published by Vintage in 2005

Vintage
Random House, 20 Vauxhall Bridge Road,
London SW1V 2SA

www.vintage-books.co.uk

Addresses for companies within The Random House Group Limited
can be found at: www.randomhouse.co.uk/offices.htm

The Random House Group Limited Reg. No. 954009

A CIP catalogue record for this book
is available from the British Library

ISBN 9780099455448

The Random House Group Limited supports The Forest Stewardship
Council (FSC®), the leading international forest certification organisation.
Our books carrying the FSC label are printed on FSC® certified paper.
FSC is the only forest certification scheme endorsed by the leading
environmental organisations, including Greenpeace. Our
paper procurement policy can be found at
www.randomhouse.co.uk/environment

MIX
Paper from
responsible sources
FSC® C016897

Printed and bound in Great Britain by Clays Ltd, St Ives PLC

Contents

Acknowledgements

The research for this book was assisted initially by a grant from the Joint Committee on Japanese Studies of the Social Science Research Council and the American Council of Learned Societies with funds provided by the National Endowment for the Humanities. I would like to thank Haruki and Yōko Murakami for agreeing to be interviewed despite misgivings about such an intrusive project. *Shinchō* editor Riki Suzuki was generous with his time and comments, and Ted Goossen was especially helpful. Ian Pindar wrestled bravely with questions of style and structure. Additional thanks go to Rakuko Rubin, Deborah Bluestein, Eizō Matsumura, Tess Gallagher, Hiromi Hashimoto, Alfred Birnbaum, Elmer Luke, Kenzaburō Ōe, Charles Inouye, Hosea Hirata, Miryam Sas, Beatrice and Paul Reiss, Howard Hibbett, Edwin Cranston, Paul Warham, Emi Shimokawa, Glynne Walley, Matthew Strecher, Kozo Yamamura, Jun Kim, Rebecca Suter and Yuki Katsura. Where matters of literary interpretation are concerned, however, I have only myself to blame.

Readme

I might as well admit it from the start: I'm a Haruki Murakami fan. I knew I would like the man himself when I read his work, and I've written this book for other fans who feel a similar kinship with him and would like to know more about his life and art, but who are prevented from doing so by the barrier of the Japanese language.

I try to provide answers to the kinds of questions I have received from readers in the years since I started translating Murakami's works. Readers' comments on the Internet have been another source of inspiration. This approach may call into question my scholarly objectivity, but I like to think that my academic experience has helped me to explain to myself and others what I feel Murakami is all about, and that includes pointing out where I think he has taken some wrong turns. It also requires me occasionally to revise quoted passages from the translated works according to my own interpretation. I do this not to cause anxiety but to provide readers with an opportunity to see just how provisional the translation of literature – especially contemporary literature – can be, as illustrated in Appendix A. Mainly, though, what I want to do here is to share the excitement I have experienced in reading and translating Murakami's novels and stories and learning more about how they came to be written. Please try to bear with me if I seem to be having too much fun.

Pintac ni derewohs, amat

JAY RUBIN

Pronunciation and Name Order

Anyone familiar with Hiroshima, Honda, Ichiro, Mitsubishi, Nagasaki, Nissan, sushi, Tokyo, Toyota, tsunami, and Yoko Ono, can safely pronounce Japanese words the way they look. Three-syllable names like "Haruki" have a slight stress on the first syllable (HA-ru-kee, rather than ha-RU-kee), but don't worry, he's used to hearing it the other way.

Readers may be surprised to see long marks (macrons) over some vowels that do not appear in the translated works: "Tōru" instead of "Toru". These are for readers familiar with the Japanese language, in which the length of a syllable changes the meaning of a word; the general reader can ignore them. Yōko Ono and Ichirō, from the above list, seem to get along fine without them.

Japanese names are given in the Western order – surname last – everywhere in the book, with one exception: in citations of Japanese-language sources and of scholarly English-language sources in the Notes and Bibliography the original Japanese order is used. Again, this is a matter of concern only to readers of Japanese.

In Memoriam

Milton Rubin (1909–63)
Frances Rubin (1913–93)
Ippei Sakai (1909–95)
Masako Sakai (1917–92)

1

Prelude

Oh Danny Boy, the pipes the pipes are calling
From glen to glen and down the mountainside.
The summer's gone, and all the roses falling,
'Tis you, 'tis you must go and I must bide.
But come ye back when summer's in the meadow,
Or when the valley's hushed and white with snow,
It's I'll be here in sunshine or in shadow,
Oh Danny Boy, oh Danny Boy, I love you so!

Awash in the sentiment of a traditional Irish melody, the "inner" hero of *Hard-boiled Wonderland and the End of the World* (*Sekai no owari to hādoboirudo wandārando*, 1985) reclaims the connection to his heart through music. This sets up resonances between himself and the hero of the "outer" world, his conscious self, in one of the most moving passages in Haruki Murakami's richly imaginative novel.[1]

Murakami is a lover of music – music of all kinds: jazz, classical, folk, rock. It occupies a central position in his life and work. The title of his first novel commands the reader to *Hear the Wind Sing* (*Kaze no uta o kike*, 1979), and one magazine went so far as to publish a discography of all the music mentioned in his writing, a project later expanded into a substantial book.[2] Murakami owned a jazz bar for seven years and he continues to add to his collection of more than 10,000 records. He is constantly going to concerts or listening to recorded music. It is a wonder that he did not become a musician himself – though, in a way, he did. Rhythm is perhaps the most important element of his prose. He enjoys the music of words, and he senses an affinity between his stylistic rhythms and the beat of jazz, as he noted in a talk at the University of California in Berkeley:

> My style boils down to this: First of all, I never put more meaning into a sentence than is absolutely necessary. Second, the sentences have to have rhythm. This is something I learned from music, especially jazz. In jazz, great rhythm is what makes great improvising possible. It's all in the footwork. To maintain that rhythm, there must be no extra weight. This doesn't mean that there should be no weight at all – just no weight that isn't absolutely necessary. You have to cut out the fat.[3]

For Murakami, music is the best means of entry into the deep recesses of the unconscious, that timeless other world within our psyche. There, at the core of the self, lies the story of who each of us is: a fragmented narrative that we can only know through images. Dreams are one important way to come into contact with these images, but often they surface unpredictably in our waking lives, are briefly apprehended by the conscious mind, then return just as suddenly to where they came from.

The novelist tells stories in an attempt to bring out the narrative within; and through some kind of irrational process these stories send reverberations to the stories inside each reader. It is a wonderful process, as subtle as déjà vu, and just as indefinable. We see it played out in full in *Hard-boiled Wonderland and the End of the World* when tiny echoes from the protagonist's core "inner" story ("The

End of the World") manage to reach the hard-boiled "outer" world of his consciousness.

Not surprisingly in a literature so full of music and storytelling, ears play an important role. Murakami's characters take extraordinarily good care of their ears. They clean them almost obsessively so as to keep in tune with the unpredictable, shifting music of life. The incredibly beautiful ears of one character, the nameless girlfriend in *A Wild Sheep Chase* (*Hitsuji o meguru bōken*, 1982) – given the name "Kiki" ("Listening") in that novel's sequel, *Dance Dance Dance* (*Dansu dansu dansu*, 1988) – turn out to have almost supernatural powers. And ears are important for Murakami's narrators because they spend a lot of time listening to stories.

In his fifth novel, *Norwegian Wood* (*Noruwei no mori*, 1987), for example, there is a moment when the narrator-hero Tōru remarks "It felt like an awfully long day"[4] – which rings true for a simple reason. This day has occupied more than 70 pages of the novel, in the course of which we have not only followed Tōru's adventures but also listened to a long story. The wrinkled old woman Reiko (she is all of 39 years old) has been telling Tōru (and us) the story of her life: her youthful ambition of becoming a concert pianist, the onset of the mental illness that shattered those dreams, her recovery through marriage, the birth of a daughter, the beginning of a new musical career as a piano teacher, but then her encounter with a malevolent pupil who threatens to destroy her equilibrium.

Just as this new element enters the story, however, Reiko realizes how late it is and leaves Tōru and the reader hanging on. Tōru compliments her as a Scheherazade, and we look forward to the continuation of her tale, which comes in Volume 2 of the original edition. It is only then that we learn about Reiko's seduction by her new pupil, a beautiful young lesbian, the shattering of her precariously re-established life, and her descent into the madness that has brought her to the sanatorium where she tells her tale to Tōru. It is a compelling, heartbreaking story and we have been hanging on every word, thanks in part to the active involvement of the narrator, who speaks up at crucial moments to ask Reiko the kind of questions we would ask if we could be there. His timing and intelligence are remarkable. He is just as curious, just as sensitive, just as intelligent and sympathetic as *we* are!

Murakami knows how stories are told – and heard. He is sensitive to the rhythms of exchange between teller and listener, and is conscious enough of the mechanics of this process to recreate it – which he often does – in a fictional setting. In 1985 he even published an entire volume of short stories purporting to be records of real-life experiences told to him by friends and acquaintances; he later confessed they were all entirely fictional.[5] Another Murakami narrator describes the storytelling process in Book Three of *The Wind-up Bird Chronicle* (*Nejimakidori kuronikuru*, 1994–95), a huge novel crammed with stories: "I discovered that she [his dinner companion] was an extremely accomplished listener. She was quick on the uptake, and she knew how to direct the flow of the story by means of skilful questions and responses."[6]

She may be a good listener, but she is primarily of interest to the reader for the story she is telling, thereby allowing the narrator to convey to us events far beyond the limits of his experience. Murakami's narrators are usually passive in their own lives, but as listeners they are 100 per cent active. This is how the narrator describes himself in the opening pages of *Pinball, 1973* (*1973-nen no pinbōru*, 1980):

I used to have a pathological fondness for listening to stories of places I had never known or seen.

At one time, some ten years ago, I used to go around collaring anybody I could find and listening to stories of where they were born or the places they grew up. Maybe it was a time when the type of person was in short supply who would take the initiative to listen to other people's stories, because everybody – just everybody – would tell me theirs with kindness and enthusiasm. Complete strangers would hear about me and seek me out to tell me their stories.

They would tell me all kinds of stories as if they were throwing rocks into a dry well, and when they were finished, every one of them would go home satisfied . . . I listened to their stories with all the seriousness I could muster.[7]

If not exactly a therapist, the narrator provides a gently humorous, reassuring voice and a sympathetic ear. "Listening to a lot of other people's stories is very healing for me," Murakami told the psychologist Hayao Kawai. "Yes, yes," Kawai replied, "that's what *we* do, we heal and are ourselves healed."[8] The "therapeutic" tone of Murakami's early works undoubtedly accounted for part of his immediate success. Narrated by an understanding 29-year-old explaining how he has survived his twenties, the early novels provide a kind of guidebook for readers about to embark on that frightening decade themselves, between leaving the stability of college or university and finding a way of life suited to their individual needs.

Murakami is a very popular writer – initially in Japan, of course, although his works have now been translated into at least 43 languages in as many countries (see Bibliography). His books sell especially well in other East Asian countries, where his cool, detached, often comical narrator seems to offer an alternative to life lived in the grim Confucian envelope of State and Family. In Taiwan, for example, in November 2000, one bookstore had a special Murakami section with almost 20 translated titles; a two-day feature story on Murakami in one newspaper called him the most important Japanese novelist since the Meiji giant Sōseki Natsume, and suggested that his face might one day grace a Japanese banknote as Sōseki's did for 20 years; and no fewer than five different translations of *Norwegian Wood* were available from the various Chinese markets. Korea leads all foreign countries for Murakami translations, with almost instantaneous translation of nearly everything, including some of the light essays and travel writing that are unlikely ever to make it into English. Ironically for a writer who has revealed himself to be highly sensitive to the horrors unleashed on the Asian continent by Japan's invading forces in the years before he was born, Murakami would find his success in East Asia described in terms redolent of military victory: "Almost as if it were deliberately retracing the itinerary of the imperial armies, Murakami's fiction has created dominions of fans in Taiwan, Korea, mainland China, Hong Kong, Malaysia, and Singapore, winning 'hearts and minds' with an ease that the architects of the Greater East Asian Co-Prosperity Sphere would have marveled at."[9]

For the past several years each October, it has become an annual ritual of the journalistic community in Japan to gear up in anticipation of the announcement of the Nobel Prize for literature, with endless rankings of Murakami against the world's other likely awardees, and educated guesses (some, perhaps, not so educated) regarding his chances in light of the political climate or the global economic situation. Whenever Murakami wins an international award that other Nobel recipients received before winning their Nobels (the Franz Kafka Award in 2006, the Jerusalem Prize in 2009), the buzz goes out that this is moving him one step closer to the big one. Critics and academics are recruited to write sage commentary ready for release the day after the announcement, and reporters wanting even fresher reactions arrange to place calls (both domestic and international) the second the word goes out – which, so far, it has not done, with a huge let-down whenever the winner is not Haruki Murakami.

In Japan, Murakami's eight-volume *Complete Works* appeared as early as 1990, marking the first decade of a writer who began to be published at the age of 30. Seven more volumes, covering the years 1990–2000, were added to the *Complete Works* in 2002–03 but the publication of one of Murakami's longest novels, *Kafka on the Shore* (2002) rendered the set anything but "complete". *Kafka* has since been followed by a volume of short stories, the short novel *After Dark* (2004), and the three-volume behemoth *1Q84* (2009–10). Murakami himself is on the verge of turning 64 (in January 2013), but his readers still need him and feed him, and he keeps writing for them and producing numerous translations from the English in his "spare" time.

Many commentators, most of them far senior to Murakami's main readership, have taken his popularity as a sign that there is something wrong, not only with Murakami's writing but with all of contemporary Japanese literature. Lamenting the current state of literature in Japan, Donald Keene, dean of Japanese literary studies in the West, has said (in reference to Kenzaburō Ōe's[10] 1994 receipt of the Nobel Prize for his "solid" novels): "If you go to a bookstore here, unless it is a very big bookstore, you won't find a real solid literary work. Authors today are writing for the passing tastes of a young audience."[11]

One especially outspoken critic of Murakami was the ever-argumentative Masao Miyoshi, who chimed in with Keene: "Ōe is too difficult, [Japanese readers] complain. Their fascination has been with vacuous manufacturers of disposable entertainment, including the 'new voices of Japan', like Haruki Murakami and Banana Yoshimoto."[12] Like Yukio Mishima,[13] said Miyoshi, Murakami custom-tailors his goods to his readers abroad. Where "Mishima displayed an exotic Japan, its nationalist side", Murakami exhibits "an exotic Japan, its international version"; he is "pre-occupied with Japan, or, to put it more precisely, with what [he] imagine[s] the foreign buyers like to see in it".

8

Miyoshi regards Murakami as a cynical entrepreneur who never wrote a word out of any such old-fashioned motives as inspiration or inner impulse. To frighten off skittish academics who might be tempted to take Murakami seriously, he warns, "only a very few would be silly enough to get interested in deep reading".[14]

"The 1963/1982 Girl from Ipanema"

All right, then, let's get silly, but let's begin by looking at one of Murakami's most musical stories, "The 1963/1982 Girl from Ipanema" ("1963/1982-nen no Ipanema-musume", 1982).[15]

A mere six pages long, the story opens with a few lines from the song lyrics, in which a "tall and tan and young and lovely" girl in a bathing suit walks down the beach at Ipanema while some unnamed "I" sings of his unrequited love for her. This "I" then blends in seamlessly with Murakami's "I" narrator, who remarks:

> This was how the girl from Ipanema looked at the sea back then, in 1963. And that's how she keeps looking at the sea now, in 1982. She hasn't aged. Sealed in her image, she drifts through the ocean of time. If she had continued to age, she'd probably be close to 40 by now . . . Inside my record, of course, she hasn't grown any older . . . I put the record on the turntable, set the needle in the groove, and there she is.

The tune reminds the narrator not only of the girl herself but of the corridor in his high school, which "was always dark. And it was almost always silent. In my memory at least." He is not sure why the song reminds him of the corridor, since the two have nothing to do with each other. "I wonder what kind of pebbles the 1963 Girl from Ipanema threw into the well of my consciousness."

Just as mysterious as the connection between the corridor and the girl in the song is the narrator's next mental association, but Murakami knows that once you start rooting about in your memory, it's hard to predict what will come out:

When I think of my high school's corridor, I think of mixed salads: lettuce, tomatoes, cucumbers, green peppers, asparagus, onion rings, and pink Thousand Island dressing. Not that there was a salad shop at the end of the corridor. No, there was just a door, and beyond that door a drab 25-metre pool.

Salads in turn remind him of a girl he knew back then. "Now, this connection is a logical one, because all this girl ever ate was salads," and when he was with her, he ate a lot of salads too. He gives an example of the salad–filled conversations he and she used to have:

"How about that (munch munch) English report (munch munch)? Finished it yet?"
"Not quite (munch munch). Still gotta (munch munch) do some reading."

Before he knows it, "I" is inside the "metaphysical" scene conjured up by the song. He sits under a beach umbrella, drinking beer from a can, as the unchanged 1963/1982 girl from Ipanema walks by. He offers her a beer, and after a moment's hesitation, she accepts, joining him under the umbrella. She gulps down half her beer, then begins to stare at the hole in the can. "It's just an ordinary can of beer with an ordinary hole, but the way she stares at the opening, it seems to take on a special significance – as if the entire world were going to slip inside," a suggestion by Murakami that the "entire world" is nothing but an accumulation of memories, something more metaphysical than physical.

10

He remarks that she has not aged at all, to which she responds, "Of course not. I'm a metaphysical girl." She insists that the endless walking on the hot sands of Ipanema does not burn the soles of her feet because they are "completely metaphysical," and when he touches one of her cool, metaphysical soles, he realizes that time itself has come to a stop. "Whenever I think of you, I think of the corridor in my high school," he decides to tell her. "I wonder why." She responds to this with a shocking display of philosophical eloquence:

"The human essence lies in complexity. The objects of scientific investigation lie not in the object, you know, but in the subject contained within the human body. In any case, you must live. Live! Live! Live! That's all. The most important thing is to go on living. That's all I can say. Really, that's all. I'm just a girl with metaphysical soles."

Their timeless time together ends as she continues walking along the beach. Every once in a while, though, he tells us, he sees her on the Tokyo subway, and they share a smile. The story ends like this:

We haven't spoken since that day on the beach, but I can tell there is some sort of connection linking our hearts. I'm not sure just what the connection is. The link is probably in a strange place in a far-off world. I try to imagine that link – a link in my consciousness spread out in silence across a dark corridor down which no one comes.

When I think about it like this, all kinds of happenings, all kinds of things, begin to fill me with nostalgia, bit by bit. Somewhere in there, I'm sure, is the link joining me with myself. Someday, too, I'm sure, I'll meet myself in a strange place in a far-off world. And if I have anything to say about it, I'd like that place to be a warm one. And if I've got a few cold

11

beers there as well, who could ask for anything more? In that place, I am myself and myself is me. Subject is object and object is subject. All gaps gone. A perfect union. There must be a strange place like this somewhere in the world.

*

The 1963/1982 Girl from Ipanema continues to walk along the hot beach. And she'll continue to walk without resting until the last record wears out.

In this brief, songlike, funny story, we encounter themes of loss and ageing, memory and music, time and timelessness, reality and the wells of the unconscious, and a melancholy longing for a special time and place when – "all gaps gone" – we come fully in touch with others and ourselves. This, as we shall see, is vintage Murakami.

2

The Birth of Boku

Kyoto was Japan's capital for over a thousand years (794–1868); in fact, the downtown streets are still laid out according to the original eighth-century plan, and the city remains today the site of the ancient palace and of numerous shrines and temples that comprise the heart of the country's religious life. Kyoto draws millions of tourists in search of the kind of ancient roots that seem to have been obliterated from Japan's contemporary capital, Tokyo.

Haruki Murakami was born in this venerable city on 12 January 1949, and spent his early years in the Kyoto-Osaka-Kobe (i.e. "Kansai") area with its ancient cultural, political, and mercantile traditions. Still a toddler when the family moved to the Osaka suburb of Nishinomiya, he grew up speaking the region's dialect and was conditioned to distrust anyone whose speech lacked its distinctive locutions and soft accents.[16]

One thinks of Murakami now as so thoroughly cosmopolitan as to be only marginally Japanese, but this meant overcoming strong regional loyalties, whether it was food (light, sweetish tastes rather than dishes heavy with soy sauce) or universities (Kyoto University being the only acceptable institution) or even baseball players (the local boy, Murayama, was the only pitcher worth thinking about). Murakami's father, Chiaki, was the son of a Kyoto Buddhist priest, and was himself a priest for some years in

13

the old family's temple,[17] but none of this veneration for antiquity rubbed off on Murakami, who practises neither Buddhism nor any other religion. His mother, Miyuki, was the daughter of an Osaka merchant, another family tradition that seems not to have taken hold.

Chiaki and Miyuki were high-school teachers of Japanese Language and Literature when they met and, although his mother became a full-time housewife when she married, the young Haruki would often hear his parents discussing eighth-century poetry or medieval war tales at the dinner table. He was an only child, and Murakami suggests this might explain his tendency towards introversion. One of his earliest memories is of falling into a stream and being swept towards a gaping culvert, a terrifying experience he recreated in Chapter 9 of Book One of *The Wind-up Bird Chronicle*, "Culverts and an Absolute Insufficiency of Electricity . . .".[18]

Murakami's parents tended to be politically liberal and, although they could be strict with him, overall they allowed him great freedom.[19] He recalls his peaceful suburban boyhood as a time of rambling in the hills and swimming with friends at a nearby beach (the shoreline has since been filled in and developed, as sentimentally recorded in the final chapter of *A Wild Sheep Chase*). He was permitted to buy books on credit at the local bookstore, as long as he avoided comic books or trashy weekly magazines.

Haruki became a voracious reader, as his parents no doubt wished him to be, but their progressive policy on books may have backfired. After the family moved to the nearby city of Ashiya (yet another suburban neighbourhood of fenced homes) when Haruki was twelve, they subscribed to two libraries of world literature, volumes of which would arrive at the local bookstore every month, and Haruki spent his early teens devouring them. Chiaki may have hoped that by helping Haruki with his Japanese Language studies each Sunday morning he would encourage his son to develop an interest in the Japanese classics, but Haruki preferred Stendhal, and went on to develop a taste for Tolstoy and especially Dostoevsky.

In recent years he has begun to read Japanese literature – though only modern fiction, not the classics. In a free-ranging 1985 discussion with the Faulkneresque novelist Kenji Nakagami (1946–92), it became obvious that Murakami had read few Japanese writers besides Nakagami himself, and that old comic master of sensuality, Jun'ichirō Tanizaki (1886–1965).[20] Yukio Mishima he actively disliked.[21] "Not once, throughout my formative years," he has said, "did I have the experience of being deeply moved by a Japanese novel."[22]

Of his middle-school years, in the city of Ashiya, Murakami has written that all he remembers is being beaten by his teachers. He didn't like them and they didn't like him because he wouldn't study – a habit he took with him to Kobe High School. He would play Mahjongg (enthusiastically, but badly) almost every day, fool around with girls, spend hours in jazz cafés and cinemas, smoke, skip school, read novels during class, and so forth, but his grades were never terrible.[23]

Given early experiences like this, Haruki Murakami could have remained just another unremarkable member of the herd. He was a nice boy from a quiet suburb that imparted no particular stresses to his life.[24] He may have been slightly introverted and he loved reading, but he was no hermit; he had no notable hobbies or vices; no obsessions or special areas of expertise; no dysfunctional family background to deal with; no personal crises or traumas; no problems of extreme wealth or deprivation; no handicaps or talents. In other words, he had none of the early life-warping experiences that seem to propel certain sensitive souls towards writing as a form of therapy for themselves or their generation. Somewhere along the way, though, he became a stubborn individualist. He has consistently avoided groups in a country where the group is the norm. Even writers have their select groups in Japan, but Murakami has never been a member.

In Kobe High, where he wrote for the school newspaper, Murakami's reading branched out to the likes of hard-boiled detective novelists Ross MacDonald, Ed McBain, and Raymond Chandler, then Truman Capote, F. Scott Fitzgerald, and Kurt Vonnegut. An international trading capital, Kobe had many bookstores with foreign residents' second-hand paperbacks, literature in the original available at half the price of the Japanese translations. Haruki was hooked. "What first attracted me to American paperbacks was the discovery that I could read books written in a foreign language," he has said. "It was such a tremendously new experience for me to be able to understand and be moved by literature written in an acquired language."[25]

That language could hardly have been anything other than English. Despite his early interest in French and Russian literature, Haruki had begun life during the American occupation of his country and had grown up in an increasingly affluent Japan that still admired America for its wealth and culture. He hungered after the "American trad" look of John and Robert Kennedy, and went to see the movie *Harper* more than ten times to admire the West Coast casual-traditional style of Paul Newman, who really knew how to wear a pair of sunglasses.[26] As absorbed as he was by English and American books, he had no patience for systematic language study and never got more than mediocre grades in English. "My teachers would be shocked to learn I do so much translation work now," he has said.[27]

American music was another source of attraction, first rock 'n' roll, which he listened to by the hour on the radio: Elvis Presley, Rick Nelson, The Beach Boys.[28] Then, after hearing Art Blakey and the Jazz Messengers at a live concert in 1964, the 15-year-old Haruki would often skip lunch to save money for jazz records.

His encyclopaedic knowledge of jazz and other facets of American popular culture are immediately apparent in his work, though he does not invest these references with weighty symbolic significance. Having spent his teenage years in Kobe, with its many foreign residents, the Occupation over and Japan drawing abreast of the United States, he took for granted what most Japanese still found exotic. A Polaroid camera is a symbol of Western decadence for Jun'ichirō Tanizaki; America is an obsessive nightmare for writer Akiyuki Nosaka (b.1930),[29] who lived through the bombing of his native Kobe and pimped for prostitutes servicing American soldiers; even the novelist Ryū Murakami (b.1952), who is three years younger than Haruki but grew up near American military bases, is regarded as a last vestige of the Occupation mentality.[30]

In contrast, Murakami has been called the first writer completely at home with the elements of American popular culture that permeate present-day Japan. He has also been seen as the first genuinely "post-post-war writer", the first to cast off the "dank, heavy atmosphere" of the post-war period and to capture in literature the new Americanized mood of lightness.[31] When readers of his generation found him quoting Beach Boys lyrics, they bonded with him instantly: he was writing about their world, not something exotic or foreign.[32] If Murakami's copious pop references represent anything, it is his entire generation's rejection of their parents' culture.

Fiction was not all that Murakami read with interest in high school. Another multi-volume set he claims to have read and re-read at least 20 times was an unabridged world history published by the Chūō Kōron company.[33] Although Murakami's works have been dismissed by critics as apolitical and ahistorical, most of them are set in carefully defined periods and, taken in aggregate, can be read as a psychological history of post-post-war Japan: from the heat of the student movement in the 1960s to the "Big Chill" of the 1970s; the emphasis on moneymaking in the 1980s; and (perhaps) a re-emergence of idealism in the 1990s. *The Wind-up Bird Chronicle* is set precisely in the mid-1980s, but it probes deeply into the pre-war years for the roots of Japan's modern malaise. The short story collection *after the quake* (*Kami no kodomotachi wa mina odoru*, 2000) is focused even more precisely, with all six stories set in February 1995 between the great Osaka-Kobe earthquake of January and the Tokyo subway gas attack in March.

One abiding area of historical interest for Murakami seems to have been inspired by his father. Murakami is generally an easy interviewee, but he avoids talking about living individuals who might be hurt by his comments, and is especially reluctant to talk about his father. (One encounters numerous uncles in his works, but rarely fathers.) However, Ian Buruma in his insightful *New Yorker* profile did manage to overcome some of this resistance:

> Before the war, [Murakami's] father was a promising student
> at Kyoto University; then he was drafted into the Army, to
> fight in China. Once, when Murakami was a child, he heard
> his father say something deeply shocking about his experi-
> ence in China. He cannot remember what it was . . . But he
> remembers being terribly distressed.[34]

As a result, Murakami has long had ambivalent feelings about China and the Chinese. These emerged in the very first short story he ever wrote, "A Slow Boat to China" ("Chūgoku-yuki no surō bōto", 1980), a delicate, strangely touching account of how the narrator came to harbour feelings of guilt towards the few Chinese people he had met. The theme would emerge again in the passages of *A Wild Sheep Chase* that touch upon Japan's violent clashes with the other peoples of Asia, and would reach their most harrowing development in the gruesome descriptions of war in *The Wind-up Bird Chronicle*.

If Murakami hated studying for exams in school, the feeling was only compounded when it came time for him to confront Japan's notorious "exam hell". A good, middle-class boy, it never occurred to him to buck the system entirely, so he sat half-heartedly for the entrance exams at several major schools of the sort that would please his parents. He chose to study Law on the assumption that he had some interest in it, but joined the high proportion of examinees who fail the first time around and become *rōnin* ("masterless samurai") preparing for entry the following year. He spent most of 1967 studying (or as he tells it, dozing) at the local Ashiya library.[35]

English was usually considered one of the most challenging areas of the entrance exams, but Haruki had no patience for the study of grammar and instead translated passages from the American thrillers he loved. However, one exam preparation book contained something that moved him in a new way: the opening passage from Truman Capote's short story "The Headless Hawk". It was, Murakami said, "my first piece of real literature after all those hard-boiled novels". He sought out a collection of Capote stories and read and re-read them.[36] This relaxed year of reading and reflection convinced him that he was far more interested in literature than law, so he took and passed the exam for the Department of Literature at Waseda University in Tokyo.

Having spoken nothing but the Kansai dialect for 18 years, Murakami was worried how he would handle standard Tokyo Japanese, but he mastered it in three days. "I'm pretty adaptable, I guess."[37]

When he first entered Waseda, he lived in a dormitory called Wakei Juku, which he would broadly caricature in *Norwegian Wood*. A private institution run by a foundation, the residence (on a wooded area high on a hill overlooking Waseda) is not affiliated to any one university but takes in students from several different schools. Murakami depicted it as comically right wing, biased in favour of students from the more elite universities, and a "horrifying" den of filth (the last being a feature that does not necessarily distinguish it from other male dormitories around the world). Foreign students of Japanese often live there, but so unappealing is Murakami's description of the place that foreigners attempting to trace his footsteps are not always given a warm reception. Whereas the protagonist of *Norwegian Wood* lives there during his first two years in Tokyo, Murakami stayed for only six months before he fled to a small apartment that allowed him the privacy he craved.

Murakami claims that, like most Japanese college students, he attended few classes. "I didn't study in high school," he has said, "but I *really* didn't study in college."[38] Instead, he spent his time in jazz clubs in the Shinjuku entertainment district or in the bars around Waseda, just down the hill from the dormitory. The campus in those days was a virtual forest of plywood political placards, which also made handy stretchers for carrying home drinking buddies too plastered to walk. Once, when a drunk Murakami was being carried up the steep concrete hillside stairway to the dorm, his makeshift stretcher cracked in two, and he whacked his head so hard against a step that he felt the pain for days.[39]

Murakami also enjoyed backpacking as a student. He fondly recalls sleeping out in the open and being offered food by kindly strangers in various parts of the country, much as would happen to the protagonist near the end of *Norwegian Wood*.[40]

Waseda, a private institution, has always been a good school for literary types with a strong tradition in Drama Studies going back to the work of the early Shakespeare scholar and translator, Shōyō

Tsubouchi (1859–1935). Murakami entered the drama programme at Waseda, though in all the time he was enrolled there he never went to the theatre, and he found the lectures disappointing. Instead, he loved the movies and wanted to be a screenwriter. When the screenplay study group proved boring, however, he began to spend a lot of time in Waseda's famous drama museum reading tons of screenplays. "This was the single most valuable experience I gained at Waseda," he has said.[41] He tried writing screenplays, but never produced anything he considered any good. "I stopped writing screenplays. I realized it didn't suit my personality because to make a screenplay into a finished product you had to work with a lot of other people."[42] He had long thought it might be nice to make a living doing some kind of writing, not necessarily fiction, and when screenwriting reached a dead end, he gave up this half-formed ambition without a struggle.[43]

One thing that Murakami thoroughly enjoyed was living alone for the first time in his life. And then there were girls – or one special girl. "I didn't have many friends – just two in college. One is now my wife. The other one was a girl, too. My only friends were girls."

Yōko Takahashi was slim and quiet with long hair and pleasant features that never quite explained her special, indefinable magnetism. She and Haruki met in the first class they both attended at Waseda in April 1968 (the Japanese academic year begins in April), and they started seeing each other. Coming from a modern middle-class background, Haruki had never known anyone like Yōko, who had grown up in an old Tokyo neighbourhood of traditional artisans and merchants, the daughter of a futon-maker who had inherited his craft from several earlier generations. Born on 3 October 1948, Yōko was three months older than Haruki. An outstanding student, she had been sent by her parents to a prep school for rich girls where she had always felt uncomfortable. Yōko once complained to a wealthy classmate about having to walk a long distance to the bath, meaning the kind of *public* bath used in those days when a bathtub in the home was a rarity in old neighbourhoods like hers. Her classmate deliberately misunderstood and remarked with undisguised sarcasm, "Oh. Your house must be *huge!*" Yōko never raised the subject again.

As their friendship began to develop, Yōko told Haruki she was already seeing someone. Soon, though, they were a couple both in and out of the classroom as the political winds began to blow.

Like the narrator of *Hear the Wind Sing*, Murakami was probably present in Shinjuku on the night of 21 October 1968, when huge demonstrations for International Anti-War Day boiled over, and train and bus routes were shut down throughout Shinjuku Station and elsewhere, leading to mass arrests.[44] Murakami's early teachers had instilled in him the idea that, poor as Japan was, it had one thing it could boast of: it was the only country in the world with a constitution that renounced the right to wage war. Students who had grown up with such a belief went on to make the "hypocrisy" of the establishment of the Self Defence Force a central issue in their struggle.[45] (Article 9 of Japan's made-in-the-USA constitution, which renounces the country's right to wage war, continues to cause problems for conservative governments caught between a largely pacifist populace and world demands for Japanese participation in military affairs, most notably in the Gulf War of 1991, and the international coalition against terrorism after the events of 11 September 2001.)

The following year, Waseda's student strike put an end to all classes for five months. Even when the barricades went up, however, the charm of collective action evaded Haruki. He always acted as himself, not as a member of any political wing.[46] "I enjoyed the campus riots as an individual. I'd throw rocks and fight with the cops, but I thought there was something 'impure' about erecting barricades and other organized activity, so I didn't

22

participate." "The very thought of holding hands in a demonstration gave me the creeps,"[47] he wrote. As the months wore on, rival radical factions had increasingly violent confrontations with each other, which alienated Haruki all the more. He would later satirize campus radicals in *Norwegian Wood*. In one scene, two student activists take over a class:

> While the tall student passed out his handbills, the round one went to the podium and started lecturing. The handbills were full of the usual simplistic sloganeering: "SMASH FRAUDULENT ELECTIONS FOR UNIVERSITY PRESIDENT!" "MARSHAL ALL FORCES FOR NEW ALL-CAMPUS STRIKE!" "CRUSH THE IMPERIAL-EDUCATIONAL-INDUSTRIAL COMPLEX!" I had no problem with what they were saying, but the writing was lame. It had nothing to inspire confidence or arouse the passions. And the round man's speech was just as bad – the same old tune with different words. The true enemy of this bunch was not State Power but Lack of Imagination.[48]

Without groups to join or classes to attend, Murakami decided there was nothing for him to do but go to the movies; he saw at least 200 films in one year.

Personal style also proved troublesome. "My hair was down to my shoulders, and I had a beard. Until college, I was strictly Ivy League, but they wouldn't let you get away with that in Waseda. I didn't care what the others thought, but you really couldn't *live* wearing clothes like that, so I adopted the messy look."[49]

On 3 September 1969, the campus authorities called in the riot police to end the deadlock. The mood of excitement and idealism collapsed all at once, leaving in its wake a terrible sense of boredom and pointlessness. The Establishment claimed total victory and the students gave in with barely a whimper. *Norwegian Wood* again:

The universities were not so easily "dismantled". Massive amounts of capital had been invested in them, and they were not about to dissolve just because a few students had gone wild. And in fact those students who had sealed the campus had not wanted to dismantle the university either. All they had really wanted was to shift the balance of power within the university structure, a matter about which I could not have cared less. And so, when the strike was crushed, I felt nothing.[50]

For Haruki and Yōko this startling shift of mood was a defining experience in their lives.[51] Later, when Murakami began to write his fictional history of the era, there would be the time before and the time after: the promise of 1969, and the boredom of 1970. The student movement in Japan and the rest of the world collapsed at almost the same time; it is this almost universal sense of loss that captured readers of Murakami's generation in and beyond Japan, and continues to attract readers too young to have experienced the events themselves, but who respond to the lament for a missing "something" in their lives. "Since life manages to come up short pretty reliably," Louis Menand has written, "each generation feels disappointment in its own way . . . and seems to require its own literature of disaffection."[52] *The Catcher in the Rye*, for instance, captured that sense of disillusionment so well that it continues to appeal to new generations of readers.

If there is any one point at which the works of Murakami overlap with those of the older novelist Yukio Mishima (one of Murakami's least favourite writers) it is in this sense of real life never quite managing to live up to its advance billing. Mishima always wanted life to have a soundtrack and wide-screen technicolour, and his works plunge lavishly (and rather cheaply) into the pursuit of Beauty with a capital B. Murakami is more like J. D. Salinger; for the most part, he stays closer to home and continues to wonder what is missing, or he experiences vague, undefined intimations of something that used to be magical. The collapse of the student movement can be seen as his generation's first exposure to emptiness. *Norwegian Wood* is Murakami's most "realistic" work in that it deals with the historical circumstances of this loss of innocence.

Things started getting serious between Haruki and Yōko in 1971, when they were both 22. They knew for certain they wanted to be with each other – not just to live together but to be married. Haruki's parents were not pleased. First of all, they didn't want him marrying someone from outside the Kyoto-Osaka area. And they especially didn't want him marrying before he had graduated from college and established himself in some "normal" career following the "normal" order of things. But Haruki was determined. In contrast to his own parents, he was caught completely off guard by Yōko's father, who asked him only one thing: "Do you love Yōko?" He came to admire Mr Takahashi for his fair-mindedness and his lack of old-fashioned authoritarianism.

So, in October, without any fuss, Haruki and Yōko went to the ward office and registered, and that was that. Or almost. There was still the question of where and how they were to live. At this point, Mr Takahashi may have regretted not having taken a firmer line – they moved in with him! By then, Yōko had lost her mother, and her two sisters had left, so the household consisted of the newly-weds and Yōko's father.[53]

Where Haruki's parents were concerned, however, the marriage left a permanent strain – one that at times took a special toll on Yōko. Shortly before she and Haruki were married, they visited his parents in Ashiya. As she tells it, she awoke in a state of *kanashibari* (literally "metal-binding") in which the victim cannot move a muscle – a condition almost unknown abroad but fairly common in Japan with its rigid social system. Yōko could do nothing but lie there until the paralysis eased enough for her to find Haruki in his room.[54]

Murakami's studies were on hold – and in the end it would take him seven years to finish his undergraduate degree. He decided to take a year out, but he knew he couldn't keep sponging off his father-in-law for ever. He thought about getting a job with a TV station and actually went for a few interviews, but "the work was just too stupid. I felt I'd rather open up a little shop and do some kind of decent work by myself. I wanted to be able to pick my own materials, make things and offer them to customers with my own hands. About the only thing I could actually imagine doing, though, was running a jazz club. I like jazz and wanted to do something that was connected with it in some way."[55]

It was bad enough that Haruki had married against his parents' wishes: now he and his new wife were proposing to enter the shady "water trade" (*mizu-shōbai*) world of bars and cabarets. Of course they had no intention of turning Yōko into a bar hostess, flirting with drunken customers, as his parents seemed to fear. Like other jazz clubs, theirs would have the music cranked up so loud that conversation would be all but impossible: it was the chance to listen to music and *not* to interact much with customers that attracted Murakami. Yōko's father agreed to lend them money for this new venture – *lend*, that is, with interest, the flip side of his fair-mindedness.[56]

To prepare for this new phase of their life, Haruki and Yōko began working part time for a record shop in the day and a coffee house at night. Murakami provides a fictional account of his experience in the record shop in Chapter 6 of *Norwegian Wood*. The couple amassed ¥2,500,000 – roughly $8,500 at the time. With an equivalent matching bank loan, they were able to open a cosy little establishment in a western suburb of Tokyo in 1974. They called it "Peter Cat" after an old pet of Haruki's. The original Peter Cat, meanwhile, had been sent to a friend's home in the country to recover from the stress of big city life. At the age of nine or more, he might have been as feeble and flatulent as the cat in *A Wild Sheep Chase*, and though he did not survive much longer, his image has remained a part of the couple's life and of Murakami's work. Cat pictures and figurines are a prominent part of their domestic decor, and cats often appear in his fiction. The loss of a couple's cat, for example, triggers the bizarre events that unfold in *The Wind-up Bird Chronicle*. The club called "Peter Cat" had Spanish-style white walls, wooden tables and chairs, and in no way resembled J's Bar in *A Wild Sheep Chase* and the earlier novels. The Murakamis worked there as truly equal partners.[57]

The photographer Eizō Matsumura was one of the early regulars and remains a friend to this day. From the start he was impressed by the intensity with which Murakami threw himself into his work – and into the reading he would do in the little niche he had set aside for himself; it was this strange intensity that made Peter Cat such an unusual place "'where time stood still'. It was a windowless underground space. During the day it was a coffee bar, and at night alcohol was served. There, in the dim light, Murakami played jazz records, prepared drinks, washed dishes, and read."[58] He read every novel he could get his hands on, American or otherwise (Dickens and Bataille, for example). "Murakami is convinced that if it hadn't been for those years in the bar he would never have become a novelist. [H]e had time to observe and to brood, and he believes that 'the hard physical work gave me a moral backbone'."[59]

The most valuable "observing" he did, he says, was of "real live human beings", with all the problems that inevitably arose from having to deal with so many customers and hired help. "Given the type of person I am, I would never have become involved with so many different people as I did under the stressful circumstances of running that place. It provided a kind of valuable discipline for living that would have been available to me no other way."[60] Because of his natural shyness, Murakami had to force himself to play the host to his customers, though apparently he did a less than convincing job of it; many of them – including the famous novelist Kenji Nakagami – regarded him as downright anti-social.[61]

The club was remarkably successful, thanks to the long hours the young couple put in. But they were still struggling to make ends meet when they set up their own independent household. The short story "Shaped More Like a Slice of Cheesecake Than Flat Broke" ("Chiizu-kēki no yō na katachi o shita boku no binbō", 1983) provides us with an amusing glimpse of what life might have been like in those early years of marriage, when Haruki, Yōko and and a successor to Peter were living on an unusual triangular plot of land in Tokyo. Bounded on two sides by the tracks of two different – and constantly running – railway lines, the place was horribly noisy, but the very undesirability of the location made it possible for them to rent a small house rather than the cramped apartment to which they would have been limited by their budget.

> "Let's take it," I said. "Sure, it's noisy, but we'll get used to that."
> "Well, all right, if you say so," she said.
> "Just sitting here like this, I don't know, it feels like I'm married and living in a home of my own."
> "But you *are* married," she protested. "To me!"
> "Yeah, well, you know what I mean."[62]

Somehow, Yōko managed to graduate from Waseda on schedule in 1972, but Haruki needed three more years. Writing in his spare time, he finished his thesis on "The Idea of the Journey in American Films" and graduated in March 1975 at the age of 26. Instead of looking for a typical salaried position, though (which would have been too "decadent" from a countercultural perspective),[63] he kept the club going, preparing one house speciality – stuffed cabbage – so often that he can't bear to eat it any more.

In 1977, they moved the club to a central downtown location. There they played the cat theme for all it was worth: a large, smiling Cheshire cat face outside, cat figurines on all the tables and on the piano, cat photos and paintings on the walls, pussy willow branches in a cat-motif vase, and matches, coasters, chopstick wrappers, and even coat-hangers bearing cat designs. When the young couple was interviewed for a cat-lovers' magazine in 1979, Yōko wore a sweater with the words *Peter Cat* and cat figures woven into the material.

Chopped Onions and Fragmented Fiction

The circumstances surrounding Murakami's debut in fiction share much in tone with the works themselves. It started in the spring of 1978, as Murakami told his audience at Berkeley:

I was 29 when I wrote my first novel, *Hear the Wind Sing*. At the time, I was running a small jazz club in Tokyo. After I graduated from college, I didn't feel like going to work for a company and becoming a salaryman, so I took out a loan and opened my club. When I was a student, I had a vague feeling that I wanted to write something, but I never did anything about it and I never thought about it while I was running my business – listening to jazz from morning to night, making cocktails and sandwiches. Every day I had to chop up a whole bagful of onions. Thanks to this experience, I can still cut up an onion without shedding tears.[64] Most of my friends in those days were young jazz musicians, not writers.

But then suddenly one day in April 1978, I felt like writing a novel. I remember the day clearly. I was at a baseball game that afternoon, in the outfield stands, drinking beer. The stadium was a ten-minute walk from my apartment. My favourite team was the Yakult Swallows. They were playing the Hiroshima Carps. The Swallows' first batter in the bottom of the first inning was an American, Dave Hilton. You've probably never heard of him. He never made a name for himself in the States, so he came to play ball in Japan. I'm pretty sure he was the leading hitter that year. Anyhow, he sent the first ball pitched to him that day into left field for a double. And that's when the idea struck me: I could write a novel.

It was like a revelation, something out of the blue. There was no reason for it, no way to explain it. It was just an idea that came to me, just a thought. I could do it. The time had come for me to do it.

When the game was over – and by the way, the Swallows won the game – I went to a stationery store and bought a fountain pen and paper. Then every day after work I would sit at the kitchen table for an hour or two, drinking beer and writing my novel. I'd stay up until three or four in the morning. The most time I could ever squeeze out of a day was an hour or, at the most, two. This is the reason my first novel has very short sentences and chapters. It's true that at the time I was fond of Kurt Vonnegut and Richard Brautigan, and it was from them that I learned about this kind of simple, swift-paced style, but the main reason for the style of my first novel is that I simply did not have the time to write sustained prose.

[This went on for six months.] When my novel was done, I submitted it to a literary magazine that offers prizes to new

30

writers in an annual competition. It was my good fortune to win the *Gunzō* Newcomers Award for 1979 – a very good way to start a career as a writer. (After that happened, by the way, I went to get Dave Hilton's autograph, which I still have at home. I feel he was a lucky charm for me.)[65] People called my novel "pop" literature and considered it something new because of its short, fragmentary, symbolic style. But in fact, it came out the way it did because I was busy. I didn't have the time to write it any other way. My only thought at the time was this: I can write a much better novel. It might take time, but I can become a much better novelist.[66]

Murakami submitted his work to the magazine *Gunzō* for one very practical reason: it had the only competition that accepted manuscripts as long as his. Also, he felt it was more receptive to new kinds of writing. Staff members of other magazines told him afterwards that, had he submitted his work to their publications, he would never have won a prize. And had he not won the prize, as he has often said, he might never have written another novel.

If I could have got by without writing anything, that would have suited me just fine, but it was as if I had received a bill at the end of my twenties for keeping too quiet all that time. I had to make some final accounting . . . I didn't have to write a novel to go on living, I felt, and in fact writing it ate up huge chunks of time I couldn't afford. After a long day's work I wouldn't get home until one in the morning. Then I'd write until the sun came up, and at noon I'd have to go to work again.[67]

For his title, Murakami took a hint from Truman Capote's 1947 story "Shut a Final Door", a much darker work than Murakami's with its bitter, manipulative protagonist, Walter. Realizing that other people's dislike of him is fully justified, Walter struggles to deny it: "So he pushed his face into the pillow, covered his ears with his hands, and thought: Think of nothing things, think of wind."[68] Murakami later regretted that his own title was far sweeter than he had intended, but he borrowed the wind image and the imperative voice.[69]

If the impetus to write *Hear the Wind Sing* seems to have come out of thin air, the book also has an unpredictable, almost random quality. Murakami has said that he didn't write it in chronological order but "shot" each "scene" separately and later strung them together. "There's a lot in *Wind* that I myself don't understand. It's mostly stuff that came out unconsciously . . . almost like automatic writing . . . I said just about everything I wanted to say in the first few pages, so the rest has virtually no 'message' as such . . . I never imagined it would be published – or go on to become part of a trilogy."[70]

This may sound like an invitation to chaos, but the book does have its traditional novelistic elements – a chronological series of events (if not exactly a "story") in the lives of identifiable characters placed in a recognizable historical setting. The narrative covers the precisely defined period of 8 August to 26 August 1970, the boring summer that followed the collapse of the student move-ment, the prelude to university business-as-usual in the new academic term. The nameless narrator is a 21-year-old biology major home for the summer who is about to return to Tokyo for the autumn semester. The year before, one of his teeth was broken by a riot policeman in what he now regards as a "pointless" student demonstration.[71]

His slightly older friend, "the Rat" (*Nezumi*), is apparently upset about a failed romance and decides not to go back to school; but it becomes clear that his real disillusionment came when he realized that being beaten by a riot policeman had accomplished nothing. The two spend a lot of time in J's Bar, drinking prodigious amounts of beer to slake an existential thirst, and sharing drunken profundities (the wealthy Rat's tirades directed against the wealthy, his own father having made a shady profit from the Second World War, the Occupation, and the Korean War).

In a great running gag, the Rat progresses from an initial disinterest in literature, to absorption in increasingly ponderous Western classics, to writing fiction himself. A postscript tells us that in the years following the action of the novel, the narrator has turned 29, has married and lives in Tokyo, and the Rat, now 30, is writing unpublished novels (containing neither sex nor death) which he sends to his friend as combined Christmas and birthday presents.

In "the Rat", we find a wry self-portrait of a writer aborning.

"How'd you get a name like that?"
"I forget. Goes a long way back. At first I really hated being called that, but now I don't even think about it. You get used to anything."[72]

It is a nickname so old – so embedded in the psychic primordial slime of once-upon-a-time (*mukashi*) – that he has "forgotten" how he came by it. This self-absorbed young man is identified with a dark, unnerving creature that burrows into shadowy hidden spaces. Murakami may not have "understood" everything in his first book, but he knew he was rooting around in his psychic past among half-forgotten memories and half-understood images that would surface unpredictably from the "other world". As the writer-narrator of one early story (to be discussed later) says: "For some reason, the things that grabbed me were always things I didn't understand." Lack of rational understanding, forgetting, free association: these open the deep wells and dark passageways to the timeless other world that exists in parallel with this one, a world that Murakami would go on to explore with increasing confidence. Even J's Bar provides an entrée into the psyche:

> A nicotine-yellowed print hung behind the counter of J's Bar, and when things got unbearably slow we'd stare at that picture for hours on end. The image was a pattern, something like a Rorschach test, in which I saw what seemed to be a face-off between two green monkeys tossing two half-deflated tennis balls through the air at each other . . .
>
> "What do you suppose it symbolizes?" I asked [J].
>
> "The left monkey is you and the right one's me. I'm tossing you a bottle of beer and you're tossing me the money for it."[73]

Murakami jokes away the animal imagery and symbolism in general. He has been stubbornly consistent in denying that there are "symbols" in his writing. But the Rorschach monkeys are typical of the images he flashes at his readers: generic animal or water or vegetative or topographical images that the author refuses to define – either in interviews or his texts – so that, like Rorschach blots, they can work on the mind of each individual reader.

If the Rat is a writer obsessed with the internal world of symbols, the narrator is the only slightly more externalized writer of "these pages".[74] He reacts to – or merely observes – the events and people that come to his attention, who are usually more interesting than he is. As a youngster, his central problem was communication with the outside world. He was so quiet that his parents took him to a psychologist. "Civilization means transmission," the man told him. "Whatever can't be expressed might as well not exist."[75] In retrospect, he agrees: "When there are no longer any things to transmit or express, civilization will end. Click . . . OFF."[76]

34

For three months at the age of 14, he began speaking as if a dam had burst, but when that ended he became "ordinary", neither reticent nor overly talkative.[77]

As a high-school senior, the narrator consciously adopted a cool, detached attitude, vowing to speak only half of what was on his mind; now, as a writer, he finds his habitual coolness something of a handicap. It certainly hampers his relationship with the Rat, who feels unable to come to him for advice. As J puts it, "You're a nice kid, but you've got this detached something about you."[78] The narrator promises J he'll have a heart-to-heart talk with the Rat, but they never really manage to say anything to each other. The two sides of the writer are never quite in touch.

As the fictional author of the novel we are reading, the narrator bequeaths his coolness to the language of the book. Unquestionably, the most attractive feature of this slight first novel is the style, Murakami's entertaining use of words. "I like the sense of fun in your style, the playing with language," said one interviewer to him after he had written a few more novels. "There is a distance between you and your words, in contrast to earlier writers." Murakami replied, "Well, that comes from my having a strong desire to write but nothing to say. There were so many things I *didn't* want to write about that when I stripped them all away there was nothing left." Murakami laughed at this point, but went on: "So I just picked the 1970 setting and started putting words together. I guess I figured, what the hell, something would come out that way, it was worth a try. Now that I think about it, I probably assumed that, no matter how I put the words together, the one doing it was me myself, so my consciousness was bound to come out in the words one way or another."[79]

In his Berkeley talk, Murakami spoke of his struggles with style, referring to his non-Japanese influences:

I suspect that there are many of you in the audience who think it strange that I have talked all this time without once mentioning another Japanese writer as an influence on me. It's true: all the names I've mentioned have been either American or British. Many Japanese critics have taken me to task for this aspect of my writing. So have many students and professors of Japanese literature in this country.

The simple fact remains, however, that before I tried writing myself, I used to love to read people like Richard Brautigan and Kurt Vonnegut. And among Latin Americans I enjoyed Manuel Puig and Gabriel Garcia Marquez. When John Irving and Raymond Carver and Tim O'Brien started publishing their works, I found them enjoyable, too. Each of their styles fascinated me, and their stories had something magic about them. To be quite honest, I could not feel that kind of fascination from the contemporary Japanese fiction I also read at that time. I found this puzzling. Why was it not possible to create that magic and that fascination in the Japanese language?

So then I went on to create my own style.[80]

The mention of Puig, author of *Kiss of the Spider Woman* and *Betrayed by Rita Hayworth*, is especially interesting. Kenji Nakagami called Puig "the Haruki Murakami of Latin America". He is one of the few Latin American writers that Murakami has enjoyed enough to read extensively.[81]

Elsewhere Murakami has written on style: "At first, I tried writing realistically, but it was unreadable. So then I tried redoing the opening in English. I translated that into Japanese and worked on it a little more. Writing in English, my vocabulary was limited, and I couldn't write long sentences. So that way a kind of rhythm took hold, with relatively few words and short sentences."

It was a tone he had sensed in Vonnegut and Brautigan.[82]

One is reminded of Samuel Beckett's experience of writing in French, and clearly the effect in both cases was a liberating coolness and distancing, not only in the language but in the humorously detached view of life – and death. But Murakami's world rarely takes on the starkness of Beckett's hard-edged clowning; it is a much more easily digestible, pastel-coloured world that at times lets the sentiment show through.

Murakami achieves this comforting level of detachment in several ways. The narrator writes of events in his early twenties from the perspective of a wiser but only slightly older self who betrays no hint of adult smugness. It is important that the word Murakami uses for "I" throughout is *boku*. Although the "I-novel" is a long-established fixture of serious Japanese fiction, the word most commonly used for the "I" narrator has a formal tone: *watakushi* or *watashi*. Murakami chose instead the casual *boku*, another pronoun-like word for "I", but an unpretentious one used primarily by young men in informal circumstances.[83] (Women never use *boku* for "I". In the few cases where Murakami creates a female narrator, they use the gender-neutral *watashi*.)

Murakami was by no means the first Japanese novelist to adopt *boku* as the "I" of a nameless male narrator, but the personality with which Murakami invested his Boku was unique. First of all it resembled his own, with a generous fund of curiosity and a cool, detached, bemused acceptance of the inherent strangeness of life. This stance normally makes Boku a passive character, which in turn gives rise to a speech habit – or "Haruki-ism" – often used by Murakami's protagonists when they are confronted by confounding situations: *"Yare-yare"*. This has been rendered into English as "Great, just great" or "Terrific" or merely a sigh, depending on the translator and the befuddling context.[84] Murakami chose to call this fictional persona *Boku* because he felt the word to be the closest thing Japanese had to the neutral English "I"; less a part of the Japanese social hierarchy, more democratic, and certainly not the designation of an authority figure.[85]

Early in his career Murakami said he was uncomfortable assuming the stance of a god-like creator, deigning to impose names on his characters and narrating their actions in the third person. The first-person Boku was an instinctive decision to eschew all hint of authority in his narrative. Boku may encounter strange stories, but he speaks to the reader in a voice that feels just as familiar and spoken – and, in a way, distanced from the events in the tale – as if a friend were telling us of his own personal experiences. Murakami's consistent use of the friendly, approachable Boku remained central to his narrative strategy for the better part of 20 years.

Having reached the age of 29, Murakami made Boku a 29-year-old writing about events in his life from nearly a decade before. In effect, this made the narrator the reader's kindly elder brother, someone who could offer some sense of what it was like to survive the turbulent twenties and achieve a degree of self-knowledge (but nothing approaching adult smugness). Boku has seen death and disillusionment, but he is above all an ordinary, beer-drinking kind of guy, not a hypersensitive artist or outstanding intellect. He is polite and well behaved, he likes baseball and rock and jazz, he's interested in girls and sex, but is not consumed by them, and he is gentle and considerate towards his bed partners. He is actually a kind of role model, the book a more or less didactic novel giving gentle advice on how to overcome the setbacks of one's teens and get on with life.

Boku is often the least interesting individual in his crowd, but a comfortable guy to be around – a kind of Charlie Brown who provides us access to the Lucys and Linuses and Schroders of the world with their various personality quirks. He is the kind of person that people trust with their innermost thoughts – a great listener and, as with an analyst, people seem to feel better once they've told him their stories. They are of interest to him, though, only as the possessors of those quirks and those stories, not as fully rounded individuals. It might be said that the only "personality" in most of Murakami's Boku-narrated works is that of Boku himself, whose perceptions never cease to fascinate. The other characters are functions of his psyche. A Murakami story focuses on a strange perception or experience of Boku's; a Murakami novel usually provides many such moments, not the extended exploration of personality or the unfolding of a tightly constructed plot. And where the pursuit of a mystery propels the narrative, the chase is always more interesting than the goose (or the sheep).

The narrator of *Hear the Wind Sing* disarms the reader early on by denying any claims to be creating high art, although his book may contain "a lesson or two in it somewhere".[86] From its title onwards, this light and playful novel is unmistakably didactic, very much in the modern Japanese tradition of providing a model for living (one thinks of Sōseki Natsume or Naoya Shiga),[87] but as lacking in parental authority figures as *Peanuts* it delivers its message in a way that immediately appeals to young readers – and that older critics often find unbearable. (Kenzaburō Ōe is quite wrong when he asserts that Murakami has failed "to appeal to intellectuals in the broad sense with models for Japan's present and future". He just doesn't happen to like Murakami's models.) While later works would become less overtly didactic, readers could almost always count on Boku to be a familiar window on Murakami's world.

Murakami claims he was confident he would win the *Gunzō* prize, especially after he made it through the first cut. The ones who were really shocked were his friends. They never expected such recognition for someone so ordinary, and at least one friend who read the book counselled Murakami never to write again, it was so bad.[88]

The note of "ordinariness" comes through often, both in Murakami's comments on himself and in what he says others have said about him. Indeed, in person he does seem quite ordinary, easygoing, a beer-and-baseball kind of guy, except perhaps in those moments when, unpredictably, he retreats inside himself and you know he is no longer there. He cautions that the person sitting opposite you chomping on a submarine sandwich is not the same person who writes the books, and the two should not be confused. The ordinary Murakami claims no credit for the accomplishments of the other one, and that is probably what has kept the everyday Murakami such a decent, unassuming guy. He doesn't put on airs, and despite some of the hype he is no Salinger-style recluse, either. He won't appear on television, and he tends to avoid PR events, but he is perfectly capable of making a roomful of people laugh, and once he is dragged to a party he can actually enjoy himself (if they let him go home to bed early so he can get up and write the next morning). But the sense of ordinariness, of familiarity, predominates in his work. Murakami's great accomplishment is to have sensed the mystery and distance of an ordinary brain looking out at the world. If the ordinary Murakami does indeed deserve credit for the creative one, it is in having taught himself the discipline required to give his creative self an opportunity to concentrate.

Discipline. Concentration. When Murakami makes up his mind to do something, he does it. Once, cross-country skiing in New Hampshire, he lost his balance going down a small incline and went face-first into an icy snowdrift. His companion, equally inexperienced at the sport, had the good sense to take off his own skis and walk downhill, where he found Murakami slightly dazed and with a bloodied lip. After a few dabs with an alcohol swab, Murakami trudged uphill and tried again – and again – and again, until he got it right. It was an impressive display of determination.

Had Murakami continued only to repeat himself, he would have been little more than a briefly popular writer for a high school and college readership. He has exhibited remarkable growth over the years, however, and the opening chapter of the work that brought him fame – in which he supposedly exhausted everything he had to say – is worth quoting in full both as a sample of what appealed to readers at the time and as a point of reference in discussing the later works. It may begin like a new novelist's affectedly self-conscious ruminations on writing, but in it we see themes and images that will come to inform Murakami's most important works.

Hear the Wind Sing

CHAPTER 1

"There's no such thing as perfect writing. Just as there's no such thing as perfect despair."

A writer I chanced to meet when I was in university told me this once. It was only much later that I caught on to the real meaning of those words, but at least I was able to find some consolation in them. That there is no such thing as perfect writing.

All the same, when it came to getting something into writing, I was always overcome with despair. The range of my ability was just too limited. Even if I could write, say, about an elephant, I probably couldn't write about the elephant's keeper. That kind of thing.

For eight years I went on wrestling with that dilemma – and eight years is a long time.

Of course, if you keep telling yourself there's something to be learned from everything, growing old shouldn't be that hard. In general.

Ever since I turned 20, I've tried to stick to that philosophy of life. Thanks to which I've been dealt smarting blows, been cheated and misunderstood – and just as often got myself into the strangest situations. All sorts of people have come my way telling their tales, trudged over me as if I were a bridge, then never come back. All the while I kept my mouth tight shut and refused to tell my own tales. That's how I came to the final year of my twenties.

Now, I'm ready to tell.

Granted, I haven't come up with one single solution to anything, and by the time I get through telling my tale, things might be the same as they were when I started. When you get right down to it, writing is not a method of self-therapy. It's just the slightest attempt at a move in the direction of self-therapy.

Still, it's awfully hard to tell things honestly. The more honest I try to be, the more the right words sink into the darkness.

I'm not making excuses, but at least this writing is the best I can do for now. There's nothing more to say. And yet I find myself thinking that if everything goes well, sometime way ahead, years, maybe decades from now, I might discover myself saved. And then, at that time, the elephant will return to the plain, and I shall begin to tell the tale of the world in words more beautiful than these.

*

I've learned a lot about writing from Derek Heartfield. Perhaps almost everything. Unfortunately, Heartfield was in every sense of the word a barren talent. Read him and you'll see. His style is difficult, the stories impossible, the themes infantile. Nonetheless, he was one of those few writers distinguished by an ability to put up a good fight with words. A contemporary of Hemingway, Fitzgerald, and that crowd, Heartfield was in my estimation no less a "fighter" than they. It was just that right through to the end Heartfield never got a clear picture of who it was he was supposed to be fighting. Ultimately, this is what it means to say that he was barren.

For eight years and two months he kept up his barren struggle, then died. One fine Sunday morning in June 1938, a portrait of Hitler clutched in his right hand and an open umbrella in his left, he leaped from the top of the Empire State Building. He was as unnoticed in death as he had been in life.

It was during summer vacation in my third year of middle school – and I'd come down with a terrible rash in my crotch – when an out-of-print work by Heartfield first found its way into my possession. The uncle who'd given me the book developed intestinal cancer three years later and died in excruciating pain, his guts all hacked to pieces and plastic pipes shoved in and out of his body. The last time I saw him, he'd shrivelled up dark and red like some crafty old monkey.

*

Altogether I had three uncles, one of whom died on the outskirts of Shanghai. Two days after the cease-fire, he stepped on a mine he himself had laid. My one surviving uncle has since become a sleight-of-hand artist who tours hot spring resorts throughout Japan.

*

Heartfield has this to say about good writing: "The task of writing consists primarily in recognizing the distance between oneself and the things around one. It is not sensitivity one needs, but a yardstick" (*What's So Bad about Feeling Good?*, 1936).

With me, it had to have been the year President Kennedy died that I took my yardstick in hand and began studying my surroundings ever so cautiously. That's already 15 years ago, and in those 15 years I've tossed out quite an assortment of things. Just as when an aeroplane has engine trouble and they start tossing out

43

the baggage to reduce the weight, then the seats, and finally even the poor flight attendants. Over these 15 years I've tossed out all kinds of things, but taken on almost nothing in the process.

I'm not entirely sure it was the right thing to do. Certainly it's made my load easier to bear, but the prospects are awfully scary: in old age, when it comes time to die, what's going to be left of me? After my cremation there won't be one bone remaining.

"Dark are the dreams of those whose hearts are dark. And those whose hearts are darker still have no dreams at all." That's what my grandmother always said.

The night my grandmother died, the very first thing I did was reach out to close her eyes. And as I drew her eyelids down, the dreams of her 79 years quietly dispersed like a passing summer shower on a paved street, leaving not a thing behind.

*

One more point about writing. And this will be the last.

For me, writing is extremely hard work. There are times when it takes me a whole month just to write one line. Other times I'll write three days and nights straight through, only to have it come out all wrong.

Nonetheless, writing is also fun. Compared with the difficulty of living, it's all too easy to give it meaning.

Back in my teens, was it? I was so startled upon awakening to this truth that for one week I couldn't say a word. All I had to do was use my brains a little and the world would go my way, all values would turn about, and time itself would change its flow. Or so I felt.

I realized what a trap this was only much later, unfortunately. I ruled a line down the middle of a notebook page, put all the things I'd gained in the meantime on the left, and on the right what I had lost. Things I'd lost, things I'd crushed under foot, things I'd abandoned long before, things I'd sacrificed, things I'd betrayed . . . I could never reach the end of the list.

44

A gaping chasm separates what we try to be aware of and what we actually are aware of. And I don't care how long your yardstick is, there's no measuring that drop. What I can set down here in writing only amounts to a catalogue. Not a novel, not literature, not art. Just a notebook with a line ruled down the centre. And maybe a lesson or two in it somewhere.

If it's art or literature you're looking for, you'd do well to read the Greeks. In order for there to be true art, there necessarily has to be slavery. That's how it was with the ancient Greeks: while the slaves worked the fields, prepared the meals, and rowed the ships, the citizens would bask beneath the Mediterranean sun, rapt in poetical composition or engaged in their mathematics. That's how it is with art.

Mere humans who root through their refrigerators at three o'clock in the morning can only produce writing that matches what they do.

And that includes me.[89]

Having entered his twenty-ninth year, Boku promises some slim hope of understanding some time in the future (perhaps even salvation for himself decades ahead if he continues to write), but he denies that he has any answers. He is no authority, and potential authority figures come in for some rough treatment. The literary authority, imaginary obscure American novelist Derek Heartfield, went mad and killed himself. The uncle who introduced him to Heartfield was reduced to a grotesque monkey (again, that animal imagery) by cancer. The uncle representing the wartime generation died a comic death, stepping on his own land mine after the war. The one surviving uncle performs as a lowly trickster.

What Boku has learned from "Heartfield" is the importance of

45

the yardstick: distance, irony. One fanciful book title suggests the comfort to be gained: *What's So Bad About Feeling Good?* This may be the only way to survive the eight years from early to late twenties (and whatever else might be left beyond the barrier of 30), though there are no guarantees: Heartfield's eight-years-plus-two-months struggle ended in suicide (one of five deaths touched upon in this short chapter). All you can do is keep telling yourself there is something to be learned from everything and measuring the distance between yourself and the things and people in the world around you. There is a deep cynicism here, but also a willingness to go on measuring and testing, a positive desire to define the relationship between the self and the world, to examine the nature of communication between the two, to observe the extent to which dreams and perceptions relate to what is "out there", to define the nature of reality – and fantasy. Murakami is an epistemologist. He wants to investigate the "gaping chasm [that] separates what we try to be aware of and what we actually are aware of".

This experiment will form the basis of all Murakami's writing. We will see him testing his powers and questioning their validity. As a writer, "All I had to do was use my brains a little and the world would go my way, all values would turn about, and time itself would change its flow." Such solipsism is, however, confounded by one nagging suspicion: in that world outside the perceiving intelligence there seem to be other perceiving intelligences with their own internal worlds. Among those "things I'd lost, things I'd crushed under foot, things I'd abandoned long before, things I'd sacrificed, things I'd betrayed" are "things" (*mono*: the Japanese term, written in phonetic *hiragana*, is exquisitely ambiguous) called people. Murakami has said that he "wasn't interested in real people in those days", which was probably true well into his career.[90] Literature was primarily a means of escape from the real world – an escape from Japanese literature and literary language. This would be paralleled in his life by an escape from Japan itself. Later, he would look back on this time and say:

All I could think about when I began writing fiction in my youth was how to run as far as I could from the "Japanese Condition". I wanted to distance myself as much as possible from the curse of Japanese . . .

Which perhaps explains why his narrator chooses the assassination of President Kennedy as an important milestone rather than an event in Japanese history. "I didn't especially admire Kennedy's politics," Murakami has said, "but I was strongly attracted to – and perhaps even influenced by – the idealistic, liberal atmosphere that he brought to the early 1960s."[91] And of his decision to leave the country:

When I was in Japan, all I wanted was to be an individual, to get away – just get away as far as I could from societies and groups and restraints. When I graduated from the university, I didn't go to work for a company. I've lived by writing entirely on my own. The literary establishment was nothing but a pain for me, which is why I have stayed by myself, writing my novels.

This is also why I went off to Europe for three years, and after a year in Japan, went to live in America for a little over four years.[92]

As Murakami and his Bokus matured, however, the degree of understanding and misunderstanding between the self and others would become increasingly the central focus in his writing; and once he rediscovered Japan as a country he wanted to know rather than to flee, "real" people would begin to populate his works.

3

Half-Remembered Tune

When he finished *Hear the Wind Sing* and sent it to *Gunzō* magazine, Murakami had satisfied the strange impulse that had come to him in a ballpark and might never have written again.[93] Winning the prize changed everything – though not at first. In 1980, aged 31, he was still the owner of a jazz club who happened to have written a well-received first novel. But the prize encouraged him to try again. He still had to write at the kitchen table after long hours at the club, and it did not always go well.

"I swear a lot while I'm writing. My wife gets mad and says she can't stand listening to me," which is a habit Murakami says he has been unable to cure to this day. Sometimes Yōko would joke, "Why don't you stop writing novels and become an ordinary husband again?"[94]

But novels were not all he was writing. Editors were eager to publish this hot new talent and he gave them short stories, translations (a handful of stories by F. Scott Fitzgerald), and essays (on Stephen King; on the theme of the generation gap in films; on his intention to continue writing despite encroaching "middle age"), while his next novel portrayed the continued adventures of Boku and the Rat.

Pinball, 1973

After an introductory summary of the years 1969 to 1973, during and after the Tokyo student uprisings, *Pinball, 1973* (1980) concentrates on the months of September to November 1973, when Boku is 24 and the Rat 25. Boku is living in Tokyo, sharing his bed with twin girls identified only by the numbers on their sweatshirts, 208 and 209, and listlessly pursuing his career as a commercial translator, working with a friend and an attractive office assistant. He feels his mid-twenties going by in a shapeless, boring blur, but when he tells the office girl that his formula for coping with the pointless routine is "not to want anything any more",[95] she is not convinced and neither is he.

Meanwhile the Rat, having quit the university, is still hanging around in J's Bar, 700 kilometres away in Kobe, trying to tear himself away from a woman with whom he has become involved, and planning to leave the town once and for all. The one hint we have that the Rat is still developing as a writer comes from the circumstances in which he met this woman: by answering a classified ad for a typewriter. (One of the few things we know about her, by the way, is that she has a Scandinavian-style bed – perhaps suggested to Murakami by the lyrics of the Beatles song "Norwegian Wood", featured on *Rubber Soul*, an album mentioned several times in the book.)

Boku and the Rat never meet in the course of the book; instead, chapters alternate (somewhat erratically) between first-person descriptions of Boku's life and third-person descriptions of the Rat's. This is the first suggestion we have that the Rat is a "made-up" fictional character, while Boku is closer to the author. The didactic element surfaces in this novel again, but rather than from Boku, who does not speak in this book as his older self, it comes most directly from the mouth of the wise "old" (45) Chinese bartender, J, who had very little to do in the first novel. Shown in the present rather than in retrospect, the 24-year-old Boku shares more with the Rat than he did in *Hear the Wind Sing*. The Rat's pain is just as raw and unrelieved as in the earlier novel, and Boku also lets us see some of the pain of his past, his coolness an inadequate defence against his feelings of loss.

The overall tone of the book, as a result, is far more sombre than that of *Hear the Wind Sing*, but rather than having Boku return to the most agonized chapter of his past, when his beloved Naoko died, Murakami has him embark on a self-consciously non-Arthurian quest for, of all things, a pinball machine on which, until it disappeared with the closing of a Tokyo arcade three years earlier, he spent many mindlessly happy hours – as he had on a similar machine in J's Bar.

The climactic scene of the book occurs in the blinding fluorescent glare of a freezing cold storage warehouse permeated with the smell of dead chickens – a distinctly inelegant stink of death – as Boku confronts the silent and timeless other world of memory; a place variously described as the legendary "elephants' graveyard"; as "the graveyard of dreams so old they are beyond remembering"; as "deep in the forest" of fairytale where Boku himself momentarily feels the threat of being turned into a motionless gargoyle; as a repository of faded adolescent dreams where every Hollywood starlet thrusts out her glorious breasts; and as a scene in outer space, where the pinball machine, "Spaceship", waits for him in the utter stillness. It is an eclectic evocation of almost every alternative "other" world of popular literature and film.

The place is permeated with the smell of dead chickens, but also with numbers: there are exactly 78 pinball machines – "78 deaths and 78 silences" – standing on "312 legs", the precise numbers being less important than the fact that the numbers are precise – hard, immutable, dead.[96] Memory is the place where everything and everyone we have ever experienced still reside unchanged, long after they have been lost to us in reality, in this silent elephants' graveyard of ours, a pinball machine may be just as real and important to us as a person who was once so real as to have that rare Murakami gift: a name – in this case (and later in *Norwegian Wood*) Naoko.

Death is a major presence in Murakami's "other world", but that world is not simply death. The mysterious "Sheep Man" in *Dance Dance Dance* will specifically deny that the other world is merely the obliteration of death. The other world exists in "reality"[97] he says – which it does of course if all "reality" is memory. The "strangely familiar" coldness experienced by the Boku of *Dance Dance Dance* may be the coldness of this particular chicken warehouse, and the animal source of the stench of death here will find its parallel in several works. "The New York Mining Disaster" (Nyū Yōku tankō no higeki, 1981), for example, a sad and funny meditation on the constant nearness of death (unreality) in everyday life, begins with a description of a man who hurries to the zoo whenever the city is hit by a torrential storm.[98] It turns out he is the owner of a suit the narrator borrows whenever he has to attend a funeral – which happens with disturbing frequency. Thanks in part to the prominence of animals, and the sense the story evokes of the interpenetratedness of human and animal life, the presence of death seems less a threat than simply another aspect of the mysteriously connected random flow that constitutes life. Animals fascinate Murakami for what they share with the unconscious life of the human mind: alive but devoid of rational thought, in touch with mysterious forces but unable to communicate. Animals – like the Rorschach monkeys of *Hear the Wind Sing* – are richly symbolic without having specific allegorical themes attached to them.

The rationale for investing so much metaphorical weight in

such an absurd, outlandish experience as being reunited with a long-lost pinball machine can be found in some earlier observations of Boku's:

> On any given day, something claims our attention [literally, "grabs our hearts": *kokoro o toraeru*]. Anything at all, inconsequential things. A rosebud, a misplaced hat, that sweater we liked as a child, an old Gene Pitney record. A parade of trivia with no place to go. Things that bump around in our consciousness for two or three days then go back to wherever they came from . . . to darkness. We've got all these wells dug in our hearts. While above the wells, birds flit back and forth.
>
> That autumn Sunday evening it was pinball that grabbed my heart. The twins and I were on the golf course watching the sunset from the green of the eighth hole. It was a par 5 long hole with no obstacles and no slope. Only a straight fairway like the corridor of an elementary school . . . Why at that very moment a pinball machine grabbed my heart, I'll never know.[99]

The passageway to the past is a long, corridor-like place reminiscent of childhood such as we saw in the story inspired by "The Girl from Ipanema".

Is life for Murakami, then, nothing but a "parade of trivia" that unpredictably "grabs" a person's "heart" for a while before marching back to where it came from? Well, yes and no. The universe is going to click off and everything in it is destined for oblivion, but in the meantime we have our lives, which can "mean" something to us, depending on our attitude. Herein lies the "lesson" of *Pinball, 1973*, as articulated by J:

Me, I've seen 45 years, and I've only figured out one thing. That's this: if a person would just make the effort, there's something to be learned from everything. From even the most ordinary, commonplace things, there's always something you can learn. I read somewhere that they say there's even different philosophies in razors. Fact is, if it weren't for that, nobody'd survive.[100]

In search of "meaning", Boku turns to Kant's *Critique of Pure Reason*, which he often reads in the course of the novel. The occasion is a "funeral" in which he is forced to play the role of the priest. The October rains drench everything in this sombre scene and the ritual is carried out with great solemnity. Never mind that this beautifully described, even moving funeral is not Naoko's but that of an electric switch-panel that has "died" and must be disposed of. Murakami plays it 100 per cent straight, until:

One of the twins took our dearly beloved switch-panel out of the paper bag and handed it over to me. In the rain, it looked more miserable than ever.

"Say some kind of prayer, will you!"

"Prayer?" I was caught off guard.

"It's a funeral, so we need to say last rites." . . .

"The obligation of philosophy," I drew on my Kant, "is to eradicate illusions born of misunderstanding . . . Oh, switch-panel! Rest ye at the bottom of the reservoir" . . .

"That was a wonderful prayer!"

"You make it up?"

"But of course," I said.[101]

An absurd ritual for a meaningless object, this funeral reveals the "illusion" of thinking that a human life has any more meaning than that of a switch-panel. What is the meaning of life? What is the meaning of the things – including the people – that enter our lives and are inevitably lost? They are all mental impressions, and they have no more – and no less – meaning than the meaning we invest them with. Boku thinks of the switch-panel again when he tries to assure his office assistant that her life is not headed for a dead end. The only response to the pain of life, he decides, is detachment: "Better just not want anything any more."[102]

The Rat seeks detachment in his own, rather more conventional ways. Endless thinking is what troubles him. At the close of the novel, he manages to tear himself away from the woman, to say a regretful farewell to J, and – for the third time in the course of this short book – to attain oblivion by falling asleep in his car (foreshadowing, perhaps, the fate of Watashi in *Hard-boiled Wonderland and the End of the World*). He talks about leaving town, but his thoughts about how warm and comforting the bottom of the sea must be suggest that he may have a more permanent solution to his anguish in mind.

The most prominent feature of Boku's present detached life is the twins, 208 and 209, with whom the action of the novel begins and ends. Although they insist on their utter distinctness, they are entirely interchangeable – to the point of assuming each other's "identities" by exchanging the numbered sweatshirts by which Boku tells them apart. They do not count in Boku's mind as girlfriends when he is asked if he has any.[103] He sleeps between them, but their presence has nothing erotic or physical about it (one strokes his inner thigh on the way to the funeral, but to comfort, not to stimulate). Indeed, they hardly exist as human beings in the world of the novel, having far less personality than the longed-for pinball machine "herself" when he finally encounters "her". Boku claims he doesn't know when the twins entered his life, only that his sense of time has since regressed to that of a one-celled organism. They are pale, abstract (if cute) embodiments of the bifurcation principle that splits the author into Boku and the Rat. Part of the "parade of trivia", 208 and 209 "bump around in" Boku's "consciousness" for a while "then go back to wherever they came from", their departure marking the end of the novel. "Where are you going?" Boku asks them. "Back to where we came from," they reply. They and Boku cross the long, straight eighth-hole fairway that originally brought the pinball machine from the depths of his memory – the same mysterious passageway from the unconscious that brought the twins themselves into existence for Haruki Murakami. They move under the gaze of birds – those creatures that freely communicate between the conscious and unconscious worlds. "I don't know how to say this," he says, "but I'm going to be really lonesome without you."

Of course he doesn't know how to say it – or explain to himself how, when the author stops writing the book and stops thinking about these figments of his imagination, their absence will make Boku feel lonely – but they have taken on an undeniable reality for him and he will miss them. "Let's meet again somewhere," he suggests. "Yes, somewhere," they reply, and their voices reverberate in his heart like an echo; for finding that special "somewhere" where he can "meet again" those people – and things and ideas and words – that have grabbed his heart for a while is Boku's quest, and the central literary project of Haruki Murakami.

Although Murakami's jazz-filled works could not at first glance appear to be more different from those of the quintessentially Japanese novelist Yasunari Kawabata (1899–1972),[104] with their geisha and tea ceremonies, both are the product of their authors' struggles to arrest the flow of time as it sweeps life relentlessly into the past, and both offer detachment as a way of coping. After he has "lost" the twins, Boku watches the day move past his window, "a November Sunday so tranquil it seemed that everything would soon be utterly transparent."[105] He is in his detached state again, his quest safely at an end, the "real" world slowly draining itself of colour in an ending reminiscent of the conclusion to Kawabata's "The Izu Dancer", in which the mind of the central character drips slowly away into Zen nothingness.[106]

"A Poor-Aunt Story"

One of the most powerful demonstrations of the force of memory in Murakami's world is a story that appeared the same year as *Pinball, 1973* and bore the odd title "A Poor-Aunt Story" ("Binbō na obasan no hanashi", 1980, rev. 1990). What inexplicably grabs the narrator's heart in this piece is the phrase "poor aunt" – the phrase itself, without referring to anything in the real world, and without any special meaning in Japanese. The reader in English must *not* assume that the phrase "poor aunt" has any more significance in Japan than it does in Britain or America.

The "Poor-Aunt" is that rarity among Murakami works (however common it may be in modern Japanese fiction): a story about a writer trying to write a story.[107] Most of Murakami's protagonists are men stuck in boring, mundane jobs – advertising copywriters, commercial translators and the like: people who have lost their 1960s idealism and accommodated themselves to the Establishment. But this story is about a writer's fascination with words, and we can safely assume that the writer depicted here is a lot like Haruki Murakami.

Murakami is a writer for whom the unpredictable process of creating something out of nothing, in words, is endlessly fascinating. Most of his stories, he has said, start from their titles. A phrase spontaneously brings an image to mind, and he "pursues" that image in writing without knowing where it will lead him.

Sometimes the process is a failure and he gives up, but us~~ ~~
the image will suggest an opening scene, from which the re~~ ~~
of the story develops. "As I write, something of which I was
unaware makes itself evident to me. I find this process tremendously thrilling and interesting," he says.

"A Poor-Aunt Story" is a perfect example. Indeed, "it is a story
that takes as its motif the very process of beginning a story from
its title ... The story has a double structure: it consists simultaneously of 'A Poor-Aunt Story' and 'The Making of "A Poor-
Aunt Story"'." In this case, the phrase "poor aunt" came up in a
conversation with his wife, Yōko, and suddenly struck him.[108]
He had no poor aunts in his family, no one to whom the phrase
could apply, while for Yōko, with her less affluent background,
the phrase was all too real.[109]

The story begins with Boku and his girlfriend sitting by a
pond outside a picture gallery, enjoying a July Sunday afternoon.
Everything is tranquil and ordinary, except that certain details strike
Boku in a recognizably Murakamiesque way: "even the crumpled
silver sphere of a chocolate wrapper discarded on the lawn gave
off a proud sparkle, like a legendary crystal at the bottom of a
lake ... Soft-drink cans shone through the clear water of the
pond. To me, they looked like the sunken ruins of an ancient lost
city ... Sitting at the edge of the pond, my companion and I
looked across the water towards the bronze unicorns on the
other shore." Suddenly the timeless world of legend intrudes
upon the "real" world. The unicorns are of particular interest.
Inspired by actual unicorn sculptures that stand by the large
fountain outside the Meiji Memorial Picture Gallery in the Outer
Garden of the Meiji Shrine in Tokyo, they will become a major
fixture in the timeless other world of *Hard-boiled Wonderland and the
End of the World*.[110]

Soon we hear music, another characteristic hint that we are

moving inwards: "The breeze carried snatches of music from a large portable radio on the grass: a sugary song of love either lost or about to be. I seemed to recognize the tune, but I could not be certain I had heard it before. It might have sounded like another one I knew."

And then it happens:

"Why a poor aunt, of all things, should have grabbed my heart on a Sunday afternoon like this, I have no idea. There was no poor aunt to be seen in the vicinity, nothing there to make me imagine her existence. She came to me, nonetheless, and then she was gone. If only for a hundredth part of a second, she had been in my heart. And when she moved on, she left a strange, human-shaped emptiness in her place. It felt as if someone had zipped past a window and disappeared."

Boku then turns to his companion and says, "I'd like to write something about a poor aunt." (To the reader he explains, laconically, "I'm one of those people who try to write stories.")

"Why?" the girlfriend asks. "Why a poor aunt?"

"Not even I knew the answer to that. For some reason, things that grabbed me were always things I didn't understand."

His girlfriend raises the issue of the relationship between the inner and outer worlds by asking if Boku actually *has* a poor aunt, and it turns out he does not. She, on the other hand, *does* have one – she even lived with her for a while – but she doesn't want to write about her.

"The portable radio started playing a different tune, much like the first one, but this I didn't recognize at all . . ." Boku is no longer in touch with his deep memories. He turns outwards now to ask if the reader happens to have a poor aunt. "But still," he says, even if the answer is no, "you must have at least seen a poor aunt at someone's wedding. Just as every bookshelf has a long unread book and every closet has a long unworn shirt, every wedding reception has a poor aunt." She is a sad figure to whom almost no one speaks, and her table manners are far from perfect.

After he has brooded on a "poor aunt" for a while, a "real" poor aunt takes shape on his back. He can't see her, but

> I first realized she was there in the middle of August. Not that anything in particular happened to alert me to her presence. I simply felt it one day: I had a poor aunt on my back. It was not an unpleasant sensation. She wasn't especially heavy. She didn't puff bad breath across my shoulder. She was simply stuck there, on my back, like a bleached shadow. People had to look hard even to realize she was there. True, the cats I shared my apartment with gave her suspicious looks for the first few days, but as soon as they understood that she had no designs on their territory, they got used to her.[111]

Boku's human friends are less accommodating. The "poor aunt" depresses them because she reminds them of depressing people and things in their own lives. He realizes that "what I had on my back was not a poor aunt with a single, fixed form: it was apparently a kind of ether that changed shape in accordance with the mental images of each observer." To one person, she appears as a dead pet, a dog that died horribly from cancer of the oesophagus; to another, she is a schoolteacher who carried burn scars from the 1944 Tokyo air raid.

The media chase after Boku, and he finds himself being interviewed on a TV talk show. After he has explained that the "poor aunt" on his back is just words, the emcee's young female assistant asks whether he is free, then, simply to expunge them. "No," he says, "That's impossible. Once something has come into being, it continues to exist, independent of my will. It's like a memory. You know how a memory can be – especially a memory you wish you could forget."[112]

By having Boku obsess on the phrase "poor aunt", Murakami in effect gives us a memory we never had. He makes us experience déjà vu ourselves by inventing a cliché – a phrase that takes on an uncanny familiarity as it is repeated until we begin to think that it is one of those idiomatic expressions we've known most of our lives but have never really thought about. Murakami makes his new cliché stand for everything unpleasant that we push out of our minds by subtly suggesting things we ought to know but have managed to suppress. For us, the "poor aunt" may be a homeless beggar on the street, or Salvadoran or Iraqi or Balkan or Afghani children crippled by American-made bombs, or tortured political prisoners, or simply relatives we avoided because we didn't like their table manners: "Each individual's response will be entirely different, of course," explains Boku.[113]

In Boku, the phrase arouses not only pity but a degree of guilt that derives from a feeling of helplessness, of being unable to assuage the suffering or loneliness of any kind of "poor aunt" in the real world. And he concludes that they sensitize us to the impact of time: "In a poor aunt, we can see the tyranny of time before our eyes, as if through an aquarium window."[114]

A "poor aunt" is a symbol, but a transparent one that may or may not be filled in with specific equivalents by the reader. The important thing for Murakami is how it feels in the mind of each of us. It should have a sense of déjà vu. It should be strange and familiar at the same time. Perhaps no other writer concerned with memory and the difficulty of reclaiming the past – not Kawabata, not even Proust – has succeeded as well as Murakami in capturing the immediacy of the experience of déjà vu. When one of Murakami's narrators tells us he is uncertain about his recollections, we can be sure he is pointing to the heart of the story.

After she has clung to Boku's back for some months, the poor aunt suddenly disappears. On a train, Boku sees a little girl being treated unfairly by her mother, and his heart goes out to her. The scene echoes an earlier discussion between Boku and his companion concerning the origins of "poor aunts" in the real world: "I sometimes wonder what kind of a person becomes a poor aunt. Are they born that way? Or does it take special poor aunt conditions? . . . A poor aunt might have a 'poor aunt' childhood or youth. Or she might not. It really doesn't matter."[115]

The little girl on the train may be a "poor aunt" in the making. Or she may not be. What is important is that she is as much of a "poor aunt" figure for Boku at that moment as the dog or the teacher or the mother is for his friends. What matters is that someone out there, in the real world, has aroused his sympathy (and the reader's: the scene is genuinely touching) and so released Boku from his obsession with the phrase in his mind.

This obsession has interfered with his personal relations as well. While he has been living his inward-looking life, his companion on that first fateful Sunday in July has become a peripheral figure: they do not see each other for three months, and winter is coming by the time they talk again. He calls her as soon as the poor aunt disappears from his back. He is relieved that she is "still alive", so far has she been from his thoughts, but she cannot respond to him with an open heart just yet. A tiny detail suggests how very close the two of them were before his obsession came between them: "In the silence at her end, I could sense her biting her lip and touching her little finger to her eyebrow."

When their call ends inconclusively, a hunger of metaphysical proportions suddenly overtakes him and, to satisfy it, he turns with shocking desperation to his readers, addressing them indirectly at first, and then directly, in the second person: "If they'd give me something to put in my mouth, I'd crawl to them on all fours.

I might even suck their fingers clean. Yes, I would, I would suck your fingers clean."[116]

What follows is a rhapsody of imagination, a free plunge into the world of word and image association that perhaps only the writer can experience – and perhaps only in those moments when he is slightly out of control, when he chooses to go with whatever his unconscious produces, unedited, unanalysed – and weirdly beautiful:

> The [poor aunts] might prefer to live quietly in giant vinegar bottles of their own making. From the air you could see tens – hundreds – of thousands of vinegar bottles lined up, covering the earth as far as the eye could see . . . And if, by any chance, that world had space to admit a single poem, I would gladly be the one to write it: the first honoured poet laureate of the world of poor aunts . . . I would sing in praise of the resplendent glow of the sun in the green bottles, sing in praise of the broad sea of grass below, sparkling with the morning dew.[117]

Aside from the vinegar bottles, the story has several of those strange, evocative Murakami images that no one will ever fully explain. The origin of one such oddity, however, may be partially traceable. Seemingly out of nowhere, Boku wonders if he might have been better off with an umbrella stand on his back rather than a poor aunt. Asked about this strange choice of objects by a student in Charles Inouye's class at Tufts University on 1 December 1994, Murakami mused that it might have come to him because the umbrella stand in his jazz bar was a constant source of trouble for him at the time. Angry customers would complain to him whenever their expensive umbrellas were taken by other customers.

In any case, it seems that here the narrator *can* provide salvation for all the poor aunts, the cancerous dogs, the scarred teachers of the world. He can sing for them as poet laureate, compensate them somehow for their loneliness, and try, as well, to salve the guilt he feels for having turned away from them.

Salvation is only momentary, however. The story has begun on a beautiful July day and ends with the approach of winter as the writer gives up on any hope that he can help anyone in the course of his lifetime. Perhaps it will happen ten thousand years in the future if at all.

The disappearance of the poor aunt has been as unpredictable as her materialization. "I had no idea when it happened. Just as she had come, she had gone before anyone noticed. She had gone back to wherever it was that she had originally existed."[118] This "original place" is where memories reside, the place from which they leap out and "grab" us, and to which they return, just as the twins in *Pinball, 1973* go "back to where we came from".[119] It is nothing less than the core of the self: "She had gone back to wherever it was that she had originally existed, and I was my original self again. But what *was* my original self? I couldn't be sure any more. I couldn't help feeling that it was another me, another self that strongly resembled my original self. So now what was I to do?"[120]

Murakami would go on after "A Poor-Aunt Story" to make his exploration of this most indefinable area of the mind, this "original place", the very foundation of his writing. Boku, the writer, is speaking for Murakami when he says, "For some reason, the things that grabbed me were always things I didn't understand."[121]

A Slow Boat to China

"A Poor-Aunt Story" was later anthologized in a book called *A Slow Boat to China* (*Chūgoku-yuki no surō bōto*, May 1983). "Most of what we could call my world is presented in this first story collection of mine," Murakami has said.[122] Indeed, "A Poor-Aunt Story" is undoubtedly one of his defining works. "The New York Mining Disaster" (March 1981), mentioned earlier, with its strangely funny angle on death, is another early exploration of one of Murakami's most central and enduring themes.

"The Kangaroo Communiqué" ("Kangarū tsūshin", October 1981) is a fair sample of the crazy stylistic fireworks that attracted attention to Murakami's early writing. Perhaps this is why it was the first piece by Murakami to be published in English translation outside Japan (see Appendix A). A better title might have been "Thirty-six Degrees of Separation". The garrulous narrator insists that even the most random-seeming events in life can be analysed to reveal the logical steps that connect them. For example, the 36 steps leading from the kangaroos at the zoo to "you". In this case, "you" is the recipient of a wildly rambling "communiqué" dictated into a tape-recorder by a 26-year-old department store employee to a female customer who has registered a complaint. In the real world, the young man's confession that he would like to sleep with this woman, whom he has never met and about whom he knows nothing, would not only cost him his job but probably land him in jail as a sex pest, but this is less a window on society than a stylistic indulgence in randomness concerning the role chance plays in human relationships. It is therefore closely related to a story that Murakami had published earlier that same year, "On Seeing the 100% Perfect Girl One Beautiful April Morning", which appeared in a later collection and will be discussed below.

Another noteworthy story from *A Slow Boat to China* is "The Last Lawn of the Afternoon" ("Gogo no saigo no shibafu", August 1982), in which Boku, looking back to his college days when he used to mow lawns for spending money, observes that "Memory is like fiction; or else it's fiction that's like memory. This really came home to me once I started writing fiction . . ."[123] The story emphasizes an important characteristic of the classic Murakami Boku: a tendency to perform some mindless physical task – ironing shirts, cooking pasta, mowing lawns – with meticulous attention to detail as an exercise in healing a wounded psyche – rather like Zen and the art of motorcycle maintenance.

The title story of the collection, "A Slow Boat to China" (April 1980), is also a defining work, though in a different sense. The first story of Murakami's to appear in print was also the first to hint at his abiding interest in China. Hint is all it does, however, so that its full significance can be grasped only in retrospect.

"When did I meet my first Chinese?" the story begins, and Boku digs into his early memory for any bits and pieces he can find there. Three brief episodes ensue.

Boku's first encounter was with the Chinese proctor at an exam he was given, a man who made an indelible impression on him by talking about ethnic difference and the importance of pride.

The second was a pretty girl he worked with at a part-time job. He asked her out on a date, enjoyed an evening of dancing, wrote down her telephone number on a matchbook cover, but then accidentally put her on the wrong train home. He had to work hard to convince her it had not been a nasty prank because she was Chinese. He promised to call her, said goodnight, then absent-mindedly threw the matchbook away after lighting up. She had just changed jobs and addresses; all his attempts to find her proved fruitless. No doubt she was convinced he *had* been making fun of her after all. His remorse and frustration are palpable – and irredeemable; this episode is the emotional heart of the story.

The third Chinese Boku met was a fellow he couldn't remember – and probably didn't want to remember – from high school, now an encyclopaedia salesman specializing in Chinese customers.

All three episodes involve uncomfortable memories, and we are left with an odd, sad feeling that, whatever it is that bothers Boku about the Chinese, it has more to do with urban loneliness than ethnic difference. Indeed, so indirect is the story that in 1983 the critic Tamotsu Aoki claimed that "the piece has nothing to do with Chinese people per se; they merely serve as milestones along the path taken by the protagonist from the 1960s into the 1980s . . . As the melody of 'Slow Boat to China' fades, an era is created, and for a little while we are reminded of our own journey down the same path."[124] This may well have been the dynamic that functioned for Murakami's early readers, but now it is possible to see his consistent awareness of China and the Chinese as an understandably difficult memory for the Japanese.

A Perfect Day for Kangaroos

Among Murakami's early stories are several short, startling mental journeys that would later be put between the covers of his second anthology, *A Perfect Day for Kangaroos* (*Kangarū-biyori*, 1983). "The 1963/1982 Girl from Ipanema" (April 1982) had its Boku wandering in the mental space created by the famous jazz song. Bolder still is "Dabchick" ("Kaitsuburi", September 1981), which foreshadows the subterranean groping of *Hard-boiled Wonderland and the End of the World*. Nothing less than a physical assault on the reader's brain, it is one of Murakami's weirdest short stories, part Beckett, part Laurel and Hardy. If some readers find themselves bewildered by Murakami's stories in general, this one bewilders

Murakami himself. Whenever it is mentioned he scratches his head and says with a chuckle, "That is one strange story", as if he still can't work out where it came from.[125]

Like "A Poor-Aunt Story", "Dabchick" requires a small warning. The original title, "Kaitsuburi", is a word that means as little to the typical Japanese reader as "Dabchick" means to most readers in English. Both words refer to real but little-known water birds; in English, "dabchick" is another word for "grebe". We are already familiar with the story's central symbol, however: the corridor. Here it receives the starkest, most abstract treatment that Murakami was able to give it. The story begins: "When I reached the bottom of a narrow concrete stairway, I found myself in a corridor that stretched on forever straight ahead – a *long* corridor with ceilings so high the passageway felt more like a dried-up drainage canal than a corridor. Lacking decoration of any kind, it was an authentic corridor that was all corridor and nothing but corridor."

Boku continues walking down the seemingly endless passageway, then suddenly finds himself at a T-shaped intersection. The crumpled postcard he fishes from his pocket tells him he will find a door here, but there is no door. Determined to get the job he has come for, he flips a coin and turns right. After numerous twists and turns of the corridor, he does come to a door, but at first no one responds to his knock. Finally, a pasty-faced young man in a maroon bathrobe appears, dripping wet from his "required" mid-day bath.

Boku apologizes for arriving five minutes late, but the young man has not been apprised of the arrival of any new hires and is unwilling to announce Boku to his boss unless Boku can give him the password.

The dialogue that follows reads like a vaudeville act, as Boku tries to gain admittance without knowing the password. The doorman, we learn, has never met his "superior" and is afraid of being fired, as his predecessor was, for letting someone in without the password. Boku whines and tries to wheedle at least a few hints out of him, then finally browbeats him into accepting the word "dabchick" as the password, though neither man is sure what a dabchick is. (They seem to agree that it is "palm-sized", i.e. can be held on the palm of one hand.) "I didn't even know I knew the word until I heard myself saying it. But 'dabchick' was the only eight-letter word I could think of that fit the clues."

"I give up," [the doorman] said, wiping his hair once again with his towel. "I'll give it a try. But I'm pretty sure it won't do you any good."

"Thanks," I said. "I owe you one."

"But tell me," he said. "Are there really such things as palm-sized dabchicks?"

"Yes. Without a doubt. They exist somewhere," I said, though for the life of me I couldn't tell how the word had popped into my head.

*

The palm-sized dabchick wiped his glasses with a velvet square and let out another sigh. His lower right molar throbbed with pain. Another trip to the dentist? he thought. I can't take it any more. The world is such a drag: dentists, tax returns, car payments, broken-down air conditioners . . . He let his head settle back against the leather-covered armchair, closed his eyes, and thought about death. Death was as silent as the ocean bottom, as sweet as a rose in May. The dabchick had been thinking about death a lot these days. In his mind, he saw himself enjoying his eternal rest.

HERE LIES THE PALM-SIZED DABCHICK, said the words engraved on the tombstone.

Just then his intercom buzzed.

He aimed one angry shout at the device: "What!"

"Someone to see you, sir," came the voice of the doorman. "Says he's supposed to start work here today. He knows the password."

The palm-sized dabchick scowled and looked at his watch.

"Fifteen minutes late."[126]

And so, with a final pinch to the reader's grey matter, the story ends. Does the doorman "know" that the boss he's supposedly never met "is" a dabchick? Is he lying to the boss when he says Boku "knows" the password? What "is" the password if not the half-known word that has sprung from nowhere in Boku's brain? What does the word "is" even mean in a story in which the protagonist has arrived on the scene by a flip of a coin, only to make a seemingly incorrect guess which turns out to be the controlling intelligence of the entire system of reality within which all the work's characters supposedly exist? A bird with a throbbing molar? A suicidal boss who somehow "is" at the same time a "palm-sized dabchick"? The story's contradictions and convolutions are unresolvable and impress for their sheer boldness.

Not all the stories in *A Perfect Day for Kangaroos* are such bewildering mind games. "Shaped More Like a Slice of Cheesecake Than Flat Broke", with its amusing peek at the Murakamis' house on the triangular plot of land, is to be found here. Three other stories from the collection are readily available in English.

In "A Window" ("Mado", May 1982; original title, "Do You Like Burt Bacharach?" ["Bāto Bakarakku wa o-suki?"]), we find the 22-year-old Boku working as a part-time instructor in a correspondence course designed to help students improve their letter-writing style. It begins:

Greetings,

The winter cold diminishes with each passing day, and now the sunlight hints at the subtle scent of springtime. I trust that you are well.

Your recent letter was a pleasure to read. The passage on the relationship between hamburger steak and nutmeg was especially well written, I felt: so rich with the genuine sense of daily living. How vividly it conveyed the warm aromas of the kitchen, the lively tapping of the knife against the cutting board as it sliced through the onion![127]

The recipient of Boku's letter, which gives her a grade of 70 for her most recent attempt, is a 32-year-old married (but childless and lonely) female student of his who offers to cook him a hamburger steak. Although company rules forbid fraternizing between students and instructors, he is about to change jobs, so he agrees to meet her, enjoys eating her hamburger steak, chatting against a background of Burt Bacharach tunes, and *not* sleeping with her.

Ten years have gone by, but whenever I pass her neighbourhood on the Odakyū Line I think of her and her crisply grilled hamburger steak. I look out at the buildings ranged along the tracks and ask myself which window could be hers. I think about the view from that window and try to figure out where it could have been. But I can never remember.[128]

Sad, sweet, funny, and deeply imbued with the sense of relationships unexplored, such a nostalgic reminiscence on hamburger steak could only have been written by Murakami.

Another of his pastel creations on the role of chance in human relationships is a very short story with a very long title: "On Seeing the 100% Perfect Girl One Beautiful April Morning" ("Shigatsu no aru hareta asa ni 100 pāsento no onna no ko ni deau koto ni tsuite", July 1981). Boku sees his perfect girl on a Tokyo street and thinks:

> Wish I could talk to her. Half an hour would be plenty: just ask her about herself, tell her about myself, and – what I'd really like to do – explain to her the complexities of fate that have led to our passing each other on a side street in Harajuku on a beautiful April morning in 1981.[129]

He goes on to imagine, in the space of two pages, a scenario involving a flu epidemic that wipes clean the memories of two perfectly matched lovers who pass each other on a Tokyo street years later with only the faintest glimmering of the deep ties they once shared. Of course, they never see each other again. A favourite of budding filmakers, the tiny story would later comprise the nucleus of Murakami's longest novel, *1Q84*.

One of the weirdest stories in the collection, not yet available in English, is "The Rise and Fall of Sharpie Cakes" ("Tongari-yaki no seisui", March 1983). "Sharpie Cakes" or simply "Sharpies" are a kind of confection that have been baked in Japan since at least the tenth century, but which, in the 1980s, are beginning to lose popularity, especially among the young. Or at least that is what Boku learns when he goes to a large, heavily attended PR gathering organized by the company. He has never heard of Sharpies, but the many young people at the meeting seem to know all about them and about the "Sharpie Crows" that have been known to attack anyone who criticizes the cookies.

Boku is unimpressed by the taste of Sharpies, but since the company is offering a big prize to the person who comes up with the best updated version, he decides to enter the contest. A month later he is summoned to the company and informed that he is the top finalist; young employees, especially, like his recipe, but some older ones insist that what he has produced is not authentic Sharpies. The final determination is to be made by none other than the Sharpie Crows themselves. When Boku asks the executive in charge what Sharpie Crows are, the man is incredulous:

"Do you mean to say you entered this competition without knowing anything about the Sharpie Crows?"

"I'm sorry, I lead a kind of sheltered life."

They go down a corridor, up an elevator to the sixth floor, and down yet another corridor, which ends in a steel door. This is where Their Holinesses, the Sharpie Crows, have lived for many years, eating nothing but Sharpies, the executive explains. The two men enter to find upwards of a hundred huge, grotesquely swollen crows on perches, all screaming "Sharpies! Sharpies!" Instead of eyes, the birds have globs of white fat, and when the man throws some Sharpies on the floor in front of them, Boku sees why: the birds pounce en masse, pecking each other to be the first to eat the cookies. Next the man throws them some losing contest entries, but these the birds spit out, crying for the real thing.

"Now let's try it with your new Sharpie Cakes," the executive informs him. "If they eat them, you win. If not, you lose." A huge mêlée ensues, in which some of the birds love the new version, but others reject it, while those birds unable to reach Boku's cakes peck the others mercilessly, splattering blood all over the place.

Boku leaves in disgust, convinced that no amount of prize money would be worth spending the rest of his life in association with such creatures. "From now on I would make and eat the food that *I* wanted to eat. The damned Sharpie Crows could peck each other to death for all I cared."[130]

A parody of the kind of corporate pride that inspires a venerable history for every cookie and pickle in Japan, a sly jab at Japan's literary establishment, a prescient satire on corporate global strategizing to attract young customers, and a critique of the sort of worshipful mentality that inspires mass devotion instead of individual decision-making, "The Rise and Fall of Sharpie Cakes" shows Murakami going into dark regions he would explore more fully later and which would involve elements of the occult.

One little anecdote connected with this story is worth appending here. The word translated as "Sharpies Cakes" is *tongari-yaki*, meaning, more or less literally, "pointy-baked-things". Some time *after* he wrote the story, Haruki and Yōko were walking along a Tokyo street when they were bowled over to see a billboard advertis-ing a new snack: *tongari-kōn* or "pointy-corn", cornucopia-shaped corn chips. "Pointy-corn" has since become far better known than Murakami's story. Just remember, though, Murakami's "pointy-baked-things" came first![131]

4

Keeping the Ears Clean

In 1981 Haruki and Yōko sold their jazz club so that he could become a full-time writer. He was 32. The business was doing well and he still enjoyed the work, but after the success of his first two novels he wanted to be able to write without having a mountain of onions to dice. The time had come to switch from the kitchen table to a proper desk.

They moved out of Tokyo to suburban Funabashi and underwent a complete change of lifestyle. Instead of working at the club until two or three in the morning, Haruki was in bed by ten and up by six, writing. He started listening to more classical music and growing vegetables in the garden with Yōko.

And the cascade of manuscript pages began. By May, Murakami had translated enough short stories by F. Scott Fitzgerald to publish a collection entitled *My Lost City*, and he has continued to produce translations ever since. What lesser mortals might have made a career, he has done for fun, in the afternoon, after exhausting himself on his novels, stories, essays, and travel writing in the morning.

Over the years, with the frequent collaboration of Professor of American Literature Motoyuki Shibata at the University of Tokyo, he has translated not only Fitzgerald but Raymond Carver (the complete works), John Irving, Paul Theroux, C. D. B. Bryan, Truman Capote, Tim O'Brien, Grace Paley, Mark Strand, jazz bassist Bill

Crow (an autobiography and anecdotes), Mikal Gilmore (the story of the life and execution of Gary Gilmore), Raymond Chandler, Geoff Dyer, collections of contemporary American short fiction and criticism, plus several illustrated children's books (see Bibliography). "Learning another language is like becoming another person," he says.[132] He has been credited with helping to jump-start a new wave of translation of American fiction in the 1980s.[133]

Murakami the translator is an important figure in contemporary Japanese letters, the popularity of his fiction drawing attention to his translations, and his translations providing him with a broad knowledge of Western (especially American) literature. In this way he became a one-man revolution in Japanese fictional style. He nurtured new, urban, cosmopolitan, and distinctly American-flavoured tastes in Japanese writing. He has spawned a host of imitators as well. The eminent critic Kōjin Karatani complained that two of the four finalists in the 1991 literary newcomers' competition (the *Gunzō* prize that Murakami had taken in 1979) had come under the "undisguised influence" of Murakami. "One Haruki Murakami is enough," added a *Gunzō* editor.[134]

By his own account, the single most important writer for Murakami was Raymond Carver, an author he loved to translate and an influence on his own work. He had never heard of Carver until he read the story "So Much Water So Close to Home" in 1982. It "literally came as a shock to me" he wrote.

There was the almost breathtakingly compact world of his fiction, his strong but supple style, and his convincing story line. Although his style is fundamentally realistic, there is something penetrating and profound in his work that goes beyond simple realism. I felt as though I had come across an entirely new kind of fiction, the likes of which there had never been before.[135]

Murakami was persuaded he had discovered a genius in Carver, and after reading "Where I'm Calling From" in *The New Yorker* he began collecting and translating Carver's works. He published his first translated collection, *Where I'm Calling From and Other Stories*, in May the following year, the same month in which *A Slow Boat to China* came out.

Hardly a household name even in America, Raymond Carver was virtually unknown in Japan until Murakami began translating him, and the response was overwhelming. "The warm, even passionate reception that Raymond Carver received from Japanese readers gave me almost as much pleasure as the reception of my own work," he wrote. He went on to translate everything of Carver's, including unpublished manuscripts and letters. Having worked so long in a void in Japan, Murakami came to feel as he translated and learned from Carver that he had found a true mentor.

> Raymond Carver was without question the most valuable teacher I ever had and also the greatest literary comrade. The novels I write tend, I believe, in a very different direction from the fiction Ray has written. But if he had never existed, or if I had never encountered his writings, the books I write (especially my short fiction) would probably have assumed a very different form.[136]

Murakami was somewhat taken aback a few years later when the American writer Jay McInerney pointed out to him certain similarities between Carver's "Put Yourself in My Shoes" and his own story "The Wind-up Bird and Tuesday's Women" (discussed below). "Until Jay mentioned this to me, I was not aware of it, but it is possible that I have absorbed the rhythm of Ray's phrasing and something like his view of the world much more deeply than I had suspected. Of course, he is not the only writer who has had an influence on me. But Ray Carver is after all the most significant writer for me. Otherwise, why would I want to translate all of his work?"[137]

If Carver has influenced Murakami, it might be said that Murakami has influenced Carver – at least in translation. As Professor Hiromi Hashimoto has pointed out, Murakami's inward-looking, pastel-coloured, Boku-centred style has been criticized as gentrifying Carver's world – especially the early works (often described as "dirty realism", "K-Mart Realism", "hick-chic", "white-trash fiction" and so on). While Carver narrates with strict objectivity, Murakami tends to introduce a more subjective tone. In "Neighbors" for example, Carver writes "He wondered if the plants had something to do with the temperature of the air", but in his translation Murakami enters the character's mind: "He toyed with the thought, 'Hmm, could the temperature be different because there are plants here?'" Professor Hashimoto concludes that this slight shift in perspective is more appropriate for Carver's later works (from "Cathedral" onwards), Murakami's translations of which are truly outstanding.[138]

Students of Japanese literature will know that this shift from outside to inside the character reflects a natural tendency of the Japanese language to interiorize. Indeed, the scholar Ted Fowler has written an entire volume on this problem, showing how Japanese lends itself to subjective modes of narration such as the "I-novel", which occupies a dominant position in the history of modern Japanese literature.[139] It may well be that Japanese readers took more eagerly to Carver than American readers because, through the medium of the Japanese language, Carver lost some of his edge and became more "naturalized" to a Japanese setting in which the distance from "he" (*kare*) to "I" (*boku*) is not very great.[140]

A Wild Sheep Chase

Murakami began working on a new novel in the autumn of 1981, completing it the following spring – which has become something of a pattern for him. He knew he wanted to write a novel about (of all things) sheep, so for the first time in his career he left home to do some research. He travelled to sheep facilities and interviewed sheep production experts in Hokkaidō, Japan's northernmost island.

Impressed by a novel called *Coin Locker Babies* by Ryū Murakami (no relation), Murakami knew that he wanted to write something equally sustained, unlike the fragmentary two books that had brought him such attention.[141] It was the sheer energy of *Coin Locker Babies* that encouraged him to think more in terms of storytelling than montage to provide narrative momentum and wholeness. Now he had the time to concentrate, and the product of that concentration took him far beyond what he had accomplished to date.[142]

At first glance, though, things look familiar. For his first full-length novel as a professional, Murakami turned once again to the central figures of *Hear the Wind Sing* and *Pinball, 1973*. When we encounter Boku, the Rat, and the Chinese barkeeper J in *A Wild Sheep Chase* (*Hitsuji o meguru bōken*, 1982) it is July 1978, although there is a Prelude labelled (in the original, not in the translation) "25 November 1970". This was the day on which the novelist Yukio Mishima attempted to rouse Japan's Self Defence Force in the name of the Emperor. When the military men refused to take him seriously, he slit open his stomach and was beheaded by one of his followers. In *A Wild Sheep Chase*, however, Mishima's harangue to the troops appears as nothing more than a series of images flashing on a silent TV screen. The volume control is broken, but the students watching are not interested anyway – another illustration of the ennui that followed the 1969 uprisings.

Boku, now 29, has since married and divorced the attractive office assistant. She had been sleeping with a friend of his, but he didn't care enough either to win her back or stop her from leaving after four years of marriage. He has expanded his translation service into a moderately successful advertising agency, but he has lost track of the Rat, who has simply disappeared, as was suggested at the end of *Pinball, 1973*; and he no longer sends novels each December, as he did in the postscript to *Hear the Wind Sing*.

The ennui so central to Boku's perception of life in the earlier works is expressed with stark simplicity here:

> I don't know how to put it, but I just can't get it through my head that here and now is really here and now. Or that I am really me. It doesn't quite hit home. It's always this way. Only much later on does it ever come together. For the last ten years it's been like this.[143]

The student demonstrations of 1969 marked the end of his youthful idealism. After that, his twenties have been nothing but the deadening routine of working life, in which a gap seems to open between "me" and "myself". Boku feels nostalgia for the time before the gulf opened. "Someday," mused Boku in the "Girl from Ipanema" story, "I'll meet myself in a strange place in a far-off world . . . In that place, I am myself and myself is me. Subject is object and object is subject. All gaps gone. A perfect union." But now Boku spends much of his time in a fog induced by cigarettes and alcohol, and lives on a diet of junk food.

For much of *A Wild Sheep Chase*, boredom and life are polar opposites, with adventure providing an escape from boredom into life. The original title of the novel means "An Adventure Surrounding Sheep", but we have the translator, Alfred Birnbaum, to thank for the hint in the English title that Boku's search for a mysterious sheep will be something of a wild goose chase. Boku begins as a bored urbanite, then plunges into an adventure that promises to alleviate his boredom, only to return to his life as a bored urbanite – with one crucial difference: he has come to realize that the mundane world of ordinary flesh and blood is far preferable to the world of memory and death, which is inhabited only by ghosts. "I'd made it back to the land of the living. No matter how boring or mediocre it might be, this was my world."[144]

The characters in *A Wild Sheep Chase* seem familiar, but they live and act in a whole new way. Murakami described his new approach at Berkeley:

> In this novel, my style underwent a major change – or two major changes. The sentences were longer, more sustained; and storytelling elements played a far greater role than in the first two books.
>
> As I wrote *A Wild Sheep Chase*, I came to feel strongly that a story, a *monogatari*, is not something you create. It is something that you pull out of yourself. The story is already there, inside you. You can't make it, you can only bring it out. This is true for me, at least: it is the story's spontaneity. For me, a story is a vehicle that takes the reader somewhere. Whatever information you may try to convey, whatever you may try to open the reader's emotions to, the first thing you have to do is get that reader into the vehicle. And the vehicle – the story – the *monogatari* – must have the power to make people believe. These above all are the conditions that a story must fulfill.
>
> When I began writing *A Wild Sheep Chase* I had no preset program in mind. I wrote the opening chapter almost at random. I still had absolutely no idea how the story would

a flashback. We learn that a package arrived from the far north last December, 1977, containing a letter from the Rat and a novel. Another letter from "some place totally different" arrived in May enclosing a photograph of a bucolic scene with sheep and a request that Boku put it on public display. The Rat also asked him to visit J and the woman he abandoned in *Pinball, 1973* and say goodbye to them for him. (Conveniently for the plot, the postmark on this second package was obliterated when Boku tore off the forwarding slip.) Boku inserted the photograph in an advertisement produced by his firm, and he dutifully made a sentimental journey to his hometown.

Returning to the present, we learn that the sinister man in black has searched out Boku because of some undeclared interest he has in the sheep photograph. The man – the lieutenant of a right-wing "Boss" ("Sensei") who is dying from a huge cyst in his brain – compels our hero to embark on a search for one particular sheep in the photo with a faintly discernible star-shaped mark on its back. Now Boku must set off in search of the Rat, who sent him the photo. He takes along his new girlfriend, a part-time call girl with an ordinary face but "perfectly formed ears", which she – like several Murakami characters – is endlessly cleaning. The astonishing charm that her ears, when revealed, lend to her appearance, is described with comic abandon:

> Several of the other customers [in the restaurant] were now turned our way, staring agape at her. The waiter who came over with more espresso couldn't pour properly. Not a soul uttered a word. Only the reels on the tape deck kept slowly spinning.[146]

It is reminiscent of those wonderful stock brokerage commercials in which rooms full of people stop what they are doing because

"When E. F. Hutton speaks, people listen." This is an unforgettable scene in the book, occupying an entire "chapter" of its own, and a crucial one, for Murakami's comic boldness utterly disarms the reader. It is only a small step from accepting this to accepting his girlfriend's extraordinary, ESP-like powers and the increasingly bizarre series of events that they open up to Boku. There are similarities here between Murakami and Thomas Pynchon, but Murakami does not cite him as an influence. Pynchon's *V*, he says, is a marvellous novel, but, "I don't know why, I've hardly read anything else of his. Maybe novelists with similar tendencies don't like to read each other's work."[147]

It is Boku's girlfriend who predicts out of the blue that he will receive an important phone call about sheep. It is she who insists they go to Hokkaidō in search of sheep, and she who, seemingly at random, picks their "metaphysical" hotel out of a phonebook (a hotel with yet another animal label – "Dolphin" – chosen by the owner for its association with *Moby Dick*, another narrative of a quest for an elusive beast). Miraculously, this building turns out to be the former Hokkaidō Ovine Hall, where the "Sheep Professor" lives, a man who, in 1935, was briefly possessed by the sheep they are searching for. He is perhaps the only person in the world who could have told Boku where the photograph was taken (in fact, a similar photo hangs in the lobby of the hotel), and he thereby provides the final clue that leads Boku to the Rat – a connection that Boku realizes he could have made himself if he had not "forgotten" that the Rat's family had a summer home in Hokkaidō.

Once Boku has this final clue, the girlfriend drops into the background, her only remaining role in the novel being *not* to have sex with him any more and then to disappear as he undergoes a process of purification.[148] Boku also conveniently fails to notice the obvious connection of the Boss to this part of Hokkaidō until after he has found his way to the Rat's summer retreat. There, *almost* by chance, he happens to read a wartime book praising Japan's continental expansion and handily containing a list of pro-expansion activists including the Boss and his home address.[149]

As shaky as these plot connections are, they are given a final jolt by the black-suited secretary, who reveals near the end that he knew all along where the Rat was hiding and sent Boku on this "wild sheep chase" because the Rat had to be lured out by someone he trusted, someone who knew nothing of the secretary's sinister plan to transfer the possessing sheep from the Rat to himself so as to exploit its super powers. Does this mean that the girlfriend was in league with the secretary, and that her own powers were a ruse? Does this mean that her choice of the Dolphin Hotel was by no means random? Were the Sheep Professor and his son also planted by the secretary? Or does it simply mean that Murakami allowed events to take their course without questioning them too closely?

Surely the ease with which the girlfriend disappears and Boku lets her go (her departure marked by the playing of the tune "Perfidia") suggests that she might have been paid off and that he is somewhat disgusted with her. ("She seemed kind of sick," the hotel owner tells Boku, who brushes him off with a "Never mind.")[150] But no: her powers are "real", and the Sheep Professor is nobody's plant. The Professor's agony is presented without irony, and it is he who proclaims the book's central message: "The basic stupidity of modern Japan is that we've learned absolutely nothing from our contact with other Asian peoples."[151] Pressing too hard for logical consistency will probably succeed only in sapping the fun from a detective story that is meant to be more outlandish than sturdily constructed and to present its political position in the least painful way.

For a "wild" novel so full of "loopy" adventures, however, *A Wild Sheep Chase* is surprisingly concerned with death and irretrievable loss. It begins with Boku hearing about the accidental death of an ex-girlfriend; then he recalls the ritual disembowelling of Yukio Mishima; later he reveals that the Rat has committed suicide; and after a meeting between Boku and Rat's ghost, the sinister man in black is killed. Along the way, there are at least four other deaths reported, including that of the right-wing Boss and the "death" of the waterfront of Boku's hometown with its headstone-like modern buildings. The girlfriend's disappearance near the end is another loss, preceded by the departure of Boku's wife and the end of his business partnership. "I'd lost my hometown, lost my teens, lost my wife, in another three months I'd lose my twenties. What'd be left of me when I got to be 60, I couldn't imagine."[152] The cool Boku tries not to take any of this too seriously. As he points out, loss comes in three forms: "Some things are forgotten, some things disappear, some things die. And there's hardly anything tragic about this."[153]

His search for the Rat – who, he hopes, will lead him to the mysterious sheep – takes him to Hokkaidō, to which the office assistant in *Pinball, 1973* once suggested an outing. (Murakami frequently pursues hints from his earlier works, and this novel is particularly rich in that regard: we even find Nat King Cole's "South of the Border" here, ten years before it would emerge in the title of a novel.)[154] While he waits in the isolated mountain cottage where the Rat seems to have been living until recently, Boku's only human contact is with a bizarre local character called "the Sheep Man" (*hitsuji-otoko*), who is not entirely human. For no apparent reason, this little (4'10") man

> wore a full sheepskin pulled over his head. The arms and
> legs were fake and patched on, but his stocky body fit the
> costume perfectly. The hood was also fake, but the two horns
> that curled from his crown were absolutely real. Two flat

ears, probably wire-reinforced, stuck out level from either side of the hood. The leather mask that covered the upper half of his face, his matching gloves, and socks, all were black. There was a zipper from neck to crotch . . . Sprouting from the rear end of his costume was a tiny tail.[155]

Wearing this outfit the Sheep Man hides out in the woods, an escapee from the world's wars and the military presence in general, a self-appointed lamb of peace as it were. We don't know if he has a cabin out there – or has any real existence apart from the scenes in which he speaks with Boku: he just materializes out of the forest and returns there, a fairytale creature with little more flesh than the *Pinball* twins.

Gradually, as Boku begins to sense the "presence" of the Rat in this weird creature, the autumn deepens, the snows begin to fall, and the coldness that permeated the scene in *Pinball*'s chicken warehouse begins to increase in severity. Boku senses that something is about to happen:

> The more I thought about it, the more difficult I found it to escape the feeling that the Sheep Man's actions reflected the Rat's will. The Sheep Man had driven my girlfriend from the mountain and left me here alone. His showing up here was undoubtedly a harbinger of something. Something was progressing all around me. The area was being swept clean and purified. Something was about to happen.[156]

As a "harbinger" of scenes to come, Murakami uses an archaic expression, *atari ga hakikiyomerareru*: "the area was being swept clean and purified", much as the sacred space of a Shintō shrine would be ritually purified in preparation for the appearance of a god. "This is no ordinary place: you should keep that much

87

in mind,"[157] the Sheep Man advises Boku, who is being physically purified as he starts eating a healthier diet (the celebration of food is central to Shintō), gives up sex and cigarettes and begins to run every day in the clear, cold air. He even purifies himself mentally: "I decided to forget everything."[158]

On one run, Boku suffers a chill and retreats to the house. The snow buries the area in white silence, and Boku sets the phonograph on repeat to intone Bing Crosby's "White Christmas" 26 times in a mantra of purification. He feels everything "flowing"[159] on without him and, as if becoming a part of the flow, he proceeds with an almost poetically described ritual of cleansing that is physically demanding but which his newly clean lungs respond well to: dusting, vacuuming, mopping and waxing the floors, scrubbing the tub and toilet, polishing the furniture, washing the windows and shutters, and finally – the most important task of all – polishing the mirror, the central object in Shintō ritual.

The mirror in this house is a large, full-length model, an "antique", and Boku cleans it so well that it seems to reveal a world as real as – or more real than – this one.[160] When the Sheep Man comes to visit, however, drawn to the house by the sound of Boku playing the Rat's guitar, his image does not appear in the mirror, and a thrill of terror runs down Boku's spine. As different physically as the tall Rat and minuscule Sheep Man are, Boku knows that his old friend is somehow present in the Sheep Man. Dramatically smashing the guitar to make his point, he urges the Rat to visit him that night and sends the Sheep Man back into the forest where he lives.

After an unsettling dream, Boku waits in the cold and darkness for his friend to arrive. He feels as if he is "crouching in the bottom of a deep well".[161] He stops thinking and gives himself up to the flow of time. The Rat speaks to him in the silence, and for a while the two return to "the old days",[162] stopping the clock during this timeless reunion, and enjoying beer together as the Rat explains how he killed himself with the malevolent sheep inside him. Boku suffers with the cold, but the Rat promises that they will meet again, "Preferably somewhere brighter, maybe in summer" – perhaps somewhere like the beach at Ipanema.[163] Afterwards, Boku spends a feverish night filled with hallucinatory dreams, opening to question the reality of his meeting with the Rat. Another brief ritual of purification – shaving and releasing an "incredible" amount of urine – follows this contact with the world of the dead.[164]

Whether we view Boku's successful reunion with his deceased friend as "real" or a product of delirium, it is the culmination of his quest. He has managed, if only for a few moments, to recapture his lost past – "the old days". When Boku is cataloguing his boring existence for the girl with the beautiful ears, he says, "I've memorized all the murderers' names in every Ellery Queen mystery ever written. I own the complete *A la recherche du temps perdu*, but have only read half."[165] The use of the French title may strike us as somewhat affected for the normally unpretentious Boku, but it is an alert translator's signal that this mention of Proust is more than just a joke about Proust being unreadable. The original English title, *Remembrance of Things Past*, would simply not do, and has since been re-translated as *In Search of Lost Time*. In this and the similarly accurate Japanese translation, Proust's title sounds like pure Murakami: *Ushinawareta toki o motomete*: "Searching for Lost Time" – which is exactly what Boku has been doing.

Murakami's adventures in the inner world of memory follow Proust's lead in trying to arrest the flow of time, but with one crucial difference: Murakami is not boring. You can get all the way through his books. He's as easy and fun to read as Ellery Queen – a refreshing taste of Proust Lite for our high-commercial, low-cholesterol times. He deals with the Big Questions – the meaning of life and of death, the nature of reality, the relationship of mind to time and memory and the physical world, the search for identity, the meaning of love – and all in an easily digestible form, not ponderous and fattening, not depressing, but honest and entirely devoid of pious illusion. He speaks to us now, in the language of our times, profoundly nihilistic and receptive to the sheer interest and excitement of being alive.

Having said all this, the question remains: Why sheep? What (if anything) does the sheep symbolize? Murakami has tried to explain it this way:

> I made no story outline for *A Wild Sheep Chase* other than to use "sheep" as a kind of key word and to bring the foreground character "I" [*boku*] and the background character "Rat" together at the end. That's the book's entire structure . . . And I believe that if the novel does succeed it is because I myself do not know what the sheep means.[166]

In a talk at the University of Washington in November 1992, Murakami finally revealed the source of the sheep image and, with hindsight, what it might signify. Discussing *Pinball, 1973*, the novelist Takako Takahashi had taken Murakami to task for describing some bushes as looking "like grazing sheep". This, she said, was "an inappropriate figure of speech because there are no sheep in Japan". But Murakami was certain there must be sheep in Japan, and he began to research the subject. He described this process in his lecture at Berkeley:

> I went to Hokkaidō to see real sheep. Almost all of the large-scale sheep ranches in Japan are concentrated in Hokkaidō. There I was able to see real sheep for myself, to talk to people who raise sheep, and to do research on sheep in government

offices. I learned that there had not always been sheep in Japan. They had been imported as exotic animals early in the Meiji period. The Meiji government had a policy of encouraging the raising of sheep, but now sheep have been all but abandoned by the government as an uneconomical investment. In other words, sheep are a kind of symbol of the reckless speed with which the Japanese state pursued a course of modernization. When I learned all this, I decided once and for all that I would write a novel with "sheep" as a key word.

These historical facts regarding sheep turned out to be a major plot element when it came time for me to write the novel. The character I call the Sheep Man is almost surely a being that floated up out of that vast historical darkness. At the time I was deciding to write a novel on sheep, however, I knew nothing about such facts. The Sheep Man was a product of a great coincidence.[167]

It is no coincidence, however, that the Sheep Man is hiding out from the military. When Boku reads the history of the area, an imaginary town called Jūnitaki (Twelve Waterfalls), he discovers that the Meiji government promoted the raising of sheep there as part of the Army's plans for continental invasion. The locals couldn't work out why the government was being so nice to them in practically giving them their first flock of sheep – until some of their sons were killed, wearing woollen coats, in the Russo-Japanese War (1904–05).

The fortunes of the town declined after the Second World War, and a period of rapid economic growth saw the local economy switch to producing wooden products for the new urban consumer – TV cabinets, mirror frames, toy animals – who lived in the sort of society in which Boku has spent his boring twenties. Boku is fascinated by the early history of Jūnitaki, but the story of this latter period is so dull (it ends in 1970, the year the numbness really set in) that it puts him to sleep.[168]

Murakami may take a fanciful slant on history, but it is significant that in this first novel of his to step beyond the narrow confines of the student movement, Murakami explores Japan's tragic encounter with the Asian mainland, an area of concern to which he would return in full force in *The Wind-up Bird Chronicle*.

Born in 1913, the shady right-wing Boss of *A Wild Sheep Chase* is described as having been sent to Manchuria, "where he fell in with the upper echelons of the Kwantung Army and became party to some plot". (The Kwantung Army, with which Japan policed its puppet regime in Manchuria, was given to hatching plots, at least one of which gave rise to hostilities that blossomed into the Pacific War.) The Boss "plundered his way all over the Chinese mainland only to board a destroyer two weeks before the Soviet troops arrived [to destroy the Kwantung Army in the final days of the war], beating a quick retreat back to Japan. In his booty – a huge, nearly inexhaustible stash of gold and silver."[169]

With his fortune, the Boss goes on to exercise covert control over "politics, finance, mass communications, the bureaucracy, culture . . . everything"[170] – by which Murakami imputes sinister motives to the key controlling elements of contemporary Japanese consumer culture, linking them with the same forces behind Japan's doomed, destructive attempt at continental expansion. Behind the Boss's all-encompassing shadow kingdom lurks a huge, individual-snuffing, totalitarian "Will" that is somehow embodied in a certain "chestnut-coloured sheep with [a] star on its back". The sheep took up residence inside the Boss's brain in 1936 and may once have possessed and inspired the bloodthirsty Genghis Khan.[171] A year after being possessed by the sheep, the Boss went to Manchuria. Here (it is hinted) he inspired the Kwantung Army to foment the notorious "Manchurian Incident" of 1937, the key event that led to Japan's rape of China, which was its primary "contribution" to the Second World War.

The sheep, then, cannot merely be a symbol of peace if it embodies the evil "Will" that has wrought such wide-scale suffering in Asia. Indeed, the sheep-embodied "Will" seems to have originated on the continent, the very continent that was victimized by Japan as far back as the Sino-Japanese War (1894–95), through the Russo-Japanese War (1904–05), the annexation of Korea (1910), and the final round of violence from 1931 to 1945, including the Manchukuo puppet regime of 1932–45. The mission of the Emperor's sacred troops was to establish the Greater East Asian Co-Prosperity Sphere. What better symbol for such high-minded violence than a lamb of peace?

The Chinese barkeeper, J, may be seen as a victim of the war and its aftermath in mainland China. He would have been 17 at the end of the war in 1945. After somehow making it to Japan, he married, only to lose his wife to illness, but he has little more to contribute to the plot than pronouncing an occasional gem of wisdom and lending his lonely presence to Boku's world. When Boku allows himself to daydream about bringing together all the important people in his life to run a restaurant in the mountains of Hokkaidō, he includes J with such intensity of feeling that the translator seems to have concluded that the passage was out of place and could be cut. Restored, it might look like this:

> Now, if we could get J to come up here, I'm sure things would work out fine. Everything should revolve around him, with forgiveness, compassion and acceptance at the centre.[172]

Language like this almost invites speculation that "J" might stand for "Jesus". Murakami is no Christian (or Buddhist, or anything else involving organized religion), but he is surely toying with the image of the lamb of peace, from which it is only a short hop to a J for Jesus. J seems to stand at the opposite extreme to the Boss, whose "Will" has run rampant over J's homeland. In the end, almost as if paying war reparations, Boku hands J the large cheque he has received from the Boss's secretary for undertaking his wild sheep chase.

Now that the Boss is dying, the mysterious sheep has left him and chosen to inhabit the psyche of none other than the Rat – though why it should have gone from a right-wing thug to a disillusioned student radical is another plot-point the author wisely refrains from probing too deeply. One might have expected it to move into someone like Yukio Mishima, whose death marks the opening of the novel with such chronological precision. Nevertheless, in a final flowering of his old, pre-1970s idealism, the Rat decides that the one contribution he can make to society is to kill himself while the spirit of the powerful sheep slumbers inside him. Boku aids him in this by connecting the bomb that will kill the malevolent secretary who is so bent on inheriting the sheep's power for himself.

Not that the killing of the sheep and the secretary is going to liberate Japan from the evil they represent or that any of this adds up to a systematic critique of Japan Inc., or its exploitation of its obedient workforce. There is little doubt, however, that many readers can relate to Boku's urban malaise and are ready to lose themselves in the novel's fantasy of striking back. Through the character of Boku they can vicariously destroy the corrupt and powerful system that controls the economic machine in which they feel trapped and exploited, and which prevents them from feeling "that here and now is really here and now. Or that I am really me."

*

Boku's "purification" in Hokkaidō was partly autobiographical. As he neared the end of *A Wild Sheep Chase*, Murakami gave up smoking (cold turkey: from three packs a day to nothing) and took up running in earnest. As he burrowed deeper inside himself for material, he felt the need for some kind of physical discipline to keep on an even keel.

The image of a typical member of the Japanese literary establishment has always been that of a hard-drinking, heavy smoking "decadent" whose physical decline is a major source of material, but Murakami decided that physical health would be the foundation stone of his professional career.[173] Just as his characters are always fixing themselves "simple" meals, Murakami's own health regimen calls for eating simply, with a heavy emphasis on vegetables (huge salads!), low-fat Japanese dishes and few starches. He does enjoy properly cooked pasta, however, like many of his characters, and, again reflected in the fiction, he has a broad repertory of cuisines that he enjoys, though Italian is probably his favourite.

His strong dislike of Chinese food has been linked to his peculiar sensitivity to Japan's atrocities in China, but in conversation he insists that the only problem for him is the flavourings and points out that he is "constitutionally incapable of eating not only Chinese food but Korean and Vietnamese as well" (not that the Japanese were angels in those countries, either).[174] Never a heavy drinker, he enjoys an occasional beer or glass of wine, and is especially fond of single-malt whiskys. "I've heard it said a million times that fiction comes out of something unhealthy, but I believe the exact opposite. The healthier you make yourself, the easier it is to bring out the unhealthy stuff inside you."[175]

By 1999 Murakami had run 16 full marathons and so completely identified himself with physical fitness that one magazine ran a 25-page spread on the connection between his running and his writing. "You've got to have physical strength and endurance," he said, "to be able to spend a year writing a novel and then another year rewriting it ten or fifteen times." He decided that he would live as if each day were 23 hours long, so that no matter how busy he might be, nothing would prevent him from devoting an hour to exercise. "Stamina and concentration are two sides of the same coin ... I sit at my desk and write every day, no matter what, whether I get into it or not, whether it's painful or enjoyable. I wake up at 4 a.m. and usually keep writing until after noon. I do this day after day, and eventually – it's the same as running – I get to that spot where I know it's what I've been looking for all along. You need physical strength for something like that ... It's like passing through a wall. You just slip through."[176] This physical discipline is inseparable from the enormous professional discipline that has kept Murakami so astonishingly productive year after year.[177] In time he would come to feel that, while jazz supplied the energy for the clipped beat of his earlier works, the sustained power of his later style owed much to his becoming a long-distance runner.[178]

In 1983, a year after he wrote *A Wild Sheep Chase*, Murakami took his first trip out of the country. He ran the course of the Athens Marathon on his own, and later that year he completed his first competitive marathon, in Honolulu. He has since run in marathons, half-marathons and triathlons both in Japan (including the 1996 100-kilometre "ultra-marathon" in Hokkaidō, which he completed in eleven hours) and abroad: Athens, New York, New Jersey, New Bedford, and Boston five times as of 1997; his best time: 3:31:04 (1991). To date, he has completed over 30 full marathons.[179]

This new urge to travel reflected a rise in his standard of living with the successful launch of his full-time career. *A Wild Sheep Chase* sold some 50,000 copies in six months. But aside from the occasional Alfa Romeo or Mercedes he allows himself, commercial success has not altered Murakami's essentially Spartan lifestyle.

He maintains his distance from the literary beautiful people and chooses not to go on TV. (In one rare public appearance, he volunteered to do some readings to benefit the libraries of the Kobe area after the 1995 earthquake.) He still walks around in sneakers most of the time, prefers plastic watches, and almost never wears any of the five suits or twenty ties he found he owned in the year 2000.[180] The walls of his apartment in an admittedly fashionable (i.e. quiet and private) area of Tokyo and his seaside house west of Tokyo are as sparsely decorated as his minimalist prose.

Murakami is definitely a workaholic in the sense that he rarely does anything that doesn't involve writing, but the fact is he thoroughly loves it. He thinks of his athletic activities as maintaining his health for writing. Most of the considerable travelling he does is "on assignment" for one magazine or another, often in the company of a cameraman (or of Yōko, many of whose excellent photos have appeared with his texts); which is to say he puts himself into situations that require him to learn more about his destinations than he might as a casual traveller, and he writes what he learns, which gives him great pleasure.

During the New Year holidays of 2000, he vowed to make himself stop work for a while. But while he resisted switching on the computer, he couldn't stand the idleness. To pass the time he began making up palindromes – sentences that read the same backwards and forwards such as "Madam, I'm Adam", to which the reply is "Sir, I'm Iris." Murakami, of course, was writing in Japanese, in which language such constructions are called *kaibun* and are not necessarily complete sentences. He managed to write one *kaibun* for each syllable in the Japanese phonetic system (a total of 44), but instead of stuffing them in a drawer as anyone else might do, he wrote silly stories explaining each one and published them in a cute little book with cute little drawings by Mimiyo Tomozawa, adding yet another volume to his ever-expanding opus.[181]

The title of the book is *Ma-ta-ta-bi a-bi-ta Ta-ma*, which reads the same backwards and forwards, syllable for syllable. "Tama" is capitalized because it is the name of a cat. There is probably no way to translate a palindrome into another language. The bare meaning of Murakami's title is "Tama, showered in catnip", which, spelled backwards, is "Pintac ni derewohs, amat".

As for work-related travel, in 1984, Haruki and Yōko toured America for six weeks that summer. Murakami had stopped off briefly in Hawaii to run in the Honolulu Marathon the year before, but on this first serious trip to the United States, he visited Raymond Carver, John Irving and Princeton, the alma mater of F. Scott Fitzgerald.

The meeting with Carver and his wife, the poet Tess Gallagher, at Sky House, their Olympic Peninsula home in Washington State, was the foremost of Murakami's literary pilgrimages that summer. Although it lasted only an hour or two, it left its mark on both couples. Carver was deeply involved in a writing project, but he was determined to make time for Murakami, so honoured was he to think that a translator would come all the way from Japan to meet him. Tess Gallagher reports that "Ray was eager, almost childlike with delight, to meet Murakami, to see who he was and why Ray's writing had brought them together on the planet."[182] Haruki and Yōko arrived in the early afternoon and were served a simple snack of tea and smoked salmon and crackers.

In his account of the meeting, Murakami notes that it took place after Carver had overcome his drinking problem.

In the waning of that quiet afternoon, I remember with what distaste he was sipping black tea. Holding the teacup in his hand, he looked as though he was doing the wrong thing in the wrong place. Sometimes he would get up from his seat and go outside to smoke. From the window of Tess Gallagher's Sky House in Port Angeles, I could make out a ferryboat on its way to Canada.[183]

Out on the deck of the hilltop house together, they lamented the death of small birds that had been crashing into a glass windbreak. They discussed why Carver's work should be so popular in Japan, and Murakami suggested it might be owing to Carver's theme of the many small humiliations in life, something to which Japanese people could readily respond. The discussion triggered just such memories in Carver, who later wrote the poem "The Projectile", dedicating it to Murakami:

> We sipped tea. Politely musing
> on possible reasons for the success
> of my books in your country. Slipped
> into talk of pain and humiliation
> you find occurring, and reoccurring,
> in my stories. And that element
> of sheer chance. How all this translates
> in terms of sales.
> I looked into a corner of the room.
> And for a minute I was 16 again,
> careening around in the snow
> in a '50 Dodge sedan with five or six
> bozos. Giving the finger
> to some other bozos . . .

A snowball fight ensues, and "dumb luck" sends one projectile "into the side / of my head so hard it broke my eardrum", the intense pain drawing tears of humiliation in front of his friends. The victorious "bozo" drove off and probably never gave the incident

another thought. And why should he?
So much else to think about always.
Why remember that stupid car sliding
down the road, then turning the corner
and disappearing?
We politely raise our teacups in the room.
A room that for a minute something else entered.[184]

Of course, in those days before English translations of Murakami's works were available, Carver could have had no inkling of how similar this mental flight into the past was to the fictional world of his Japanese translator. Tess Gallagher recalls that Murakami presented himself only as a translator, and that his still relatively untested spoken English led to some silences, but that "he was obviously very moved to be in Ray's presence". Afterwards, she and Carver agreed that they had just met an extraordinary couple to whom they felt somehow connected.

Murakami was impressed at first by Carver's imposing physical presence, and he also had a feeling of kinship with the American, whose honest, simple prose was so close to his own. Despite fundamental differences in the tone of their literary worlds (Carver's so focused on the emotional strains inherent in relationships, Murakami's burrowing deep into the isolated psyche and its fantasies), Carver's style has inspired Murakami to translate the complete works.

In 1987, the Murakamis went so far as to have an extra-large bed built into their new home in anticipation of the 6'2" Carver's arrival in Japan, at the invitation of the Chūō Kōron Company publishers. The bed frame was constructed by a furniture maker, and the futon mattress (5' × 7') was made by the shop that Yōko's late father had owned. By then, however, Carver's cancer made such a trip impossible. Surgery on 1 October involved the removal of three-quarters of a lung, and the following year he died.

Murakami could hardly believe it when the news reached him. "I imagined what an ordeal it must have been for so large a person to die over such a long period of time. I thought it must be something like the slow fall of a giant tree."[185] He felt that Carver's death had cost him a good friend, and he and Yōko have maintained close ties with Tess Gallagher ever since. She, in turn, aware of how much Carver meant to Murakami, sent him a pair of Carver's shoes as a memento. A portrait of Carver and Tess is one of the few photos hanging in the Murakamis' Tokyo apartment.[186]

Having heard that fame had made John Irving both difficult to contact and more difficult as a person, Murakami had all but given up any hope of meeting him. But while in Washington, D.C., that summer of 1984, he applied through the State Department and received a most welcoming response. Irving said he would be glad to meet Murakami – in New York – because he was only the third person to have asked to translate his never very popular first novel, *Setting Free the Bears*, into a foreign language. (Murakami's translation was published in 1986.) Irving knew from Murakami's curriculum vitae that he was a runner, so he suggested they go for a jog together.

The novelist and his Japanese translator met on a steaming hot June 14th afternoon at the entrance to the Central Park Zoo dressed in running gear. They jogged an easy six miles, talking all the while, Murakami later reporting the experience without benefit of camera or recorder. Their shared athleticism, their similar heights (5'7"), Irving's strikingly clear gaze, and of course Murakami's admiration for his work helped them hit it off well, Irving frequently cautioning Murakami about the "horse shit and taxi drivers" in Central Park. They talked about film adaptations of Irving's books, and he told Murakami about his new novel, *The*

Cider House Rules. He also praised Raymond Carver as an underrated first-rate writer who was finally getting the attention he deserved. After a circuit of the Park, they parted, sweating, Irving going off to wrestling practice, and Murakami to down three beers in a nearby bar.[187]

Murakami enjoyed meeting Carver and Irving on this trip, but overall his encounters with American novelists have not been entirely satisfactory. They have always given him a sense that, the language barrier aside, he was not quite able to communicate with his American counterparts. Some fundamental – and perhaps indefinable – difference between their grasp of the novel and his stood in the way of complete understanding and left him feeling frustrated.[188]

Murakami would take home several permanent impressions of Princeton, where he strolled the campus and visited the library to see original F. Scott Fitzgerald manuscripts. First there were the squirrels – because Japanese are always fascinated by the squirrels that run free in American cities, especially in such park-like places as university campuses. The squirrels – and the rabbits he saw when jogging in the morning – were part of the university's peaceful, pastoral atmosphere. This attractive memory would lure him back seven years later.[189]

5

Études

Back from America in the summer of 1984, Haruki and Yōko moved from the eastern working-family Tokyo suburb where they had been living to the older, quieter suburb of Fujisawa in the west. The disruption of moving seems to have had little impact on Murakami's prolific output as an author or translator. He had become an important enough writer to be invited that December to take part in a one-on-one discussion with the major novelist Kenji Nakagami for an authoritative literary journal.[190] Nakagami had first known Murakami as the rather aloof owner of Peter Cat; now the two men met on a nearly equal footing. Eight years later, Murakami would be shocked to hear that Nakagami had died of cancer of the kidney before he could complete the novel they had discussed that day.

The years between *A Wild Sheep Chase* (1982) and Murakami's next novel, *Hard-boiled Wonderland and the End of the World* (1985), were productive even by Murakami's standards. In addition to writing a good deal of literary and film criticism and many impressionistic essays, he brought out two collections of older stories, published enough new stories to fill a third collection, and continued translating American literature. From his translation work, especially, Murakami always says "I learn a lot."[191] His edition of Raymond Carver's *Where I'm Calling From* appeared in July 1983, the year before his trip to the States. He began serializing John

Irving's *Setting Free the Bears* in April 1985, bringing out the book in 1986. Carver's *At Night the Salmon Move* was published in Murakami's Japanese in June 1985, the same month in which *Hard-boiled Wonderland and the End of the World* appeared, as did Murakami's fourth collection of stories, plus his translation of the Truman Capote story that had so moved him as a teenager, "Headless Hawk".

Firefly, Barn Burning and Other Stories

Murakami's third short story collection, *Firefly, Barn Burning and Other Stories* (*Hotaru, Naya o yaku, sono-ta no tanpen*, 1984), contains many noteworthy pieces that he wrote after *A Wild Sheep Chase*. They show him moving in several directions at once, and they suggest progress in his career, appearing as they did in establishment journals rather than the offbeat magazines that had carried most of his stories before. (The respected literary journal *Shinchō*, was one exception: it printed Murakami's work almost from the beginning.)

The long title story, "Firefly" ("Hotaru", January 1983), appeared in *Chūō Kōron*, the prestigious liberal general-interest magazine that had underwritten the career of Jun'ichirō Tanizaki and was bringing out Murakami's complete works of Raymond Carver. Followers of the cool Murakami may have had second thoughts about both the venue and the rather sentimental piece itself, which is devoid of any excursions into the surreal. Based on Murakami's own early college years, the story is almost unreadable today because most readers will be familiar with the far more fleshed-out version in Chapters 2 and 3 of *Norwegian Wood*.

For the first time Murakami describes the filthy dormitory in which he lived. It is also the story in which he created both the stuttering, map-loving roommate and the troubled girlfriend (though still without a name here), whose former boyfriend (Boku's best friend) had killed himself when they were all still at high school. When the girlfriend abandons Boku and enters a sanatorium after a single episode of love-making, he is consumed with remorse.

The depiction of the roommate as a stutterer is not just a cheap gag. His affliction is greatest when he tries to pronounce the word "map", which is ironic for a geography major and can be taken as a sign of stress involving the discipline. In *Norwegian Wood*, the roommate will be given the nickname "Storm Trooper" for his right-wing style, and in *The Wind-up Bird Chronicle* the importance of map-making and logistics to Japanese imperialist aggression will be made explicit.

The firefly of the title is given to Boku by his roommate. As in the novel, he goes to the dorm roof and releases it from its jar into the darkness. This mournful scene survives intact in *Norwegian Wood*:

> Long after the firefly had disappeared, the trail of its light remained inside me, its pale, faint glow hovering on and on in the thick darkness behind my eyelids like a lost soul.
>
> More than once I tried stretching my hand out in that darkness. My fingers touched nothing. The faint glow remained, just beyond their grasp.[192]

"Barn Burning" ("Naya o yaku", January 1983) is another story that keeps its feet on the ground, though in describing the odd relationship of a 30-something married novelist (Boku) and a 20-something bohemian girl, Murakami leaves so many loose threads hanging, not least the girl's disappearance at the end, that the mood of the piece can hardly be anything but bewilderment.

The key scene is a rambling, abstract, marijuana-inspired conversation between the girl's new boyfriend and Boku. The phrase "barn burning" is repeated like a mantra as the boyfriend reveals his penchant for burning empty barns and the novelist later goes on a methodical (logical) but fruitless (mysterious) search for a burnt barn in his neighbourhood. Undoubtedly, the piece was Murakami's "exploration" of whatever the phrase – from William Faulkner's short story "Barn Burning" – happened to summon to mind in the course of writing.[193]

The most striking piece in the collection is "The Dancing Dwarf" ("Odoru kobito", January 1984). If the magic of Murakami's early stories lies in their straining at the bounds of reality and common sense, this one crosses that line by a mile:

> A dwarf came into my dream and asked me to dance.
> I knew this was a dream, but I was just as tired in my dream as in real life at the time. So, very politely, I declined. The dwarf was not offended but danced alone instead.

As only a Murakami dream dwarf would do, he dances to records of the Rolling Stones, Frank Sinatra, Glenn Miller, Maurice Ravel and Charlie Parker. (As eclectic in his musical tastes as Murakami himself, the dwarf keeps his LPs in any random jackets he happens to pick up.) His beautiful dancing has surprising political overtones. He is from "the north", where dancing is forbidden.

> I wanted to dance like this. And so I came south. I danced in the taverns. I became famous, and danced in the presence of the king. That was before the revolution, of course. Once the revolution broke out, the king passed away, as you know, and I was banished from the town to live in the forest.

Boku feels himself waking up, and so he bids the dwarf goodbye, but the dwarf tells him, somewhat ominously, that they will surely meet again.

Awake, Boku seems – until the end of the next paragraph – to have returned to an utterly mundane world:

> I washed my face with great care, shaved, put some bread in the toaster, and boiled water for coffee. I fed the cat, changed its litter, put on a necktie, and tied my shoes. Then I took a bus to the elephant factory.

The elephant factory? So casually does the narrator drop this on us that the reader's instinctive reaction is to explain it away, to assume he must be talking about a toy factory or something. But Murakami doesn't let us off the hook so easily. He keeps us wondering:

> Needless to say, the manufacture of elephants is no easy matter. They're big, first of all, and very complex. It's not like making hairpins or coloured pencils. The factory covers a huge area, and it consists of several buildings. Each building is big, too, and the sections are colour-coded.[194]

As this matter-of-fact description of the factory progresses, describing how the colour-coded sections of the plant assemble the elephants part by part, it dawns on the reader with mounting wonderment that Boku's elephant factory is exactly what it sounds like: a factory that makes elephants. *Real* elephants. There he goes again, playing with our grey matter. But he does have a purpose. Whereas the depths of the unconscious were labelled an "elephants' graveyard" in *Pinball, 1973*, here the elephant is associated with a creative process, the power of the imagination. This will not be Murakami's last word on elephants, however.

At work the next day, Boku tells his partner in the Ear Section about the dwarf in his dream. The normally reticent partner surprises him by saying he thinks he has heard about this particular dwarf before. He advises Boku to ask an old worker who has been at the factory since before the revolution. (Aha, so there was a revolution in *this* world, too!) By this point in "The Dancing Dwarf" we know that the two worlds of dream and "reality" (a "real" world with an elephant factory requires quotation marks) are going to do more than just casually intersect. The rest of the story plays itself out with all the implacable certainty of a fairy-tale, rising to a crescendo of horror as a beautiful young girl is transformed into a mass of squirming maggots. "The Dancing Dwarf" is a marvellous demonstration of Murakami's ability to use traditional storytelling motifs in startling ways, and it is something of a preparation for the bifurcation of worlds on a grand scale that will come in *Hard-boiled Wonderland and the End of the World*.

Dead Heat on a Merry-Go-Round

One more volume of post-*A Wild Sheep Chase* stories, *Dead Heat on a Merry-Go-Round* (*Kaiten mokuba no deddo hiito*, October 1985), is fascinating both for what it is and for what it pretends *not* to be. Unlike the earlier collections, it is not a random assemblage of unrelated stories that have appeared in magazines. For this volume, Murakami wrote a substantial introductory essay linking the works in theme and conception, and stating unequivocally that they were not fictional – or at least not *very* fictional. Speaking as Boku and thus blurring the line between fact and fiction, he says:

> I hesitate to call the pieces assembled in this volume fiction.
> They are not fictional stories (*shōsetsu*) in the proper sense
> of the word . . . Rather, they are without exception based on
> fact. I have simply written down here various stories that

I have heard from a number of people. Of course, I have altered some details to protect certain people from embarrassment . . . but the general thread of each story is factual. I have not exaggerated nor added anything to make the stories more entertaining . . .

I first started to write these pieces – call them sketches – as a kind of "warming up" before taking on the task of writing a full-length novel, on the assumption that the process of recording facts as facts would later serve some kind of purpose. Which is to say, I originally had no intention of putting these into print.[195]

All of the stories in the collection, then, are presented within a frame: Boku hears them from people who decide to open themselves up to him. Some of his informants even call him "Murakami", further enhancing the impression that Boku and Murakami are one and the same. Only when the fifth volume of the *Complete Works* appeared in 1991, however, did he confess that the entire volume was made up. "None of the characters here is modelled on anyone," he declared. "I was very clear in my own mind about what I wanted to accomplish in this series . . . This was training for me to write realistic prose . . . I needed the camouflage of verbatim note-taking. The character of Nick Carraway, the narrator in Fitzgerald's *The Great Gatsby*, had always interested me, and that was the most immediate reason for my adopting the device . . . I would never have been able to write *Norwegian Wood* without this practice."[196]

The stories tend to be a little wordy as they strive for a sense of detailed accuracy; they are given an unpolished, fragmentary quality to enhance the appearance of realism, and where the reader might expect Boku to offer some wise insight or advice to the perturbed teller of the story, he is usually just as confused as the other person is, and the two part company without any clear-cut conclusions. The volume's very success at creating a drab realism perhaps makes it less attractive than some of his other story collections, but it is a special, quietly absorbing work that might one day merit a complete translation. At present, Murakami would rather see a few of the more finished pieces appear as independent stories.[197]

In *Dead Heat on a Merry-Go-Round* (the title borrowed from the 1966 film with James Coburn), Murakami pursues his fascination with the frightening ease with which people's lives and personalities can change. Fortunately, the story that Murakami justifiably considers the most successful one, "Lederhosen" ("Rēdāhōzen, October 1985), is available in translation (with the framing device abbreviated) in *The Elephant Vanishes* along with "The Silence" ("Chinmoku", January 1991).[198]

"Lederhosen" tells the story of a woman whose life undergoes a profound change during the 30 minutes it takes to have a pair of lederhosen custom-designed for her husband. She realizes that she wants a divorce as all the years of lingering resentment towards him – mostly for his infidelities – combine with her newfound sense of autonomy on a trip to Europe. This is also one of the more vivid and economical realizations of the theme of the disappearing woman to which Murakami would return again and again.

The next story in the collection, "The Man in the Taxi" ("Takushii ni notta otoko", February 1984), portrays another woman who, in a foreign country, decides to abandon her husband and child and make a life for herself without them. The catalyst is a painting she buys from a Czech artist in New York. Though technically mediocre, its depiction of the loneliness and emptiness of a young man riding in a taxi conjoins with her sense of failure and lost youth at the age of 29. She burns the picture and goes back to Japan. Years later, in Athens, she finds herself sitting next to the very man depicted long ago in the painting, still young, dressed as he had been back then.

She says nothing to him about the painting, of course, but feels that she has left a part of herself in the cab with him. Boku admits it has been difficult keeping this story to himself, and is relieved to have had the chance to tell it. It is a rare foray into the mysterious for such a supposedly realistic collection.

In another story, "Poolside" ("Pūrusaido", October 1983), Boku sits by a marvellously clear pool in which swimmers seem to float in space, listening to the story of a man who, through systematic exercise and diet, struggles against the ravages of middle age. The man wonders why, despite a happy marriage and a successful life, he feels there is something inside him that he cannot grasp. The story might be regarded as a precursor of *South of the Border, West of the Sun* (*Kokkyō no minami, taiyō no nishi*, 1992).

A novelist named Murakami (who calls himself Boku) recalls having become sexually aroused when pressed up against a beautiful young woman he disliked, but who fell asleep on his arm during a college outing. Years later he meets her husband, who tells him how unprepared she was, as a spoiled rich girl, for the loss of their baby daughter. Boku feels too confused to follow the husband's suggestion to give her a call. And so ends "One for the Queen, Who Is No Longer With Us" ("Ima wa naki ōjo no tame no", April 1984).

In "Ōto 1979" (*"La Nausée 1979"*, October 1984), a young illustrator with whom Boku/Murakami worked on a magazine assignment (and with whom he occasionally trades jazz records) begins vomiting on 4 June 1979, and continues vomiting once a day until 14 July (his diary is very precise). During this time he also receives mysterious phone calls from an unfamiliar male voice pronouncing his name and hanging up. This may have something to do with the guilt he feels (or ought to feel) about his favourite hobby of seducing his friends' wives and girlfriends, but nothing is ever explained. The story thus portrays a mundane phenomenon carried to surreal extremes, with only hints at a psychological cause, as we see so often in Murakami's fiction. Similar devices are at work in "The Ball Field" ("Yakyūjō", June 1984), in which a college student becomes an obsessive voyeur and, once cured, can no longer be sure what comprises his real self.

"Ama-yadori" ("Taking Shelter from the Rain", December 1983) depicts a beautiful female editor who gave Boku/Murakami his first interview as a novelist, but shortly afterwards found herself without a job or a lover. Luxuriating in her first free time in years, she quickly became bored and ended up selling her body to several men, until she started a new job a few weeks later. This episode appears to have left her entirely unmarked. Murakami frequently depicts sex in which there seems to be a clean split between mind and body, the psychological far outweighing the physical in importance.

"Hunting Knife" ("Hantingu-naifu", December 1984) contains lengthy and seemingly inconclusive descriptions of a seaside resort at which Boku observes a mother in her late fifties and her wheelchair-bound son in his late twenties about whom we learn only that the mother has occasional bouts of emotional collapse and her son carries a finely made hunting knife. It is no coincidence, however, that Boku and his wife, both in their late twenties, are trying to decide once and for all whether or not to have children, and the example set by this odd couple is hardly encouraging. A remark that Boku drops about his attitude towards socializing is of some autobiographical interest: "I uncrossed my legs under the table and looked for a chance to get away. It seems that's what I'm always doing: looking for chances to get away. I guess it's my personality."[199]

"The Silence" vividly recalls the psychological strains of high school as an amateur boxer tells Boku about his experience of having been subjected by his classmates to the silent treatment for an offence he never committed. What most bothers him, even in adulthood, is the ease with which one charismatic – if shallow – individual was able to influence the entire class. Murakami would pursue this theme in The Wind-up Bird Chronicle's portrayal of a wily but popular media figure, and in his investigations into Aum Shinrikyō's sarin gas attack on the Tokyo subway.

The stories from this period, then, show Murakami using short fiction as a staging ground for longer efforts. In his postscript to Firefly, Barn Burning and Other Stories, he writes: "People often ask me whether I am more comfortable writing short stories or novels, but I don't know the answer to that. After I finish a novel, I feel a vague, lingering regret, and after I've written a number of stories, an oppressive feeling makes me take on a full-length work. That's my pattern. I *may* stop alternating between short and long forms some day, but I know I want to keep writing fiction. It's what I enjoy most."[200]

6

Song of My Self

Hard-boiled Wonderland and the End of the World

Murakami won the prestigious Noma Literary Newcomer's Prize for *A Wild Sheep Chase*. His next novel, *Hard-boiled Wonderland and the End of the World* (1985), won the still more prestigious Tanizaki Literary Prize, named after the great novelist Jun'ichirō Tanizaki (1886–1965), author of *The Diary of a Mad Old Man*, *The Key*, *The Makioka Sisters*, and a host of other modern classics. It was fitting that Murakami should be honoured by association with Tanizaki, a novelist who helped establish a precedent in Japanese literature for wholly imagined fictional worlds. In *Hard-boiled Wonderland and the End of the World* Murakami would create not one but two utterly different – though subtly interrelated – fictional worlds.

The distinguished writers who awarded Murakami the Tanizaki Prize were hardly unanimous in their praise of the book, but among them Kenzaburō Ōe wrote how "wonderfully invigorated" he felt that the "young" Murakami had won the prize for having so painstakingly fabricated this adventurous fictional experiment. He also noted that it could be read as a new *In Praise of Shadows* [*In'ei raisan*])", suggesting, by reference to Tanizaki's most famous essay, that an aesthetic link could be made between Murakami and Tanizaki.[201]

These words probably came back to haunt Ōe, who later complained that Murakami's works fail to "go beyond their influence on the lifestyles of youth to appeal to intellectuals in the broad sense with models for Japan's present and future".[202] Ōe's remarks are reminiscent of critics of Tanizaki, who said that his works were devoid of ideas or divorced from the real world.

If *A Wild Sheep Chase* was a major advance over Murakami's first two books, *Hard-boiled Wonderland and the End of the World* is an even bigger leap forwards in scope and imaginative bravura. It was the first novel he wrote expressly for book publication rather than for a magazine, and it is his most successful attempt to create a novel with an overarching structure. One might assume from the novel's sheer scale and complexity that he spent all of his time after *A Wild Sheep Chase* writing it. In fact, he did not begin the book until after his trip to America, and wrote it in the five months between August 1984 and the following January. The process took all his powers of concentration, and he finished it with a considerable sense of relief on the evening of his thirty-sixth birthday. He was taken aback when Yōko advised him that he should rewrite the entire second half, but he calmed down and spent another two months revising it, rewriting the ending five or six times.[203]

At this point in his career Murakami had a substantial backlog of stories, as we have seen, but when the Shinchōsha publishing house asked him to write a novel for their prestigious "Belletristic Book-Publication Series"[204] he turned to a long story he had written after *Pinball, 1973*: "The Town and its Uncertain Walls" ("Machi to sono fu-tashika na kabe", 1980), which he considered such a failure that he later excluded it from the *Complete Works*. His powers as a writer had simply not been up to the task, he has written, but he felt that his subsequent experience had given him the confidence to try again.[205]

Short as it is, the story "Dabchick" discussed above is probably

115

the one most compelling piece of evidence that, for Murakami, all reality is memory, and that fiction is strictly the interplay of words and imagination. And this is just as true for the lengthy *Hard-boiled Wonderland and the End of the World*, which Susan Napier has correctly labelled "solipsistic".[206] As Murakami told an interviewer after the novel received the Tanizaki Prize, there is nothing that he enjoys so much as the process of describing in ever finer precision the details of a thing that does not exist.[207]

In retrospect, it seems inevitable that Murakami should have written a book like *Hard-boiled Wonderland and the End of the World*. If not so clearly in *Hear the Wind Sing* with its Martian wells, certainly by the following year's *Pinball, 1973* he was thinking in terms of a timeless "original place" inside the deep wells of the mind. This repository of legend and dream is inaccessible to conscious thought, but, mysteriously and unpredictably, there emerge from it highly idiosyncratic images and words associated with a particular lost past (and the things and people one has lost in the past). They travel down dark passages and occupy the conscious mind for a while before returning to that timeless original place.

Murakami has said that a tendency to contrast "existence" with "non-existence" or "being" with "non-being" is fundamental to his work. His writings tend to posit two parallel worlds, one obviously fantastic and the other closer to recognizable "reality".[208] In *Hear the Wind Sing*, for example, he created a cool, this-worldly Boku and an anguished, inward-burrowing writer called the Rat. In *Pinball, 1973*, Boku and the Rat never meet, separated not only by the geographical distance between Tokyo and Kobe but also by the epistemological distance between a seemingly autobiographical first-person narrator and a more overtly fictional character depicted in the third person. They live in two parallel worlds that are revealed to the reader in roughly alternating chapters. In *A Wild Sheep Chase*, the point of view remains entirely with Boku, and the

116

only means he has to contact his dead friend in the other world is through a possibly delirious experience that occurs in impenetrable darkness.

This psychological bifurcation emerged again when Murakami turned to writing full-length fiction after a three-year hiatus following the publication of *A Wild Sheep Chase*. Now, however, instead of giving the other psyche a name (or a nickname), Murakami split his narrator-hero into Boku and Watashi, assigning the formal Watashi-"I" to the more realistic world of a vaguely futuristic Tokyo, and the informal Boku-"I" to the inner, fantastic world of "The Town and Its Uncertain Walls".

The words "Watashi" and "Boku" give very different impressions in Japanese, such that the Japanese reader can open the book at any point and know immediately which narrative is spread out on the page. Unfortunately for the translator, the only word that can be used to translate either "Watashi" or "Boku" into English is "I". Alfred Birnbaum solved this problem by translating the "End of the World" sections into the present tense, thereby making a distinction between the two narrators' worlds that is natural in English. It also imparts a timeless quality that may be more appropriate than the normal past-tense narration of the original.

As narrators, Boku and Watashi remain absolutely separate, but in dialogue Watashi speaks to other characters in the book as a young man normally would, routinely referring to himself as "Boku". This becomes dramatically significant near the end of the book as the two characters begin to merge. When Watashi demands to know "what the hell's going to become of me (*boku*)?" he is in effect asking what is going to become of Boku in the other world.[209]

The two narratives progress in alternating chapters, Watashi's "Hard-boiled Wonderland" and Boku's "The End of the World". Each narrative creates a different world, each echoing the other at first in only the tiniest details (such as the odd prominence in

117

both of paper clips), but obvious parallels begin to emerge. Both narrators become involved with librarians, and both visit the library in connection with unicorns. (The more "realistic" affair is highly physical, but the woman in question has an enormous appetite for food that goes far beyond the bounds of realism.) The great adventure of reading the novel is to discover how the two worlds are interrelated.

Murakami keeps a tight rein on the process of that discovery through careful control of detail and structure. The tiniest details in the opening chapter – a poorly whistled song, a whiff of cologne – turn out to have great bearing on the unfolding of the plot. None of his other novels before or since has been worked out with such attention to an overall fictional architecture. The two separate but simultaneous narratives are deliberately kept apart. The rationale for this is the inability of the individual to know his own inner mind.

That inner mind is called many things in this novel: the "core consciousness", the "black box", and, in the words of the character known as the Professor, a "great unexplored elephant graveyard". The Professor quickly corrects himself, however:

"No, an 'elephant graveyard' isn't exactly right. 'Tisn't a burial ground for collected dead memories. An 'elephant factory' is more like it. There's where you sort through countless memories and bits of knowledge, arrange the assorted chips into complex lines, combine these lines into even more complex bundles, and finally make up a cognitive system. A veritable production line with you as the boss. Unfortunately, though, the factory floor is off-limits. Like *Alice in Wonderland*, you need a special drug t'shrink you in."[210]

Thus the elephant of *Hear the Wind Sing* has evolved through the elephant graveyard of *Pinball, 1973* and the elephant factory of "The Dancing Dwarf" to become an image of the unconscious that sees the inner mind as an all-but-inaccessible factory engaged in the manufacture of elephants, those inscrutable masters of memory. "Nobody's got the keys t'the elephant factory inside us," says the Professor, not even Freud or Jung.[211] In his hard-boiled wonderland, however, Watashi will learn more about his own elephant factory than he ever wanted to know and will "succeed" in the Proustian search for lost time.

The image of the well is flashed at the reader on the first page of the book, and soon the protagonist of the "Hard-boiled Wonderland" narrative, Watashi, is walking down a long, gloomy corridor, led by an attractive (but chubby) young woman in pink whose voice does not seem to work. Like the narrator of "Dabchick", Watashi is here for employment, and he apologizes to the mute receptionist for arriving late. The fruity scent of her cologne fills him with "a nostalgic yet impossible pastiche of sentiments, as if two wholly unrelated memories had threaded together in an unknown recess",[212] at which point she forms the word "Proust" on her lips. Reminiscent of the backhanded citation of Proust in *A Wild Sheep Chase*, this typically wacko Murakami-ism (try reading the single word "Proust" on anybody's lips, outside of any context, and more especially in the Japanese pronunciation, "Purūsuto"!) suggests that Watashi is about to embark on a journey into the "unknown recesses" of his own memories as serious as anything Proust ever attempted. Seemingly confident that he is forging into Proustian territory but that no one would ever suspect him of harbouring such pretensions, Murakami decides to have some fun.

Considering the possibility that he has misread the girl's lips, Watashi experiments with other words. Did she say *"urūdoshi"* ("intercalary year": a word connected with ancient ways of keeping time)? Or *"tsurushi-ido"* ("dangling-well": a word Murakami seems to have made up to add to his inventory of wells)? Or was it *"kuroi udo"* ("large black tree": a potentially powerful vegetative image joining the upper and lower worlds)?[213]

> One after the other, quietly to myself, I pronounced strings of meaningless syllables, but none seemed to match. I could only conclude that she had indeed said, "Proust". But what I couldn't figure out was, what was the connection between this long corridor and Marcel Proust?
>
> Perhaps she'd cited Marcel Proust as a metaphor for the length of the corridor. Yet, supposing that were the case, wasn't it a trifle flighty – not to say inconsiderate – as a choice of expression? Now if she'd cited this long corridor as a metaphor for the works of Marcel Proust, that much I could accept. But the reverse was bizarre.
>
> A corridor as long as Marcel Proust?
>
> Whatever, I kept following her down that long corridor. Truly, a long corridor.[214]

With his literary credentials thus both established and denied in a single stroke, Murakami sets his protagonist upon a new but familiar quest down a long corridor with comic overtones reminiscent of "Dabchick".

The girl shows Watashi to a bare, modernistic office, hands him a rain cape, boots, goggles, and a flashlight, and shows him to a black opening inside a large wardrobe, from which emanates the roar of a river. Following her silent instructions, he climbs down a long ladder into the darkness and begins to walk along a river bank, at the end of which he is supposed to find a waterfall behind which is the laboratory of the girl's grandfather – all of this in the middle of Tokyo!

The grandfather unexpectedly meets him halfway. Somehow "turning down" the sound of the river so that they can hear each other, he warns Watashi of the danger of the INKlings (*yamikuro*: literally "darkblacks") who live down there under the city – indeed, directly under the Imperial Palace – devouring the flesh of the occasional human who wanders into their realm.

We learn later that the grandfather, known as the Professor, has situated his laboratory in this dangerous place to keep out both the "Calcutecs" and the "Semiotecs", who want access to his work, and he keeps the INKlings away by controlling the sounds in the vicinity. (He also realizes that he has absentmindedly left his granddaughter's voice "off" from an earlier experiment and has to go correct his mistake while Watashi works in his laboratory.) Watashi himself is a Calcutec and, it turns out, so was the Professor – but a far more prominent figure in the Calcutec "System" than Watashi. Apostate Calcutecs are usually recruited by the enemy Semiotecs and their "Factory", but the Professor is not aligned with either side in the ongoing information war.

Watashi has been hired by the Professor for his ability as a Calcutec: men whose brains have been split to allow them to perform complex calculations. This has been done for security purposes since, unlike computers, brains cannot be electronically tapped – at least not yet, though the ruthless Semiotecs keep trying. Once, in fact, they kidnapped five Calcutecs, sawed off the tops of their skulls, and attempted, unsuccessfully, to extract data directly from their brains. This "cyber-punk" aspect of Watashi's identity bears a striking resemblance to one element in William Gibson's 1981 story, "Johnny Mnemonic", but Murakami denies that Gibson's work was a source for the novel.[215]

Watashi's world stands in stark contrast to Boku's. Watashi's is one of words and sounds; Boku's is one of images and song, many of them half-remembered, their significance all but lost. (As the barrier between the two begins to break down, however, Watashi experiences déjà vu, recalling both images and songs.) The garrulous Watashi is constantly cracking jokes, even to himself; the elevator in the opening scene is so big "You might even squeeze in three camels and a mid-range palm tree." Very much a "hardboiled" type, he keeps the world at a distance through sardonic humour. The dreamy Boku has no such distancing sarcasm. He feels vibrations from a past that he can barely recall, and sees the world as a poet might ("Particles of yellow light seem to swell and contract as they fall").[216]

Time passes differently in the two worlds. We get practically an hour-by-hour report of Watashi's actions, which take place over a period of precisely five days, 28 September to 3 October. The passing of the season from autumn into deep winter is what marks time for Boku. The two move implacably towards a final crescendo. As Boku rediscovers music and warmth, Watashi feverishly absorbs his last sense impressions of the real world in an eclectic rhapsody of pop- and high-culture trivia, falling asleep in a car to the strains of Bob Dylan.

The setting of the Boku-narrated part of the story, "The End of the World", seems to be a medieval walled town, but later references to abandoned factories, electric lights, obsolete army officers and empty barracks, suggest something more like a post-nuclear (or perhaps simply post-war) world with ruined reminders of a past that cannot quite be remembered. The clock in the tower is frozen at 10.35 (though other timepieces in the town do work). The wall that surrounds the town is enormous – "almost 30 feet high, which only birds can clear".[217] The entire town is, in effect, an elaborate well of the unconscious, as in *Pinball, 1973*: "We've got all these wells dug in our hearts. While above the wells, birds flit back and forth." Only birds can travel freely between the conscious and unconscious worlds, so they act as symbols for all the delicate psychological phenomena that interest Murakami – déjà vu, images of half-remembered things, flashes of memory, and – their opposite – sudden memory blanks. Murakami provides a map of the town, which seems to be shaped rather like a brain. (He says he drew it as he wrote, so that he could keep the layout of his imaginary town in mind.)[218]

In "The End of the World", a herd of unicorns spends its days inside the town walls and is let outside at night by the gatekeeper, who seems to have tyrannical powers over the residents. (See the discussion of "A Poor-Aunt Story" above for the source of the unicorns.) Boku is not a native of the town, and when he first arrived, the gatekeeper (who spends most of his time sharpening knives) insisted upon cutting Boku's shadow off at the ankles, though he promised to take care of the shadow and let Boku visit him. The loss of his shadow signals the beginning of the loss of everything that allows him to think and feel as an individual. Boku soon learns that, detached from him, his shadow will not survive the coming winter.

Significantly, Boku's primary informant regarding matters of the shadow and forgetting is a retired army officer, the Colonel. Stephen Snyder suggests that "the walled, amnesia-stricken community [is] a metaphor for a Japan that hesitates to come to terms with its past or actively define a global role for its future (though such a reading would be crediting Murakami with greater political consciousness than he is usually allowed)."[219] Murakami's use of the Colonel would seem to confirm this, at least where the past is concerned, and many still find the "wall" surrounding Japan a source of frustration. "It is not easy to surrender your shadow and simply let it die," the Colonel tells Boku. "The pain is the same for everyone, though it is one thing to tear the shadow away from an innocent child who has not gotten attached to it, and quite another to do it to an old fool. I was in my sixty-fifth year when they put my shadow to death. When you reach that age, you have lots of memories."[220]

The Colonel also seems to echo pre-war conservative Japanese fears of "dangerous thoughts" from abroad when he warns Boku to keep away from the woods, for it is there, we learn later, that the few people live who have not fully surrendered their hearts and minds and memories: "Their existence is wholly different from our own," he says. "They are dangerous. They can exert an influence over you." The wall is another potential source of danger for Boku, he warns. Not only does it hold everyone in with a ferocious tenacity, "It sees everything that transpires within," as much on the lookout for those who threaten to step out of line as is Japanese society itself.[221]

Intent on permanently separating Boku from his memories, the gatekeeper becomes an increasingly malevolent character. After Boku commits himself to living in this town where the residents are forbidden to have shadows, he discovers that neither he nor anyone else will ever be allowed to leave. During one furtive visit, the shadow orders Boku to scout the town and draw a detailed map, concentrating especially on the wall and its portals. (This becomes the book's brain-shaped map.) The gatekeeper also assigns Boku on his arrival to the profession of "Dream Reader", marking him as such by painlessly cutting slits in his eyeballs. This makes Boku sensitive to light and requires him to sequester himself on bright days, and do his dream reading at the town "library" at night.

The town's "old dreams" are contained in its vast store of unicorn skulls, and when Boku touches a skull the dreams come to him as vivid, disconnected images, the meaning of which he cannot fathom. Neither he nor the lady librarian with whom he becomes passionlessly involved know why he must perform this task, but eventually he realizes that he is releasing into the atmosphere the very qualities of personality and memory that permit of passionate feelings – feelings towards other individuals and towards the world itself.

In exchange for eternal life, the residents of the town must sacrifice their hearts and minds (their *kokoro*, in Japanese). This is the only route to salvation. As the gatekeeper puts it, when he is boasting to Boku of the wall's "perfection" and the impossibility of escape:

> I know how hard it is for you [to lose your shadow]. But this is something that everybody goes through, so you'll just have to endure it, too. After that comes salvation. Then, you won't have any more worries or suffering. They will all disappear. Momentary feelings aren't worth a thing. I'm telling you this for your own good: forget about your shadow. This is the End of the World. This is where the world ends. Nobody goes anywhere from here – you included.[222]

Living under the sway of the gatekeeper, the people of the town have only the palest feelings for each other and for the world. The young librarian loved by Boku cannot return his love because her shadow died years ago when she was 17 (the age of the chubby girl in pink, who is perhaps her "shadow" in the outside world), and she no longer has the *kokoro* to feel deeply for him. This numbers her among the "saved", rather in the way *Pinball*'s Boku concluded that the only route to peace was "not to want anything any more".

Here, Boku asks the librarian –

> "Did you meet with your shadow before she died?"
> She shakes her head. "No, I did not see her. There was no reason for us to meet. She had become something apart from me."

"But your shadow might have been you yourself."

"Perhaps. But in any case, it is all the same now. The circle is closed."

The pot on the stove begins to murmur, sounding to my ears like the wind in the distance.

"Do you still want me even so?" she asks.

"Yes," I answer. "I still want you."[223]

What we have here, is a full-scale exploration of the "gap" mentioned in the "Girl from Ipanema" story: "Somewhere in [my consciousness], I'm sure, is the link joining me with myself. Someday, too, I'm sure, I'll meet myself in a strange place in a far-off world . . . In that place, I am myself and myself is me. Subject is object and object is subject. All gaps gone. A perfect union. There must be a strange place like this somewhere in the world."

The townspeople's lack of deep feeling is seen most clearly in their having lost the power to appreciate music. Indeed, there is a storeroom in one isolated part of the town where old musical instruments are kept as curious gadgets, their use forgotten. The librarian vaguely recalls that her mother used to "talk" in a peculiar way:

"Mother would draw words out or she would make them short. Her voice would sound high and low like the wind."

"That is singing," I suddenly realize.

"Can you talk like that?"

"Singing is not talking. It is song."

"Can you do it too?" she says.

I take a deep breath but find no music in my memory.[224]

As the snows of winter deepen (again the coldness of the chicken warehouse in *Pinball, 1973*), Boku struggles to make himself remember a song until he manages at last to extract music from "a box hinged with leather folds" that has "buttons for the fingers".[225]

After a time, I am able, as if by will, to locate the first four notes. They drift down from inward skies, softly, as early morning sunlight. They find *me*; these are the notes I have been seeking.

I hold down the chord key and press the individual notes over and over again. The four notes seem to desire further notes, another chord. I strain to hear the chord that follows. The first four notes lead me to the next five, then to another chord and three more notes.

It is a melody. Not a complete song, but the first phrase of one. I play the three chords and twelve notes, also, over and over again. It is a song, I realize, that I know.

Danny Boy [the very song Watashi had been trying unsuccessfully to recall in Chapter 1].

The title brings back the song: chords, notes, harmonies now flow naturally from my fingertips. I play the melody again.

When have I last heard a song? My body has craved music. I have been so long without music, I have not even known my own hunger. The resonance permeates; the strain eases within me. Music brings a warm glow to my vision, thawing mind and muscle from their endless wintering.

The whole Town lives and breathes in the music I play. The streets shift their weight with my every move. The Wall stretches and flexes as if my own flesh and skin. I repeat the song several times, then set the accordion down on the floor, lean back, and close my eyes. Everything here is a part of me – the Wall and Gate and Woods and River and Pool. It is all my self.[226]

127

Only when he realizes that the town is his very self, does Boku sense his "responsibilities" towards it, which vastly complicates his plan to escape to the "real" world with his shadow.[227] The pull between the two worlds – one real but on the verge of death, the other timeless but also soulless – keeps the reader in suspense until the very end. The choice that Boku makes may be one that is open only to the artist, who inhabits a marginal space somewhere between the two.

(This summary has been left deliberately obscure at crucial points for readers who have not yet read *Hard-boiled Wonderland and the End of the World*. The pleasure this book affords is something quite special.)

Hard-boiled Wonderland and the End of the World is Murakami's most elaborate exploration of the relationship of the brain to the world it perceives. He had an opportunity to expand on this question when interviewed about the spontaneity of his style. The interviewer didn't quite buy his assertion that he had "nothing to write about", as he had claimed with reference to *Hear the Wind Sing*. "If you have nothing to write about," asked the interviewer, "how do you account for your ability to write such long novels?"

I think it's precisely because I have nothing I want to write about that I can write long novels. The less there is I want to say, the simpler the structure gets. If you know beforehand "I want to say this or that", then structure naturally begins to become oppressive and to interrupt the spontaneous flow of the story . . . "Theme" is strictly a secondary matter . . . Basically, I believe in the inner power of the human being.

Q: Hmm, that sort of reminds me of Keith Jarrett's performances of improvisational music.

A: Except that I have no concept of a god being involved.

Q: Right, his idea is religious. He says he is being guided by God as he plays.

A: I'm a little more . . . what? . . . pragmatic? . . . physical? That's why the brain keeps coming up in my works. I feel that somewhere I'm tying together the brain and that inner power. So, as in *A Wild Sheep Chase*, you get this blood cyst in the boss's brain. I don't believe in the existence of God, of course, but I think I do believe in something like that kind of power in the human *system*.[228]

About a month before he finished writing the last part of *Hard-boiled Wonderland and the End of the World*, Murakami justifiably felt a strong sense of accomplishment as a novelist. "I *have* to write novels," he told the writer Kenji Nakagami. "For me, a story is more or less a springboard for a novel." When Nakagami pointed out that Murakami's reputation at this point rested primarily on his short stories, Murakami insisted: "The way I feel about it, a short story can be either a preparation for a novel or a kind of gleaning – a way to write something that didn't quite fit into a longer work."

He then told Nakagami he was planning to spend 1985 translating and writing stories, then go abroad for a while the year after. He had enjoyed meeting American writers but wasn't especially attracted to the US as a place to live. He thought he would try Greece or Turkey, which he had enjoyed visiting.[229] It would be another four months before he completed his novel and the rewrites, but otherwise things would go pretty much according to plan.

When Nakagami asked him the title of the new novel, Murakami just chuckled: "I'm too embarrassed to say." He revealed why to his Berkeley audience:

Next I wrote a novel with a very long title: *Hard-boiled Wonderland and the End of the World*. My Japanese editor

129

asked me to shorten this title to *The End of the World*. My American editor asked me to shorten it to *Hard-boiled Wonderland*. Alfred Birnbaum, who translated it, thought the title was simply ridiculous and asked me to find something completely different. But I resisted them all. *Hard-boiled Wonderland and the End of the World* may be a long, ridiculous title, but it is the only possible one for that book.

The double title reflects the fact that there are two separate stories in the novel, one called "Hard-boiled Wonderland" and the other called "The End of the World", told in alternating chapters. In the end, these two totally different stories overlap and become one. This is a technique often used in mystery stories or science fiction. Ken Follett, for example, is a writer who often uses this approach. I wanted to write a large-scale novel using this method . . .

Writing this novel was a sort of game for me, since for a long time I myself had no idea how the two stories would come together. It was a thrilling experience, but one that left me exhausted. I knew it would be a long time before I tried something like that again.[230]

7

Wagner Overtures and
Modern Kitchens

After the sustained effort of writing a novel, Murakami began writing short fiction again. Several of his finest stories date from this time between *Hard-boiled Wonderland and the End of the World* (June 1985) and *Norwegian Wood* (September 1987). Two of the best appeared in August 1985: "The Second Bakery Attack" ("Pan'ya saishūgeki") and "The Elephant Vanishes" ("Zō no shōmetsu"). The stories from this period would be anthologized in Murakami's fifth short story collection, *The Second Bakery Attack* (April 1986), and no fewer than five of them would be featured in his first English-language anthology, *The Elephant Vanishes*.

"The Second Bakery Attack"

A young husband and wife are awakened one night by an onslaught of hunger pangs. "For some reason, we woke up at exactly the same moment," the man (Boku) tells us. "A few minutes later the pangs struck with all the force of the tornado in *The Wizard of Oz*." Their "tremendous, overpowering hunger pangs" are reminiscent of the lady librarian's in *Hard-boiled Wonderland and the End of the World*, and suggest an unverbalized inner need. The couple's newlywed status couldn't have anything to do with it – could it?

As the story unfolds it becomes clear that the uncertainty surrounding their new commitment to one another is precisely what the story is about. But Murakami handles his material with such comic inventiveness, delicacy, and indirectness that the couple's relationship comes to stand for all the things in life that baffle us and take us by surprise. Brief as it is, "The Second Bakery Attack" is perhaps the most perfect poetic distillation of Murakami's vision.

The couple (he is 28 or 29, working for a law firm; she "two years and eight months younger", a design school secretary) have not lived together long enough to establish a mealtime routine in their new household, so they have run out of food. "Our refrigerator contained not a single item that could be technically categorized as 'food'. All we had was a bottle of French dressing, six cans of beer, two shrivelled onions, a stick of butter, and a box of refrigerator deodorizer." He suggests they look for an all-night restaurant, but she refuses: "You're not supposed to go out to eat after midnight." He merely answers, "I guess not," and dwells upon an image of an undersea volcano that his extreme hunger has aroused in him. Mentally, he floats in a little boat, looking down at the volcano through crystal clear water.

> Which is when it occurred to me that I had once before had this same kind of experience. My stomach had been just as empty then . . . When? . . . Oh, sure, that was –
> "The time of the bakery attack," I heard myself saying.
> "The bakery attack? What are you talking about?"
> And so it started.

The episode that pops into Boku's mind may be familiar to the dedicated Murakami reader as well. This story is called "The Second Bakery Attack" in part because four years earlier Murakami had published a piece called "The Bakery Attack" ("Pan'ya shūgeki").[231] The episode that Boku stumbles into recounting to his wife in "The Second Bakery Attack" is an outline of that first story.

The event occurred during Boku's college years – or, more precisely, when he was temporarily out of college. For Murakami, this almost certainly means that golden age when the universities were shut down because of the student riots. In a weirdly twisted version of student idealism, Boku and a friend decided – for financial and also "philosophical" reasons – to "attack" a local bakery and thereby satisfy their hunger rather than resort to getting a job. "We didn't want to work. We were absolutely clear on that." When Boku's wife points out that he has since compromised and is now working, he takes a swig of beer and muses, "Times change. People change," then suggests they go back to bed. But she wants to hear more about the bakery attack: "Was it a success?"

"Well, it was kind of a success. And kind of not. We got what we wanted. But as a hold-up, it didn't work. The baker gave us the bread before we could take it from him."

"Free?"

"Not exactly, no. That's the hard part." I shook my head. "The baker was a classical-music freak, and when we got there he was listening to an album of Wagner overtures. So he made us a deal. If we would listen to the record all the way through, we could take as much bread as we liked. I talked it over with my buddy and we figured, Okay. It wouldn't be work in the purest sense of the word, and it wouldn't hurt anybody. So we put our knives back in our bag, pulled up a couple of chairs, and listened to the overtures to *Tannhäuser* and *The Flying Dutchman*."

So Boku and his friend got enough bread for several days without compromising on their "principles", such as they were. Since then, however, he has wondered whether the baker put some kind of "curse" on him and his friend: "It was kind of a turning point. Like, I went back to the university, and I graduated, and I started working for the firm and studying for the bar exam, and I met you and got married. I never did anything like that again. No more bakery attacks."

That compromise, in other words, was the beginning of Boku's accommodation with ordinary middle-class life, and it still nags at him. Something from his past remains inside him like an undersea volcano, threatening to erupt at any moment, and his new wife is wise enough to know that these unresolved elements from his past could be a threat to their marriage. Their surreal hunger, she tells him, must be a result of the curse. There is only one thing to do: "Attack another bakery. Right away. Now. It's the only way."

This is where Murakami's comic imagination comes most wildly into play. Like any new husband, Boku learns things about his new wife that he could never have imagined: she owns a Remington automatic shotgun and two ski masks, with which they are to carry out Boku's second bakery attack. "Why my wife owned a shotgun, I had no idea. Or ski masks. Neither of us had ever skied. But she didn't explain and I didn't ask. Married life is weird, I felt." Even more impressive is the professional way she handles herself in the "attack", which is itself a comic tour de force.

Afterwards, she seems to have been right: the curse has been lifted, and she can go to sleep, leaving Boku with his thoughts:

Alone now, I leaned over the edge of my boat and looked down to the bottom of the sea. The volcano was gone. The water's calm surface reflected the blue of the sky. Little waves – like silk pajamas fluttering in a breeze – lapped against the side of the boat. There was nothing else.

I stretched out in the bottom of the boat and closed my eyes, waiting for the rising tide to carry me where I belonged.[232]

The ending of "The Second Bakery Attack" may be the closest Murakami has come to offering a moment of "salvation" to his characters and his readers. Even in works that deal with occult or "otherworldly" material, Murakami is always talking about this world and our ultimately undefinable place within it, but here he manages to do so in an economical form through delicate comic exaggeration. In order to succeed, the technique requires that certain elements are never fully explained, which is why it is better suited to the short story than the novel.

Murakami will never tell anyone the "meaning" of the symbols in his works. In fact, he usually denies they are symbols at all. He did this when he joined a discussion of "The Second Bakery Attack" in the class of Japanese Literature Professor Howard Hibbett at Harvard the day after the 1991 Boston Marathon. When the students were asked what they thought the undersea volcano symbolized, Murakami interrupted to insist that the volcano was *not* a symbol: it was just a volcano.

One of the academics attending the class shouted to the students "Don't listen to that man! He doesn't know what he's talking about!" and a lively debate ensued. Murakami's response was characteristically ingenuous: "Don't *you* see a volcano in your mind when *you* get hungry? I do."[233] He was hungry when he wrote the story; hence, the volcano: it was as simple as that.

Whatever mental images Murakami might see when he happens to be hungry, within the context of "The Second Bakery Attack" the undersea volcano is clearly a symbol of unresolved problems from the past, things that linger in the unconscious and threaten to explode and destroy the calm of the present. Calling it a symbol and defining it like this, however, only drains it of much of its power as far as Murakami is concerned. Like other writers, he would prefer to leave it a volcano and let it do its work, unexplained, in the mind of each reader.

"The Elephant Vanishes"

The other short masterpiece in *The Second Bakery Attack* is "The Elephant Vanishes", which draws the reader immediately into a world of quotidian detail: "When the elephant disappeared from our town's elephant house, I read about it in the newspaper. My alarm clock woke me that day, as always, at 6:13. I went to the kitchen, made coffee and toast, turned on the radio, spread the paper out on the kitchen table, and proceeded to munch and read."

Boku goes on to summarize the news reports of the sudden disappearance of both the elephant and its keeper. Dedicated Murakami readers will almost certainly be reminded of the lines in his first novel, *Hear the Wind Sing*, written seven years earlier: "When it came to getting something into writing, I was always overcome with despair. The range of my ability was just too limited. Even if I could write, say, about an elephant, I probably couldn't write about the elephant's keeper." In "The Elephant Vanishes" Murakami succeeds in writing about both – not by providing lengthy characterizations, as might be required in a novel, but by giving us a few vivid glimpses of the two before spiriting them away.

The newspaper (Boku has an unusually complete collection of clippings) provides detailed information on how the town happened to acquire its own pet elephant, a delightful parody of local (and not-so-local) politics that culminates in a celebration:

I joined the crowd at the elephant-house dedication ceremonies. Standing before the elephant, the mayor delivered a speech (on the town's development and the enrichment of its cultural facilities); one elementary-school pupil, representing the student body, stood up to read a composition ("Please live a long and healthy life, Mr Elephant"); there was a sketch contest (sketching the elephant thereafter became an integral component of the pupils' artistic education); and each of two young women in swaying dresses (neither of whom was especially good-looking) fed the elephant a bunch of bananas. The elephant endured these virtually meaningless (for the elephant, entirely meaningless) formalities with hardly a twitch, and it chomped on the bananas with a vacant stare. When it finished eating the bananas, everyone applauded.

Boku tells us about the heavy chain connecting the elephant's hind leg to a concrete slab, about Noboru Watanabe, the "small, bony old man" with huge (elephantine?) ears who was the elephant's keeper, and about their almost telepathic ability to communicate with each other. More details support Boku's conviction that "the elephant had in no way 'escaped'. It had vanished into thin air." Faintly disgusted at the politicians' unwillingness to countenance such a possibility, Boku decides not to contact the police with what he "knows" about the disappearance. "What good would it do to talk to people like that, who would not even consider the possibility that the elephant had simply vanished?" Months go by without a clue, and the elephant is gradually forgotten by everyone – except Boku, who has still not revealed to us his special knowledge about the disappearance.

Suddenly the narrative shifts into a new and seemingly disconnected direction: "I met her near the end of September." The woman who arouses his interest is the editor of a magazine for young housewives. She comes to a press party organised by Boku, who, we learn only now, works "for the PR section of a major manufacturer of electrical appliances". He is "in charge of publicity for a matching set of kitchen appliances that was scheduled to go on the market in time for the autumn wedding and winter bonus seasons". Showing her around the display, he explains the need for a modern "*kit-chin*", for which only an elegant imported English word will do. She questions his advertising lingo, and he steps out of his professional role long enough to admit that, in this "pragmatic" workaday world, selling the product is all that matters. By staying within the bounds of the pragmatic, he adds, "you avoid all kinds of complicated problems".

But Boku is the only one who knows that the elephant has vanished, and this knowledge quickly comes to impinge on his relationship with the editor. Just as Boku in "The Second Bakery Attack" almost inadvertently crossed into unknown territory the moment he told his wife about the first attack, this Boku also lets something slip. They get chatting in a bar about their college days, music, sports, and so on until "I told her about the elephant. Exactly how this happened, I can't recall."

As always in Murakami's work, things that happen on the edge of memory are the very things that matter. The moment the words escape his mouth, Boku is sorry, but the woman insists on knowing more. Then he tells her what he has not told us: he was probably the last one to see the elephant and its keeper before they disappeared.

The evening before they vanished, Boku was looking down at the pair through an air vent from a little-known vantage-point on a cliff. He had the feeling that "something about the balance between them" had changed. Once the conversation has ventured into otherworldly territory, things on this side can never be the same. Their remarks dissolve into awkward fragments. A few minutes later, they say goodbye, and he never sees her again. They talk once on the phone about business, and he considers asking her out to dinner, but changes his mind. "It just didn't seem to matter one way or the other." He finds this to be true about practically everything in life now, "after my experience with the vanishing elephant".[234]

If elephants never forget, they are of particular fascination to a writer for whom memory and the incommunicable inner life are so central. They are large, dark embodiments of mystery, but "People seem to have forgotten that their town once owned an elephant", just as something magic died after the student movement, and the "pragmatic" world reestablished its primacy. Boku in "The Second Bakery Attack" achieves a kind of salvation by coming into contact (however wackily) with his old idealism once again, and "A Poor-Aunt Story" leaves us with some hope that Boku and his companion will renew their relationship now that he has shaken off his obsession with his "poor aunt", but in "The Elephant Vanishes", after his brush with the transcendent, nothing seems to matter any more.

The narrator of "Family Affair" ("Famirii-afea", November–December 1985) is another appliance manufacturer PR type. This Boku is a joker who has no direct exposure to other worlds, but he is concerned with questions of value that transcend the daily routine. He fears the loss of the one person who has ever meant anything to him: his younger sister. She is about to marry a nerdy computer engineer, Noboru Watanabe.

Noboru Watanabe? Wait a minute, wasn't that the name of the elephant's keeper? The name pops up in one story after another in *The Second Bakery Attack* attached to an astonishing range of characters: the elephant keeper in "The Elephant Vanishes"; the brother-in-law-to-be in "Family Affair"; the translation agency business partner of Boku in "The Twins and the Sunken Continent"

139

("Futago to shizunda tairiku", December 1985); the nondescript brother-in-law in "The Wind-up Bird and Tuesday's Women" ("Nejimaki-dori to kayōbi no onna-tachi", January 1986); and, more importantly in the same story, the cat named after the brother-in-law.

When Murakami first wrote the stories for this collection, he was just having fun with the real name of a good friend, the famous illustrator Mizumaru Anzai. But six years later when he decided to mine the "The Wind-up Bird and Tuesday's Women" for its dark potential, turning the brother-in-law into the embodiment of national evil, he felt he ought to at least change the surname – to Wataya. The name Watanabe, quite common in Japan and probably used by Murakami precisely because of its ordinariness, would also be given to the protagonist of *Norwegian Wood*, though his "first" name would be "Tōru".

"Family Affair" is a very funny story that also contains a far more realistic exploration of character than is usual in Murakami's work. Boku himself is different, a more aggressive personality than most Bokus. He entertains us by describing the changes in his sister's style and behaviour as she prepares herself for marriage to her humourless computer engineer (an uncritical cog in the machinery of the electrical industry). But Boku's wit and sarcasm incompletely mask his fear at the approaching end of youth (he is 27, she 23). Much of the story involves lively bickering between brother and sister as they fight over the fiancé "by proxy" – for example, arguing about the quality of spaghetti in an Italian restaurant.

If much of Murakami's writing sees him delving into genres such as detective novels and science fiction, "Family Affair" – written for a young female readership – is an amusing foray into situation comedy – a little more risqué than what we might see on television, but full of wisecracks and fairly predictable plot twists.[235]

The story does have an edge, however. Tired of his constant jokes as she hosts a nice dinner party, Boku's sister accuses him of being immature and selfish. Later, he has mechanical sex with a girl he picks up in a bar, and afterwards out on the street he throws up his dinner. "How many years had it been since I last vomited from drinking? What the hell was I doing these days? The same thing over and over. But each repetition was worse than the one before."[236]

At home, he finds his sister alone, worried she has been too severe with him. They open up to each other as they have not done for some time, if ever, and reach a kind of truce. Murakami manages to keep the laughs going almost to the story's touching conclusion.

One manifestation of Murakami's sense of humour is the number of weird and funny titles he gives his works. In *The Second Bakery Attack* there is a story entitled "The Fall of the Roman Empire, the 1881 Indian Uprising, Hitler's Invasion of Poland, and the Realm of the Raging Winds" ("Rōma teikoku no hōkai, 1881-nen no Indian hōki, Hittorā no Pōrando shinnyū, soshite kyōfū sekai", January 1986). This would be long enough for an encyclopaedia, but the piece itself is barely seven pages; a game played with words and memory, it is memorable primarily for its outsized title – and its mysteriously raging winds.[237]

"The Wind-up Bird and Tuesday's Women" begins with Boku cooking spaghetti and ends with a feuding married couple refusing to answer the endlessly ringing telephone – exactly as in Chapter 1 of Murakami's longest work, *The Wind-up Bird Chronicle*, which would not be serialized for another six years. Like "Firefly", "The Wind-up Bird and Tuesday's Women" can hardly be read on its own merits now that it has grown into a three-volume novel, although when he first wrote it Murakami had no thought of expanding it. As far as he was concerned it was a finished story.[238] One scholar, however, reads it as the middle work in a trilogy that begins with "The Second Bakery Attack" and ends with *The Wind-up Bird Chronicle*, partly because Boku is a law-office employee in all three, but mainly because together they trace married life from the earliest days through growing difficulties and finally to the wife's sudden departure and its consequences.[239]

As an independent story, "The Wind-up Bird and Tuesday's Women" seems little more than a quirky story about an out-of-work law clerk who finds himself bewildered by all the women he comes into contact with one Tuesday, including his own wife. An anonymous female caller shocks him by asking for ten minutes of his time so that they can "come to an understanding . . . of our feelings", and later attempts telephone sex with him. His wife shocks him by suggesting during a call from work that he should try to earn money writing poetry, then switching to assurances that he can simply live as a house husband on her income. She also reminds him to go and look for their lost cat, Noboru Watanabe, at a vacant house in a back alley, which makes him wonder how she came to be so familiar with such a place. When he ventures out, he encounters a neighbourhood Lolita who tells him of her fascination with death. She "draws" a mysterious diagram on his wrist with her fingertip (an occult gesture that Murakami frequently employs to evoke a sense of the subconscious at work) and, when he awakes from a nap sometime afterwards, she is gone.

Throughout the story (and more frequently than in Chapter 1 of the novel) Boku hears the call of a bird he has never seen and which his wife has nicknamed "the wind-up bird" because of its ratchety cry; supposedly, it "is there every morning in the trees of the neighbourhood to wind things up. Us, our quiet little world, everything."[240] It is not the only bird in the story, however. As he cooks spaghetti, he listens to the overture of Rossini's *La Gazza*

Ladra (*The Thieving Magpie*). In the garden of the vacant house where he hopes to find the cat, there is a stone figurine of a bird that looks desperate to fly away. Pigeons are cooing. What does it all mean? Murakami probably wondered that himself, and he was using birds, as earlier noted, to symbolize some kind of inexplicable contact between the conscious and unconscious worlds. At the time he wrote the story he wanted only to give the reader a sense of unease and disequilibrium by solving none of the questions the piece raises.[241] In retrospect, it seems almost as if subsequent rereading made him want to explore the many mysteries he had thrown at the reader in the space of these 30 pages.

8

Pop Melody

The House of the Rising Sun

The last of the stories in *The Second Bakery Attack* appeared in journals in January 1986, and the collection appeared in April. A volume of short fiction by Paul Theroux, *World's End and Other Stories*, was Murakami's major translation work that year.

And then there was the side of Murakami that, for an English-speaking audience, is almost impossible to understand, as if Hemingway and Dave Barry and Ann Landers were one and the same person. Almost from the beginning of his career he was writing light essays and related pieces that were published after 1984 under the playful title *Murakami Asahidō* or *Murakami's House of the Rising Sun*, with cartoon drawings supplied by illustrator Mizumaru Anzai (real name Noboru Watanabe, as we saw in the previous chapter).

In his *House of the Rising Sun* Murakami is just having fun, and some of his lighter stuff can get downright cute and cuddly. Take for instance *The Sheep Man's Christmas* (*Hitsuji-otoko no kurisumasu*, 1985), not part of the *Rising Sun* series but in the same spirit. Here, Maki Sasaki provides illustrations not only of the Sheep Man and Sheep Professor from *A Wild Sheep Chase*, but also the twins from *Pinball, 1973* and other fanciful creatures, all of whom come together at the end to wish each other a Merry Christmas (a Japanese Christmas, of course, with trees and presents and vapid good cheer, but Christ nowhere in sight or mind). We are unlikely to see this side of Murakami in English, although a German translation of *The Sheep Man's Christmas* was produced at the behest of one professor fascinated by the Japanese practice of Christmas.[242]

Murakami would later use *Murakami's House of the Rising Sun* as the title of his website. Yes, for three years (June 1996–November 1999) he had a website sponsored by the *Asahi* (*Rising Sun*) newspaper, complete with a cute cartoon portrait of him that you could click to make it say, in his own voice: "I'm Haruki Murakami. Hello there!" Though the site has since been discontinued, the entire contents (including the talking Murakami) have come out in books and on CD-ROMs with titles even wilder than the ones Murakami gives his fiction: *Murakami's House of the Rising Sun: Surf City of Dreams*; *Murakami's House of the Rising Sun: Smerdyakov vs. Warlord Oda Nobunaga's Retainers*; and *"That's It! Let's Ask Murakami!" Say the People and They Try Flinging 282 Big Questions at Haruki Murakami, But Can Murakami Really Find Decent Answers to Them All?*[243]

The website had various departments, but the most important ones that have been preserved for posterity are *Murakami Radio*, in which the author kept his readers up to date with his latest projects, and a readers' forum in which he answered readers' questions – some of which involved serious personal problems, and others public events such as the sarin gas attack on the Tokyo subway.

While most of the *House of the Rising Sun* electronic "chatting" is just that – "What do you use to scrub your body in the shower?" – "What if you were to see a naked woman come out on a veranda?" – "How do you translate 'Fuck you' into Japanese?" – "Where should I go for my graduation trip?" – "Do squids have *legs* or *arms*?" – Murakami proved an earnest and faithful correspondent with his fans, some of whom addressed him by his first name, which is shockingly familiar in a country as formal as Japan, and he replied in a chatty conversational style.

The transcripts are enjoyable to read because they convey a sense of fun and of genuine two-way communication – the readers are thrilled to have direct access to their favourite writer, and Murakami is touched by their honesty. Until the workload became too much for him and he regretfully gave up the site, Murakami dealt with some 6,000 e-mails from a broad array of correspondents, from high school and college students to housewives and labourers and salarymen in their thirties and forties. It was another important learning experience for Murakami as he came into contact with the hopes and fears of ordinary people, while at the same time maintaining his solitude. The Internet offered him a means of accepting the traditional role of the pontificating *sensei* or mentor expected of the Japanese writer by his society, but to do so on an intimate one-to-one basis devoid of pomposity. (In answer to the squid question, for instance, he advised the reader to present the creature with ten gloves and ten socks, and to see which it chose. And in the shower, should anyone be interested, he prefers bare hands to a flannel.)[244] Murakami probably was, as the Asahi publicity suggests, "the first writer in history" to engage in e-mail correspondence with his readers. The medium was as perfectly suited to him as the word processor.

Murakami is serious about all of his writing (more serious about some than others), but he has no preconceived barrier in his mind between what is "popular" and what is "art". With truly disarming candour, he once explained the situation faced by any writer in the late twentieth century who hopes to reach a wide audience. Nowadays, with the growing diversity of activities and interests available to the modern urbanite, he said, novels have to compete

146

with sport and the stereo and TV and videos and cooking and a host of other enjoyable pastimes. The novelist can no longer expect readers to put the time and energy into trying to understand difficult fiction: now the writer has to work hard to draw the reader into the novel. The burden is on the writer to entertain, to tell stories in simple, easy-to-understand language.[245]

And indeed, aside from Murakami's tantalizing tendency to leave certain major images and events in his works unexplained, he does write simply, he does explain a great deal for us, in language that is lucid and lively and funny. It's all there, in the words, for the reader to take at face value, sometime between dinner and the latest Van Damme video.

For all of Murakami's readiness to situate the novel among the multifarious forms of entertainment available to us, he is not suggesting that it is simply another kind of DVR. The novelist must strive to gain the reader's interest amid a host of competing distractions, to draw the reader into what he calls "the cognitive system unique to the novel form".[246] For a writer like Murakami, the interplay of words and the imagination is everything. If literature is dead, someone forgot to invite Haruki Murakami to the funeral.

Norwegian Wood

1986 marked the beginning of a time of wandering for Haruki and Yōko that would last for nine years. From Fujisawa they moved closer to the sea to a home that would prove to be one of their more permanent abodes; but on 3 October, Yōko's thirty-eighth birthday, they left for Europe, stopping ten days in Rome before continuing to the Greek island of Spetses and thence to Mykonos in November. In January 1987 they moved to Palermo, Sicily, took a short trip to Malta, then returned to Rome in February, before journeying to Bologna, Mykonos again, and finally Crete.

Murakami had been having a great time writing stories, but he was beginning to wonder if he still had the energy for a longer work, so exhausted was he after writing *Hard-boiled Wonderland and the End of the World*. A trip to Europe had long been an ambition, and he prepared for it systematically by studying Greek for a year. In the end, however, he left Japan in search of new, unfamiliar surroundings in which he could concentrate on writing a novel.[247] Above all, this meant getting away from the telephone and incessant requests for product endorsements, talks at colleges, favourite recipes, round-table discussions, and comments on everything ranging from sex discrimination to environmental pollution, dead musicians, the return of the miniskirt, and ways to quit smoking.[248]

Once they arrived in Rome, it took Murakami a fortnight to recover from the sheer exhaustion caused by all of these demands, and sustained work was out of the question. Finally, in the off-season cold and wind of Mykonos, after completing his translation of C. D. B. Bryan's *The Great Dethriffe*, Murakami sensed it was time to give himself to the novel that was waiting inside him asking to be written.

He soon realized that the book, as yet untitled, would be much longer than the 350 manuscript pages he had in mind. (He had not yet converted to writing with a word processor, and was still using a fountain pen to fill in the 400 little squares on a standard Japanese manuscript page.) He reached the 60 per cent mark writing amid the "hellish" noise and filth of Palermo – an experience that tested his powers of concentration to the limit, but he was contracted to stay there to write a travel article for a magazine. When he finally finished the novel in Rome in March 1987, after transferring it from the unruly pile of notebooks and letter paper he had been using for the first draft, it had grown to 900 manuscript pages.[249] The Murakamis returned to Japan in June, mainly so that Haruki could meet editors and read galley proofs. When they went back to Rome in September, as the book was reaching bookstores, they had no inkling that this publishing sensation would change their lives for ever.

The novel was, of course, Murakami's runaway bestseller, *Norwegian Wood*. The Japanese title, *Noruwei no mori*, means literally "A Forest in Norway", or "Norwegian Woods", which is not Murakami's but the standard Japanese mistranslation of the title of The Beatles' song "Norwegian Wood".[250] Hence, the female lead's maudlin remark, less incongruous in Japanese than English: "That song can make me feel *so* sad . . . I don't know, I guess I imagine myself wandering in a deep wood. I'm all alone and it's cold and dark, and nobody comes to save me."[251] Even with its mistaken premise, however, the Beatles reference seems far more suited to the novel as we know it than the title that Murakami first considered, *Gardens in the Rain*, after the Debussy piano piece, which in the end did not rate a mention in the book.[252]

In *Hear the Wind Sing* Murakami had indirectly suggested that he would not be writing about sex or death in his fiction. For one thing, he said later, the great literary star of his teenage years, Kenzaburō Ōe, had grappled so successfully with sex and death and violence that Murakami wanted to do something else.[253] When, in his fifth novel, he opened his world to those elements in an entirely different way, the result was one of the most popular Japanese novels of all time.

I next wrote a straight boy-meets-girl story called *Norwegian Wood* after The Beatles' tune. Many of my readers thought that *Norwegian Wood* was a retreat for me, a betrayal of what my works had stood for until then. For me personally, however, it was just the opposite: it was an adventure, a challenge. I had never written that kind of straight, simple story, and I wanted to test myself.

Indeed, Murakami found this new kind of novel an absolute "bone-grinder" at times.[254]

> I set *Norwegian Wood* in the late 1960s. I borrowed the details of the protagonist's college environment and daily life from those of my own college days. As a result, many people think it is an autobiographical novel, but in fact it is not autobiographical at all. My own youth was far less dramatic, far more boring than his. If I had simply written the literal truth of my own life, this two-volume novel would have been no more than 15 pages long.[255]

The author may joke away its autobiographical features, but the book *feels* like an autobiography, it favours lived experience over mind games and shots at the supernatural, and it does indeed tell us much more straightforwardly than any of his other novels what life was like for the young Haruki Murakami when he first came to Tokyo from Kobe.

Murakami's primary response to the "challenge" of writing a realistic novel is to fill the scenes with concrete descriptive detail of a kind rarely seen in his spare, abstract landscapes. The precise descriptions of dormitory life and Tokyo neighbourhoods are based on first-hand experience, included not for symbolic value or plot significance but because the author was writing to recreate an important stage in his youth from memory, the turbulent years of the student movement, 1968–70, that occupy the bulk of the novel.

Like other Murakami protagonists (and the author himself) Tōru Watanabe comes from Kobe, and the unnamed private university he attends in Tokyo is transparently modelled on Waseda, the school that Haruki and Yōko attended. As part of his technique, Murakami invites his readers to make connections between his protagonist and himself when, for example, he gives his fictional hero his own well-known reading habits:

I read a lot, but not a lot of different books: I like to read my favourites again and again. Back then it was Truman Capote, John Updike, Scott Fitzgerald, Raymond Chandler, but I didn't see anyone else in my classes or the dorm reading writers like that. They liked Kazumi Takahashi,[256] Kenzaburō Ōe, Yukio Mishima, or contemporary French novelists, which was another reason I didn't have much to say to anybody but kept to myself and my books.[257]

Far more important than such factual parallels, however, is Murakami's narrative strategy. Tōru is presented as writing directly to the reader, which intensifies the impression of sincerity. *Norwegian Wood* begins with a dramatization of Tōru's struggle a year earlier with a sudden rush of memories, then quickly reveals how his desire not to let those memories fade has prompted him to record them:

There is no way around it: my memory is growing ever more distant . . . Which is why I am writing this book. To think. To understand. It just happens to be the way I'm made. I have to write things down to feel I fully comprehend them . . . Writing from memory like this, I often feel a pang of dread. What if I've forgotten the most important thing? What if somewhere inside me there is a dark limbo where all the truly important memories are heaped and slowly turning into mud?

151

Be that as it may, it's all I have to work with. Clutching these faded, fading, imperfect memories to my breast, I go on writing this book with all the desperate intensity of a starving man sucking on bones.[258]

In this way the reader is made to feel almost present at the process of composition, as if the book were a long intimate letter addressed to us alone. Murakami's greatest technical achievement in *Norwegian Wood* may be the success with which he exploits the conventions of the autobiographical Japanese I-novel to write a wholly fictional work. He succeeded so well in creating a sincere-seeming, honest-seeming, quasi-confessional novel full of nostalgic lyricism and the pangs of young love that his name spread far beyond the bounds of his established readership to become a household word. George Burns ("The most important thing is sincerity. If you can fake that, you've got it made") would have been proud of him.[259] The "Murakami phenomenon" had begun.

Ironically, over the years, this very success has caused both Haruki and Yōko pain by giving rise to false expectations among a Japanese readership accustomed to reading fiction as autobiography.[260] Murakami himself readily admits that certain features of the character Midori Kobayashi were modelled on Yōko Takahashi, but he flatly rejects the proposition that this in any way constrained his freedom to give the character other traits and to put her through a purely fictional series of events.[261] In Midori we can see Yōko's intelligence and intensity – and perhaps even her speech patterns. Like Yōko, Midori comes from an old merchant-class neighbourhood of Tokyo (Yōko's father was a futon-maker, Midori's the owner of a corner bookstore), and she is a few months older than Tōru, who was born in November – not January – 1949. Her background as the only girl from an ordinary family in a school for the daughters of wealthy families is also taken from Yōko. And when Midori has to write a note to get through to Tōru, who is sitting right next to her, it resonates with Yōko's later half-joking complaints that Murakami can be locked up inside himself at times. Finally, however, Midori is a composite fictional character, with traits drawn from many sources and no particular source. Her excruciatingly bad folk singing, for example, is based not on Yōko but another friend (or perhaps ex-friend!) of Haruki's.

This seems even truer of the depressive Naoko, who, Murakami insists, is *not* modelled on the one other girl he befriended in college. So often and convincingly does Murakami write of losing young friends to death that readers naturally begin looking for parallels in his life and models for his characters, especially in a "realistic" work like *Norwegian Wood*, but Murakami always denies such connections. Only one character in *Norwegian Wood* was directly modelled on a particular individual, he says: the stuttering roommate nicknamed "Storm Trooper" who first appeared in "Firefly" discussed above.[262]

The impression of autobiography is further strengthened by the mood of nostalgia that pervades the book. It carries a dedication of sorts to F. Scott Fitzgerald (FOR MANY FÊTES, echoing the dedication of *Tender is the Night*: TO GERALD AND SARA: MANY FÊTES) and mentions *The Great Gatsby* several times, a book that lingers in the memory as a sad lyric. Most of the omnipresent music mentioned in *Norwegian Wood* is sentimental. Indeed, the tone of the entire book resembles nothing so much as a sweet, sad pop tune. In English translation, Murakami's style lends itself to the language of a pop melody, and readers may sense a deliberate attempt to impart such resonances to the language. Of course, a *good* pop song is hard to write. It has to use conventional ideas and images and musical turns to appeal to a wide audience but at the same time manage to say something true about human experience in a fresh way. If Murakami plays with genres – the detective novel (*A Wild Sheep Chase*), science fiction and fantasy (*Hard-boiled Wonderland*

and the End of the World), and the sit-com ("Family Affair") – popular music is the model for *Norwegian Wood*.

Anchored as it is in a time of adolescent first love and courtship, *Norwegian Wood* has some of the sweetest, teasingest teenage love scenes ever written, and this contributed to the book's phenomenal success. Young readers love it for depicting the games they are learning to play with hands and lips and genitals, and older readers (those few who can stand the sugar) may find themselves nostalgic for a lost innocence. Indeed, the central declaration of love and commitment takes place amid the children's rides on a department store roof, after Tōru and Midori have dined in the restaurant below, a place they both associate with childhood. Nostalgia, innocence, sincerity, honesty, and plenty of good, clean, physical playing with bodies that usually stops short of grown-up intercourse (in contrast to a kind of pointless promiscuity that is shown to be a poor alternative for loving sex) make *Norwegian Wood* a novel that appeals to anyone eager to be told that the sexual revolution can lead to something meaningful rather than merely sordid. Tōru persuades us he is a nice guy because he refuses to go "all the way" with Midori until he can commit to her with a clear mind and an open heart. He wants his sex to mean something and, at the very end, that is what he gets, though in a way that comes as a surprise to the reader and involves a good deal of ambiguity.

Tōru's age also explains the book's appeal to a young audience: though 38 as he writes "his" book, he is 18 as the main action gets underway, and a few weeks short of his twenty-first birthday as the novel ends. He is an extraordinarily self-possessed young man, a good storyteller (no doubt aided by the writing skills of his older self), and an even better listener to other people's stories, notably those of the wrinkled, "old" (39) former mental patient, Reiko, with whom he shares some faintly incestuous love-making at the end of the book. This and the music they make are intended to "memorialize" Naoko, Tōru's other great love, who has committed suicide after a lengthy stay in the sanatorium from which Reiko has been released. Although the novel begins as the recollections of the 38-year-old Tōru called forth a year before upon hearing the song "Norwegian Wood", it ends with his younger self standing in a windswept phone booth wondering where he is: the dead centre of a place that is no place.

What little we know of Tōru's later life suggests he is unhappy. In the opening paragraph, at the age of 37, he is flying into Hamburg, without enthusiasm, probably on business: "So – Germany again." Later he recalls a beautiful (but heart-wrenching) sunset he saw in Santa Fe, where he had gone to interview a painter a dozen years after the main action of the book (around 1982, when he would have been 33). He appears to be some kind of globe-trotting journalist (which might explain why he writes so well), but there is no suggestion that he and Midori ever stayed together, and he comes across as a glum and lonely wanderer.

Hamburg is never alluded to again, but it probably appears in the opening paragraph for two reasons. First, it is the birthplace of Hans Castorp, the central character of Thomas Mann's novel *The Magic Mountain*, which is mentioned several times in *Norwegian Wood*. Tōru reads it on his trip to Ami Hostel, where Naoko is being treated, and Reiko chides him for his insensitivity at having brought such a book. In Mann's novel, Hans is visiting his cousin at a Swiss sanatorium specializing in TB and psychological problems (although the mention of "psycho-analysis" in these days before the First World War is enough to make Hans break into uncontrollable laughter), and the prevailing mood of the book is one of waiting for death. His cousin mentions how bodies are brought down in the winter on toboggans, and the room in which Hans is to spend his three weeks at the sanatorium (in the end much longer) has lately been occupied by an American woman who died a few days earlier.

The second and probably more important connection is that Hamburg was the scene of a crucial turning point for the success of The Beatles (with Pete Best on drums and Stu Sutcliffe on bass when they arrived in 1960). They performed at several clubs and made their first recordings as a group there.

Although on the face of it *Norwegian Wood* appears to be an all-too-realistic love story, the book's symbolism marks it out as something different. Tōru's obsession with the suicidal Naoko brings out certain parallels we have seen before between "being" and "non-being", between this world and another interior world of death and memory, which Murakami had so clearly articulated in *Hard-boiled Wonderland and the End of the World*.

A few pages into *Norwegian Wood*, Naoko is associated with Murakami's most consistent symbol of bottomless interiority, the well:

Let's see, now, what was Naoko talking about that day?

Of course: the "field well". I have no idea whether such a well ever existed . . . It lay precisely on the border where the meadow ended and the woods began – a dark opening in the earth a yard across, hidden by the meadow grass. Nothing marked its perimeter – no fence, no stone curb (at least not one that rose the slightest bit above ground level). It was nothing but a hole, a mouth open wide. The stones of its collar had been weathered and turned a strange muddy-white. They were cracked and had chunks missing, and a little green lizard slithered into an open seam. You could lean over the edge and peer down to see nothing. All I knew about the well was its frightening depth. It was deep beyond measuring, and crammed full of darkness, as if all the world's darknesses had been boiled down to their ultimate density.[263]

The well is frightening for its depths and for the threat it holds out of a slow, painful, and lonely death. If you fell in by accident, says Naoko, you

> probably wouldn't be lucky enough to be killed instantaneously, you'd probably just break your leg and then you couldn't do a thing. You'd yell at the top of your lungs, but nobody'd hear you, and you couldn't expect anybody to find you, and you'd have centipedes and spiders crawling all over you, and the bones of the ones who died before are scattered all around you, and it's dark and soggy, and way overhead there's this tiny, tiny circle of light like a winter moon. You die there in this place, little by little, all by yourself.[264]

Ami Hostel itself, a place deep in the woods and surrounded by a wall, has several parallels to the well-like town of *Hard-boiled Wonderland and the End of the World*. The patients are all seeking relief from the stresses of life in the outside world, the sort of transcendence available to the mind-less (or heart-less) inhabitants of the walled town.[265]

Tōru is attracted to both the lively, life-affirming Midori and the death-obsessed Naoko. Midori is frequently associated with elevated locations such as a laundry deck or a rooftop, while Naoko thinks of wells. Naoko could be seen as a reincarnation of the suicidal Naoko of *Pinball, 1973*, another character familiar with wells, whose fixation on the past prevents her from committing fully to the real world and ultimately claims her life. This is how Murakami describes his initial conception of the book:

> Aside from the first-person protagonist, I created five characters, two of whom were to die. Not even I knew which of the five would live and which would die. The protagonist is

in love with two different women, but not until the very end did I find out which of them would be his. Of course there was always the possibility that they would both die and he would be left alone.[266]

Exactly which five characters Murakami has in mind it is difficult to say. Aside from the protagonist there are at least seven foregrounded characters in Norwegian Wood, four of whom die or (in the case of Tōru's schoolfriend Kizuki) have died before the action begins. The number of women involved with Tōru is also difficult to calculate, especially if we include the one-night stands he has on outings with his college friend, the cynical Nagasawa. The most problematic female occupies the last few pages of the book: Reiko. Tōru has been bouncing between the polar opposites of Midori and Naoko, but Reiko is the only woman with whom he experiences adult sex between two equal partners.

Why does Murakami have Tōru sleep with Reiko at the end? It is a warm and cosy scene, and both partners feel good as they consummate their private memorial for Naoko, but it is unsettling and morally questionable. Tōru has supposedly committed himself to Midori by this time (in fact, even before Naoko's suicide), but he has sex with the older woman (38 in October 1969; 39 at the end when he is on the eve of his twenty-first birthday) with very little prompting. Moreover, the narrator specifies that they make love exactly "four times".[267] Because the number four can be pronounced the same way as the word for "death" (shi), the Japanese avoid sets of four as scrupulously as we avoid the number 13, so capping a night of love-making with that number would seem to have ominous implications.

It is only with Reiko that the question of pregnancy is raised. She pleads with him to be careful and to spare her the embarrassment of falling pregnant at her age, but when he is unable to control himself she laughs it off. This passing mention of the consequences of sex helps make their love-making the only truly adult sex in the book.

But there is some question whether Reiko can be regarded as a mature adult, which raises another ethical objection to their love-making. She is, after all, the second mentally unstable woman with whom Tōru has chosen to have sex. He could be accused of an almost callous disregard for the vulnerability of such women, a wanton ignorance of the fragility of people with mental problems. He continues to wonder whether it was "the right thing" or not to sleep with Naoko; if it was not, he might justly be blamed for her suicide.

This dark view of Tōru's character is probably an unintended complication. More likely, Murakami hoped to bring Tōru's relationship with Naoko to some kind of completion by having Reiko stand in for her (wearing her clothes, looking like her). She also reveals to him Naoko's side of the story when Tōru made love to her: she felt pleasure rather than fear. This reassures Tōru (and us) that he did the right thing.

Now, with Naoko dead and sex with her surrogate having wiped the slate clean, as it were, there appears to be nothing standing in the way of Tōru's union with Midori. But his decision to make love to Reiko leaves the situation ambiguous. He is at a loss to answer the final existential question "Where are you now?" and it seems the 38-year-old narrator knows the answer no better than his 20-year-old self. The older Tōru we glimpse in Hamburg and Santa Fe is by no means the happy husband of his perfect soul-mate, Midori. By sleeping (four times) with Reiko, a sexually functional surrogate for the sexually dysfunctional Naoko, he implicitly chooses death and negativity (Naoko) over life (Midori); Tōru will live with his memories of Naoko rather than give himself over to the vitality of Midori.

*

159

With the 1987 publication of *Norwegian Wood* Murakami was transformed from a writer into a phenomenon. Girls in their teens and early twenties were the primary readers, and a special term for them was quickly coined: "The Norway Tribe", defined by one newspaper as "young girls dedicated to the book who want to talk more seriously about love and how to live". The Norway Tribe would show up in droves at DUG, the Shinjuku nightspot mentioned in *Norwegian Wood*, clutching copies of the novel. They were also buying the red and green volumes as Christmas presents (many hoping that the kind and thoughtful Tōru Watanabe would be a good role model to improve the behaviour of their own boyfriends).[268] To sell 3,500,000 volumes by the end of 1988, however, there had to be a greater demographic impact than that. The Japanese newspapers reported that it was selling to teenage girls and women in their sixties, to young men in their twenties and to men in their forties. Younger readers, it was said, were enjoying the novel as a love story, while older ones were attracted to the depiction of the student movement against a Beatles backbeat.

The advertising industry was quick to capitalize on the fever. Illustrations of comforting green forest scenes were everywhere. Against such a background, one lightweight carpet sweeper was promoted for use "on those days when you are simply *not* going to clean house" but instead want to pamper yourself with "*Norwegian Wood*, Beaujolais Nouveau, a silk slip, a barefoot stroll, and unanswered phone calls". A new brand of cute little green-tea-flavoured, green-tree-shaped chocolates "with that pure love forest taste" went on sale with the name on the package in Japanese and English: *Noruwei no Mori (Forest of Norway)*.

The music industry saw a great opportunity as well. One record company issued a CD featuring "a sweet orchestral cover version of 'Norwegian Wood'", as described on the first page of the novel. It quickly went to the top of the charts. Company representatives denied charges of opportunism. After all, they had spelt Norway "Noruwee", as in the Japanese title of the song, whereas Murakami had spelt it "Noruwei". The original Beatles song had never been a big hit in Japan, but after *Norwegian Wood* there was a significant rise in sales of *Rubber Soul*, the album on which it appears. The lyric sheet included with the album has the girl whispering to the boy in the song: "Isn't this room good? Just like Norwegian Woods."[269]

HARUKI MURAKAMI HAS ONCE AGAIN ESCAPED FROM JAPAN declared one weekly magazine reporting the madness in December 1988. A Kōdansha Publishing Company representative expressed sadness that "the work is being read primarily as a commercial product based on its popularity", but the article went on to note that Murakami's next novel, *Dance Dance Dance*, was benefiting from the fever to the tune of 900,000 sold. However, some readers who knew only *Norwegian Wood* were finding the new book "too difficult". Established Murakami fans, on the other hand, were glad to see him back in familiar territory; the "excessive" sales of *Norwegian Wood* had robbed them of their cult hero and given him to "everybody". It was even said that an advertising executive had tracked down the reclusive author in Europe to plead with him to appear in commercials, but was sent packing. Several film deals were also rejected.[270] (*Hear the Wind Sing* had been made into a film, but such a bad one that Murakami vowed never to go through that embarrassment again.)[271]

The two-volume set went on to sell more than 2,000,000 copies in hardback and a total to date of over 5,500,000.[272] It would be years before Japan's literary establishment could even begin to forgive Murakami for writing a bestseller – if indeed it ever has.

At the time, the furore only served to prolong Murakami's residence abroad. Staying out of the country was no guarantee of anonymity, however. He was in the Big Time Brewery in Seattle in November 1992, relaxing over a pitcher of amber ale with some University of Washington graduates and their professor after having discussed his work with them, when two pale, grim-faced Japanese girls edged up to the table. One of them tried to calm her trembling and to speak, in Japanese, the words catching in her throat: "Par . . . pardon me, sir, but . . . would you . . . by any chance . . . be . . . Haruki Murakami?"

"Yes, I'm Murakami," he said with the hint of a smile.

For a moment, the girls just stood there, thunderstruck, as if they had almost hoped they were wrong.

The bravest spoke again: "Would you . . . could you possibly . . . shake my hand?"

"I don't mind," he said simply, and reached out to shake the hand of first one girl, then the other.

After expressing their profuse thanks, they returned to their table, but were back minutes later with slips of paper and a pen for autographs. Signing the first one, Murakami asked the girl her name so that he could personalize it.

"You'd do that for *me*?" she gasped.

When he had finished, the awestruck, overjoyed pair all but crawled across the sawdust-strewn floor, bowing as they went.

The whole thing was as embarrassing to Murakami as it was amusing to his companions, but it is a small example of what life can be like for him – almost anywhere in the world – since the publication of *Norwegian Wood*.

The third thing I want to have in my style [after spareness and rhythm] is humour. I want to make people laugh out loud. I also want to make their hair stand on end, make their hearts pound. It is important to me that my writing should accomplish that. When I wrote my first novel, several friends called me up to complain to me – not about the book itself, but because the book made them want to drink a lot of beer. One friend said he had to interrupt his reading to go out to buy beer. He drank his way through the rest of the book.

When I heard these complaints, I was overjoyed. My writing, I realized, was having an effect on people. With nothing but my writing, I had succeeded in making a number of human beings want to drink beer. You have no idea how happy this made me. And then there were a few people who complained that they had embarrassed themselves by laughing out loud when they were reading my novel on the subway. I suppose I should feel sorry for what I put them through, but such reports only fill me with pleasure.

Because it is a love story, *Norwegian Wood* had a very different effect on people. I received many letters from people saying that the book made them want to make love. One young lady said she read the book all night and when she was finished she wanted to see her boyfriend immediately. At five o'clock in the morning she went to his apartment, pried open his window, crawled inside, and woke him up to make love. My sympathies went out to the boyfriend, but the young woman's letter made me very happy. Somewhere in this world, my writing was influencing the behaviour of real people. Rather than writing that requires complex interpretation and footnotes, I want to write words that actually move people like this.[273]

It was while writing *Norwegian Wood*, however, that Murakami came to see most clearly what a dangerous game he was playing as he mined his inner world for visions to share with his audience. "A Little Death at 3:50 in the Morning" was a chapter he penned on the subject:

I think I can say that writing a novel is, for me, an extremely peculiar activity . . . whenever I am writing one, in some corner of my brain I am always thinking about death.

I *never* think about death under ordinary circumstances. It is extremely rare for me – as it is for most healthy men in their late thirties – to see death as a daily imminent possibility. But once I get involved in writing a long piece of fiction, there is nothing I can do to prevent an image of death from taking shape in my mind . . . and the sensation never leaves me until the moment I have written the last line of the book.

It always happens this way. It's always the same. While I write, I go on thinking to myself, "I don't want to die, I don't want to die, I don't want to die. At least until I get this novel finished, I absolutely do not want to die. The very thought of dying with it still unfinished is enough to bring tears to my eyes. It may not turn out to be a great work that will live in literary history, but it is, at the very least, *me myself*. To put it in still more extreme terms, if I don't bring this novel to completion, my life will no longer properly be my life." These are more or less the kinds of thoughts I have every single time I write a novel, and it seems that the older I get, and the more I build upon my career as a novelist, the stronger these feelings become. I sometimes stretch out on the floor, hold my breath, close my eyes, and imagine myself dying . . . and I just can't stand it.

Sometimes, waking in the early morning, Murakami says, he finds himself praying: "Please let me live just a little longer. I need just a little more time." Is he praying to a god? he wonders. Or to fate? Or is he just sending his prayers off into space like those scientists who hope their radio transmissions will be picked up by aliens? In this violent, imperfect world we are surrounded by death. "When you stop to think about it coolly, it's a wonder we've survived as long as we have."

And so I go on praying in random desperation: "Don't let me be run down at an intersection by a Fiat whose driver is looking the other way." "Don't let a policeman's automatic pistol go off at me because he's absentmindedly fiddling with it while he stands there gabbing." "Don't let the potted plants lined up on a fifth-floor apartment's shaky railing fall on my head." "Don't let a madman or a junkie on the rampage shove a knife in my back."

. . . If, a hundred years from now, this novel of mine dries up and fades away like a dead worm, I tell myself, there's nothing I can do about it. That's not the point at all. What I am hoping for is neither eternal life nor a deathless master-piece. What I am hoping for is something right here and now. I just want to be allowed to stay alive long enough to finish this novel. That's all.

Murakami goes on to recount a blood-drenched dream he had in Rome from which he awoke at 3.50 a.m. on Wednesday, 18 March 1987. He thought first about F. Scott Fitzgerald's sudden death from a heart attack before he finished *The Last Tycoon*. He is convinced that, however instantaneous it might have been, Fitzgerald spent his last moments tormented by the thought of the novel that was already complete in his mind but would now remain forever unfinished.

He had dreamed of the severed heads of cattle lined up by their hundreds in a row opposite their oozing carcasses in a cavernous room. Their blood ran in rivulets over the edge of a cliff, staining the sea red. Outside the windows of the room, an insect-like swarm of seagulls swooped to drink the blood and snatch up the tiny gobs of flesh suspended in it, but they were not satisfied with that. They wanted the flesh of the dead animals and of the dreamer himself and persistently hovered outside, waiting for the chance to satisfy their hunger.

In these "small hours" before the morning comes, I feel the surge of death. Like a distant roar of the sea, the surge of death sets my body to trembling. Things like this happen often when I am writing a full-length novel. By writing it, I descend little by little into the depths of life. One step at a time, I go down my little ladder. But the closer I draw to the centre of life, the more clearly I can feel it: just the tiniest half-step beyond in the darkness, death too is displaying its own simultaneous surge.[274]

9

Dancing to a Different Tune

Dance Dance Dance

Murakami began writing his next novel in Rome on 17 December 1987. After *Norwegian Wood* he was determined not to struggle with reams of paper and copying machines any more, and bought himself a dedicated Japanese word processor on his last trip home.[275] If word-processing has been a blessing to those of us who use a mere 26 letters, imagine what a relief it is to writers who deal with a couple of thousand Chinese characters, as well as two sets of phonetic symbols, plus Roman letters and Arabic numerals. Kōbō Abe (1924–93) was probably the first major Japanese writer to convert to a PC in 1984, and once Murakami made the switch in 1987 he never looked back.[276]

Unlike *Norwegian Wood*, Murakami's new novel began life with a title. He took it from the old-fashioned rhythm and blues number "Dance Dance Dance" by a group called The Dells. Once its relaxed music had brewed for long enough inside him, he decided quite suddenly that *that* was the day he should start writing. The book practically wrote itself from beginning to end.

> *Norwegian Wood* was a kind of book that I had never written before, and so I kept wondering as I was writing how it would

be received. In the case of *Dance Dance Dance*, though, I had absolutely no such thoughts. I just went on writing what I wanted to write the way I wanted to write it. The style was all mine, and many of the same characters appeared who had been in *Hear the Wind Sing*, *Pinball, 1973*, and *A Wild Sheep Chase*. It was enormous fun for me, as if I had come back to my own backyard. It's rare for me to write with such simple joy.[277]

Dance Dance Dance is a sequel to *A Wild Sheep Chase* in the sense that it tells "what happened next" to Boku after he blew up the evil man in black and returned from Hokkaidō to Tokyo. But there was no way the man who had written *Hard-boiled Wonderland and the End of the World* could recapture the innocence with which he had approached *A Wild Sheep Chase*, any more than the author of *A Wild Sheep Chase* was the same jazz club owner who had written the first adventures of Boku and the Rat in *Hear the Wind Sing* and *Pinball, 1973*. The struggle to regain that kind of innocence and spontaneity – to empty the mind, to banish logical thought, to let the inner story well up – is the central problem of *Dance Dance Dance*, both in terms of what it is about and the way in which Murakami dealt with his material.

A Wild Sheep Chase had come as a revelation. It bowled him over that he had been able to go inside himself and come up with something as wild and crazy as the little Sheep Man. "I just reached out and pulled him into this world," he said.[278] And just as the young man with the "poor aunt" on his back insists that "Once something has come into being, it continues to exist independent of my will," the Sheep Man had become for Murakami a separate being, a person of sorts, and someone he felt he would like to meet again. He actually *missed* him. There was only one way to see this old friend once more, of course, and that was for him to descend into that "original place" from which the Sheep Man had emerged.

It is one thing to encounter something wholly unexpected when you are burrowing around inside your brain and quite another to go looking for something you think is down there. This is like the problem faced by the Zen practitioner who must *not* be consciously seeking enlightenment if he ever hopes to find it. The only answer, both for the Zen non-seeker and for Murakami, is to put yourself in a position in which something is likely to pop into your brain, stop thinking, and wait. And wait. And wait.

The trouble with *Dance Dance Dance* – and, to a lesser extent, with *The Wind-up Bird Chronicle* – is that the reader has to wait with Boku while Murakami waits for something to come to him. Instead of déjà vu, we get Been There Done That: strolling the city streets, making light meals, going to the fridge for cold beers. The one new element is horror, but the eerie roomful of skeletons that Boku finds in downtown Waikiki has a creaky artificiality about it.

In *Dance Dance Dance*, Boku, now 34, returns to the Dolphin Hotel, the base of operations in Hokkaidō for his sheep chase five years earlier. The year is 1983. In the hotel, Boku hopes to find clues to the whereabouts of his old girlfriend with the magical ears, here given the name Kiki ("listening"). The tattered old hotel has been transformed into a modern hi-tech wonder, but in an undefined dimension it also "contains" the chilling world of the Sheep Man, who speaks to Boku on the importance of his ties with other people: life has never had any "meaning", he says, but you can maintain your connectedness if you "keep dancing as long as the music plays".[279]

In the course of the novel Boku encounters a wide variety of individuals in his search, most notably a lovely young hotel employee named "Yumiyoshi", with whom he – rather unconvincingly – falls in love. If she seems to be one of Murakami's least realized characters, it may have something to do with the process by which Murakami chose her unlikely name. In *Breakfast at Tiffany's*, Truman Capote gave the utterly impossible "Japanese" name "Yunioshi" to the Japanese cameraman who lives on the top floor of Holly Golightly's building. Murakami decided to take it two steps closer (though not quite all the way) to something authentically Japanese.[280]

Aside from this rather artificial love interest, the other relationships that grow out of Boku's quest are tainted by money. *Dance Dance Dance* can be read as Murakami's critique of what he calls the "high capitalism" of the mid-1980s, when everything and everyone was reduced to the status of a commodity, including bankable authors like Haruki Murakami (as parodied in the character Hiraku Makimura). Again, boredom is the dominant mood of modern urban existence, and Boku spends an inordinate number of pages in this 600-page novel experiencing just that. Ultimately, Boku learns from a clairvoyant friend that Kiki has been murdered by an old classmate named Gotanda, now a movie star who has sacrificed his personal life to his professional image. It is never made clear why Boku needs supernatural help to realize what should have been obvious to him all along.

If *A Wild Sheep Chase* was a surreal attack on right-wing extremists and continental adventurism, *Dance Dance Dance* is a more systematic pursuit of what it means to find a profession and make a living in a culture in which meaning is dominated by the mass media. Although still fascinated by the big existential questions of life and death and memory, Murakami concentrates more than ever before on the ills of modern society. There is a new level of seriousness in *Dance Dance Dance*, a growing sense that the writer has a certain responsibility towards the society in which he lives.

As in *Hard-boiled Wonderland and the End of the World*, however, the Boku of *Dance Dance Dance* does have another world that belongs exclusively to him. It functions as a link to which, as the Sheep Man tells him, "you are tied. This place is tied to everything. It is your link . . . to what has been lost and what has not yet been lost."[281]

Dance Dance Dance might also be the first of Murakami's novels in which the typically "hard-boiled" Boku finally blows his cool and talks openly about his sadness. In retrospect, Murakami admits that *Dance Dance Dance* is not one of his stronger works, but "it was something I absolutely had to write as an act of healing following all the fuss in the aftermath of *Norwegian Wood*. In that sense, I can say with certainty that I enjoyed writing *Dance Dance Dance* more than any other novel."[282]

"TV People" and "Sleep"

Until the publication of *Norwegian Wood* in 1987, Murakami had enjoyed the psychological and material satisfaction of writing for a solid, faithful readership of perhaps 100,000. But the intrusion on his private life of sudden fame sent the normally unflappable author into a mild depression and the closest thing to writer's block he had experienced since his debut. For seven months during the latter part of 1988, owing to what he called "the after-effects of the uproar over *Norwegian Wood*", he was unable to write, though he remained productive as a translator.[283]

Murakami has gone so far as to call 1988 "The Year of the Blank". So busy was he in Rome at the beginning of the year writing *Dance Dance Dance* that he couldn't even find time for the little travel sketches he had been making in Europe. The writing may have gone smoothly, but the bone-chilling cold in the poorly heated apartment in Rome took its toll on both him and Yōko. They tried to warm themselves by talking about Japanese hot tubs and trips to Hawaii. In fact, the choice of a Hawaiian setting for much of the novel was an attempt to "think" away the cold of a Roman winter.[284]

Again, Murakami felt drained after the effort of writing a novel. Returning to Japan in April did little to counteract this feeling. For one thing, he had many chores to deal with. First, there was the checking of *Dance Dance Dance* galley proofs, and then the final touches on his next F. Scott Fitzgerald translation. He also attended driving school for a month in preparation for a planned trip to Turkey and to make travel more convenient in Europe. (In Tokyo, with its outstanding public transportation system, he had never needed a car, but the Italian non-system forced him to take the plunge – and so opened up a whole new world for him.)[285] Once these tasks were out of the way, the Murakamis spent a month in Hawaii, where they hoped to overcome the winter chill that seemed to be lingering in their bones. Haruki practised his driving skills in Hawaii – smashing the rear light of his rented Accord against a car park post.

None of this interfered with his writing – and his mental equilibrium – so much as the shock of coming back to Japan to find out what it means to be a bestselling author. The red and green volumes of *Norwegian Wood* and advertisements for them were everywhere. He felt terribly embarrassed that the publishers, Kōdansha, had draped their headquarters in bright red and green banners, and he tried not to look at them whenever he had to visit their offices. Squeezed into crowded subway carriages on the way to and from driving school, he could not escape his fans who immediately recognized him. He began to feel there was nowhere in Japan he could relax, that he had lost something terribly important.

I was happy, of course, when the book sold half a million copies. What author wouldn't be happy to have his work accepted by a broad range of people? But quite honestly, I was more shocked than happy . . . I could imagine 100,000 people, but not 500,000. And it got even worse: a million, a million and a half, two million . . . the more I thought about such huge figures, the more confused I became . . . When my novels were selling in the 100,000 range, I felt that I was being loved and favoured and supported by a great many people, but having sold a million-plus volumes of *Norwegian Wood* made me feel totally isolated. Now I felt loathed and hated by everyone . . . Looking back now, I realize that I was not suited to *be* in such a position. I didn't have the personality for it, and I probably wasn't *qualified* for it, either.

During this period [from April to October], I was confused and irritated, and my wife's health was poor. I had absolutely no desire to write anything. After we got back from Hawaii, I spent the summer translating. Even when I can't write my own stuff, I can always do translation. Cranking out translations of other people's novels is a kind of therapy for me, which is one reason I do it.

Leaving Yōko behind in Japan, Haruki went with photographer friend Eizō Matsumura and a Shinchō company editor on a physically taxing but ultimately rewarding three-week backroads tour of Greece and Turkey to produce a book on the region. He returned to Rome in October, where Yōko joined him. Their depressing basement apartment prompted them to go back to Japan once more in January 1989, a few days after the death of Hirohito, the Emperor who had reigned since 1926 and overseen Japan's disastrous war in the Pacific. The whole of Tokyo seemed mesmerized by the event, and policemen were everywhere on the lookout for terrorists.

This "madness" sent the Murakamis running to a hot spring in the south, but when they received word that a better apartment had become available for them in Rome, they returned to Italy.[286] The running back and forth was beginning to seem frantic.

Finally, though, my recovery – my real and final recovery as a writer of fiction – came after I completed my translation of Tim O'Brien's *The Nuclear Age*. As I said earlier, translation is a kind of therapy for me, and the act of translating this particular novel was for me nothing less than a spiritual rehabilitation. I gave every ounce of strength I had in translating this marvellous, mesmerizing book. Any number of times, as I worked, I found myself deeply moved, and filled with a new sense of courage. Sometimes, too, I found its wonders overwhelming to the point where I felt powerless. The heat contained in this novel warmed me from the depths of my being and dispelled the deep chill that had stayed in my bones. If I hadn't translated this work, I might have moved off in a completely different direction. Unfortunately, though, in spite of its greatness, and in spite of all the energy I put into translating it, O'Brien's novel didn't sell as much as I had hoped it would. I do know several people, though, who have truly loved and supported the book.

Once I had finished the translation, I found myself wanting to write fiction again. It seemed to me that the very thing that could authenticate my existence was for me to go on living and writing. Even if that meant that I would have to experience continued loss and the loathing of the world, all I could do was to go on living this way. This was me; this was my place.[287]

Murakami did not immediately launch into a long novel. In fact, he would not begin to write another full-length piece of fiction for almost four years, and even the number of stories he produced in the meantime was small. He does, however, credit two stories he wrote following his translation of *The Nuclear Age* as the works with which he finally broke through his writer's block. In these short pieces – again, some of his best writing – Murakami investigated areas of dread and terror that had begun to surface in *Dance Dance Dance* and would go on to occupy an important place in his fictional world.

He wrote "TV People" ("TV Piipuru") in his apartment near the Vatican City.[288] Originally called "The TV People Strike Back" ("TV Piipuru no gyakushū"), it appeared in June 1989. It reveals Murakami's uneasiness about the invasive power of television. When a strange collection of tiny humanoids plant a TV set in a couple's apartment it soon takes over their lives. The apartment door is locked, but the silent creatures somehow slip inside, bearing an ordinary Sony TV. "They act as if I don't exist," Boku says. It is clear that, like most couch potatoes, his own boredom and inertia have left him vulnerable to such an attack. His normally fastidious wife is not even aware of the presence of the new TV or of the TV people's rearrangement of the room to accommodate it. Boku switches it on to see nothing but a blank screen. He tries to return to the book he has been reading, but he can no longer concentrate on the printed word. The mere presence of a TV set, and its broadcasting of nothing, are enough to transform his life.

Like Boku in "The Elephant Vanishes", the narrator works "in the advertising department of an electrical-appliance manufacturer. I dream up ads for toasters and washing machines and microwave ovens." At the office the next day, the TV people on his mind, he can't concentrate on his work, but his colleagues compliment him on his excellent contributions to meetings. Boku's wife, like the wife to come in *The Wind-up Bird Chronicle*, edits "a natural-food and lifestyle magazine" for a small publisher, and like her, too, she simply does not come home from work that day. We last see Boku at home alone with nothing but the TV people for company – inside the TV, outside the TV, everywhere. He himself may be shrinking to their size . . .[289]

The first short story Murakami wrote following the madness surrounding *Norwegian Wood* is one of his most effective and gripping: "Sleep" ("Nemuri", November 1989). "This is my seventeenth straight day without sleep," says the female "I" (*watashi*) narrator at the outset of the story. Her wakefulness, she is certain, is different from mere insomnia, which she once experienced in college. "I just can't sleep. Not for one second. Aside from that simple fact, I'm perfectly normal. I don't feel sleepy, and my mind is as clear as ever. Clearer, if anything."

As her tale progresses, this note of an improved state of awareness – of her mind, of her body, of her place in society and in the family (her dentist husband and their young son) – comes to dominate everything, and she withdraws into her own superior little world.

It all began one night when she woke from a particularly disgusting dream to find an old man dressed in black standing at the foot of the bed. As she watches in horror, he produces a white pitcher and pours water over her feet until she is sure they are going to rot away. She tries to scream, but the sound remains bottled up inside her. A moment later the man is gone, and the bed is dry – except for the sweat soaking her body.

When she has washed herself and calmed down she thinks, "It must have been a trance." The Japanese term for "trance" here is *kanashibari*, more or less literally "metal-binding" (as discussed on page 26). The great Meiji Period novelist Sōseki Natsume describes it as becoming the "prisoner of the sleep demon".[290] There is no English equivalent for *kanashibari*, which is far better known in Japan than the English medical term "sleep paralysis".[291]

Unable to find any rational explanation for the event, Watashi starts to deal with the realization that she is not sleepy. Her first thought is to find her old high school copy of a novel, and she chooses *Anna Karenina*. "When had I really read a book last? And what had it been? I couldn't recall anything. Why did a person's life have to change so completely? Where had the old me gone, the one who used to read a book as if possessed by it? What had those days – and that almost abnormally intense passion – meant to me?" Then she finds something stuck between two pages:

As I looked at the whitened flakes of chocolate from over a decade ago, I felt a tremendous urge to have the real thing. I wanted to eat chocolate while reading *Anna Karenina*, the way I did back then. I couldn't bear to be denied it for another moment. Every cell in my body seemed to be panting with this hunger for chocolate.

She goes out and buys this treat forbidden by her dentist husband, gorging herself on chocolate and *Anna Karenina*. The days of wakefulness go by as she performs her household duties with maximum efficiency and reads and swims at the local pool with mounting energy and a burgeoning sense of her own superiority.

My mind was in deep concentration, and expanding. If I had wanted to, I could have seen into the uttermost depths of the universe. But I decided not to look. It was too soon for that.
If death was like this, if to die meant to be eternally awake and staring into the darkness like this, what should I do?

To calm herself, she goes out for one of her nighttime drives, parking her car by the waterfront. She thinks about an old boyfriend, but "All the memories I have from the time before I stopped sleeping seem to be moving away with accelerating speed.

It feels so strange, as if the me who used to go to sleep every night is not the real me, and the memories from back then are not really mine. This is how people change. But nobody realizes it. Nobody notices. Only *I* know what happens." Her megalomanic thoughts mount in intensity, until two shadowy human forms emerge from the darkness and begin to rock her car from side to side. We don't know at the end whether she is about to die or to lose her mind.[292]

There had been plenty of dark imagery in Murakami's writing before – one thinks of the tunnels beneath Tokyo and the INKlings (*yamikuro*) who lurk there, waiting to devour human flesh – but these had always stayed safely in the realm of fantasy. Now Murakami was getting into something truly unnerving because it was closer to home. It is no coincidence that this new horrific element emerged in Murakami's first attempt to narrate from a woman's point of view, in which a revived sense of self-discovery and autonomy is taken, in classic Murakami style, a step or two beyond the bounds of common sense.

"Sleep" was a genuine turning point, marking a new level of intensity, an almost total loss of the old coolness and distancing, and a distinct shift towards horror and violence, elements that seemed increasingly unavoidable as Murakami came to embrace what he saw to be his responsibility as a Japanese writer. One other aspect of intense psychological states that interests him is a split between mind and body:

> I went through the motions – shopping, cooking, playing with my son, having sex with my husband. It was easy once I got the hang of it. All I had to do was break the connection between my mind and my body. While my body went about its business, my mind floated in its own inner space. I ran the house without a thought in my head, feeding snacks to my son, chatting with my husband.

Such extreme states of self-alienation would come to figure prominently in *The Wind-up Bird Chronicle*.

Murakami has claimed several times that he never dreams. In conversation with the Jungian psychologist Hayao Kawai, however, he revealed that he does have one recurring dream in which he sees himself levitating. It is a wonderful feeling, he said, and just as wonderful is the sense of confidence he has in the dream that he knows exactly how to do it. Kawai interpreted this as a symbol of Murakami's confidence as a storyteller. Murakami replied that sometimes while writing he has a strong sense of the power of the dead. "I feel that writing fiction is very close to the sense of going to the land of the dead."[293]

"TV People" and "Sleep" appeared in a collection called *TV People* (*TV Piipuru*, January 1990), which is notable for its forays into ghostly and horrific territory. The bloody "Creta Kanō" ("Kanō Kureta", first published in this collection) introduces a pair of sisters, named after the islands of Malta and Crete, who would emerge as clairvoyants in *The Wind-up Bird Chronicle*. The narrator of the story is the ghost of Creta Kanō, a gorgeous woman (and Japan's premier designer of fire-powered electricity generating plants) who has spent her life being raped by countless men irresistibly drawn to the "mismatched" water in her body.

She and her elder sister, Malta, kill a policeman who is attempting to rape her. They are careful to drain all of his blood and slit his throat, measures intended to prevent the spirit of the victim from returning as a ghost, but to no effect. His ghost comes to haunt the cellar where they store jars containing samples of water from all the regions of Japan. (These are used by Malta to keep her ear trained to hear the water in people's bodies, which is her line of work.) Murakami seems to have been experimenting here with some of the elemental imagery (water, fire, blood) and themes (rape, life-changing physical transformations) that he would incorporate into *The Wind-up Bird Chronicle*.

"Zombi" ("Zonbi", also first published in *TV People*) is a grotesque comedy in which a young man turns into a vicious zombie in his fiancée's dream, which is inspired by Michael Jackson's music video *Thriller*. This and another story in the collection, "Airplane – or How He Talked to Himself as if Reading Poetry" ("Hikōki – aruiwa kare wa ikanishite shi o yomu yōni hitorigoto o itta ka", June 1989; translated in 2002 as "Airplane") are notable as early attempts by Murakami to use a third-person narrator instead of having Boku do all the talking.

"Tony Takitani"

Busy with travel writing, editing his first *Complete Works*, and furiously translating, Murakami published only one piece of original fiction in 1990, but it is one of his truly great stories, the sad and beautiful "Tony Takitani" ("Tonii Takitani"). A rare venture into third-person narration, it was abridged for magazine publication in June and only appeared in its entirety the following year in a volume of the *Complete Works*.[294] An English translation appeared in *The New Yorker* in 2002.

As with so many of his stories, Murakami got the title for "Tony Takitani" before he knew what the story would be about. He was fascinated by the name, which was printed on an old T-shirt he had bought in Hawaii for a dollar. From that name, he dreamed up Tony's father, a pre-war jazz trombonist named Shōzaburō Takitani who spent the war years womanizing and giving concerts in Shanghai until he was locked up by the Chinese army after the Japanese were expelled.

In a few pages, Murakami does a remarkable job of evoking the decadence of Japanese expatriate life on the continent and the chaos of war and its aftermath. None of this is strictly necessary for telling the story of Shōzaburō's son, but the vivid description of the world that Murakami creates around Shōzaburō is utterly engrossing and draws from both his knowledge of jazz and his reading on the history of the Second World War.

Shōzaburō narrowly escapes being executed by the Chinese and is sent back to Japan, where he becomes involved with a distant cousin. Tony's mother dies three days after giving birth to him, and Shōzaburō has no idea what to do with the baby or even what to name him. A jazz-loving Italian-American army major from New Jersey offers his own name: Tony. (The glimpse of Occupation Period Japan given here is another small triumph.) Shōzaburō accepts the offer, but –

> For the child himself, though, living with a name like that
> was not much fun. The other kids at school teased him as
> a half-breed, and whenever he told someone his name, he
> would get a look of puzzlement or distaste. Some people
> thought it was a bad joke, and others reacted with anger.
> For certain people, coming face to face with a child called
> "Tony Takitani" was all they needed to feel old wounds
> reopening.[295]

Spurned by his society, Tony grows up with minimal attention from his self-centred father, becoming a self-reliant and utterly detached and seemingly passionless industrial illustrator (in marked contrast to the superficially "idealistic" rebels of the 1960s, in yet another deft evocation of an era). Then one day it happens: Tony falls in love, and the shell in which he has lived is shattered.

The object of Tony's affections is a rather ordinary girl, except for one small thing: her love of clothing. Here, the story evolves into pure Murakami as Tony's new wife becomes obsessed with building her wardrobe, for which Tony converts an entire room into a walk–in closet. But a relentless turn of fate brings him back from marital bliss to his original loneliness in a heart-breaking conclusion. No summary can do justice to the sweep of history, from the expansive years of the Japanese empire to the years of empty affluence in the wealthy suburbs and boutiques of Tokyo (Murakami's own Aoyama neighbourhood), that Murakami manages to cram into 20 pages through the judicious choice of detail. Perhaps only *The Wind-up Bird Chronicle* displays his mastery of modern Japanese history as well, but that work consists of three volumes. "Tony Takitani" can be seen as a preparation for the longer work, both in its attention to historical detail and its use of third-person narration.

Murakami's low output of new fiction continued into 1991: only four stories and the full-length version of "Tony Takitani" appeared in print. The majority were included in the most recent volumes of the *Complete Works*. Volume 5 was published in January with "The Silence" (discussed in Chapter 5 above) appended to the stories in *Dead Heat on a Merry-Go-Round*. Volume 8, in July, contained "Tony Takitani" and a story called "Man-Eating Cats" ("Hito-kui neko").

Depicting the life of a couple who have run off to a Greek island together after their affair has been discovered by their spouses, "Man-Eating Cats" is primarily of interest as an early exploration of motifs that would surface again in three novels: *South of the Border, West of the Sun* (a female character named "Izumi"; abandoning a near-perfect marriage in pursuit of some indefinable missing ingredient); *The Wind-up Bird Chronicle* (running off to the Mediterranean with a woman after the collapse of one's routine life); and especially *Sputnik Sweetheart* (inexplicable disappearances, going over to the "other side" on a Greek island to the tune of *Zorba the Greek*, fracture of the self). Not only do cats and Boku's girlfriend disappear mysteriously in this story, but Boku himself somehow manages to "disappear" – twice!

Flying over Egypt on the plane to Greece, he tells us, "I suddenly felt as if I had vanished. It was the weirdest sensation. The person sitting on that plane was no longer me." And later, on the island, while looking for the vanished Izumi: "Just then – without warning – I disappeared. Maybe it was the moonlight, or that midnight music. With each step I took, I felt myself sinking deeper into a quicksand where my identity vanished; it was the same emotion I'd had on the plane, flying over Egypt."[296] Even in fiction, saying something doesn't always make it so.

The other noteworthy story from 1991 was "The Little Green Monster" ("Midori-iro no kedamono", April 1991), included in a special "Haruki Murakami Book" issue of a major literary journal and running to just over four pages in *The Elephant Vanishes*.

"My husband left for work as usual, and I couldn't think of anything to do," says the first-person female Watashi ("I"). Like the Watashi of "Sleep", she spends time inside her own mind when her husband is away – perhaps too much time. As she stares out at the garden, a little monster with green scales burrows up from underground ("At first I thought it was coming from a place deep inside me") and asks her to marry him. She is horrified to realize that this ugly embodiment of male desire can read her mind, but she quickly realizes she can use this against him. She begins to think terrible, hateful thoughts, and the creature writhes in agony. "See, then, you little monster, you have no idea what a woman is. There's no end to the number of things I can think of to do to you." Before long, it shrivels up and dies, and "the room filled with the darkness of night".[297]

10

On the Road Again

Murakami may have been able to avoid a lot of unpleasant experiences by remaining abroad, but one thing he could not avoid was the advent of his fortieth birthday on 12 January 1989. For a writer who had focused so intensely on the decade between 20 and 30, and with a predominantly youthful readership, that milestone fell with a thud. He saw death approaching and began to feel how little time he had left in which to write with real concentration. The last thing he wanted was, some time in the future, to regret that he had wasted part of his life when he was still mentally and physically capable of concentrated work. He wanted to feel that he had given it everything he could. This would certainly explain his astonishing productivity at this time. Murakami writes of this turning point in his life with passion – and with surprising frequency.[298]

For Haruki and Yōko turning 40 meant any thoughts they might have had about raising a family were all but gone. It had been out of the question when they were working long hours in the jazz club, and the intensity with which they both concentrated on his writing career had pushed thoughts of having children into the background. Murakami decided he would continue to concentrate on his career, and he has stuck to that decision without regret.[299] Besides, he and Yōko had long had misgivings about the whole undertaking. Their early lives had taught them to distrust family bonds. Nor did a more impersonal assessment of society offer encouragement: "I can't have children," he had told an interviewer in 1984. "I simply don't have the confidence my parents' generation had after the war that the world would continue to improve."[300]

In any case, with nothing tying them down, the Murakamis continued their life on the move. In May 1989 they travelled to Rhodes where the beaches, the charming old city, and relaxing with a good book or two helped them to forget about the outside world. On 6 June, however, this idyll was interrupted when Murakami bought the first newspaper he had seen in weeks. It was filled with reports of the Tiananmen Square Massacre. He read of the shooting, stabbing, and crushing of thousands of student demonstrators. "The more I read, the more depressed I got," he wrote, thinking back to his days of protest as a student. He imagined what it would have been like had he been among the students in Tiananmen Square, to feel the bullets ripping through his flesh and shattering his bones, and then the gradual descent of darkness.[301] This was as far as his imagination took him, however: inside.

In July Haruki and Yōko travelled to south Germany and Austria by car. In October they spent some days in Japan, then quickly left for New York in connection with the impending publication of the English translation of *A Wild Sheep Chase*. They returned to Japan in January 1990 – this time, supposedly, for good.

But now, as all know who have lived abroad for an extended period, there was reverse culture shock to deal with. Far from the joy it had been in Europe, driving a car in Tokyo, with its constant traffic jams, yielded little more than stress.[302] Japanese politics, too, had developed a new and unsettling undercurrent. In February the leader of the Aum Shinrikyō cult, Shōkō Asahara, stood for election in the Lower House of the Japanese Diet. Near his Tokyo apartment Murakami witnessed the Aum campaign: "Day after day strange music played from big lorries with sound-systems, while white-robed young men and women in oversized Asahara masks and elephant heads lined the pavement outside my local train station, waving and dancing some incomprehensible jig." This "odd piece of theatre" left a sickening impression, but he could never have anticipated the devastation Aum would cause five years later on the Tokyo subway.[303]

The difficulty of living in Tokyo made life abroad seem even more attractive. A complex network of social obligations in Japan served only to rob Murakami of opportunities to write. As Ian Buruma has noted, in Japan "the writer is a *sensei*, a teacher or master, as well as a prima donna . . . Writers [are] still seen as masters, and [are] expected to hold forth on everything from nuclear defence to the desirability of birth-control pills."[304] An endless stream of TV producers, magazine editors, and publishers beat a path to Murakami's door, where they usually had to deal with Yōko – in itself an affront to Japan's male-dominated society and to the equally male-chauvinistic literary establishment.

Murakami has absolutely refused to have anything to do with TV, but dealing with the literary scene has not been so simple. "Editors represent the publishing companies, but they come to you as friends. If you say no to them, they lose face, and feel hurt. They think I'm arrogant and insensitive, and this makes life very hard for me in Japan. If you wish to please the editors, you will be liked and Japanese harmony will prevail, but your work will suffer. As a result, I'm an outcast in the Tokyo literary world."[305]

This may be an exaggeration, but the fact is that in choosing to reject the usual methods of interacting with the elitist literary establishment, as well as the mass media, Haruki and Yōko have had to deal on a daily basis with an endless series of small but nagging problems that take a cumulative toll. Haruki sees this as preventing him from doing the one thing he wants to do, which is to write.[306]

A writer in Japan is expected to treat all publishers equally, to be available for socializing, to produce a text on demand for anyone who requests it. There seems to be little sense on the part of publishers that a writer might burn out under the pressure. A small publisher's grovelling approach is usually along the lines of "I don't suppose you could possibly deign to write for a press as insignificant as ours, but . . ." When an author turns down such a request – especially one so self-abasing – because he feels he is already working hard enough, he is accused of arrogance.[307] And when the writer's wife is as involved in her husband's career as Yōko, the reactions can be vicious. (Murakami reports that, with a weakening in Japan's male chauvinism, a rise in the number of female editors, and the increased use of e-mail between editors and writers, the situation has improved markedly in recent years.)[308]

Publishers may not like Murakami's way of doing business, but they like the business his books do. In the spring and summer of 1990, the first volumes of his *Complete Works* appeared along with two volumes of his *Complete Works of Raymond Carver*; a book on Murakami's European travels (*A Distant Drum* [*Tōi taiko*], with photographs by Yōko); and Murakami's translation of Tim O'Brien's *The Things They Carried*, following hot on the heels of *The Nuclear Age* the previous year.

That autumn, in conversation with Elmer Luke, an American editor friend in Tokyo, Murakami suddenly recalled his visit to Princeton six years before. "Someday," he said wistfully, "I'd like to write fiction in a quiet place like that, without any interruptions." Luke took him at his word and contacted Princeton Professor of Japanese History, Martin Collcutt, who immediately invited Murakami to stay in Princeton as a Visiting Scholar – in effect, an artist-in-residence, with no teaching duties. Luke told Murakami he was expected to show up in Princeton by the end of January, and that a place had already been designated for him to live on campus.[309]

Just back from three years of travelling around Europe, Haruki and Yōko were reluctant to uproot themselves again. Towards the end of their time abroad they had found themselves longing for Japan's hot springs and buckwheat noodles, and were more than ready to stay home for a while. But turning 40 put a different complexion on the matter: why not take advantage of this unique opportunity while they were still young enough to enjoy it?[310] As unpleasant as their dealings with the literary establishment and the mass media had been, this alone was not enough to send them abroad again. Often asked "Why did you leave Japan?" Murakami wants to shoot back "And why *shouldn't* I have left Japan? I can work anywhere: I don't have to be in Japan. I left because I wanted to see new places, to explore a broader world." Maybe, too, the image of Hemingway and F. Scott Fitzgerald writing some of their best work abroad was at the back of his mind.[311] If nothing else, the pastoral image of Fitzgerald's alma mater was too alluring to pass up.

Princeton's invitation had not come out of a vacuum. On his first visit to the States Murakami had been regarded as nothing more than a translator. Now his work had begun to be translated into English and his reputation preceded him. With the Japanese economy booming and the yen seemingly invincible, Japan's gargantuan Kōdansha publishers had actively promoted Japanese literature abroad. To help them in this they had hired some established New York editors, including Elmer Luke.

When he arrived in Japan in 1988, Luke discovered that one minor Kōdansha project was the Kodansha English Library: translations of popular contemporary novels into English, with grammar notes at the back. They were intended as language-learning aids for Japanese high-school students. One of the translators of this series was Alfred Birnbaum, a young American living in Tokyo. His translation of Murakami's *A Wild Sheep Chase* was in preparation for the Kodansha English Library project, but Elmer Luke realized it had far greater potential than just a set text for Japanese students of English. Birnbaum had come to this conclusion long before.

He had been translating art books for Kodansha International, but really wanted to do fiction. He brought in his translation of Murakami's short story "The New York Mining Disaster" as a sample of what he could do, and mentioned *A Wild Sheep Chase* as a novel he particularly liked. After a month or so of indecision, however, the company concluded that *A Wild Sheep Chase* was "too thick", but they liked his suggestion and gave him Japanese editions of *Hear the Wind Sing* and *Pinball, 1973* to read.

Birnbaum decided to do *Pinball* first, and handed in the manuscript, assuming Kodansha International would promote and distribute the book in the United States. He was disappointed to find that the parent company, Kōdansha, published it in the English Library series instead, complete with grammar notes by somebody else.[312]

If Alfred Birnbaum can be credited with having discovered Murakami for an English-speaking readership, Elmer Luke can be credited with having saved his discovery. He began working with Birnbaum to improve the appeal of *A Wild Sheep Chase* to an international readership. They removed dates and other signs linking the action to the 1970s, giving it a more contemporary feel – even going so far as to include a Reagan-era chapter title, "One for the Kipper", that chimed with the translation's hip new style, if not to the book's chronology. (Set in 1978, the novel should not have contained – and does not in the original – this allusion to the famous movie line "Make it one for the Gipper", which flourished during the Reagan years after 1980.) The novel's catchy title was Birnbaum's invention, though, and it matched the lively style of the translation perfectly.[313]

Luke called Murakami while he was still in Rome to tell him about these new plans for his work. "I suspect that he was rather dubious of the whole proposition at the time," says Luke, "though, obviously, he was tantalized by the interest and possibilities involved." Luke and the other foreign editors strongly urged Kōdansha to support the project, which they finally did, to the tune of a $50,000 advertising budget. "For a house like Kōdansha, that was extraordinary. They had never done anything like that before," says Luke.

But the time was right. Everything Japanese was of interest in America now, especially the story of a cool young guy who didn't buy in to the economic mystique; and from America the interest spread to Europe. (It had already spread to China and Korea, where Murakami has an enthusiastic readership.) In 1989 Murakami became the first Japanese writer since Kōbō Abe to attract a substantial audience beyond the small field of Japanese literary studies in America.

And so by the time Luke contacted Princeton in autumn 1990, Murakami's importance on the Japanese literary scene was becoming known in the States. *The New Yorker* of 10 September 1990 published Birnbaum's translation of the creepy new story "TV People" (discussed in the previous chapter), and the 26 November issue carried "The Wind-up Bird and Tuesday's Women" (see Chapter 7).

Things were happening quickly – perhaps too quickly. That January Yōko and Haruki were in a taxi heading for the American Embassy in Tokyo to pick up their visas when they heard the news on the radio that America had just bombed Baghdad. It seemed a bad omen. Neither of them liked the idea of living in a country at war – however distant it might be from America itself. Murakami voiced his concerns to Luke, who was convinced he would back out and stay in Tokyo. Everybody had put so much effort into the arrangements by that time, however, that Murakami felt he had no choice. When he and Yōko arrived in the United States some days later they found an ugly atmosphere of macho patriotism running rampant.

Arriving at the Princeton campus, Murakami felt a pleasant sense of nostalgia when he walked straight into an anti-war demonstration – until he looked more closely at the placards and realized the students were demonstrating in *support* of the war. And later, when a few students finally protested against the carnage in the Middle East, a pro-war faction attacked the demonstrators and smashed up their placards. The war mood seemed to be everywhere. Even when Murakami ran his first Boston Marathon that April he noticed that in the peaceful town of Hopkinton, Massachusetts, where the race began, a side-show encouraged people to smash a car labelled SADDAM with a sledgehammer for one dollar a blow, the proceeds going to the town's scholarship fund.

As the months passed this chauvinistic attitude abated, only to be replaced by rising anti-Japanese feeling with the approach of the fiftieth anniversary of Pearl Harbor. Murakami and other Japanese left their homes as little as possible. He was at home most of the time anyway, working hard on his next novel. His strict schedule was in keeping with the Spartan faculty housing provided by the university and which he and Yōko found most congenial. It was here that Murakami switched from a dedicated word processor to a computer under the tutelage of Japanese Literature Professor Hosea Hirata.[314]

Aside from the heightened political atmosphere (including being called a "Jap", almost innocently, by an old soldier), Murakami began to enjoy his simple life in America. He drank Bud Dry without feeling the need to consume something more fashionable;

he wore his favourite T-shirts and trainers that blended in with the casual look of the students; he drove a second-hand Honda Accord (later a Volkswagen Corrado) without anyone remarking that as a well-off bestselling novelist he ought to drive something more glamorous. "What I like about America is I'm really free here," he told the *Los Angeles Times Magazine*. "I'm free to do anything; I'm not a celebrity here. Nobody cares."[315]

This was almost true. Japanese Literature specialists at various American universities cared, and soon the invitations were coming thick and fast. The day after the Boston Marathon, Murakami arrived at Harvard University to discuss "The Second Bakery Attack". He went on to attend classes at Michigan, Amherst, Tufts, Berkeley, Austin, Stanford, Dartmouth, Montclair State College, William and Mary, Penn, Irvine, Pomona, and especially the University of Washington, where he was astonished at the high standards of Japanese literary studies.[316] Murakami's greatest pleasure during these visits was the time he spent talking to students, and he was willing to put up with the presence of their professors. (In July 1991 he briefly visited Seattle and made another visit to Tess Gallagher, across Puget Sound in Port Angeles.)

Murakami's attitude to America changed. In Japan he had once craved Ivy League clothes and American-made goods, but now he began to realize that almost everything in his Princeton home had been manufactured elsewhere: Denon stereo, Sony TV, Sharp VCR, Panasonic microwave oven – all made in Japan; Bang and Olufsen turntable from Denmark, headphones and coffee mill and iron from Germany; and even his seemingly "American-made" AT&T fax machine was made in Japan. A search around the apartment turned up the major parts of his bicycle, a notebook and a wallet as the only American-manufactured goods he owned. "As uninformed as I am about economic matters," he says, "I couldn't help thinking that there was more of a problem with America's economy than could be explained by mere economic globalization." But then he realized he did all of his writing on a Macintosh Power Book.[317]

Murakami felt so at home in America that he asked to have his year-long appointment as Visiting Scholar extended for another six months. This was agreed and after that he prolonged his stay for another year by agreeing to teach a seminar on modern Japanese writers as a visiting lecturer. It was the first time he had ever drawn a salary, and also the first opportunity he had ever had to read his literary predecessors in a systematic way. He chose to concentrate on the so-called "Third New Generation" of Japanese writers active in the late 1950s and early 1960s (the period when, as a young man, he had preferred Dostoevsky and Raymond Chandler).

Never having taught anything to anyone (or, for that matter, done much formal studying himself), Murakami found it a daunting task – and one that made it impossible for him to write fiction while he was under contract. Nevertheless, he truly enjoyed discussing literature with his students and he learned a lot in the process.

Constitutionally incapable of wasting an opportunity to write, Murakami produced a book from the experience: *A Young Reader's Guide to Short Fiction* (*Wakai dokusha no tame no tanpen shōsetsu annai*, 1997), in the preface to which he went to great lengths to deny that he was an authority on the subject. The one thing that Murakami cannot abide is to be identified in any way with authority. Needless to say, he uses the word "Boku" in this book, too, when he finds it necessary to refer to himself, and he addresses his "young readers" in almost comically polite language. Rather than lecturing them, he says, "I am reading these works with you, so if you have any questions, please don't hesitate to raise your hands." In addition to his fresh views on the writers under study, he encourages his readers in their love of literature: "To be able to talk to your heart's content about a book you like with someone who feels the same way about it is one of the greatest joys that life can offer."[318]

Murakami also used his free time on campus to add to his knowledge of modern Japanese history. As Ian Buruma tells it, Murakami "researched the [1939] Battle of Nomonhan at the Princeton University library. It struck him as the perfect example not only of irrational violence but also of the sacrifice of individuals to a crazy collective enterprise."[319]

Murakami was no stranger to research. He had done a great deal for *A Wild Sheep Chase* and "Tony Takitani", which demonstrated his sensitive understanding of Japan's recent past, but at Princeton the depth and intensity of his reading on the Second World War surpassed anything he had done before. Although 1990 and 1991 were years in which Murakami published only a handful of stories, he was always *thinking* about writing. He had a big novel in mind – perhaps too big, for "through a mysterious process of cell division" it became his next two novels, *South of the Border, West of the Sun* (*Kokkyō no minami, taiyō no nishi*, 1992) and *The Wind-up Bird Chronicle*. The former would tie up loose ends from his earlier work, while the latter, a product of his historical research, is regarded by many as his masterpiece.[320]

South of the Border, West of the Sun

This slim novel might appear initially to be a return to the world of *Norwegian Wood*, the sexual experiences of a teenaged protagonist occupying much of the book. But whereas *Norwegian Wood* only hints at the life of its 38-year-old narrator, *South of the Border, West of the Sun* concentrates on the later Boku around the same age.

Hajime (another narrator who calls himself Boku) is the owner of a successful jazz club and bar. We see him at the age of 36 (soon to be 37), the happily married father of two daughters, the eldest of whom he drives to a private kindergarten every day in his BMW.

While waiting outside to pick her up in the afternoons, he often chats to another affluent, Mercedes-driving parent about wine sales and supermarket parking problems. While his daughter is in school, he swims and works out with weights to keep his middle-aging body in trim. He has a second country home in Hakone. In fact, Hajime's life is so good he even gets along with his father-in-law! The older man's money helped him break out of his dead-end company job and transform himself into an elegant, successful worldly-wise proprietor who spends his well-dressed evenings overseeing his fashionable establishments, much like Humphrey Bogart in *Casablanca*.

But *South of the Border, West of the Sun* is the ultimate novel of yuppie mid-life crisis. As perfect as Hajime's life may appear – not only to us but to Hajime himself – there is something missing, some ideal, indefinable quality that waits for him in a half-imagined world "south of the border" or even more impossibly "west of the sun". As we might expect by now, this realm lies in Hajime's past and is associated with his early sexual experiences.

The first hint that Hajime might be troubled after all comes when he confesses to himself a sense of guilt over the shortcut that his father-in-law's money gave him to financial independence. A member of the late 1960s, early 1970s generation of rebellious students who said "no" to "the logic of late capitalism", he now lives in a world that functions according to "the very same capitalist logic". Listening to Schubert one day in his BMW, it hits him that "I was living someone else's life, not my own."[321] Still, no matter what, he would never go back to his twenties.

Then along comes Shimamoto-san, once his closest friend in grammar school when they had been strongly drawn to each other as only children. They were forced to part when they went to separate middle schools. Hajime and Shimamoto-san are lonely outsiders (a congenital limp prevented her from joining in many school activities), but although almost inseparable for a time, they were never involved sexually. Rather, Hajime's fondest memory is of often listening to Nat King Cole's "South of the Border" with her. The song had such mysterious, otherworldly overtones for Shimamoto-san that she later admits to being disappointed when she discovered it was about Mexico.

Almost from the moment she re-enters his life one rainy night, Murakami invites us to wonder whether Shimamoto-san is "real" or a figment of Hajime's imagination. Described in lavish Hollywood-style terms, her beauty is literally incredible (even her old limp has been surgically mended). She "vanishes" into the night after her first visit, and Hajime can only reassure himself she was actually there by finding her glass and ashtray still on the bar. He recalls another dreamlike incident eight years before, when he followed a woman who reminded him of (and, as it turns out, actually was) Shimamoto-san, only to be restrained by a mysterious man as he was about to approach her. The man, who seems to have assumed Hajime was a hired detective, gave him an envelope containing ¥100,000 and warned him to stop following her. Even then, Hajime had wondered if the event actually happened, but the envelope is still in his desk, untouched, the sight of which reassures him that his mind is not playing tricks.

These continual appeals to dream and illusion, plus Shimamoto-san's insistence that Hajime must not ask her anything about the intervening years, suggest that she will remain an enigmatic figure to the end. She has grown into a beautiful, seductive woman, but all he knows about her derives almost wholly from his childhood. She is "Shimamoto-san" ("Miss Shimamoto") from beginning to end, both in the retrospective narrative and in dialogue when he is passionately declaring his love for her. "Shimamoto" is a family name, and "-san" is the polite suffix used for almost all people (a kind of unisex "Mr", "Miss", and "Mrs"). "Shimamoto-san" is what she would have been called in grammar school, and therefore the expression carries a heavy dose of nostalgia for the time they spent together.

She calls him "Hajime-kun", as he was known back then, the "-kun" suffix an endearing version of "-san" most often used in childhood and teenage contexts, more often with males than females. Even Japanese reviewers have found it curious to have these late-30-something lovers addressing each other as though they were still in the sixth grade, but the effect is to reinforce the importance to the mature protagonist of those idealized moments in childhood. The subtle superiority of "-san" to "-kun" also parallels their sexual relationship, in which she is the more active partner.

Shimamoto-san continues to enter and leave Hajime's life unpredictably, but he learns almost nothing of her past. At one point, at her request, he takes her to a river where she discards the ashes of a day-old baby she lost a year earlier, but she divulges none of the circumstances of its conception. When, at last, in the novel's climactic chapter, she gives him the original copy of Nat King Cole's "South of the Border", they go to his country home to listen to it and make love for the first time. Afterwards he demands that she tell him "everything" about herself so that they have no secrets from each other. "Tomorrow," she assures him, but just as she insisted that their first act of love should be a masturbatory enactment of the sex they had missed with each other in their teens, there will be no "tomorrow" with Shimamoto-san, only the past. Hajime wakes alone, and aside from a slight impression of her head on the pillow next to his, there is no physical evidence in the house that Shimamoto-san was ever there. Even the Nat King Cole record is gone. She has vanished as mysteriously as the town pet in the story "The Elephant Vanishes".

Murakami practically invites the reader to conclude that the affair

197

with Shimamoto-san has all been in Hajime's head. The "reality" Hajime awakes to is "different" from the reality he perceived before then, he thinks. "She exists nowhere but in my memory."[322] Not only is the record gone, but he can no longer find the envelope with the money in it that he has kept all these years in a locked drawer of his desk.

Has he been hallucinating? Have we been reading the confessions of a man losing his mind? If so, no "fact" in the novel can be relied upon. Does he really own a bar and a jazz club? Is he really married? Does he have two little girls? Hajime himself begins to lose track: "once I acknowledged that the envelope had disappeared, its existence and non-existence traded places in my consciousness . . . To what extent facts we recognize as such really *are* as they seem, and to what extent these are facts merely because we label them as such, is an impossible distinction to draw."[323]

"Facts" are what Hajime most wants from Shimamoto-san and they are what she resolutely refuses to provide. Without them, she will remain an enigma to him. And yet how much more does he really know about anyone else – most notably, his wife, Yukiko, about whom he once assumed he had all the "facts" he might ever need? "You actually believe you know what I'm thinking?" she asks him after he has confessed to her his (possibly hallucinatory) affair with Shimamoto-san, and much of the final chapter is devoted to exploring what has hardly crossed Hajime's mind until now: the inner life of his own wife.[324]

Yukiko suddenly emerges as a forceful character with a world of thoughts that he has never guessed. (There is a distinctly feminist slant here, as in Shimamoto-san's aggressive sexuality: *she* strips *him*.) Shimamoto-san remains an enigma, but she is only an extreme version of all Others, and even of ourselves. Everyone we "know" is an assemblage of our remembered perceptions of them. As Boku's wife said in *A Wild Sheep Chase*, "Most everything you think you know about me is nothing more than memories."[325] We may think we "know" other people when we know superficial facts about them, when we think they have no secrets from us, especially when we intuitively feel so close to them – love them – so intensely that their very existence is the one indispensable element we think we need to make our lives meaningful and complete. It is the one thing Hajime thinks he can get from Shimamoto-san, for which he is willing to sacrifice his family and his yuppie lifestyle, without which all of his material comfort amounts to "the airless surface of the moon".[326] But this completeness exists only "south of the border" or "west of the sun", in another world, a place so deep down inside ourselves that we may never gain access to it.

Shimamoto-san is no more nor less a hallucination than anyone else: she "really" exists in the world of the novel; Hajime is not mad. Did the elephant in the story "really" exist? If we accept that the townsfolk "really" celebrated its arrival and the newspaper "really" reported its coming and going, we have to conclude that Boku did not imagine the whole thing. But Haruki Murakami certainly did imagine the whole thing. Shimamoto-san is – and must remain – as great a mystery as the elephant. She and Yukiko and Hajime are constructs, ideas, dreamed up by Haruki Murakami. The "solution" to this mystery lies outside the fictional world of the novel. Murakami has deliberately made it internally inconsistent. The novel stands apart from "life" as a totally artificial assemblage of words and, in self-destructing, it propels us outside its hermetic universe into our own. Faced with the question of what is "real" for Hajime, we are asked to question what is "real" for any of us. The answer is far from certain.

South of the Border, West of the Sun is a bold book. It dares to put the most sickly sweet words of love into the hero and heroine's mouths, promising "meaning" in a life that is lacking only this one element to make Hajime's success complete. It then takes away this one unattainable ideal, leaving the hero in the desert (Walt Disney's *Living Desert*!) of his happy marriage and financial security. Hajime-Humphrey Bogart and his Ingrid Bergman are torn apart, but he is not left with a higher love to idealize for the rest of his life: he is left "only" with a perfect marriage from which some indefinable "something" seems to be missing. "It can't end like this," he thinks, but of course it does, with the hero still in full-blown mid-life crisis, filled with the "nothingness" he sees in the eyes of Izumi, a woman he betrayed in their high school days.[327]

Just as Boku's encounter with the mysterious other world of the disappearing elephant left him a better refrigerator salesman than ever, but feeling that human relationships "didn't seem to matter one way or the other",[328] after his affair with Shimamoto-san Hajime finds that in his business "Everything ran like clockwork, but the thrill was gone." He observes, "On the surface, my days were the same as ever."[329] But he has changed inside.

At the jazz club, Hajime asks the pianist not to play Duke Ellington's "Star-Crossed Lovers" for him any more. "Sounds a little like *Casablanca* to me!" the man observes, and every now and then, a mischievous twinkle in his eye, he plays his boss "As Time Goes By".[330] Hajime doesn't want to hear his old Ellington favourite not because it reminds him of Shimamoto-san but because it no longer moves him. The book ends in middle-aged defeat. Hajime recognizes that, as Wordsworth wrote, "there hath past away a glory from the earth".

11

Overture to *The Thieving Magpie*

Most of Murakami's visits from Princeton to other universities were brief one or two day affairs, but in November 1992, a month after *South of the Border, West of the Sun* was published in Japan, he went to Berkeley for four weeks as the Una's Lecturer in the Humanities (in honour of Berkeley alumna Una Smith Ross). This prestigious role required him to deliver one public lecture and to present four weekly seminars. He found the academic expectations a real challenge, for which the small seminar at Princeton had hardly prepared him. He really sweated over the lecture, which had to be delivered in English to a sizeable general audience, not just a room of Japanese-speaking students.

Years of translating had given him a solid command of English grammar, and living at Princeton had forced him to develop his spoken English to the point where he could manage most daily interactions with confidence, but now he was being asked to pontificate like one of those professors who always seem to think too much. He decided to accept the challenge, writing in Japanese before translating it into English. The result was an eloquent and revealing lecture entitled "The Sheep Man and the End of the World". In it Murakami provided a lot of interesting background information about the two novels that by then had been published in English translation, but he also spoke more generally about his role as a Japanese novelist in the modern world. Here is his conclusion:

It seems to me that in a country like America, with its ethnic variety, communication is a matter of special importance. Where you have whites and blacks and Asians and Jews and people of all different cultural and religious backgrounds living together, what is needed to convey one's ideas clearly is not in-group complacency but writing styles that can have an effect on a broad range of people. This calls for a broad range of rhetorical devices and storytelling and humour.

In Japan, with its relatively homogeneous population, different literary customs have evolved. The language used in literary works tends to be the kind that communicates to a small group of like-minded people. Once a piece of writing is given the seal of approval with the label *jun-bungaku* – "pure literature" – the assumption takes hold that it only needs to communicate to a few critics and a small segment of the populace. There's nothing wrong with writing like that, of course, but there's nothing that says that *all* novels have to be written this way. Such an attitude can only lead to suffocation. But fiction is a living thing. It needs fresh air.

That fresh air was something I found in foreign literature.

The fact remains, of course, that whatever I may have found in foreign literature, I wanted to write – and I continue to write – Japanese fiction. Using new methods and a new style, I am writing new Japanese stories – new *monogatari*. I have been criticized for not using traditional styles and methods, but, after all, an author has the right to choose any methods that feel right to him.

I have been living in America for almost two years now,

and I feel very much at home here. If anything, I am more comfortable here than in Japan. I am still very much aware, however, that I was born and raised in Japan, and that I am writing novels in Japanese. Furthermore, my novels are always set in Japan, not in foreign countries. This is because I want to portray Japanese society using the style that I have created. The longer I live abroad, the stronger this desire of mine becomes. There is a tradition whereby Japanese writers and artists who have lived abroad come home with new feelings of nationalism. They undergo a re-conversion to Japan and sing the praises of Japanese food and Japanese customs. My case is rather different. I like Japanese food and Japanese customs, of course, but what I want to do for now is live in a foreign country, observe Japan from here, and write what I see in novels.

I am now writing a new novel, and as I write I am aware that I am changing bit by bit. My strongest awareness that I have changed is this new awareness that I must change. Both as a writer and as a human being, I have to become more open to the world around me, I know. And I know, too, that in some cases I am going to have to engage in a struggle.

For example, until I came to America, I had never spoken like this before an audience. I had always assumed that there was no need for me to do such a thing because my job is to write, not to speak. Since coming to live in America, however, I have gradually begun to feel that I wanted to speak to people. I have come to feel more strongly that I want the people of America – the people of the world – to know what I, as one Japanese writer, am thinking. This is an enormous change for me.

I feel certain that novels from now on will have a far more diverse mixture of cultural elements. We see this tendency in the writings of Kazuo Ishiguro, Oscar Hijuelos, Amy Tan, and Manuel Puig, all of whom have taken their works beyond the confines of a single culture. Ishiguro's novels are written in English, but I and other Japanese readers can feel in them something intensely Japanese. I believe that in the global village, novels will become in this way increasingly interchangeable. At the same time, I want to go on thinking about how, in the midst of such a powerful tide, people can manage to preserve their identities. What I must do, as one novelist, is to carry this thought process forward through my work of telling stories.

The Wind-up Bird Chronicle

The "new novel" of which Murakami speaks is, of course, *The Wind-up Bird Chronicle* which had just begun to be serialized in the Japanese magazine *Shinchō*. This massive project would occupy most of his time and energy for the next three years. Having grown out of the story "The Wind-up Bird and Tuesday's Women", Books One and Two of the novel were published simultaneously on Tuesday, 12 April 1994; the 500-page Book Three, however, finally appeared on Friday, 25 August 1995.[331] Murakami was exhausted, as he had been after writing *Hard-boiled Wonderland and the End of the World*.[332]

South of the Border, West of the Sun and *The Wind-up Bird Chronicle* may have separated from each other "through a mysterious process of cell division", but the points of contact lie in the shared theme of the difficulty of one person's knowing another and the affluent 1980s setting. Where *South of the Border, West of the Sun* might be seen as a novel-length exploration of the mystery of "The Elephant Vanishes", *The Wind-up Bird Chronicle* opens up new areas of exploration. It is a sprawling work that begins as a domestic drama surrounding the disappearance of a couple's cat, then transports us to the Mongolian desert, and ends by taking on political and supernatural evil on a grand scale. Longer than *Hard-boiled Wonderland and the End of the World*, it was clearly a turning point for Murakami, perhaps the greatest of his career. As Murakami said, this is where he finally abandons his stance of cool detachment to embrace commitment,[333] and though much of the action still takes place in the mind of a first-person Boku narrator, the central focus of the book is on human relationships.

This was a bold move for a writer who had built his reputation on coolness, but Murakami had come to feel strongly that "mere" storytelling was not enough. He wanted to care deeply about something and to have his hero's quest lead to something.

In many ways *The Wind-up Bird Chronicle* can be read as a re-telling of *A Wild Sheep Chase*. It is as if Murakami had asked himself: "What if the Boku of that novel had *not* been so cool about the breakup of his marriage?"[334] And where the tragic history of Japan's continental depredations had only been hinted at in the fanciful story of Jūnitaki Village and the government's exploitation of its farmers (turning them into sheepherders to aid the war effort against the Russians in China), here the scene shifts for many pages at a time to wartime action on the Manchurian-Mongolian border to explore the violent heritage of modern-day Japan.

Much of *The Wind-up Bird Chronicle* borders on the exotic, including never-explained elements of the occult, and scenes set far from modern Japan in both time and space. If we strip away the mystery and colour, however, it turns out to be the story of a somewhat sexually repressed husband whose even more repressed wife leaves him when she awakens to her true sexual appetite in the arms of another man.

Neither partner in the marriage is a prude, although the wife's perfectionism and neatness border on the extreme (as with the wife in *A Wild Sheep Chase*, to comic effect). She and her possessions – and her handwriting – are constantly described in terms of their neatness and precision.[335] Never a grand passion even at the outset ("not one of those strong, impulsive feelings that can hit two people like an electric shock when they first meet, but something quieter and gentler"),[336] their marriage has at least given them six years of sensual intimacy, as well as what seems like genuine love (marred only by some unexplained secret on the wife's part surrounding an unexpected pregnancy and abortion three years earlier). Nevertheless, in all their time together they never gave themselves so fully to sexual pleasure that they lost control. Something was always held back.

When the wife strays into the dark realm of desire and begins sending her husband ambiguous cries for help from that unknown world, he is understandably confused. Afraid to follow her into that darkness, he waits for a sign to tell him what to do. He receives a letter from her asking for a divorce and containing a graphic description of her affair. This would have been more than enough evidence for most men to end the relationship, but still he hesitates to act. He considers escaping to Europe with another woman and leaving all of his troubles behind, but in the end he decides to stand and fight.

Tōru, the husband, works through his anger by directing it at someone else, beating up the folk singer he saw perform on the night of his wife's abortion. The loss of this child, he finally realizes, signalled the beginning of the end of their marriage. But the love they shared for six years is too important to abandon. If it was meaningless, then his life at the time was meaningless, too, and perhaps his whole life has been meaningless. This he cannot accept and he vows to fight for his wife's return.

Tōru decides to pursue his wife, Kumiko, to preserve the integrity of his own personality as much as the continuity of his marriage. "I had to get Kumiko back. With my own hands, I had to pull her back into *this world*. Because if I didn't, that would be the end of me. This person, this self that I think of as 'me' would be lost."[337]

Thus, rather than doing anything so practical as hire a private detective or search the streets himself, Tōru launches his quest inwards. He goes down into the earth, into a well, to brood on his past. What he finds there has implications that go far beyond his own inner world. As his young friend May Kasahara tells us (almost too directly), in choosing to fight for his wife Tōru will become a kind of culture hero, fighting battles not only for himself as an individual but "fighting for a lot of other people" as well.[338] In trying to find out who he is, Tōru discovers elements of his identity that have wide-ranging cultural and historical significance.

The psychologist Hayao Kawai reads Kumiko's disappearance as an allegory for the kind of emotional barrenness that can overtake a modern marriage when one partner psychologically withdraws from the relationship; this in turn can be seen as emblematic of human relations in general, which call out for the often painful process of "well-digging" on both sides.[339]

The well thus holds out the promise of healing, which is why Tōru goes to inordinate lengths to assure himself of an opportunity to spend time inside it, but the process of "well-digging" is by no means pleasant. Indeed, it suggests the threat of a slow, painful, and most of all lonely death, as we saw in *Norwegian Wood*, and as May Kasahara reminds Tōru after she has pulled up his rope ladder:

> If I just walked away from here, you'd end up dead. You could yell, but no one would hear you. No one would think you were at the bottom of a well . . . they'd never find your body.[340]

Tōru spends so much time in the well in *The Wind-up Bird Chronicle* that many readers want to know if Murakami himself has been down one. The answer, quite simply, is no. He would be "too scared" to do such a thing he told Laura Miller in an interview for the web magazine *Salon*, adding that he associates the well with the story of Orpheus descending to the land of death. He also became visibly excited when he told an audience at a benefit reading he did after the Kobe earthquake that he had recently read about a hunter who had survived several days trapped down a well. Many of the details of sound and light in the report matched what he had written entirely from his imagination.[341]

The name "Tōru" (literally "to pass through") was used in *Norwegian Wood*, perhaps to indicate that the protagonist was making his passage into adulthood. In *The Wind-up Bird Chronicle*, however, Tōru learns to "pass through" the wall separating the ordinary world from the world of the unknown. In the original, his name first appears in the *katakana* phonetic script, though it is later written with a Chinese character meaning "to receive", which suggests passivity.[342] It therefore seems to imply both activity and passivity. Most of the time, Tōru is a typical Murakami Boku, a first-person narrator of interest to us less for himself than for the stories he hears – the stories he "receives" through his ears – from the more colourful, even bizarre characters who surround him. Tōru listens to one "long story" after another, and one of the major attractions of the novel is the stories themselves.

His wife's name is also significant. The "kumi" of "Kumiko" could have overtones of neatly bundling things together, arranging things, or, from another "kumu", to draw water from a well. The connection with water and wells brings to a kind of culmination the well symbolism we have seen since Murakami's earliest works.

If the well is a passageway to the unconscious, the water at the bottom represents the contents of the psyche. When Tōru goes down into the dry well, he takes on the role of its water, becoming almost pure psyche. In the darkness, he all but loses track of his physical existence and becomes pure memory and imagination, floating in and out of consciousness, unsure of where he ends and the darkness begins. Only the wall against his back seems to provide a barrier between the physical world and that deeper darkness he seeks. But then Tōru passes through the wall, and he discovers his fears concentrated in a place known only as Room 208, which is reminiscent of Room 101, the repository of every person's greatest fear, in George Orwell's *1984*. (The Orwell connection may not be accidental.)

The number 208 may also strike the reader as strangely familiar: the twin girls 208 and 209 in *Pinball, 1973*. In that early novel, the cute twins evoke the mystery of memory. Without any explanation, they show up in Boku's bed one day and go back just as suddenly to their "original place" in the depths of his mind.

Room 208 exists in Tōru's (or perhaps even Kumiko's) mind and is accessible only through a dreamlike state. For Tōru, Room 208 is a place of irresistible sexual allure, where the faceless telephone sex woman lies in bed, seemingly naked, waiting for him amid the suffocating fragrance of flowers; a place where his half-conscious attraction for Creta Kanō blossoms into a sexual fantasy so intense it causes him to ejaculate in "reality", an adolescent throwback perhaps related to Creta's Sixties-style hair and clothes. (Though, born in April 1954, Tōru would have been only nine in 1963 when Kennedy was assassinated.) Finally, Room 208 is a place of danger where there is a threat of death involving sharp knives and it is somehow related to his brother-in-law, the evil Noboru Wataya.

Tōru hesitates to confront his fears, but he is determined to wrench some kind of "meaning" out of his existence. Whereas most of Murakami's earlier characters were content to leave things unexplained and even relished their absurdity, Tōru wants answers.

He wants to understand another person, the woman to whom he is married – and, by extension, himself:

> Is it possible, finally, for one human being to achieve perfect understanding of another? . . .
>
> That night, in our darkened bedroom, I lay beside Kumiko, staring at the ceiling and asking myself just how much I really knew about this woman . . .
>
> I might be standing in the entrance of something big, and inside lay a world that belonged to Kumiko alone, a vast world that I had never known. I saw it as a big, dark room. I was standing there holding a cigarette lighter, its tiny flame showing me only the smallest part of the room.
>
> Would I ever see the rest? Or would I grow old and die without ever really knowing her? If that was all that lay in store for me, then what was the point of this married life I was leading? What was the point of my life at all if I was spending it in bed with an unknown companion?[343]

The problem is set out implicitly in Chapter 1 and overtly in Chapter 2, but it is not until Book Three, some 600 pages later, that Tōru is ready to take action. His Hamlet-like indecision is at an end. At this point his quest takes on the overtones of legend – both Japanese and Western. He becomes a modern-day Theseus, advancing into the dark convoluted labyrinth of linked computers, guarded by the half-human, half-bull Minotaur named Ushikawa (Bull River). Or he is Orpheus or Japan's earth-creating god Izanagi, pursuing his dead wife into the depths of the underworld, where she forbids him to gaze on her physical decay.[344] "I want you to think about me this way if you can," Kumiko writes to Tōru from her end of the computer hookup: "that I am slowly dying of an incurable disease – one that causes my face and body gradually to disintegrate."[345] And when, after wandering blindly through the maze of corridors of his inner world, he pursues her into Room 208 with a torch, she commands him, "Don't shine that light on me."[346]

Going down into the well – into himself – is the ordeal Tōru must face to be worthy of marital commitment. Mozart's *The Magic Flute*, another story of an ordeal undertaken for love, provides a motif for Book Three, "The Birdcatcher".[347] Murakami has said of marriage: "For a long time after I got married, I used to have this vague idea that the purpose of marriage was for each partner to fill in what the other lacked. Lately, though, after 25 years of marriage, I've come to see it differently, that marriage is perhaps rather an ongoing process of each partner *exposing* what the other lacks . . . Finally, only the person himself can fill in what he is missing. It's not something another person can do for you. And in order to do the filling in, you yourself have to discover the size and location of the hole."[348]

Before Tōru can bring Kumiko back with him from the darkness into the real world he must face his greatest fear: the evil embodied by Noboru Wataya. Noboru, his political success made possible by his smooth manipulation of the media, is heir to the continental depredations of his uncle's generation. He represents the very same evil that appeared in the form of the right-wing boss in *A Wild Sheep Chase*. Murakami associates it with the authoritarian tradition of the Japanese government responsible for the murder of untold numbers of Chinese, the sacrifice of millions of Japanese in the war, and for suppressing the student idealism of the late 1960s, leading to the boredom and overwork of the consumer culture that dominates modern Japan. This element expands the scope of the novel far beyond the story of a failed marriage. In search of his wife and his self, Tōru finds more than he bargained for. He finds ugly aspects of his country's recent history, much of it violent and horrible and lying just beneath the surface of everyday

211

life. He also finds the violence inside himself as he nearly kills the folk singer, beating him bloody with a baseball bat.

"Violence," Murakami has said, is "the key to Japan."[349] For Westerners who live in fear of the random violence of their own society and who see the safety of a megalopolis like Tokyo as something of a miracle, this statement comes as a surprise. But Murakami was speaking – and always writes – as a historian. *The Wind-up Bird Chronicle* is, indeed, a chronicle, a book of history in which chronology matters, a story set precisely in the mid-1980s, but probing deeply into the violence of the wartime years for the root causes of Japan's modern malaise. Each Book is labelled with the dates of its action: June and July 1984; July to October 1984; October 1984 to December 1985 – the very heart of the 1980s, the decade when the consumer culture seemed to obliterate everything but the pursuit of wealth.[350] Tōru has chosen to withdraw from the pointless dead-end job this culture has offered him and to think about his life and where it is heading.

The central symbol of this era is the alley behind Tōru's house. Sealed at both ends, it leads nowhere. At the far end is a vacant house, where Tōru has been ordered by Kumiko to search for their missing cat. Images of emptiness abound in the book, echoing the description of the empty house. In the garden of the house stands a stone statue of a bird, "its wings open as if it wanted to escape from this unpleasant place as soon as possible".[351] The scene is as dead as the centre of Jūnitaki in *A Wild Sheep Chase*, where there is "a bird-shaped fountain with no water in it. The bird looked vacantly up at the sky with an open mouth."[352] If Murakami's birds represent a lively communication between the conscious and unconscious worlds, these frozen birds suggest a kind of amnesia.

Jūnitaki had once flourished under the government-subsidized programme to raise sheep in order to produce wool for coats that would enable Japan's military to wage war in China. The yard of the empty house in *The Wind-up Bird Chronicle*, we learn later, has a well that has gone as dry as the bird fountain in Jūnitaki. This old well beneath an ancient tree becomes the site of Tōru's inner quest.

The 1980s, then, are presented as a vacant, stagnant, dissatisfying decade, just beneath the surface of which lurks a violent history. They are much like the "boring" 1970s of *A Wild Sheep Chase*, the emptiness a legacy of pre-war authoritarianism. There are other symbolic parallels between *A Wild Sheep Chase* and *The Wind-up Bird Chronicle*: the star-shaped mark that distinguishes the malevolent sheep and the stain-like mark, the size of a baby's palm, that appears on Tōru's cheek when he passes through the well wall separating this world from the other, a mark that links him with the fate of the veterinarian who witnessed the war in Manchuria. The one violent act in their marriage is an abortion that Kumiko chose to have. Tōru had wanted the child (whose palm print comes to grace his cheek), but she believes there is something evil in her family's blood that must not be allowed to reproduce itself. Her decision to end the life inside her is reminiscent of the Rat's suicide in *A Wild Sheep Chase*, an attempt to kill the malevolent spirit of continental plunder lodged within him.

What does all this talk of war and imperialism have to do with an unemployed paralegal whose marriage is on the rocks? Well, nothing – except that he is Japanese. And he is looking inside himself. Murakami has always written about half-remembered things that lurk in the mind until they unexpectedly jump out and grab us. In *The Wind-up Bird Chronicle*, Murakami's most ambitious novel to that point, what leaps out at his narrator from the depths of his individual memory is Japan's dark and violent recent past. "It's all there, inside me: Pearl Harbor, Nomonhan, whatever," Murakami has said of himself.[353]

The Wind-up Bird Chronicle continues a debate that still rages in Japan today about the official recognition of the crimes Japan committed against the other peoples of Asia. After decades of official silence in which history textbooks hid the unpleasant facts from schoolchildren, Japan has begun to face up to its past, and *The Wind-up Bird Chronicle* can be seen as part of that painful process. The Japanese now recognize that they were not simply the innocent victims of the atom bomb, that Japanese soldiers carried out the Rape of Nanking, and that this was but one episode in Japan's rape of an entire continent. Murakami was indirectly hinting at this truth in his very first short story, "A Slow Boat to China".

Searching deep down in the least accessible areas of memory after a head injury, Boku in "A Slow Boat to China" comes up with the totally inexplicable words: *That's OK, brush off the dirt and you can still eat it.* In themselves, they are meaningless, but their very lack of logical connection to anything implies they have somehow surfaced from his unconscious.

"With these words," he writes, "I find myself thinking about . . . Death . . . And death, for some reason, reminds me of the Chinese."[354]

At the end of the last episode in the story, which illustrates Boku's ambivalence towards the Chinese, he declares: "I wanted to say something . . . I wanted to say something . . . about the Chinese, but what? . . . Even now, I still can't think of anything to say." He continues in an epilogue: "I've read dozens of books on China . . . I've wanted to find out as much about China as I could. But that China is only my China. Not any China I can read about. It's the China that sends messages just to me. It's not the big yellow expanse on the globe, it's another China. Another hypothesis, another supposition. In a sense, it's a part of myself that's been cut off by the word *China*."[355]

In the end, Boku cannot explain what it is that causes him to feel so ambivalent towards China and the Chinese, but *The Wind-up Bird Chronicle* is far more direct. One of the last images in the book is "a young moon, with a sharp curve like a Chinese sword", by which point China has come to stand for the horrifying slaughter perpetrated by Japanese soldiers in the war.

While writing Book Three, Murakami was asked in an interview: "Why should your generation take responsibility for a war which ended before it was born?" He replied:

> Because we're Japanese. When I read about the atrocities in China in some books, I can't believe it. It's so stupid and absurd and meaningless. That was the generation of my father and grandfather. I want to know what drove them to do those kinds of things, to kill or maim thousands and thousands of people. I want to understand, but I don't.[356]

Beneath the curved Chinese moon, Tōru finds in the water of his heart's well the sins committed by the generation of his "uncle" – or rather, the dangerous, media-exploiting Noboru Wataya's uncle. An elite army officer, Noboru's uncle can be seen as the heir to *Norwegian Wood*'s "Storm Trooper", the roommate who stuttered every time he tried to pronounce the word "map". Noboru's uncle believes wholly in the science of logistics, for which maps are an indispensable tool. He comes under the influence of the actual historical figure Kanji Ishiwara (1889–1949), a believer in Japan's mission in Asia and notorious leader of the Manchurian Incident, the Japanese Army-manufactured "attack" on Japanese troops that started the Pacific War. By inheriting this uncle's seat in the National Diet, Noboru somehow inherits his legacy of imperialism. Thus it is China that lurks behind his appearance as a modern intellectual on TV, an image that gives Noboru such power over a superficial society. In "TV People" the television screen was blank, filling people's lives with a numbing nothingness; here, the threat of the invasive medium is tied to the darkest aspects of Japan's recent history.

Boku of "A Slow Boat to China" may not know what to say about that country, but in *The Wind-up Bird Chronicle* Murakami knows exactly what he wants to say. Japan's recent history is alive inside Tōru, even though he is one of the most apolitical beings imaginable. This is hinted at in a scene in Book One, Chapter 5, when Tōru's 16-year-old neighbour, May Kasahara, asks him his name:

> "Tōru Okada," I said.
>
> She repeated my name to herself several times. "Not much of a name, is it?" she said.
>
> "Maybe not," I said. "I've always thought it sounded kind of like some pre-war foreign minister: Tōru Okada. See?"
>
> "That doesn't mean anything to me. I hate history. It's my worst subject."[357]

In fact, Keisuke Okada (1868–1952), Prime Minister from July 1934 to March 1936, was a key player in events leading to the ideological extremism that led to Japan's disastrous decision to go to war. A retired admiral, Okada headed a government that promoted the worship of the mystical "national essence" (*kokutai*) and of the Emperor, and quashed the more rational, widely accepted "organ theory" of the Japanese state; nevertheless, he was still not considered right-wing enough for the renegade young officers who staged a coup on 26 February 1936. They tried to assassinate him, but killed his brother-in-law instead. Okada resigned after this incident. He never served as Foreign Minister, but Tōru's vague reference to pre-war politics hints at dramatic events such as these.

The 30-year-old Tōru Okada recognizes a certain indefinable bond with Japan's pre-war government and displays some interest in the history of the war, but the shadow of history has yet to fall on the young May. She remains a virgin to the end, uninitiated into the ways of either sex or history. The young readers that Murakami has cultivated, however, may lose their historical "virginity" with regard to the war as they follow him from the sunlit beach at Ipanema into Tōru's dark room.

Some commentators have criticized Murakami for fabricating fictional wartime episodes rather than using specific incidents, but this misses the point. The "war" in *The Wind-up Bird Chronicle* is not presented as a series of historical facts but as an important part of the psychological baggage of Murakami's generation and beyond. For most Japanese, the war exists in the same half-known realm as Rossini's opera *The Thieving Magpie*, the title of which occurs on the first page of the novel and is the title of Book One. All Tōru knows about the opera is the overture and the title: it is a thing half-remembered from childhood, something he has taken for granted, but never questioned or pursued.

What kind of opera was *The Thieving Magpie*? I wondered. All I knew about it was the monotonous melody of its overture and its mysterious title. We had had a recording of the overture in the house when I was a boy. It had been conducted by Toscanini. Compared with Claudio Abbado's youthful, fluid, contemporary performance, Toscanini's had had a blood-stirring intensity to it, like the slow strangulation of a powerful foe who has been downed after a violent battle. But was *The Thieving Magpie* really the story of a magpie that engaged in thieving? If things ever settled down, I would have to go to the library and look it up in a dictionary of music. I might even buy a complete recording of the opera if it was available. Or maybe not. I might not care to know the answers to these questions by then.[358]

The opera features prominently in the book not because its plot provides a key to the novel but precisely because it is just out of reach, on the periphery of most people's consciousness. Parts of the overture can be heard in TV commercials, and some readers may associate it with the violent Stanley Kubrick film *A Clockwork Orange*, but for Tōru *The Thieving Magpie* will always be something he hasn't quite understood. It is familiar, and yet its meaning eludes him. This is one instance when Murakami and his Boku are almost indistinguishable. I was with Murakami when he bought a video of *La Gazza Ladra* [*The Thieving Magpie*] in San Francisco in November 1992. He wanted to find out once and for all what it was about – long after he had written Book One of *The Wind-up Bird Chronicle*.

Rather than writing about historical facts, then, Murakami examines the Pacific War as a psychological phenomenon shared by generations of Japanese too young (like Tōru) to have experienced it first-hand. History is a story. By exploiting the power of storytelling, Murakami takes his readers to the edge of the cliff and makes them hang there while he switches to another narrative line.

This happens most effectively in Book Three, when war episodes alternate with those in which Tōru does battle in the darkness against the violence and evil in his own psyche. Chapter 30, for example, tantalizes the reader by cutting short Lieutenant Mamiya's story of "Boris the Manskinner" (the Russian officer who skins people alive) almost before it has begun. Chapter 31 drops that story completely and switches to Tōru climbing down into the well. This chapter also ends by tantalizing the reader, for after Tōru has followed the whistling hotel waiter to Room 208, we learn only that "the door began to open inward".[359] At this moment of heightened suspense Chapter 31 ends, and the story of Boris the Manskinner is picked up again in the next chapter with the sub-title "The Story of Boris the Manskinner, Continued", like an old movie serial.[360] With his entertaining chapter titles, Murakami throws out any pretence at reportage and steps forth as a per-formative novelist in the tradition of Richardson or Fielding. He is unashamedly pulling the strings, switching his reader back and forth between parallel narratives as we have often seen him do before. Lieutenant Mamiya's story of Boris, told in a letter to Tōru, has no direct connection to Tōru's adventures in the dark corridors of his mind.

But how is Lt Mamiya's letter interrupted by Chapter 31 on Tōru's final confrontation in Room 208? Has Tōru suddenly leapt back to his desk and resumed reading? Of course not. He is still down in the well. The only answer is that Murakami has put the new chapter there so that we will absorb alternating episodes of the two narratives in what he deems to be the most effective way. As the apparently unrelated stories appear in alternate chapters, a relationship takes shape in the mind of the reader: the war becomes part of what Tōru finds inside himself.

In *The Wind-up Bird Chronicle* Murakami relies heavily on story-telling. At several points he leaves Tōru behind in favour of a third-person narrator. For all of Murakami's supposed discomfort at assuming the role of a god-like creator, he is a master of third-person fiction. This is obvious in Book Three, particularly Chapters 9 and 26 of the translation, "The Zoo Attack (or, A Clumsy Massacre)" and "The Wind-up Bird Chronicle No. 8 (or, A Second Clumsy Massacre)". These two stories are narrated by the mother and son known as Nutmeg and Cinnamon.

Nutmeg tells her story to Tōru as they dine in an expensive

restaurant. Later, Tōru *reads* the sequel on a computer – supposedly entered there by Cinnamon. In fact, Tōru only reads it once and can't access it again, which means that we get it either because we are somehow looking through his eyes as he reads – which in turn means that *we* have access to the text again anytime we like because it is in the book, but Tōru can never see it again – or he has a superb memory and has somehow recalled it all for us later. Where the Tōru of *Norwegian Wood* tells us he is writing it all down from memory, in *The Wind-up Bird Chronicle* things are never so simple.

Nutmeg, whose alias is suggested to her by salt and pepper shakers on the restaurant table,[361] is a kind of shaman or medium, telling her story in a semi-conscious trance-like state. She represents the function of storytelling in its most primitive form, drawing on the depths of what might be called the collective unconscious. When Tōru interrupts her to ask about something she has said, she has no memory of having said it.[362] Her son Cinnamon, whose alias is chosen by Nutmeg through free association with her own, comes from a long line of mute Murakami story-spinners going back to the child Boku of *Hear the Wind Sing*. Their lack of eloquence is more than compensated for by their facility with the written word. Cinnamon is the next evolutionary step in storytelling, replacing the oral recitation with a computer keyboard. When Tōru is frustrated in his attempt to access any files on the computer other than the sequel to Nutmeg's story, entitled "The Wind-up Bird Chronicle No. 8", he begins to wonder about Cinnamon's role as a storyteller in ways that might reflect Murakami's own deliberations:

But why had Cinnamon written such stories? And why *stories*? Why not some other form? And why had he found it necessary to use the word "chronicle" in the title? . . .

I would have had to read all 16 stories to find the answers to my questions, but even after a single reading of No. 8, I had some idea, however vague, of what Cinnamon was pursuing in his writing. He was engaged in a search for the meaning of his own existence. And he was hoping to find it by looking into the events that had preceded his birth.

To do that, Cinnamon had to fill in those blank spots in the past that he could not reach with his own hands. By using those hands to make a story, he was trying to supply the missing links . . . He inherited from his mother's stories the fundamental style he used, unaltered, in his own stories: namely, the assumption that *fact may not be truth, and truth may not be factual*. The question of which parts of a story were factual and which parts were not was probably not a very important one for Cinnamon. The important question for Cinnamon was not what [a person] *did* but what [that person] *might have done*. He learned the answer to this question as soon as he succeeded in telling the story.[363]

Of all the characters in this long novel, Cinnamon appears to be the closest thing to an alter-ego for the author. He "was engaged in a search for the meaning of his own existence . . . by looking into the events that had preceded his birth". It is as if the cool, detached Murakami had begun to write as a way to explore his own detachment, and rather than be satisfied with amusing himself, had used the process to feed his deep curiosity. He began to probe into his life and times and the history of his country to try to figure out what was missing in them that might explain why he himself didn't feel more. Nowhere has he come closer to confessing his own emotional void than in *Norwegian Wood*, through the voice of the cold-hearted seducer of women, Nagasawa:

We're a lot alike, though, Watanabe and me . . . Neither of us is interested, essentially, in anything but ourselves. OK, so I'm arrogant and he's not, but neither of us is able to feel any interest in anything other than what we ourselves think or feel or do. That's why we can think about things in a way that's totally divorced from anybody else. That's what I like about him. The only difference is that he hasn't realized this about himself, and so he hesitates and feels hurt . . . Watanabe's practically the same as me. He may be a nice guy, but deep down in his heart he's incapable of loving anybody. There's always some part of him somewhere that's wide awake and detached. He just has that hunger that won't go away. Believe me, I know what I'm talking about.[364]

Cinnamon is the storyteller who probes most deeply into the historical past to explain the emptiness of the present. For a time, visitors to Murakami's Tokyo office used to find the name "Cinnamon" on his mail-box, and a variation on the name was part of the office e-mail address. Like Cinnamon, Murakami was engaged in a creative act of self-examination in *The Wind-up Bird Chronicle*, as he brought stories out of the depth of his being that were suggested to him by his country's history, especially its military activities in China.

Murakami traced his own inward search in a series of articles written after visiting the site of the Nomonhan Incident on the border between Manchuria and Mongolia in June 1994. The timing is significant. Books One and Two of *The Wind-up Bird Chronicle* had just appeared, while Book Three was still growing in his computer. Which is to say that Murakami had never set foot on the Asian continent or seen the Khalkha River or Nomonhan before he conceived of Mr Honda, the mystic who survived the Nomonhan slaughter, or before he wrote the scenes of cross-border espionage that bring Book One to its horrifying close with the flaying of the still-living Yamamoto. Only Book Three can be said to have benefited from Murakami's first-hand observation of a battlefield that had haunted him as a schoolboy.

From a history book he read as a child Murakami remembered certain photographs of weird, stubby, old-fashioned tanks and planes from what he calls the Nomonhan War (generally referred to in Japan as the Nomonhan Incident and in Mongolia as the Khalkha River War), a fierce border clash that took place in the spring and summer of 1939. It involved Japanese soldiers stationed in Manchuria and a combined force of Soviet and Outer-Mongolian troops. The images of the event remained vivid in his memory for reasons he could never explain to himself, and he read the few books he could find on the subject.

Then, almost by chance, he came across several old Japanese books on Nomonhan in the Princeton library and realized he was as mesmerized by the event as ever. He sought out Alvin Coox's massive two-volume study and was particularly pleased to discover that Coox, too, had been fascinated by the subject since childhood but found it hard to explain why. Continued rumination, however, led Murakami to a tentative explanation for his own unflagging interest: perhaps, he thought, "the fascination for me is that the origin of this war was all too Japanese, all too representative of the Japanese people".[365]

The same could be said of the Second World War, he admits, but that war is just too big, too much of a towering monument to grasp in its entirety. It *was* possible to get a handle on Nomonhan, however: a four-month undeclared war staged in a limited area that may have been Japan's first experience of having its un-modern worldview – its "warview" – trounced by a country that knew how to establish supply lines before going to war rather than simply hoping for the best. Fewer than 20,000 Japanese troops lost their lives in Nomonhan, but the number soared to over 2,000,000 in the Second World War. In both cases, they were the victims of a system that will make any sacrifice to preserve "face" and that blindly trusts to luck rather than efficient modern planning. "They were murdered," says Murakami, "used up like so many nameless articles of consumption – with terrible inefficiency within the hermetically sealed system we call Japan." It happened first in Nomonhan, but Japan learned nothing from that harsh experience, and so it went on to fight the Second World War. "But what have we Japanese learned from *that* dizzying tragedy?"

This clearly echoes one of the themes of *A Wild Sheep Chase*: "The basic stupidity of modern Japan is that we've learned absolutely nothing from our contact with other Asian peoples." True, the Japanese now "love" peace (or rather, they love *being* at peace), but the "sealed system" was left virtually untouched by the bitter experience of the war.

We did away with the pre-war emperor system and put the Peace Constitution in its place. And as a result we have, to be sure, come to live in an efficient, rational world based on the ideology of a modern civil society, and that efficiency has brought about an almost overwhelming prosperity in our society. Yet, I (and perhaps many others) can't seem to escape the suspicion that even now, in many areas of society, we are being peacefully and quietly obliterated as nameless articles of consumption. We go on believing that we live in the so-called free "civil state" we call "Japan" with our fundamental human rights guaranteed, but is this truly the case? Peel back a layer of skin, and what do we find breathing and pulsating there but the same old sealed national system or ideology.[366]

As far as Murakami is concerned, nothing has changed in all the decades since Nomonhan. Perhaps the peeling of the skin of the spy and nationalist zealot Yamamoto is a metaphor for the need to look beneath the outer layer to discover why Japan, even in peacetime, continues to regard its own people as expendable commodities.

The border dispute in which the Japanese military became embroiled in 1939 was still very much alive when Murakami made his visit in June 1994. In order to get to the village of Nomonhan, he and Eizō Matsumura had to take a plane, then two trains, and eventually a Land Cruiser, to see the Chinese side of the Khalkha River. They then had to go all the way back to Beijing, take another two planes and a long journey by jeep across the steppe to see the Mongolian side. Direct border crossings were impossible between China's Inner Mongolian Autonomous Region and the independent nation of Mongolia.

But it was worth it. Having overcome these difficulties, Murakami found himself standing on one of the best preserved battlefields in the world – preserved not by government mandate for historical research but by nature. The place was so fly-ridden, remote, arid and useless to anyone that tanks and mortars and other detritus of war had been left where they had been abandoned under the vast sky, rusting but still intact, more than half a century later. Seeing this vast graveyard of steel, where so many men had suffered and lost their lives for no good reason, Murakami wrote:

I suddenly realized that in historical terms we probably belong to the later iron age. The side that managed to throw the greater amount of iron more effectively at the enemy and thereby destroy the greater amount of human flesh would achieve victory and justice. And they would be able to take victorious command of one section of this drab plane of grass.[367]

There were more metal scraps of war on display at a large war museum in a nearby town, but a power cut hid most of them from view. On the way back to the military guest quarters where they were to spend the night, Murakami and Matsumura clung on amid the reek of petrol fumes from the extra tanks on board the bouncing jeep as their chain-smoking Mongolian Army guides took a detour to hunt down and kill a she-wolf. They arrived at one o'clock in the morning, and Murakami flopped into bed exhausted, but unable to sleep. He felt the presence of some "thing", and began to regret bringing back a rusty mortar and other war souvenirs that now lay on the table in his room.

When I awoke in the middle of the night, *it* was causing the whole world to pitch wildly up and down, as if the room were in a shaker. The darkness was total. I couldn't see my own hand, but I could hear everything around me rattling. I had no idea what was going on, but I jumped out of bed to turn on the light. The quaking was so violent, though, I couldn't stay upright. I fell, and then managed to pull myself to my feet by holding onto the bed frame . . . I made it to the door and felt for the light switch. The instant I turned it on, the shaking stopped. Now everything was silent. The clock showed 2.30 a.m.

Then I realized: it was not the room or the world that was shaking: it was me. At that moment, a chill froze me to the core. I was terrified. I wanted to cry out, but my voice wouldn't come. This was the first time in my life I had ever experienced such deep, violent fear, and the first time I had ever seen such utter darkness.

Too frightened to stay where he was, Murakami went to Matsumura's room next door, and sat on the floor by his sleeping friend, waiting for the sun to come up. As the sky began to lighten after 4 a.m., the chill inside him began to abate, "as if a possessing spirit had fallen away". He went back to his room and fell asleep, no longer afraid.

> I have thought about this incident a great deal, but could never find a satisfactory explanation for it. Nor is it possible for me to convey in words how frightened I was at the time. It was as if I had accidentally peered into the abyss of the world.
>
> In the [month or so] since it happened, I have come to think of it more or less this way: It – that is, the shaking and the darkness and the terror and that strange presence – was not something that came to me from the outside, but rather may have been something that had always been inside me, that was part of who I am. Something had seized a kind of opportunity to rip open this thing inside me, whatever it was, just as the old photos of the Nomonhan War that I had seen in a book as a grammar school boy had fascinated me for no clear reason and brought me some 30-odd years later to the depths of the Mongolian steppe. I don't know how to put it, but it seems to me that no matter how far we go – or rather, the farther we go – the things we discover are more likely to be nothing more than ourselves. The wolf, the mortar, the war museum darkened by a power cut, all of these were parts of me that had always been there, I suspect: they had been waiting all this time for me to find them.
>
> I do know this much, though: I will never forget those things that are there – that *were* there. Because that is probably all I can do: to keep from forgetting.[368]

Reading this description in a supposedly factual essay, it is hard not to share Ian Buruma's reaction when he heard the story from

Murakami: "I was sceptical. The scene sounded too much like one from his novels. It was as if he had started to take his metaphors literally."[369] However, Murakami insists that he described the event exactly as it happened to him, and he even repeated it to the psychologist Hayao Kawai, stipulating at the outset that he did not believe it was a paranormal phenomenon, but resulted from his "utter commitment" to (or perhaps we could say "obsession with") Nomonhan. Kawai could reply only that he believed such experiences could happen, but that one had to resist interpreting them with "phoney science" – for example, claiming that there was some "energy" in Murakami's battlefield souvenir.[370]

Eizō Matsumura had no idea Murakami had come into his room that night. He only found out about the whole strange experience when he read about it in Murakami's magazine article. He had no difficulty in believing it to be true. He too had felt very strange about the Nomonhan battlefield. Athough he knew nothing about its history, it had given him goose flesh (something he says almost never happens to him), and for weeks after going there he dreamed about the place. That night, although Murakami found him fast asleep, Matsumura had had difficulty sleeping, despite the fact he was absolutely exhausted, and had drunk a beer to knock himself out.[371]

Once, asked if he believed in the sort of paranormal phenomena depicted in *The Wind-up Bird Chronicle*, Murakami laughed. "No," he said, "I don't believe in that stuff." He enjoyed writing about such things, he said, but in his own life he was strictly a realist. Having said that, he added without irony that if he "concentrated" on people he could tell a lot about them – for example, how many siblings they had, or what kind of relationship they had with their parents. This was the technique that palmists used, he said. "Reading" the lines on the palm was just a bit of fakery. But this kind of "concentration" takes enormous energy and is extremely draining, so he reserves it for his writing. As for Malta Kanō's practice of divination using the water in a person's house, this was not, as far as he knew, a venerable (if suspect) practice like palmistry. He had simply made it up for the book.[372]

Murakami also has evocative things to say about the relationship between the world of the living and the world of the dead. After telling a British interviewer about Japan's version of Orpheus descending to Hades to find Eurydice (the story of Izanagi and Izanami), he claimed it was his "favourite myth", before adding, with regard to certain deceased friends: "I feel the dead people around me sometimes. It's not a ghost story. Just a kind of feeling, or, a kind of responsibility. I have to live for them."[373] Asked by a reader if he believes in reincarnation, Murakami replied: "My stock answer for that is: 'I'll think about it when I'm dead.'"[374]

In other words, Murakami sits on the fence as far as the supernatural is concerned. He is quick to deny belief in it, and yet feels the mind is capable of things science cannot explain. And so his visit to Nomonhan is of some value in illuminating what he went on to write: the third book of *The Wind-up Bird Chronicle*. Here Tōru encounters the war and violence inside himself, as if they had been waiting for him all that time.

Murakami was still hard at work on *The Wind-up Bird Chronicle* when he moved from Princeton to Cambridge, Massachusetts, in July 1993. He lived 15 minutes' walk from the Harvard campus (and the great second-hand record stores in Harvard Square), but his primary affiliation was with Tufts, a university in the neighbouring town of Medford.

Charles Inouye, a professor of Japanese Literature there had arranged for him to be Writer in Residence for a year and Murakami accepted. He was not yet ready to relinquish the special perspective on Japan that living in America had given him. Indeed, he says that he could not have written *The Wind-up Bird Chronicle* if he had not been living in the United States.[375] It was there that he had begun to see more clearly the connections between the history of the Second World War and the realities of modern Japanese society, and it was there that he began to think seriously about his responsibility as a Japanese writer.

He stayed in Cambridge for two years and was still there in 1994 when the first two volumes of *The Wind-up Bird Chronicle* were published in Japan. It was from Cambridge that he travelled to Manchuria and Mongolia, and it was in Cambridge that he completed the final volume of the novel a few months after a massive earthquake in January 1995 devastated much of his home region around Kobe. (It was also in Cambridge that his Volkswagen Corrado was stolen and dismantled – but that is another story.)[376]

On the evening of 22 October 1994, Murakami was exhausted after a three-hour interview with a graduate student named Matthew Strecher who was writing a Ph.D. thesis on him, and for once he showed his fatigue.[377] A remark to this effect sparked an unusually voluble justification for his working so hard all the time. Writing *The Wind-up Bird Chronicle* had been a particularly intense experience, he said, to the point of keeping him up all hours and throwing out his routine. He spoke about the sense of impending death that struck him when he turned 40 and his desire to write with full concentration while he still could, but he also spoke about his growing sense of responsibility to Japan.

Novelists have a serious responsibility towards the culture of their society, he said. They must stand for something, and as they enter their later years they need to clarify what it is their work stands for as a whole. He voiced great admiration for Kenzaburō Ōe, who had fulfilled his responsibility as a believer in (and a central figure of) Japan's mainstream "pure literature", which Murakami had rejected. He was pleased, too, that Ōe had recently been awarded the Nobel Prize. Ōe thoroughly deserved this recognition for living up to his responsibility as a writer. Murakami was equally impressed by the way Ōe had demonstrated his consistency as a counterculture figure by rejecting the Japanese Emperor's Order of Cultural Merit, awarded hastily by the Imperial Household Agency in the afterglow of the Nobel Prize. As a believer in "pure literature", however, said Murakami, Ōe was the Last of the Mohicans.

But for this very reason Ōe had given Murakami and his contemporaries some breathing space: by defining the mainstream, Ōe and the other great novelist of that older generation, Kenji Nakagami, had prevented the literary scene from descending into chaos, while new writers like Murakami went on groping around for whatever it was they wanted to say. Ōe and Nakagami had been buffers for them. Murakami had assumed that he had another ten good years during which he could continue to search around, but Nakagami's sudden death the year before came as a terrible shock: now he felt he had no more than five years left to be relatively free and irresponsible. Soon, as a "top runner" ("*toppu-rannā*") among Japanese writers, he would have to clarify his political stance and also decide for himself what his work was about. His groping would more or less have to come to an end.[378] This is not to say that he was planning to become a politician or a social worker: through writing he hoped to contribute to an evolutionary change in the ideas and attitudes of society at large.[379]

The Wind-up Bird Chronicle can be seen as the first product of this newly serious, self-conscious attitude. Not that it is entirely devoid of fun (the survey of bald heads, for example) or that its historical worldview came out of a vacuum, as we have seen in his earlier novels and stories, but Murakami is more focused than ever on the problems of his own society.

The one thing I can say in all earnestness is that since coming to America I have begun to think with absolute seriousness about my country, Japan, and about the Japanese language. All I could think about when I began writing fiction in my youth was how to run as far as I could from the "Japanese Condition". I wanted to distance myself as much as possible from the curse of Japanese . . .

As I have aged, though, and have begun to feel at home with my own kind of accommodated Japanese style as a result of my struggles with the language, and as the years have mounted up in which I have lived away from Japan, I have come more and more to *like* the act of writing fiction in the Japanese language. I'm actually *fond* of Japanese now: I need it. This is by no means a "Return to Japan" with a capital R. There are plenty of examples of worshippers of the West who go abroad and come back touting the superiority of all things Japanese, but this is not what I mean. There are many people, too, who declare that Japanese as a language possesses a special genius and is far more beautiful than any foreign language, but I believe they are wrong . . . It is my unswerving belief that all languages are of fundamentally equal value, and without such a recognition, there is no possibility of genuine cultural exchange.[380]

With little more than six months left to spend abroad, Murakami could write this way about his "accommodation" with the Japanese language and the country of his birth. The distance had only sharpened his focus on Japan while it reinforced his respect for other cultures. He no longer felt the need to include overt references to foreign foods and brand names in his fiction. His readers had been either charmed or puzzled by such references. They either bemoaned the absence of cherry blossoms and geisha or found his work a welcome relief from obsessive Japaneseness. They had been a way for Murakami to overcome the "Japanese Condition". Names of foreign items are particularly prominent in Japanese as they are written in the distinctive *katakana* script, lending them a cool foreign air. With the lessening of Murakami's coolness, however, came a decrease in the number of references to American popular culture. *The Wind-up Bird Chronicle* is noteworthy for this shift in both style and attitude.

It is important to note how shocking Murakami's cultural relativism is in the context of Japanese literature. Readers unfamiliar with the quasi-religious rhapsodizing about the spiritual superiority or unique magic of Japanese that has passed for serious intellectual commentary in Japan (and not just at the height of the Second World War) may not realize that Murakami's cosmopolitanism is almost revolutionary. His website comments are a good example of how refreshing Murakami can be on the subject.

This question came from a 30-year-old "graduate school graduate (i.e., unemployed person)" married to a woman studying Asian Literature in a certain graduate school. A friend of theirs, a Japanese studying American literature, often says to her: "Any Japanese person, even an amateur when it comes to literature, is bound to be able to read Japanese literature way more deeply than any foreigner." This invariably angers his American wife, but he wants to know what "Haruki-san" thinks.

Murakami replied:

> I'm not going to call your friend a single-celled fascist or anything, but I do think he tends to oversimplify things. I've had a lot of experience discussing Japanese literature with American students, and true, there are those who come up with crazy stuff, but there are plenty, too, who have given me tremendously sharp and fresh views that strike at the essence

of what they are reading. There are lots of Japanese who might be able to understand the so-called "subtle nuances and unique expressions" of Japanese but who don't have the slightest idea of what literature is all about.

The world of literature is probably 85 per cent feeling and desire, things that transcend differences of race or language or gender, and these are basically things that admit of mutual exchange. I suspect that when people say "There's no way an American can understand Japanese literature", they're just revealing a complex. It's my belief that Japanese literature has to open itself much more broadly than it now does to the scrutiny of the world at large.[381]

The Wind-up Bird Chronicle did much to change the attitude of the Japanese literary establishment towards Murakami. Having deliberately distanced himself from the cliques that control most of the serious literary production in Japan, Murakami tended to be dismissed as a "pop" novelist. He has never been awarded the Akutagawa Prize (memorializing the writer Ryūnosuke Akutagawa [1892–1927]), receipt of which represents a seal of approval from the literary establishment and is the traditional entrée to a successful career. Murakami forged ahead nonetheless, and not winning the Akutagawa Prize has became something of a point of pride for him. But *The Wind-up Bird Chronicle* changed everything.

In spite of his lack of contacts inside the elite Tokyo literary world, Murakami was awarded the prestigious Forty-Seventh Yomiuri [Newspaper] Literary Prize for 1995, joining a long line of distinguished authors going back to 1949, including Yukio Mishima, Kōbō Abe, and Kenzaburō Ōe. Almost as remarkable as the award itself was the prize-giving ceremony. The chief spokesman for the prize committee was none other than Murakami's most prominent and vocal critic, Nobel Laureate Kenzaburō Ōe.

While Murakami was still living in Cambridge, Ōe had spoken at Harvard on a post-Nobel book tour in May 1995, but neither had taken the opportunity to meet the other. In Tokyo on the evening of 23 February 1996 Murakami had the strange experience of standing in the same room as his long-time critic, listening to him praise *The Wind-up Bird Chronicle* as "beautiful" and "important". Ōe went on to read aloud the striking passage in Book Two, Chapter 4, "Divine Grace Lost", portraying Lieutenant Mamiya's failure to experience a revelation in the light that floods down into the Mongolian well in which he has been left to die.[382] Murakami, said Ōe, was able to respond to the expectations of a huge audience while remaining utterly faithful to the exploration of themes that were purely and deeply his own.[383]

When the ceremony was over the guests raised their glasses in a toast and turned their attention to the lavish buffet. A long line of admirers formed to beg individual audiences with Ōe, who was hardly given a chance to enjoy the beer, wine, noodles, sushi and skewered oysters. Once he had regained his freedom, however, he took the initiative to approach Murakami, whose crowd of well-wishers parted to let the Nobel Laureate through.

Ōe was beaming and seemed truly delighted to have the opportunity to introduce himself to Murakami, who managed only a nervous smile in response. Much of the remaining tension dispersed as the conversation turned to jazz, a passion for both writers. Ōe wore a blue pin-stripe suit and his trademark round glasses, while Murakami had come to the ceremony in white tennis shoes, a baggy sports coat and chinos. Photographers swooped to capture the moment for posterity. Murakami and Ōe could hardly say anything very intimate or profound while surrounded by onlookers, and ten minutes of cordial conversation later the two men parted amicably. They have not been in touch since.

But although their lifestyles and fictional worlds are radically different, Ōe and Murakami have far more in common than either might wish to admit. Having announced his intention around the time of the Nobel Prize to stop writing novels and concentrate on non-fiction, Ōe later changed his mind and wrote his longest novel ever, featuring a dangerous religious cult. Murakami on the other hand turned to non-fiction, completing a lengthy volume of interviews with victims of the sarin gas attack on the Tokyo subway by members of the Aum Shinrikyō cult, later followed by a volume of interviews with members and ex-members of the Aum cult. Both writers examine questions of memory and history, of legend and storytelling, and both continue to probe into the dark forest of feeling in search of who they are as individuals, as citizens of the world, and as Japanese.

12

The Rhythm of the Earth

Underground

If researching and writing *The Wind-up Bird Chronicle* made Murakami look at his country and its history in a whole new way, it also marked a return to Japan after more than nine years of living mostly abroad. Haruki and Yōko had left for Europe in October 1986, spent an unsettled year in Japan from January 1990 to January 1991, then fled to America to escape Murakami's fame. Their planned one-year stay in Princeton, New Jersey, became two-and-a-half, followed by another two years in Cambridge, Massachusetts.

Having avoided Japan for so long, Murakami found himself wanting to know more about his own country. This urge to understand Japan better began to haunt him during his final two years of "exile". He "could feel the change inside" himself, "an ongoing 'revaluation'" of his values that called for him to go back and take his place in Japanese society. He felt, too, that in this connection he wanted to write some major piece of work other than a novel. Perhaps by doing so he might find a new role for himself – a new position in his society. The problem was deciding what it should be.

"I spent my last year abroad in a sort of fog when two major catastrophes struck Japan: the Great Osaka-Kobe earthquake and the Tokyo gas attack . . . [These were] two of the gravest tragedies in Japan's post-war history. It is no exaggeration to say that there was a marked change in the Japanese consciousness 'before' and 'after' these events. These twin catastrophes will remain embedded in our psyche as two milestones in our life as a people."[384]

The Osaka-Kobe area was home territory for Murakami. Calling from America he learned that his parents' house had been destroyed but his parents were safe. He made arrangements for them to move to a condo in nearby Kyoto, which had suffered little damage. Then, during Tufts' spring break in March, Murakami spent two weeks in Japan. He was listening to records and organizing the books in his seaside retreat on the morning of the twentieth when a friend called with the news that something terrible had happened in the Tokyo subway system involving poison gas. The obvious suspects were members of the Aum Shinrikyō cult whose campaign tactics had disturbed him so much in 1990. "Better steer clear of Tokyo for the time being," said the friend.[385]

As the news came out, it became apparent how much damage the cult had done. Some 5,000 people on the Tokyo subway that morning had inhaled the deadly gas called sarin. Some of them had been crippled for life, eleven had died. Cult members travelling in separate carriages on five different subway lines had dropped newspaper-wrapped plastic bags of liquid sarin on the floor, then punctured them with the sharpened points of their umbrellas before leaving. The gas was released under the busiest parts of Tokyo at the height of the rush hour. Commuters were struck down with dizziness, convulsions, vomiting and in some cases blindness. Hospitals in the area overflowed with victims seeking help, but the emergency services were slow to respond and unprepared.

Having been away from Japan for so long, and having been so deeply involved in writing his longest novel, Murakami was unaware of an earlier incident in the city of Matsumoto involving

Aum and sarin gas that caused the police to suspect their involvement immediately. This, too, brought home to him how out of touch he was.

Murakami returned to Cambridge as scheduled for the final weeks of the semester, but little remained for him to do besides preparing for departure. He and Yōko left in June. That September, Murakami gave two public readings in the earthquake zone to benefit severely damaged libraries – in one of which, the Ashiya Public Library, he had spent many days as a middle-school and high-school student and "dozing" in preparation for his entrance exams.[386]

Beginning that January and continuing all through 1996, Murakami began doing what he so often has Boku do in the novels: listening to people's stories. He was convinced that if he could get victims of the gas attack to tell him about their experiences, it would be a quick way for him to learn more about Japan, and might even help him fulfil his growing sense of responsibility towards Japanese society. The first product of these efforts was *Underground* (*Andāguraundo*, 1997) a 700-page book of Murakami's interviews with victims of the attack, to which he added his comments and vivid character sketches of the interviewees. Murakami followed this with a second volume, *The Place That Was Promised: Underground 2* (*Yakusoku-sareta basho de: underground 2*, 1998), a book of interviews with members and former members of the Aum Shinrikyō cult. In both volumes (abridged and combined in English translation), Murakami attempts to convey how little separates the sick world of Aum from the everyday world of ordinary Japanese.

The individuality-crushing pressures of Japanese society can lead highly educated, ambitious, idealistic young people to abandon the places that have been promised them in search of worlds of unknown potential under misguided religious leaders. In a similar way, young members of the elite abandoned the positions offered

239

them in pre-war Japanese society to join the government's mis-guided ventures in Manchuria in the name of utopian slogans that masked a bloody reality. The greatest distinction between victims and perpetrators is that the latter are desperate enough to try to do something about the emptiness that both feel.[387]

The postscript to *Underground* discusses the historical, social, and literary interests that led Murakami to write his first major non-fiction piece. In particular, the literary ties recall the imagery we have seen developing throughout his work, most notably in *Hard-boiled Wonderland and the End of the World* and *The Wind-up Bird Chronicle*: "Subterranean worlds – wells, underpasses, caves, underground springs and rivers, culverts, subways – have always fascinated me, both as an individual and as a novelist. The image, the mere idea of a hidden pathway, immediately fills my head with stories . . ."[388]

That two such enormous events, the earthquake and the gas attack, occurred so close together was astonishing, he writes. They came with impeccable timing, just as the bubble economy burst so spectacularly, as the age of confidence in Japan's unstoppable development came to an end, as the Cold War structure fell apart, as values were faltering on a worldwide scale and when the foundations of the nation of Japan were being subjected to close scrutiny.

The one element these two different events shared was their "overwhelming violence". To be sure, one was natural and unavoid-able, the other man-made and avoidable, but from the point of view of the victims the result was not so different. "Both were nightmarish eruptions beneath our feet – from underground – that threw all the latent contradictions and weak points of our society into frighteningly high relief." In the face of this sudden, raging violence, Japanese society had proved itself utterly powerless and defenceless.[389]

True, the earthquake and the gas attack brought forth many admirable examples of grass-roots volunteerism and even heroism – especially on the part of subway workers who sacrificed their lives – but the system as a whole was thrown into chaos. High-ranking officials of the subway authority, the fire department and the police came nowhere near the conscientiousness of the workers on the line, either in terms of immediate response or follow-up. Instead they succumbed to that deplorable (and not wholly Japanese) instinct to cover up errors of judgement, to hide embarrassments, to keep the locus of responsibility deliberately unclear. No obvious gag orders were issued, but the superiors let their employees know that they had best keep quiet about something that was "over and done with". The more he learned about the way the gas attack was dealt with by the so-called emergency services, the more Murakami found himself feeling the same sort of anger he had felt with regard to the Nomonhan Incident.

In preparing to write my latest novel, *The Wind-up Bird Chronicle*, I did in-depth research into the so-called "1939 Nomonhan Incident", an aggressive incursion by Japanese forces into Mongolia. The more I delved into the records, the more aghast I became at the recklessness, the sheer lunacy of the Imperial Army's system of command. How had this pointless tragedy been passed over in the history books? Again, researching the Tokyo gas attack, I was struck by the fact that the closed, responsibility-evading ways of Japanese society were really not any different from how the Imperial Japanese Army operated at that time.[390]

Simply stated, the soldiers on the line with their rifles were the ones who suffered, while the officers and General Staff in the rear took no responsibility whatever. They thought only of saving face, of denying defeat, of glossing over their mistakes with official propaganda in the name of "military secrecy". These tendencies do not, of course, distinguish them from other organizations throughout the world, military or otherwise, but the Japanese system is perhaps more effective in shielding the men at the top from blame.

The causes of the defeat at Nomonhan were never fully or effectively analysed by the upper echelons of the Army. Nomonhan never became a vital lesson for the future. The Army did nothing but transfer a few of the Kwantung Army General Staff, and they sealed all intelligence with regard to this limited war. Two years later, Japan plunged into the Second World War, and the tragic errors of Nomonhan were repeated on a massive scale.

Underground shows Murakami approaching the subway attack from different angles. The interviews with victims are generally modelled on Studs Terkel's *Working*, a book of interviews with ordinary Americans. Simple in plan and approach, they are part of Murakami's attempt to learn more about Japan after his long absence. He wants to know about the lives of ordinary Japanese and how they function within society, and for that reason many of the interviews range well beyond the events of 20 March 1995. They provide a composite portrait of the ordinary Japanese men and women who comprise the Tokyo workforce. One mother of a man who was killed by sarin, for example, tells Murakami about the easy labour she had giving birth to him. This may not tell us much about the gas attack, but it adds an unexpected human dimension to the picture we are given of the victims. Precisely because they are so unremarkable, Murakami seems determined to set down the facts of their lives.

A portrait also begins to take shape of the interviewer himself. Murakami shares the active curiosity of his Boku narrators in his many novels. It is one of the features that makes them so appealing – and Murakami such an engaging interviewer. "Of course, if you keep telling yourself there's something to be learned from everything, growing old shouldn't be that hard. In general. Ever since I turned 20, I've tried to stick to that philosophy of life," says Boku of *Hear the Wind Sing*.

In the second part of *Underground* Murakami is also engaged in a learning process, but he made a conscious decision to be more argumentative in his discussions with the cult members and not just to sit back and let them have their say. Here, Murakami intervenes, raising several themes that inform his own novels. The Aum members fascinate him because they have tried to do what his characters usually give up any hope of doing. Through religion, they have sought out regions "south of the border" or "west of the sun" where they hope to find that missing something, that absolute certainty of "liberation" or "enlightenment" that will give their lives meaning. Unlike the more passive victims of the attack, the cult members have dared to probe into the black box at the core of themselves. In the process, some have temporarily been unable to distinguish between dream and reality, another familiar Murakami motif. At times Murakami seems to sense danger, perhaps recognizing how his own inner investigations might have taken a wrong turn: ". . . talking to them so intimately made me realize how their religious quest and the process of novel writing, though not identical, are similar. This aroused my own personal interest as I interviewed them, and it is also why I felt something akin to irritation at times as well."[391]

What most irks him is their willingness to surrender their egos to a guru who offers to think and make decisions for them, as Aum Shinrikyō's leader, Shōkō Asahara, surely did. It is a comforting illusion that someone can think for you, but Murakami objects to it as an individualist and as a writer who sees the world in terms of narrative:

If you lose your ego, you lose the thread of that narrative you call your Self. Humans, however, can't live very long without some sense of a continuing story. Such stories go beyond the limited rational system (or the systematic rationality) with which you surround yourself; they are crucial keys to sharing time-experience with others.

Now a narrative is a story, not logic, nor ethics, nor philosophy. It is a dream you keep having, whether you realize it or not. Just as surely as you breathe, you go on ceaselessly dreaming your story. And in these stories you wear two faces. You are simultaneously subject and object. You are the whole and you are a part. You are real and you are shadow. "Storyteller" and at the same time "character". It is through such multilayering of roles in our stories that we heal the loneliness of being an isolated individual in the world.

Yet without a proper ego, nobody can create a personal narrative, any more than you can drive a car without an engine, or cast a shadow without a real physical object. But once you've consigned your ego to someone else, where on earth do you go from there?

At this point you receive a new narrative from the person to whom you have entrusted your ego. You've handed over the real thing, so what comes back instead is a shadow. And once your ego has merged with another ego, your narrative will necessarily take on the narrative created by that other ego . . .

Asahara was talented enough to impose his rehashed narrative on people . . . Asahara was a master storyteller who proved capable of anticipating the mood of the times . . . [392]

In October 2001, an interviewer for The *New York Times* sought out Murakami in Tokyo, noting the applicability of his analysis of Aum to the previous month's terrorist attacks on New York and Washington. Murakami compared the closed world of Aum Shinrikyō with that of Islamic fundamentalist groups. In both cases, he said, "If you have questions, there is always someone to provide the answers. In a way, things are very easy and clear, and you are happy as long as you believe." In the open-ended world of everyday life, however,

> Things are very incomplete . . . There are many distractions and many flaws. And instead of being happy, in most cases we are frustrated and stressed. But at least things are open. You have choice and you can decide the way you live . . . What I write are stories in which the hero is looking for the right way in this world of chaos . . . That is my theme. At the same time I think there is another world that is underground. You can access this inner world in your mind. Most protagonists in my books live in both worlds – this realistic world and the underground world.
>
> If you are trained you can find the passage and come and go between the two worlds. It is easy to find an entrance into this closed circuit, but it is not easy to find an exit. Many gurus offer an entry into the circuit for free. But they don't offer a way out, because they want to keep followers trapped. Those people can be soldiers when they are ordered to be. I think that is very much like what happened with those people who flew the planes into those buildings.[393]

Murakami does not adopt an attitude of "us versus them", however. In *Underground* he challenges the reader – and himself – to avoid such complacency:

> Most of us laughed at the absurd off-the-wall scenario that Asahara provided . . . So, then, what about you? (I'm using

the second person, but of course that includes me.)

Haven't you offered up some part of your Self to someone (or some thing), and taken on a "narrative" in return? Haven't we entrusted some part of our personality to some greater System or Order? And if so, has not that System at some stage demanded of us some kind of "insanity"? Is the narrative you now possess *really and truly* your own? Are your dreams *really* your own dreams? Might not they be someone else's visions that could sooner or later turn into nightmares?[394]

Murakami challenges his readers to think for themselves and not simply and uncritically to accept the narrative offered by society or religion or the state, however "mainstream" and uncontroversial it may appear to be. In this, he echoes the post-war writer Ango Sakaguchi (1906–55) who challenged his countrymen to shake off the spell of the deified Emperor and Way of the Warrior (*Bushidō*) that had led them to devote themselves to an insane war, and instead to substitute for them their *own* interior Emperor and their *own* Way of the Warrior.[395] According to Sakaguchi, the Japanese had loved the war because it offered them the comfort of not having to think for themselves – something to which we are all susceptible.[396] The first time Murakami had encountered the Aum cult in 1990 he had looked away in disgust, but on reconsideration he concludes that it was precisely the *bond* he felt with them – the almost universal longing to have all our questions answered – that had revolted him.[397]

Of course, Murakami's Aum interviewees are not those who committed the atrocities on the Tokyo subway. Many of them doubt they would have followed orders to kill people, though a few ascribe this more to their own spiritual shortcomings than to their strength of character. In a sense, they are victims as well.

They are for the most part social misfits, drop-outs, losers; manipulated by Aum's elite leadership, they knew nothing of Asahara's murderous intentions. Murakami has this to say about the people at the top of the cult's hierarchy:

> The fact that such upwardly-mobile people easily rejected the positions in society that were promised them and ran off to join a new religion is a serious indication, many have said, that there is a fatal defect in the Japanese education system.
>
> However, as I went through the process of interviewing these Aum members and former members, one thing I felt quite strongly was that it wasn't *in spite of* being part of the elite that they went in that direction, but precisely *because* they were part of the elite.[398]

With a new sense of himself as a writer engaged with society's ills, he concludes his analysis of the problem with a call for action:

> I believe that the government should convene experts from all fields as soon as possible and create a fair and open committee to investigate the subway gas attack, to clarify facts that have been hidden, and to conduct a thoroughgoing revision of the relevant systems. Where were the mistakes made? What prevented the system from responding as it should have? A rigorous and meticulous pursuit of the answers to these questions would be the greatest tribute we could pay to those unfortunate enough to have lost their lives in the attack. Indeed, we owe it to them to do no less. The information gathered in the process must not be allowed to be sealed up inside each administrative branch, but must be made widely available to the entire public. Until this is done, the danger persists of our repeating the same systemic errors.[399]

We are a long way from the author who dreamed of meeting the Girl from Ipanema. Neither he nor anyone else could have predicted the growth he was to undergo as a writer and as a person. Which is not to say that Murakami was suddenly stepping forth as the leader of a social movement or that this more overt political stance should be seen as a rejection of his earlier work (though it might be pointed out here that he contributed a portion of his *Underground* royalties to a victims' fund).[400] He was still very much a writer of fiction, as he would make clear in his handling of the other catastrophe of 1995, the Kansai earthquake.

The Lexington Ghosts

Involved as he was with his non-fiction writing, Murakami did not publish another novel for almost four years after the last volume of *The Wind-up Bird Chronicle* appeared in August 1995. In the meantime, his short fictions were a kind of summing up. *The Lexington Ghosts* (*Rekishinton no yūrei*, November 1996) contained stories that had appeared in magazines as long ago as 1990 ("The Little Green Monster", "The Silence", and "Tony Takitani", all discussed earlier) but also a piece from as recently as the month before.

The title story, "The Lexington Ghosts" (October 1996, published first in an abridged version) is a rarity for Murakami in its use of a foreign setting, the town of Lexington, Massachusetts, a few miles west of where he had been living in Cambridge from July 1993 to June 1995. "This is something that actually occurred a few years ago," Boku begins his tale. "I have changed only the names of the people involved, but everything else is fact."[401]

Boku is a Japanese novelist who was living in Cambridge, Massachusetts for two years, during which time he did some house-sitting for an architect friend. Late one night he became convinced that some ghosts were throwing a noisy party behind the closed doors of the parlour in the venerable old house, but he never saw them, and now the events, which happened relatively recently, feel as though they happened in the "far distant past". "Frustrating" and "inconclusive" are two words that come to mind in describing this story; perhaps it is another Murakami warm-up piece for writing on ghosts and evoking a sense of something spiritual hovering in places with a history. Murakami had seen such a house in the area; the "facts" of the story are entirely fictitious.[402]

The other new creation from this time, "The Seventh Man" ("Nanabanme no otoko", February 1996), has its own hoary old narrative trappings (reminiscent of Chaucer, perhaps, or Boccaccio) as a group of people sit around telling each other stories on a dark and stormy night.

> "A huge wave nearly swept me away," said the seventh man, almost whispering. "It happened one September afternoon when I was ten years old . . . [The wave] just barely missed me, but in my place it swallowed everything that mattered most to me and swept it off to another world. I took years to find it again and to recover from the experience – precious years that can never be replaced."[403]

The themes of loss and emptiness are familiar Murakami territory, but what follows is a gripping piece of old-fashioned, doom-driven storytelling about a boy who loses his best friend and his reason for living.

Murakami told his web page readers that he had "ground [his] bones down" with the effort of writing *Hard-boiled Wonderland and the End of the World* and *The Wind-up Bird Chronicle*, and he wrote his next novel, *Sputnik Sweetheart* (*Supūtoniku no koibito*, April 1999), "in order to replenish the bone" he had lost to those earlier works.[404]

> I think of *Sputnik Sweetheart* as a kind of experiment in style – a "summation", perhaps, or a "leave-taking", or a "fresh start". I wanted to see how far I could go with style in that book. In that sense, I think I was able to make a clean break in it. It would be like testing yourself as a runner by seeing if you can run full out to a certain point, or if you can run from here to there without drinking any water – that kind of thing. As an experiment in style, it may have been like another *Norwegian Wood* for me.[405]

In some ways *Sputnik Sweetheart* is a new departure. It concentrates on a female character swept away by a lesbian passion. Sumire (pronounced Soo-mee-reh) is a cute, lively, and driven (but unsuccessful) writer, whose presence naturally colours much of the book. Especially when her writing is quoted, the cuteness quotient can go off the charts.

Sumire's story is told by a lovelorn Boku narrator known to us only as "K.", who functions primarily as a window on her. The use of K. as a device enables Murakami to write in the third person for long stretches at a time. His struggles to overcome the restrictions imposed by first-person narration in *The Wind-up Bird Chronicle* led him thereafter to experiment with a broader perspective.

It is K., aged 24, who narrates the wonderfully hyperbolic opening passage on the tornado of first love that sweeps away the

22-year-old Sumire and crosses the sea to destroy the temples of Angkor Wat, and it is K. who reports events involving Sumire and her 39-year-old beloved, the beautiful Korean-Japanese Miu. He also places before the reader various written documents he has discovered, most notably those contained in Sumire's computer. A schoolteacher, K. turns to the mother of one of his pupils for the sexual fulfilment he cannot hope for with Sumire. Sumire, meanwhile, accompanies Miu, her employer, on a glamorous trip to Europe. But when the frigid Miu rejects Sumire's sexual advances while they are holidaying on a Greek island, Sumire suddenly disappears without a trace.

K. flies to the island to join Miu in a search that turns up – nothing at all. Lured out one night by mysterious music coming from a hilltop (just as in "Man-Eating Cats"), K. feels himself being drawn into the other world where he is convinced (all too easily) Sumire has disappeared. Nevertheless he resists and returns to his humdrum life in Tokyo. When his lover's young son is caught shoplifting, K. attempts to cure the boy's psychological problems by telling him of his own loneliness (in a sentimental passage involving a run-over puppy). He then ends his relationship with the boy's mother. K. continues his lonely, Sputnik-like existence, but the book ends with an ambiguous phone call from Sumire, who is either back in Tokyo or calling from the "other side" or just a figment of K.'s imagination.

The story of Miu, as read by K. on Sumire's computer, carries echoes of "The 1963/1982 Girl From Ipanema". As the narrator of that story had said:

I try to imagine . . . a link in my consciousness spread out in silence across a dark corridor down which no one comes . . . Somewhere in there, I'm sure, is the link joining me with myself. Someday, too, I'm sure, I'll meet myself in a strange place in a far-off world . . . In that place, I am myself and myself is me. Subject is object and object is subject. All gaps gone. A perfect union. There must be a strange place like this somewhere in the world.

And when Miu finds herself inexplicably split into two separate selves, one "on this side" and the other "on the other side", she knows she will never be able to reunite them. But then, on second thoughts: "I guess *never* is too strong a word. Maybe someday, somewhere, we'll meet again, and merge back into one."[406] In the pivotal scene in which Miu is trapped in a Ferris wheel and looking in through the window of her distant hotel room, the trained Murakami reader knows long before it ever happens that she is going to see her "other" self there.

In the soft, jazzy, beery atmosphere of a short story, Murakami has no trouble convincing the reader of that sense of imperfection, the incompleteness of self-knowledge that underlies so much of his fiction. The meeting with the Girl from Ipanema is an enjoyable conceit carried off with great aplomb and over a short enough distance that we don't think about it too deeply. In *Sputnik Sweetheart*, however, we hear Astrud Gilberto singing from the same album "Take me to Aruanda", the exotic place name standing for everything "south of the border", "west of the sun", and "on the other side". Murakami's lengthy, over-literal evocation of that other realm as the best explanation of Sumire's mysterious disappearance makes us long for the skilful brevity of the Girl from Ipanema story.

In one of the worst lines in the book, K. actually thinks to himself: "Sumire went over to the *other side*. That would explain a lot."[407] Indeed it would, just as the existence of gremlins would explain how my glasses moved from my desk to the dining-room table. Murakami turns up the hilltop music *loud* in an attempt to give K.'s brush with the "other side" some sense of urgency and conviction, and he lays on the heightened emotional prose to "explain" K.'s deep (if temporary) bond with Miu, but admirers of the cool Murakami of old might find the last 50 pages of *Sputnik Sweetheart* heavy going.

Everyday life is full of the kind of mystery that Murakami so beautifully evokes in stories like "The Second Bakery Attack" or "The Elephant Vanishes". We experience it all of the time, and in his stories Murakami makes it special by going one step further, by crossing the line through sheer force of imagination and humour, making his characters experience things that are just barely beyond belief, just slightly outrageous.

It is a delicate balancing act, far more subtle and demanding than the techniques Murakami began using in *Dance Dance Dance*, with its roomful of skeletons near Waikiki Beach, and even *The Wind-up Bird Chronicle*, with its forays into the occult. He was uncertain what he wanted to do with these elements in the latter novel, so he just dropped some of them. That is why the clairvoyant Kanō sisters – with their special ability to divine something-never-very-explicit about their clients from samples of water taken from their homes – simply disappear, and the protagonist's spiritual cures of rich but neurotic housewives remain unexplained and undeveloped.

Even the image of the wind-up bird itself smacks of this gimmickry as it lends its cry to decisive turning points in the lives of individuals. Its intrusion into the Manchuria chapters is saved, however, by the third-person narrator's assumption of a god-like stance, his bold pronouncements of the future fates of the doomed characters reminding us that we are dealing here not with a clairvoyant but with a *writer* – a storyteller who has taken on total responsibility for the past, present and future of the lives he has created. It is a stunning performance that stands in strong contrast to the predictable machinery of *Sputnik Sweetheart*, in which characters conveniently lose consciousness whenever they might be required to provide rational explanations for the mysterious events that befall them. In the final analysis, *The Wind-up Bird Chronicle* is a compilation of self-contained short stories, its great power deriving more from cumulative effect and variety than structural wholeness.

Another over-familiar element in *Sputnik Sweetheart* is the almost obsessive use of brand names and references to popular (and not-so-popular) culture. K. never just drinks a beer, he lets us know it's an Amstel. Miu carries a Mila Schön shoulder bag. K. jokes at one point that the wealthy Miu must own "Marc Bolan's favourite snakeskin sandals in a glass case . . . One of the invaluable legacies without which the history of rock and roll cannot be told." The account of Sumire and Miu's trip to Europe brims with references to food and wine and classical music that verge on the precious.[408]

Because its central character is an aspiring author, *Sputnik Sweetheart* continues Murakami's investigation into the function of the writer that began in the opening paragraphs of *Hear the Wind Sing*. It is important not to write too soon, Sumire is told; she needs more "time and experience". And when she does later resume her writing, she says: "In order for me to think about something, I have to first put it into writing . . . On a day-to-day basis I use writing to work out who I am." Expanding somewhat on the insight of the author in "A Poor-Aunt Story", Sumire says: "I see now that my basic rule of thumb in my writing has always been to write about things as if I *didn't* know them – and this would include things that I did know, or thought I knew about."[409]

One early theme pursued somewhat more fully in this novel is lesbianism, which emerges more frequently in Murakami's works than male homosexuality. In *Norwegian Wood*, Reiko's sanity was destroyed by a vindictive lesbian pupil, and in the sanitarium she and Naoko can't help laughing at their awkward experiments with lesbianism. Perhaps the theme relates to Murakami's fascination with the mind-body split, in which the reality of what occurs in the mind is always more convincing than anything that occurs on the physical plane.

Sputnik Sweetheart was discussed by readers in a special "Forum" on Murakami's website just before it was discontinued in November 1999. One reader was convinced the call from Sumire at the end of the book was a hallucination, but others were equally certain it was a happy ending and Sumire would return. "I'm not asking you to tell me which is right," said the reader, and true to form Murakami did not. Deciding whether or not it was a happy ending was a "difficult problem" for him, he said, "because it impinges upon my place as a human being in this world. Inside me, those two values are always in opposition, struggling with each other, and finally blended together in appropriate proportions. I can't explain it any better than this. So if you felt you couldn't believe the novel had a happy ending, then it's a non-happy-ending type story."[410]

after the quake

In August 1999, Murakami began to serialize five stories indirectly linked to the Kansai earthquake. The title of the series, *Jishin no ato de*, means "after the quake", although the pieces would be joined by one additional story and published in a volume called *Kami no kodomotachi wa mina odoru* (*All God's Children Can Dance*, 2000) after the title of one of the six.[411] Later, Murakami decided that *after the quake* (which he insisted should be all lower-case) was a more appropriate title for the English translation. All the stories are set in February 1995, the quiet month between the January earthquake and the March gas attack in Tokyo.

The stories in *after the quake* are remarkable in several ways. For one thing, they are all narrated in the third person, a perspective Murakami had rarely adopted – in *The Wind-up Bird Chronicle*, *Sputnik Sweetheart*, and a few earlier pieces, notably "Tony Takitani". The many voices of *The Wind-up Bird Chronicle* show Murakami struggling to overcome the narrowness of a first-person perspective in grappling with large historical questions, and *after the quake* represents a decisive move towards greater objectivity. By abandoning the limited focus of Boku, Murakami implies that the malaise he is diagnosing goes beyond the privileged few who live on the periphery of national events and who observe them from afar: in *after the quake* he examines the very fabric of everyday life. The result is a glum panorama of mid-1990s Japanese in which the earthquake is a wake-up call to the emptiness of their lives in a society in which most people have (or recently had, until the bubble burst) more money in their wallets than they knew how to spend.

That emptiness may be what Murakami discovered in the hearts of the ordinary people he interviewed as victims of the gas attack: a vague sense (like Hajime's in *South of the Border, West of the Sun*) that there is some indefinable thing missing from their lives. Indeed, the 38-year-old shrimp import buyer, Mitsuteru Izutsu, interviewed in *Underground*, may have been an inspiration for some of the stories:

> [T]he day after the gas attack, I asked my wife for a divorce . . . After being gassed I phoned home from the office to tell the wife what had happened and my symptoms and everything, but I got almost no reaction from her. Perhaps she couldn't really grasp the situation, exactly what had occurred. But even so, well, I knew then that we'd come to a turning point. Or else, the state I was in had got me all worked up,

maybe that's what it was. Maybe that's why I came straight out with it and said I wanted a divorce. Perhaps if this sarin thing hadn't happened, I wouldn't have been talking about divorce so soon. I probably wouldn't have said anything. It was a shock to the system and at the same time a kind of trigger.[412]

The central characters in *after the quake* live far from the physical devastation, which they witness only on TV or in the papers, but for each of them the massive destruction unleashed by the earth itself becomes a turning point in their lives. They are forced to confront an emptiness they have borne inside them for years.

In the first story, "UFO in Kushiro", the wife of a stereo component salesman called Komura suddenly leaves him after spending five days glued to the TV watching scenes of destruction from Kobe, a city with which she has no obvious connection. (This story seems almost prophetic after the coordinated attack on the World Trade Center and the Pentagon on 11 September 2001.) Komura had been satisfied enough with his job and his wife, but she tells him in a letter that she felt being married to him was like "living with a chunk of air".

At the behest of a work colleague, Komura seems to carry a small box containing that very emptiness with him when he flies north to Hokkaidō for a break. Distracted by images of the earthquake, he abandons a listless attempt to have sex with an attractive young woman, and stays in bed talking with her about this feeling of emptiness. "I may have nothing inside me," he says, "but what would *something* be?" The woman agrees: "Yeah, really, come to think of it. What *would* something be?" When she jokes that the box he brought with him may have contained the "something" he used to have inside, Komura feels a wave of anger come over him, as if he were "on the verge of committing an act of overwhelming violence".[413] Unlike the Aum perpetrators, however, Komura stays on the commonsense side of the line.

And so the mood is set for the rest of *after the quake*, perhaps Murakami's most conventional story collection. It explores the lives of realistic people in realistic situations, people whose outwardly satisfactory lives leave them feeling unfulfilled and who live on the edge of some devastating discovery.

In "Landscape with Flatiron" ("Airon no aru fūkei"), a young woman clerk in a convenience store is ready to die with a middle-aged loner who has abandoned his wife and children in Kobe and refuses to check on their well-being after the quake. He visits the convenience store often because he doesn't like refrigerators – they seem to hold out to him the threat of a slow, painful death in a sealed box, rather like the death feared by Tōru in *The Wind-up Bird Chronicle*. He paints symbolic pictures and builds driftwood bonfires that remind the heroine of Jack London's story "To Build a Fire", the central character of which "was fundamentally longing for death. She knew that for sure. She couldn't explain how she knew, but she knew it from the start. Death was really what he wanted. He *knew* that it was the right ending for him. And yet he had to go on fighting with all his might. He had to fight against an overwhelming adversary in order to survive."[414] Her own sense of emptiness, however, is leading her to give up the fight.

In "All God's Children Can Dance" ("Kami no kodomotachi wa mina odoru"), Yoshiya, a young publishing company employee, fears sexual involvement with his beautiful single mother, a religious cult member who has tried unsuccessfully to convince him that he is the son of God. While she is off ministering to the victims of the earthquake, he spots a man on the Tokyo subway whom he believes to be his actual father. The man disappears after a lengthy pursuit that leads to a deserted baseball pitch at night, and Yoshiya is left alone to reassess the situation:

What was I hoping to gain from this? he asked himself as he strode ahead. Was I trying to confirm the ties that make it possible for me to exist here and now? Was I hoping to be woven into some new plot, to be given some new and better-defined role to play? No, he thought, that's not it. What I was chasing in circles must have been the tail of the darkness inside me. I just happened to catch sight of it, and followed it, and clung to it, and in the end let it fly into still deeper darkness. I'm sure I'll never see it again.[415]

Reconciled to the mystery of his birth and of his inner self, Yoshiya dances in a kind of religious ecstasy, thinking about an old girlfriend who had nicknamed him Super-Frog for his ungainly movements on the dance floor. He loves dancing, however. He feels as if he is moving in time with the rhythms of the universe:

How long he went on dancing, Yoshiya could not tell. But it was long enough for him to perspire under the arms. And then it struck him what lay buried far down under the earth on which his feet were so firmly planted: the ominous rumbling of the deepest darkness, secret rivers that transported desire, slimy creatures writhing, the lair of earthquakes ready to transform whole cities into mounds of rubble. These, too, were helping to create the rhythm of the earth. He stopped dancing and, catching his breath, stared at the ground beneath his feet as though peering into a bottomless hole.[416]

In "Thailand" ("Tairando"), Satsuki, a menopausal physician, struggles with fantasies of violent death for the Kobe man who destroyed her hopes of ever becoming a mother. The Thai driver, Nimit, who arranges for Satsuki's comforting private swims wonders if his taste for jazz is really his own or if he gave up his independent self by becoming a chauffeur for a jazz-loving Norwegian for 33 years – surely an echo of Murakami's concern for the loss of self to a guru. (There is a hint as well that he might have been the passive partner in a homosexual relationship. It may be that he is "half dead" because he has lost the love of his life.)[417] A touch of the occult emerges at the end of the story when Nimit drives Satsuki to a backward village where a clairvoyante advises her how she can remove the "stone" of hatred from inside her by wrestling with a large snake in her dreams.

"Super-Frog Saves Tokyo" ("Kaeru-kun, Tokyo o sukuu") is the only story in *after the quake* to abandon the realm of the everyday and it does so with comic panache. In a scene reminiscent of Kafka, an under-appreciated, un-promoted, overworked bank collection officer named Katagiri returns home to find a giant frog waiting for him. This huge and highly intelligent amphibian quotes Nietzsche, Conrad, Dostoevsky, Hemingway, and Tolstoy, and repeatedly (to comic effect) corrects Katagiri's formal manner of address ("Mr Frog"). Frog (as he prefers to be called) soon makes it clear that he needs Katagiri's help to save Tokyo from an earthquake much larger than the one in Kansai: together, they are to go underground to do battle with Worm, a gigantic creature boiling with undefined rage that he is about to unleash beneath Tokyo. (This is reminiscent of the giant catfish of Japanese legend that causes earthquakes by thrashing its tail.)

The "Super-Frog" of "All God's Children Can Dance" and the "slimy creatures writhing, the lair of earthquakes ready to transform whole cities into mounds of rubble" evoked there have been wildly elaborated in this story by Murakami (the pieces were written in the order given here and in the book),[418] using echoes from story to story in a way that recalls his use of the name "Noboru Watanabe" for unrelated characters in *The Second Bakery Attack*.[419] In *after the quake* Murakami can be as playful as ever, even after the solemnity of *Sputnik Sweetheart*, and is able to use something as horrifying and significant to him as the earthquake to evoke the ominous emptiness "beneath the feet" of a bank employee like Katagiri. As seriously and respectfully as he has dealt with ordinary people in *Underground*, Murakami is still able to sketch Katagiri's "ordinariness" with comic skill:

> "To be quite honest, Mr Katagiri, you are nothing much to look at, and you are far from eloquent, so you tend to be looked down upon by those around you. *I*, however, can see what a sensible and courageous man you are. In all of Tokyo, with its teeming millions, there is no one else I could trust as much as you to fight by my side."
>
> "You know, Mr Frog . . . I'm an absolutely ordinary guy. Less than ordinary . . . I live a horrible life. All I do is eat, sleep, and shit. I don't know why I'm even living. Why should a person like me have to be the one to save Tokyo?"
>
> "Because, Mr Katagiri, Tokyo can *only* be saved by a person like you. And it's *for* people like you that I am trying to save Tokyo."[420]

With Katagiri's moral support, Frog does succeed in saving Tokyo from the earthquake. Before he finally departs, however, in a vivid scene of decomposition reminiscent of "The Dancing Dwarf", he evokes the spiritual vacuum in which the Katagiris of Japan do their jobs while the more desperate ones throw themselves at the feet of a guru:

> Fyodor Dostoevsky, with unparalleled tenderness, depicted those who have been forsaken by God. He discovered the precious quality of human existence in the ghastly paradox whereby men who had invented God were forsaken by that very God.[421]

In the final story, "Honey Pie" ("Hachimitsu pai"), Junpei is a writer of short fiction who long ago lost his secret love to his best friend. The couple have since divorced, and he finds himself drawn closer to her. He tries to help her calm her little daughter, Sala, when she has nightmares caused by TV images of the Kobe earthquake. Sala is frightened by The Earthquake Man, who lives inside the TV (somewhat like the "TV people" who take over people's lives) and keeps a little box into which he threatens to stuff all the people he can get his hands on (the same fear of a gradual death in a sealed space of the artist in "Landscape with Flatiron").

Ever since the divorce, Junpei had hesitated to propose marriage, but the earthquake's images of death seem to provide the proper catalyst. Not only will he make this long-delayed move and become the protector of Sala and her mother, but he will also from now on "write stories that are different from the ones I've written so far", stories "about people who dream and wait for the night to end, who long for the light so they can hold the ones they love."[422] This is exactly what Murakami has done in this moving and richly imagined collection rooted in the kind of everyday Japanese experience that Murakami almost had to re-learn when he ended his self-imposed "exile" in 1995.

It is almost as if, in *after the quake*, he has begun to realize what he foresaw in the opening pages of *Hear the Wind Sing*. Back then, as he told BBC producer Matt Thompson, "I wasn't interested in people",[423] though he was, paradoxically, interested in their stories. As his first young Boku puts it: "I find myself thinking that if everything goes well, sometime way ahead, years, maybe decades from now, I might discover myself saved. And then, at that time, the elephant will return to the plain, and I shall begin to tell the tale of the world in words more beautiful than these." After he had returned to Japan he began to engage with ordinary people in a way that was entirely new for him – to the extent that he could openly declare his "love" for them (again on the BBC broadcast).

In "Honey Pie" Junpei is "a born short story writer" whose work lacks "novelistic sweep".[424] Murakami says he deliberately created Junpei as "a type of writer entirely different from me". He considers himself "a born novelist, someone whose worth is to be evaluated by the full-length novels I write. I think it's important to write short stories, and I enjoy doing so, but I believe strongly that if you take away my novels, there is no me."[425]

To be sure, Murakami's long fictional works succeed in drawing the reader in for the duration of unique and often mind-altering journeys. They have the paradoxical magic of novels in that they force the reader to rush through many pages towards an end that is dreaded because the reader will be evicted from their mesmerizing worlds by the turn of the last page. With the exception of *Hard-boiled Wonderland and the End of the World*, however, Murakami's long novels are more often compilations of shorter narratives rather than large architectonic structures. They stun and startle and amuse and enlighten along the way, but they rarely draw their disparate threads together at the end. In this, they may be said to share tendencies toward shortness and fragmentation that have often been remarked in Japanese fictional forms.

13

You Give Me Fever

Turning 50 on 12 January 1999 did not seem to bother Murakami as much as turning 40 had. He continued to run in marathons and produce novels and stories and translations and non-fiction at such an undiminished pace that no book written close to the fact can hope to be more than a progress report.

The Yomiuri Prize for *The Wind-up Bird Chronicle* was followed in July 1999 by the Kuwabara Takeo Prize, named in honour of a great literary scholar and awarded for outstanding non-fiction. In this case, the work was Murakami's second volume on the sarin gas attack, *The Place That Was Promised*.

As we saw in Chapter 12, Murakami published his reaction to the Kobe earthquake in the form of short fiction, which emerged in the collection *after the quake* in 2000. By then he was working on his tenth novel, which appeared as the massive, two-volume *Kafka on the Shore* (*Umibe no Kafuka*) in the autumn of 2002. In November of that year, the Kōdansha publishers began to bring out a continuation of Murakami's collected works in seven volumes, providing another level of canonization to his oeuvre.

Murakami the translator fulfilled a long-standing dream in April 2003 with the publication of his translation of J. D. Salinger's *The Catcher in the Rye*. It and *Kafka on the Shore* almost had to compete for display space in bookstores, and soon they were joined by *Young*

Kafka (*Shōnen Kafuka*), Murakami's fourth compendium of email correspondence with readers. This differed from the earlier email volumes both in its bold "cartoon book" format and in being focused on a single novel.

In a move emblematic of Murakami's acceptance as a world-class literary figure, the British publisher Harvill Press brought out *Birthday Stories: Selected and Introduced by Haruki Murakami*, containing eleven American, British and Irish short stories plus one new story by Murakami himself. The release of this book of stories on the birthday theme was timed to coincide with Murakami's own fifty-fifth birthday on 12 January 2004.

Murakami is no closer now than he ever was to becoming a media darling, but thanks to the Internet, he has taken on a more public persona. The kindly elder brother of his early fiction has grown up to be the wise and sympathetic (but still funny) uncle who can be turned to for advice on a wide range of questions. Some of his Japanese publicity can get warm and fuzzy. For instance, the blurb on a handsome little volume published in June 2001 assures us that "Deeply, softly, this long-awaited collection of essays will sink into your heart with a tiny thud."[426] Fortunately, Murakami remains as humorous and down-to-earth as ever. Through the medium of the Internet, he has provided his fans with rare glimpses of his private life. Take, for example, this exchange from his website published with the outrageous title, *"That's It! Let's Ask Murakami!" Say the People and They Try Flinging 282 Big Questions at Haruki Murakami, But Can Murakami Really Find Decent Answers to Them All?*:

Big Question No. 18

Did Mrs Murakami ever think that one day you would be famous?

(2-2-97, 11.58 p.m.)

Here are three questions from my wife to Mrs Murakami.

"Back when your husband was dicing onions at the jazz club, did you ever think that he would become famous?"

"When you two were moving all over the place in foreign countries before your husband became a bestselling author, I suppose you had lots of pleasant things happen to you, but didn't *un*-pleasant things happen, too?"

"Do you enjoy taking those beautiful photographs that appear in your husband's books? (The ones in *Twistercat*[427] were especially beautiful, I thought. Do you have some tricks?)"

These are all such presumptuous questions, please forgive us. (I'm 32, and like me my wife is a Virgo, blood type O.)

Hello, there. No no, your questions are not presumptuous at all. I tried them out on my wife, and here are her answers:

I never imagined for a second that he'd be famous, and I still think it's weird. He thinks he's so special, he's got this cool look on his face like "It was bound to happen."

To tell you the truth, I had almost no fun the whole time we were in Europe. Living in foreign countries involved more pain and inconvenience than anything. I would *much* rather have stayed in Japan, soaking in a hot tub, petting our cat and taking it easy. Italian, English: I really hated the whole language-learning thing.

I'm not that crazy about photography. My husband orders me to take pictures because he needs them in his work, so

I do my best, that's all. I would much rather draw or paint.

Sorry for giving you such *cynical* answers. I don't know, they make me sound like an insensitive brute of a husband, but really, I'm not like that at all. She's kind of exaggerating: don't take her answers at face value.[428]

Murakami doesn't try hard to convince us that these are actual answers from Yōko. In the "popular" writings he gives her the persona of a loveable contrarian and milks it for laughs. Here is another one:

Big Question No. 15

What kind of person *is* Mrs Murakami?
(25-1-97, 1.35 p.m.)

You often write about your wife, but as far as I know, there don't seem to be any photos of her available.
I imagine it's because she is opposed to having her photo released to the public, but just once, I would *really* like to see what she looks like. (Age 32)

Hello, there. My wife doesn't like the idea of appearing in the mass media (like in a magazine or something just because you happen to be a member of somebody-or-other's family), and neither do I, so we just don't do it. In my case, though, I have to do it sometimes in connection with my work.

But, really, even if you saw her, it wouldn't do a thing for you, believe me.

267

All right, now I'm started on this, let me tell you something about her. When we first got married, she had long, straight hair down to her waist, but it's been getting shorter and shorter over the years, and now, mainly because she swims a lot, it's super short. She's really unusual: except under very special circumstances, she has never once had her hair curled or worn make-up. She says these are what she likes: David Lynch, Mozart K491, surf clams, salmon skin, Carson McCullers' fiction, Motoka Murakami's *Red Pegasus* [an adventure cartoon for boys], Porsche Targa 911s (whoa, too expensive for us).

The TV programmes that influenced her most when she was little were *Sucharaka shain* [a company sit-com] and *Beverly Hillbillies*. She wanted to grow up to be a Ninja.

You want a picture? It'll never happen.[429]

 Not all of the readers' Big Questions are silly and playful, and Murakami can answer a serious request for advice with a thoughtful response. On 9 November 1997, two days after losing her uncle to cancer, a 30-year-old woman posed a question that continues to plague the Japanese (as seen in Akira Kurosawa's great film *Ikiru*): whether or not to inform terminal cancer patients of the truth of their illness. The woman's aunt had died the year before, and the couple were almost second parents to her. In the midst of the depression that followed this great double loss, she regretted having lied to her uncle during his final illness, though she suspected that, given the chance, she would probably make the same choice all over again. After acknowledging the "great blow" this loss must have been to her, Murakami replied:

 The last poetry collection of Raymond Carver, which I

translated, is called *A New Path to the Waterfall*. Carver wrote this book by wringing out every last ounce of strength he had *after* he had been informed that he was dying of cancer. It is an absolutely marvellous set of poems. Opinions differ as to whether or not people should be told they have cancer, but every time I take this book in hand, it reaffirms my belief that people have a right to know. People should not be deprived of this lofty opportunity to surmount their fear and despair and leave behind them some tangible something. I know there are those who think they wouldn't want to know,
but I myself would definitely want to be told.[430]

At this stage in his career, with several assistants dependent upon him for a living as they work in Tokyo to keep his one-man literary industry going, Murakami no longer feels free to tramp around other parts of the world. Writing assignments that involve travelling are another matter, however. He followed the two gas attack volumes with *Sydney!*, a delightful book on the Sydney Olympics in 2000 that contains not only vivid descriptions of the action on the field and gripping inner portraits of athletes in action but, among other things, a humorous primer on the life of the koala, detailed observations on the Sydney aquarium and the toilets of the Brisbane soccer stadium, and a good deal of local history – almost certainly researched and not made up like Midori's map notes in *Norwegian Wood*.[431]

When Murakami wants to write without interruption for a few months at a time, he and Yōko go abroad, far from the demands that his success has brought him, but still in daily electronic touch with his staff. As in their jazz café, Yōko works as a genuine (if not exactly equal) partner. She is the one who keeps the administrative side of things running smoothly, but she also continues to be his first reader, an insightful critic he knows he can trust to be totally honest with him. Perhaps most important of all, through her honesty, Yōko helps to keep Murakami firmly in touch with his own fundamental ordinariness.

For this valuable service, those of us who enjoy Murakami's fiction should be grateful to Yōko. Surely it is Murakami's ability to remain convincingly ordinary as he ventures into other worlds that enables the rest of us to tag along for the ride.

Kafka on the Shore

As he did on 18 March 1987 when he experienced "A Little Death at 3:50 in the Morning", Murakami continues to believe that "The deepest part of writing fiction involves going to (and coming back from) *the other world*, which is a place that inevitably overlaps with the image of death. I always experience that feeling when I write a novel. That has not changed for me in the least."[432] *Kafka on the Shore* is a book in which the traces of that journey are particularly distinct.

Murakami had long been wanting to write a sequel to *Hard-boiled Wonderland and the End of the World*, and *Kafka on the Shore* was as close as he felt he could come. Too much time had gone by, he said, for it to be an immediate sequel, and so it followed the earlier work more "in spirit" than as a continuation of the story, but the echoes are unmistakable. As in *Hard-boiled Wonderland*, there are two parallel narratives from beginning to end, and the reader is held in suspense as the developments seem to draw the separate groups of characters in each narrative closer together in time and space towards an anticipated climactic intersection. Unlike *Hard-boiled Wonderland*, however, the separate narratives do not occur on different levels of reality. Indeed, in both stories a more or less "real" world and a distinctly metaphysical or metaphorical "other world" intersect on several occasions so that, in effect, the reader is drawn into four separate levels of existence.[433]

The central character in the odd-numbered chapters is a troubled boy who runs away from his Tokyo home on Monday, 19 May 1997 (or 2003)[434], the eve of his fifteenth birthday. We never learn his real given name, but he tells people that it is Kafka; his family name is Tamura. The background of Kafka Tamura becomes somewhat less obscure on 3 June, in Chapter 21, when he reads a newspaper report on the recent bloody murder of his father, a well-known sculptor named Kōichi Tamura. He discovers that the police are searching for him in connection with the murder, but he makes no move to reveal himself, and to the end he remains "Kafka", the name he chose to replace the one given to him by his parents.

The news of his father's death does not grieve young Kafka. Indeed, it comes as something of a relief.[435] This, after all, was the father who saddled Kafka with an oft-repeated curse – that, like Oedipus, he would kill his father and sleep with his mother. This vile man (he is said to pollute and destroy all those who come in touch with him) also predicted that Kafka would sleep with his only sibling, the sister that Kafka's mother took away with her when she fled from her husband, abandoning her four-year-old son.

Kafka thus ventures out into the world with a combination of longing and dread that he might meet his actual mother and sister. He wonders about every likely female he meets if *she* is the one missing from his life, and having had such a terrible relationship with his father, he fantasizes about older males, what kind of fathers they might have been for him. He is thus not merely a 15-year-old protagonist of interest to 15-year-old readers but a surrogate for all who feel rootless in the world. He is perhaps too ready to conclude that the women he meets by chance are the right ones: Sakura, the "sister" with whom he has sex in a dream that fills him with the guilt of a rapist, and Saeki, the "mother" with whom he sleeps both

271

physically and metaphorically to therapeutic effect. So full of need is he that he might have met the "right" ones wherever he went. Was it instinct or chance that drew him to the one place in Japan where there lived a wounded woman with a "Kafka" of her own in her past?

Because he runs away to a town near the sea on the island of Shikoku, where some important scenes take place on the shore, and because his one surviving childhood photo shows him on a beach, it is not hard to imagine the boy as the "Kafka on the Shore" of the title, but he is not the book's only "Kafka on the Shore": both a song and a painting share the title. The other Kafkas are not Franz Kafka, either, and the significance of this name choice, by both Murakami and his protagonist, is never entirely clear. Young Kafka surmises that Saeki, the middle-aged woman he loves and who might be his longed-for mother, gave the name to the painting of a young man on a shore (her lost lover) because the special mood of loneliness in the painting was something she associated with Franz Kafka's fiction.[436] This would suggest that his own reason for choosing to label himself "Kafka" was an expression of this same loneliness.

In an interview, Murakami voiced his great admiration for Franz Kafka, who is only one of many writers, musicians, and artists cited in the novel. Echoing remarks in *Kafka on the Shore*, Murakami's interviewer mentions "In the Penal Colony", which accomplishes its eerie effect through a seemingly objective description of a grotesque apparatus used for executions. Murakami responds: "What Kafka gives us in his writing, I think, is the narrative of a nightmare. In the world in which he lived, real life and nightmare were, in a sense, closely bound together." Kafka conveys the true terror of a nightmare, he says, not by concentrating on the reactions of the protagonist but on the fine details of the nightmare itself. What Murakami says he most likes about Kafka is "his abnormal fixation on the details of the world of dream or imagination". This is a quality that Murakami perhaps shares with Kafka, suggests the interviewer. Indeed, the remark is reminiscent of Murakami's own earlier quoted comment regarding *Hard-boiled Wonderland and the End of the World* that there is nothing he enjoys so much as the process of describing in ever finer precision the details of a thing that does not exist.[437]

Young Kafka has a kind of alter ego, "the boy named Crow" (*Karasu to yobareru shōnen*), who speaks to him at certain critical moments in the story, calling him "you". We learn at one point that "Kafka" means "crow" in Czech, and a crow motif derived from the letterhead of Franz Kafka's father is used to decorate both the title page of Volume 1 and certain unnumbered sections where the "boy named Crow" speaks to the protagonist.[438] In fact, the novel opens with just such a speech:

> "So you're all set for money, then?" the boy named Crow asks in his characteristic sluggish voice. The kind of voice you have when you've just woken up and your mouth still feels heavy and dull. But he's just pretending. He's totally awake. As always.
>
> I nod.
>
> "How much?"
>
> I review the numbers in my head. "Close to ¥400,000 in cash, plus some money I can get from an ATM. I know it's not a lot, but it should be enough. For the time being."
>
> "Not bad," the boy named Crow says. *"For the time being."*
>
> I give him another nod.
>
> "I'm guessing this isn't Christmas money from Santa Claus."
>
> "Yeah, you're right," I reply.
>
> Crow smirks and looks around. "I imagine you've started out by rifling drawers, am I right?"[439]

Kafka is preparing to leave home, and he has helped himself to some of his father's money from a drawer in the study. He is another "Boku" narrator, and he tells his story largely in the present tense, rather like the "Boku" in the dreamier chapters of the English translation of *Hard-boiled Wonderland and the End of the World*. One wonders if Birnbaum's device, which worked so well in the translation of that novel, was Murakami's inspiration here. Young Kafka's world is not so dreamlike as that earlier Boku's, but near the end the boy does enter a timeless alternate reality that has many features reminiscent of the earlier novel's walled town. More important, he is trapped throughout between hazy memories of a past abandonment by his mother and the all-too-clear prospect of a future fulfilment of his father's prophecy: suspended between the past and the future, he has only the present in which to find himself.[440] The central event in his maturation is his decision not to remain in the other world's suspended state but to go back, present himself to the police, and take his place as a responsible member of society. The novel ends with him travelling back to Tokyo on Friday 13 June, three weeks and four days after his largely internal journey began.

This clear-cut decision to abandon the attraction of lotus-land stands in stark contrast to the conclusion of *Hard-boiled Wonderland and the End of the World*. Boku's decision was a compromise: he decided to linger for ever in the forest while his shadow returned to the real world. As Murakami says, "I have no regrets about that now. It was the most honest conclusion I could come up with at the time . . . If I were to write that story now, it would turn out differently . . . probably because my view of the world and maybe of the function of the novel has changed. It's a simple matter of a sense of responsibility."[441]

Aboard the bullet train carrying him back to Tokyo, Kafka has a good cry and asks himself, "Did I do the right thing?" The book ends:

274

"You did the right thing," the boy named Crow says. "You did what was best. No one else could have done as well as you did. After all, you're the genuine article: the toughest 15-year-old in the world."

But I still don't know anything about life," I protest.

"Look at the painting," he says. "And listen to the wind."

I nod.

"I know you can do it."

I nod again.

"You'd better get some sleep," the boy named Crow says. "When you wake up, you'll be part of a brand new world."

Eventually you fall asleep. And when you wake up, it's true. You are part of a brand new world.[442]

The book thus ends (in Chapter 49) on a hopeful note – one that, coincidentally, recalls the inadvertently "sweet" title of Murakami's first novel. The reader assumes that Kafka will not be prosecuted for the murder of his father, though in fact neither he nor we can be entirely sure that he is innocent. For on the very night of the father's murder, 28 May, just eight days after Kafka's arrival in Shikoku, the boy awoke in the grounds of a Shinto shrine after four unexplained hours of unconsciousness to find his T-shirt soaked with blood and his shoulder in pain. He realized that he was not wounded – that the blood belonged to someone else – but he had no memory of any violent encounter. Nor was it possible that, during the four blank hours, he could have travelled back to Tokyo, killed his father, and then returned to this Shinto shrine in Shikoku.

Shinto (or, more accurately, Shintō, "the Way of the Gods") is Japan's so-called "native religion", a far more earthy faith than the Buddhism imported from India through China, with its abstract teachings of detachment and Nirvana. Murakami's association of the shrine with dark, disturbing – and finally inexplicable – forces is relatively conventional. Shinto celebrates food, fertility, and the divinity of the land, and many of its innumerable gods represent the awe-inspiring forces of nature. Much Shinto ritual involves purification, especially when there has been "polluting" contact with death or blood.

Having read the narrative in the even-numbered chapters that run parallel to Kafka Tamura's story, the reader has a fairly good idea of who might have killed Kafka's father, but the circumstances of the killing are anything but clear. Given clues relating to "living spirits" seen in the eleventh-century Japanese masterpiece *The Tale of Genji*, the reader can only surmise that Kafka's hatred for the man who sired him somehow left his body, flew to Tokyo, and possessed a mentally handicapped old man living in the neighbourhood, causing him to do the deed.

This old man, Nakata, is the main protagonist of the story in the even-numbered chapters (which are narrated in the third person and the past tense). He does not enter the action at his present age, however, until Chapter 6, when we find him in a Tokyo neighbourhood talking to the local cats. He is a gentle old fellow beloved by the residents of the district for his uncanny ability to find missing cats, though no one realizes that he can actually understand their speech. Chapters 2, 4, 8, and 12 provide background material suggesting (but never really explaining) how he got that way in his childhood.

Those chapters drop back to 1946 and 1972 to provide written testimony concerning mysterious events that occurred in rural Yamanashi Province in 1944, the penultimate year of the Second World War. A 26-year-old woman named Setsuko Okamochi testifies to Allied occupation authorities that she was guiding a group of schoolchildren on a hike in the hills when something (possibly involving an American warplane) caused all the children to pass out. All but one of them, a nine-year-old boy named Nakata, came

276

out of their swoon unscathed, but Nakata spent three weeks in a coma and was so severely affected that he lost the ability to read and write, and his memory and capacity for learning were nearly non-existent thereafter. The teacher's follow-up letter of 1972, addressed to a Tokyo psychologist who had been an expert witness in the case, reveals that the carefully compiled documents that comprise those earlier chapters had been based on her false testimony. In fact, she had had a wildly erotic dream the night before that brought on a premature menstrual flow during her outing with the chidren, and she used a towel to stanch the unusually heavy rush of blood. When the children went into the woods to hunt for mushrooms, the Nakata boy came out holding the bloody towel, and she was so mortified and filled with sexual guilt that she beat him into unconsciousness. The other children were so shocked by the spectacle that they went into a group swoon and conveniently forgot everything that had happened.

Nakata's mental strangeness, then, began with blood and erotically tinged violence. And although he is a sweet, simple soul, his killing of Kafka's father (if that is what it is) is a horrendously violent and bloody scene. In fact, coming as it does after several chapters looking back to the Second World War and after Kafka's reading (in the other narrative, of course) of a book about Adolph Eichmann's bureaucratically brilliant extermination of the Jews, this chapter (16) is a searingly visceral demonstration of the impossibility of ending violence with violence. In a move that perhaps only Murakami could have pulled off, it raises the intensity of its unspoken – but intensely felt – message by introducing the reader to talking cats.

This business about the talking cats, plus the note of doubt in the previous paragraph, questioning whether what we take to be Nakata's killing of Kafka's father really is that, need some explaining. When he first enters the action at his present age of 60 plus,

Nakata really is just talking to a cat, the first of several with which he communes, speaking in his special stilted style. Chapter 6 begins:

"Hello there," the old man called out.
The large, elderly black tomcat raised its head a fraction and wearily returned the greeting in a low voice.
"A very nice spell of weather we're having."
"Um," the cat said.
"Not a cloud in the sky."
". . . for the time being."
"Is the weather going to take a turn for the worse, then?"[443]

If anything, the cat speaks more naturally than Nakata, whose idiosyncratic speaking style is one of the most widely admired features of the novel. He rarely uses personal pronouns to refer to himself, for example: he calls himself "Nakata". He is a gently comical character (in contrast to the deadly serious Kafka, who rarely smiles in the book),[444] and the many scenes involving cat talk are sweet and amusing. Given the third-person narrative and the lack of intrusive commentary by the narrator, however, there is nothing to call into question the reality of the cat's talk. We are not seeing the world through Nakata's eyes, and the seeming objectivity forces us either to accept the reality of what is presented or to throw up our hands in exasperation. Murakami never flinches as he brings on a cast of highly individualized cats, including the lovely Siamese Mimi (named for *La Bohème*'s heroine, she lives in a house with a cream-coloured BMW 530 parked out front)[445] and the well-meaning Kawamura-san, whose ineptness with language produces hilarious nonsense ("I don't mind at all, the tallest of heads").[446]

Nakata has been commissioned by a neighbourhood lady to find a missing cat called "Goma", but Mimi tells him the other cats think a local cat-catcher has got her. Several more cats have been captured recently by this "bad person".[447] When the naive Nakata can't imagine what such a person would do with snatched cats, Mimi enlightens him regarding the various scientific, musical instrument and gourmet possibilities, plus torture for its own sake, because "there are twisted people like that in this world".[448] She describes the cat-catcher as being very tall, wearing a strange tall hat and long leather boots. She also warns Nakata that he is an extremely dangerous man, adding, "This world is a terribly violent place. And nobody can escape the violence. Please keep that in mind."[449]

Nakata, however, cannot fully grasp what she means, though he is soon to find out. His fuddled, innocent mind is not much different from those of the placid souls living in peaceful democratic societies unaware that violence can attack them at any moment – in the form of Aum-style terrorism or the forces of nature or the intrusions of a self-righteous right-wing government. Nakata feels he has nothing to fear from the cat-catcher because he himself "was a person, not a cat".[450] In retrospect, however, this recalls the famous words attributed to German pastor Martin Niemöller (1892–1984): "In Germany they first came for the Communists, and I didn't speak up because I wasn't a Communist. Then they came for the Jews, and I didn't speak up because I wasn't a Jew. Then they came for the trade unionists, and I didn't speak up because I wasn't a trade unionist. Then they came for the Catholics, and I didn't speak up because I was a Protestant. Then they came for me, and by that time no one was left to speak up."[451]

The one who "comes for" Nakata is a big, black dog with bloodstains and chunks of flesh on his fangs. He guides Nakata to an old-fashioned house in an unfamiliar neighbourhood, and Nakata begins to feel uneasy. The dog shows him into a dark reception room or study, which could be the same room where Kafka took ¥400,000 of his father's money from a drawer.[452] The tall man

279

sitting in the shadows of this room, however, cannot possibly be Kafka's father, the famous sculptor Kōichi Tamura. His clothing comes straight out of nineteenth-century Europe. He wears a black silk top hat, a long-skirted, tight-fitting red jacket over a black waistcoat, flesh-tight white trousers and long black boots. His left hand grips a black walking stick with decorative gold knob.

"You know who I am, I assume?," he says to Nakata and is disappointed with Nakata's negative reply. He then strikes the pose of a man jauntily striding down the street, but still Nakata has no idea who he is. "Perhaps you're not a whisky drinker, then," he says, and Nakata affirms the accuracy of this observation.[453]

The man gives up and reveals his identity to Nakata: he is Johnnie Walker, the whisky icon. This still means nothing to the illiterate, non-drinking Nakata, but by this time, most readers are probably open-mouthed in amazement. Johnnie Walker?! What is *he* doing in this book? As if this in itself were not shocking enough, Johnnie Walker has the dog guide Nakata to the kitchen, where he finds a freezer full of decapitated cats' heads. Back in the study Johnnie Walker congratulates Nakata on the good timing of his arrival: Johnnie Walker says he is about to harvest a new crop of cats' heads, and among them will be Goma, the young female that Nakata has been hired to find. If, however, Nakata will do Johnnie Walker the favour of killing him, Goma will be allowed to escape unharmed. "First you fear me. Then you hate me. And finally you kill me," he says.

"But why – why ask *me*?" Nakata asks. "Nakata's never ever killed anyone before. It's not the kind of thing I'm any good at." Johnnie Walker replies:

"I know. You've never killed anyone, and don't want to. But listen to me – there are times in life when those kinds of excuses don't cut it any more. Situations when nobody cares whether you're suited for the task at hand or not. I need you

280

to understand that. For instance, it happens in war. Do you known what war is?"

"Yes, I do. There was a big war going on when Nakata was born. I heard about it."

"When a war starts people are forced to become soldiers. They carry guns and go to the front lines and have to kill soldiers on the other side. As many as they possibly can. Nobody cares whether you like killing other people or not. It's just something you have to do. Otherwise *you're* the one who gets killed." Johnnie Walker pointed his index finger at Nakata's chest. "Bang!" he said. "Human history in a nutshell."[454]

Johnnie Walker demands that Nakata make up his mind to kill him immediately. "The knack to killing someone, Mr Nakata, is not to hesitate. Focus your prejudice and execute it swiftly."[455] He then begins pulling cats out of a leather case one at a time, eviscerating them, and yanking out and eating their still-beating hearts. Goma will be the last one, he says. Like Adolph Eichmann, Johnnie Walker works methodically, but with an added touch: he whistles "Heigh-Ho!" like Disney's Seven Dwarfs. Nakata does not know the first cat, but the horror rises as his friends begin to emerge from the case. Suddenly the killing takes on a highly personalized aspect. This is no longer the disposal of faceless victims by an anonymous Kafkaesque machine but the slaughter of recognizable individuals. Now we know why Murakami let us become so intimately acquainted with his varied cast of cat characters. Those sweet, silly chapters prepared us to share Nakata's horror. First comes Kawamura, the cutely mixed-up speaker. Nakata has been feeling something inside himself changing, but still he cannot bring himself to kill Johnnie Walker before he kills Kawamura and savours his heart. Will Nakata kill to stop the killing? And if so, what will he gain? "This is war," Johnnie Walker reminds him. Then he pulls Mimi out of the bag.

"Johnnie Walker." Nakata groans. "*Please*, stop it. If you don't Nakata's going to go crazy. I don't feel myself any more."

Johnnie Walker answers calmly: "So, you're no longer yourself . . . That's very important, Mr Nakata. A person not being himself any more."[456]

Now it is time for even the gentle Nakata to act. He snatches up a large knife and plunges it into Johnnie Walker's stomach and then his heart. Johnnie Walker laughs aloud, coughs up the cats' hearts he has just eaten, and collapses at Nakata's feet. Everything and everyone are smeared with blood. Gathering up Mimi and Goma, Nakata sits on a sofa and sinks into darkness. He has killed to stop the killing, he has saved his friends from death, but in doing so he may have ceased to be the sweet old man we know as Nakata and instead joined with "human history in a nutshell", perpetuating the endless cycle of murder. What will he be like when next we meet him? Will he have regained his memory, killed so as to become a "normal" human being? Will he be able to read and write like normal civilized killers? Will he still be able to talk to cats? Murakami could have lectured his readers on the subject of war, but instead he has created this spellbinding surreal drama – using cats and a whisky logo! – to make us *feel* the dilemma faced by those who want peace but also human justice.

The bloody Chapter 16, then, is one of the most intense and profound pieces of writing that Murakami has ever produced, raising questions that haunt the memory of the blood-soaked twentieth century and continue to plague mankind in the twenty-first, which has got off to such a heartbreakingly violent start. The value – or success – of the novel must hinge on what Murakami does with the universal issues to which he has given such urgent expression.

Nakata's killing of Johnnie Walker has occurred at the exact time (and perhaps in the same house) as the killing of Kafka's father on 28 May – the time when Kafka, hundreds of miles away in Shikoku, loses consciousness for four hours and wakes in a shrine compound with blood on his hands and clothing. Although we will read "real" newspaper reports of the death of the sculptor Kōichi Tamura, this phantasmagorical narrative is all we will ever see of Nakata's or Kafka's involvement in the murder.

Johnnie Walker has to be one of Murakami's boldest challenges to the forces of high seriousness in the evaluation of literary art. Readers will face an equally bold challenge in later chapters with the sudden appearance of Kentucky Fried Chicken's Colonel Sanders as a pimp with supernatural powers. This second strange creature, who appears only to the truck driver Hoshino, looks just like Colonel Sanders, with the white suit and glasses and string tie, but he explains his supernatural powers by pointing out that "I'm neither a [Shinto] god nor a Buddha nor a human being. I'm something else again – a *concept*."[457] Murakami has latched on to these familiar – even beloved – symbols of worldwide corporate penetration and imbued them with unimaginable powers of evil, violence, and depravity. Johnnie Walker Black Label has long been a preferred gift in Japan from duty-free shops abroad, and because Kentucky Fried Chicken restaurants in Japan all have slightly evil-looking plastic models of Colonel Sanders standing out front, the Colonel may be an even more familiar figure there than in his native country. The healthy-eating Murakami is probably conscious, too, that the Colonel's fried chicken and other fast food, much of it exported to Japan, may be a significant contributor to American – and now Japanese – obesity. Japanese readers were shocked and confused by these enigmatic creations, said an interviewer, but Murakami draws some interesting parallels between them and his earlier writing:

The first character to come out of me like that was the Sheep

Man in *A Wild Sheep Chase*. I was not planning to bring such a character onstage: he just popped out while I was writing. This was something from the world of darkness, a being that lives in the other world. Johnnie Walker and Colonel Sanders are the same kind of thing – "performers" who appear from the darkness. There were a few who showed up in *The Wind-up Bird Chronicle*, too: Boris the Manskinner, say, appears to be a realistic character, not something from the other world, but I think he's probably the same kind of thing. Because he is there, the story is able to move off in a new direction.

While I'm writing, I'm not thinking: I don't know if they are good or evil. I still don't know whether the Sheep Man is good or evil, and it's the same with Johnnie Walker. What he does is surely evil, but I don't know how much of that is true. And Colonel Sanders? I have no idea what he's all about. Both of them give a kick to the flow of the story, help it to move along. Rather than whether they themselves are good or evil, the really big question for me is, What kind of direction do they give the story as they help it to move along? It may be that, depending on how you look at them, Colonel Sanders and Johnny Walker are the same thing appearing with different faces. This is a very real possibility. I don't know, though . . . I think the story would not have proceeded so successfully had those two icons not been present. I think, too, though, that there are a lot of people out there who can't accept such things.[458]

Murakami's interviewer agrees that most of the numerous negative reviews of the book complain that these figures are undecipherable. We need not appeal to Murakami's critics to fault his use of such devices, however: his own remarks all but confess that he makes them up to solve difficulties with the plot. If your story needs

Character A and Character B to meet at some point but you have described them as strangers living in different cities, you can work out some mundane real-world developments that bring them together (work schedules, plane connections, a taxi with a flat tyre), or you can have an exotic supernatural being appear in the dream of Character A telling him to dial the phone number of Character B as soon as he wakes up. All too often in this book, it seems as though Murakami has chosen the latter approach. When it becomes important at one point for Colonel Sanders to contact Nakata, for example, he calls him on his friend Hoshino's switched-off mobile phone, defying the laws of physics. (It is at this point that he calls himself a "concept".)

Kafka on the Shore uses such devices in ways that seem quite arbitrary, and its characters often move around more by rules of authorial convenience than by any consistent system of either fantasy or realism. Murakami appears to be making up the rules as he goes along, as if, say, in a vampire novel, we were suddenly to learn in the last chapter that vampires are vulnerable not only to garlic and the sign of the cross but *also* to ketchup, which allows the hero to defeat the vampire villain by feeding him a hamburger. Anything goes. More disappointing, however, is the novel's failure to answer the questions it raises at the end of the brilliant cat-killing scene in Chapter 16. What does it mean for a peaceful human being to participate in the ugliest core of human history by killing another person, even if the killing is meant to stop the other person from killing? How do killing and war change people, make them no longer who they once were? Everything in the first 15 chapters of the book leads to that bout of horrific bloodletting, but nothing in the subsequent 33 chapters rises to that level of enquiry, and the meticulously composed chapters concerning the wartime events in Nakata's childhood never figure in the narrative again.

Instead of changing into a virtually new human being (for which

Murakami has given us plenty of precedents: take *The Wind-up Bird Chronicle*'s Creta Kanō for example), Nakata remains the same mentally weak old sweetheart. He *does* lose his ability to talk to cats, but now he acquires the ability to talk to rocks (which, thankfully, do not make audible replies), and suddenly, in Chapter 24, he can diagnose and cure back pain. He is possessed by an inexplicable desire to travel westward and cross a bridge, and he can summon such creatures as fish or leeches to rain down from the sky. He has certainly "changed", but only in diverse ways that make him bizarre without adding up to a critique of violence in society. Murakami, it seems, failed to see what a profound document he had produced in the first 16 chapters of the book, and he lost the chance to make this novel a great comment on the human condition. Having emerged as the world's foremost killer in the name of peace and justice, the United States – the primary source of Murakami's literary vision – could have benefited from such a lesson most of all. Devoid of imagination, America's leaders know only the ethic of kill or be killed in a black-and-white world of good and evil.

Nakata's need to travel westward propels him through the rest of the novel. He has no idea where he is going, but "something" (never explained) draws him to Takamatsu, the exact same Shikoku city to which the young Kafka has fled, and his instincts bring him and his newly acquired travelling companion, the truck driver Hoshino, to the library where Kafka lives and works. Though he and Kafka are from the same Tokyo neighbourhood, they have never met. When Nakata and Hoshino arrive at the library on 10 June, Kafka is off in the deep woods of Shikoku, preparing to tramp his way into the other world in the company of ghostly Second World War soldiers, so the anticipated encounter between Nakata and Kafka never happens.

At the library, Nakata feels the need to meet Kafka's middle-aged lover, Saeki, head of the library and writer of the hit song from 25 years earlier, "Kafka on the Shore", a dreamy ballad full of enigmatic poetic imagery that just happens to relate to Nakata's raining fish and to the magical stone that marks his own entryway into the "other world". (The song also contained two unusual chords that contributed to its wide appeal.) They meet for the first and only time in their lives in the climactic Chapter 42, but Saeki declares that she has been waiting for him, and he apologizes for having taken so long to find her, as if he knew all along that she was his destination. She is a person trapped inside the memories of her past (she spends her time writing her voluminous memoirs with her Mont Blanc pen), while he is all but devoid of memory and lives only in the present.

"I feel as though I've known you for ages," she says. "Weren't *you* in that painting? A figure in the sea in the background?"[459] This was the picture of "Kafka on the Shore" that featured the one true love of her youth. The two also share knowledge of the "entrance stone". This was merely an evocative phrase in her song, but it took on great reality for Nakata when his companion Hoshino, guided by Colonel Sanders, found the miraculous stone in the grounds of a Shinto shrine (probably the same shrine in which Kafka had awakened after his four-hour blackout). In a ritual Nakata performed during a dramatic storm, he had "opened" the stone and, presumably, the entrance to the other world. He confesses to her that he killed a man in Tokyo. "I didn't want to kill anybody, but Johnnie Walker was in charge and I took the place of a 15-year-old boy who should've been there, and I murdered someone. Nakata had to do it."

Saeki then wonders, "Did all that happen because I opened the entrance stone a long time ago?" Nakata does not know the answer to her question, but he does know that "My role is to restore what's here now to the way it *should* be". It was for this purpose, he says, that he "left Nakano, went across a big bridge and came to Shikoku."[460]

How the two know all the things they know is by no means clear.

The level of contrivance here is mind-boggling, but Murakami seems comfortable with it:

> In the context of a story as I conceive it, everything can occur quite naturally. Even something like this long-distance killing of the father is naturalistic realism in the world as I conceive it, so there is nothing at all strange about, say, Nakata's doing the killing and the blood showing up on Kafka's hands. I would be hard-pressed to explain why this is so, but it's something that can happen as a matter of course.
>
> A lot of readers, though, say they don't get it. *Why* does Kafka have blood on his hands even though Nakata committed the murder? Because it can happen, that's why. *How* can such a thing happen? Because a story can express things at a level that transcends explanation, things that cannot be explained in an ordinary context. Because a story expresses things in a way that is different from other kinds of expression.[461]

One's reception of *Kafka on the Shore*, then, depends heavily on the degree of one's willingness to "go with the flow" of the story. To a reader less willing, Murakami seems to be relying far too heavily on contrivance and coincidence, and he too easily overlooks inconsistencies on the realistic plane. Take, for example, the amount of publicity concerning the murder of Kafka's father. It is in all the newspapers and on TV, but for some reason none of Kafka's Shikoku acquaintances know anything about it with the single exception of the young assistant librarian, Ōshima. He has been closely following the reports, many of which mention the desire of the police to question the dead Kōichi Tamura's son, whose name certainly would have been mentioned in the media, but still Ōshima remarks that he does not know Kafka Tamura's real name.[462] The degree of Nakata's memory loss is also inconsistent. After reading several times that his memory had been wiped out, we find him at points talking about "the occupation" and "bombs", and he experiences at least one flashback that leads into a detailed narrative of his childhood.[463] Nakata is stupid where the situation calls for him to be stupid, and he is almost eloquent when he needs to be more verbally expressive.

This is not to say that Murakami completely ignores all matters of realism. The composition of the Allied occupation authorities' documents on the "Rice Bowl Hill Incident" is accomplished with meticulous attention to verisimilitude, and often the narrative will spell out the minutiae of ordinary life to give rational explanations for how or why characters do what they do – matters such as the Japanese equivalent of birth certificates (*koseki*) or the downloading of information from the Internet, or getting discounts at a hotel, or lining up room reservations at the YMCA, or the differences in traceability between prepaid and subscribed mobile phones, or weight training at the gym (Kafka works hard to toughen himself physically). We know a good deal more than we need to about Nakata's finances and also about his bowel movements – sometimes to low comic effect.[464]

For long stretches of the novel, then, Murakami seems to accept the conventions of realistic fiction, but this only makes his departures from the rules of consistency (or physics) all the more disconcerting. And for scenes involving out-and-out encounters with the supernatural, the amount of purple prose thrown at the reader exceeds even the loud music played during *Sputnik Sweetheart*'s close encounters with the other world. When Nakata invokes the magic powers of his "entrance stone" to the other world, the thunder crashes and the wind blows with all the ferocity of a Bulwer-Lytton "dark and stormy night".

Another feature of the book that has been remarked upon, both approvingly and disapprovingly, is the extremely large number of references to works of literature and music – large even for Murakami, and with a surprisingly high proportion of nods to high culture rather than jazz or pop music (although Duke Ellington, John Coltrane, McCoy Tyner, the Beach Boys, Prince, and Cream are briefly mentioned). In this, the character Ōshima plays a major role. Having taken Kafka under his wing and arranged for him to live in the library, the 21-year-old Ōshima never misses an opportunity to wax eloquent on any topic that arises between them, be it high culture or the meaning of life. He speaks profoundly on Franz Kafka and "In the Penal Colony" (actually young Kafka himself is the one who comes up with an incredibly sophisticated comment on that story); the Japanese novelist Sōseki Natsume; the best colours for automobiles; the relationship of man and nature; Greek tragedy; Plato; issues of gender, sexuality, and love; Franz Schubert; the search for identity; T. S. Eliot; the art of sculpture; the subtleties of metaphor and symbolism; the psychology and ontology of ghosts; *The Tale of Genji*, its depiction of "living spirits", and the question of whether deep resentment can leave the body and inflict injury on the object of hatred (which, we are invited to conclude, is probably how Kafka killed his father); the Edo-period fabulist Akinari Ueda (1734–1809); opera; the Spanish Civil War; Rousseau; Australian Aborigines; the nature of human freedom; Hansel and Gretel; and the guts as the original model for the interior human labyrinth. Some of these topics come in for repeated discussion by Ōshima's ever-open and active mouth. (Yeats, Mozart, novelist Jun'ichirō Tanizaki, Adolph Eichmann, and the Richard Burton translation of *The Thousand and One Nights* are commented upon elsewhere. Beethoven comes in for extended treatment, too, but that mainly happens in the Nakata narrative, as the truck driver Hoshino opens his soul to this elevating source of spiritual enrichment.)

Earlier, we noted Murakami's tendency towards an indirect didacticism, but here the didactic element is anything but indirect. Asked if he had consciously loaded this novel with so many references, Murakami answered:

> Of course . . . Citation and erudition were extremely important for me in this novel. After all, the protagonist is a 15-year old boy, so it's important for him to pass through lots of different things. I myself crammed in knowledge from many areas as I grew up; the knowledge really comes pouring in at that time of life, like rain soaking into parched earth . . . If you do something like this in the story of a mature adult, it can come off as affectation, but for a young person it's really important . . . Ōshima imparts his erudition regarding Schubert's piano sonata while he's driving. Some people might think he's just showing off his knowledge and be repelled by it, but he's using this to convey something to the boy Kafka.[465]

In a conversation with the psychologist Hayao Kawai, Murakami has said:

> Since passing the age of 50, I've become increasingly conscious of the question of generation. This may sound a little heavy, but after a point, something like "a generational sense of responsibility" begins to enter your field of vision as a matter of course. I myself don't have any children, but if I did, they would be somewhere around 20 years old, and it would be time for me to pass something on to them
>
> **Kawai:** Many of your readers are the age that your children would be, aren't they?
>
> **Murakami:** That's true. "Passing something on" sounds fairly formal, though, like looking down from above, but that's not what I mean. It's more like having naturally become conscious of it as a personal problem for myself: "What do I

want to pass on?" It's more of a feeling than a stiff posture.[466]

Readers fond of the cool, detached Murakami of old may bridle at this growing sense of high purpose and the accompanying preponderance in *Kafka* of high culture, but most readers have reacted well to this and to the prime didactic fountainhead, Ōshima. Respondents to a survey posed on Murakami's *Kafka on the Shore* web page ranked Ōshima as the character they would most like to play if the book were ever staged as a drama.[467]

This is a little bit surprising, since Ōshima is a rather odd sexual stew. When two grim feminists visit the library to critique everything from its supposedly sexist cataloguing techniques to its failure to provide a separate ladies' room, Ōshima puts them in their place with a sarcastic lecture on the difference between gender and sex and a revelation that is meant to shock everyone – the feminists, Kafka, and the reader. He can't be a typical unconscious male chauvinist, he says, because he is not a male. Providing rather more information than anyone really wants to know, he says:

"My body is physically female, but my mind's completely male . . . Emotionally I live as a man . . . But I'm not a lesbian, even though I dress this way. My sexual preference is for men. In other words, I'm a female but I'm gay. I do anal sex, and have never used my vagina for sex. My clitoris is sensitive but my breasts aren't. I don't have periods. So, what am I discriminating against? Could somebody enlighten me?"[468]

Exactly what Murakami is getting at here it is hard to say. Ōshima's sexuality seems directly relevant only in this chapter (Chapter 19) to provide a startling put-down to the cartoon-like one-dimensional feminists. The scene, however, is a poorly conceived critique of doctrinaire feminism (and prejudice in general) because it seems to adopt a male-chauvinist position that suggests that all feminists are humourless prigs. One otherwise enthusiastic female reader took Murakami to task for this on his web page, earning an apology and explanation from the author to the effect that he was satirizing narrow-minded, self-righteous, judgemental people in general and did not believe that all feminists were like the ones in the book.[469]

Concerning Ōshima's sexuality, Murakami told an interviewer that he had almost no choice but to make him sexually strange:

I needed a certain degree of "deformity" in Ōshima. A face that combined a fish and a cat, say, would have been a kind of deformation, but that wouldn't work in a novel. He plays the role of a clean-cut youth, which means that his deformity has to be internal – i.e., sexual, genital. Or so it seems to me. Ōshima is by his very nature innocent, lacking any kind of impurity. I'm not sure how to put this, but I have a strong sense of purity in hermaphroditism . . . Only a person like this could be a guide for Kafka, I think.[470]

The nearly unrelieved seriousness of the young Kafka chapters might be another disappointment for fans of the lighter, brighter Murakami, but the even-numbered Nakata chapters are full of horseplay, especially after the Forrest Gumpish Nakata teams up with the young truck driver Hoshino, loved by readers for his ponytail and Chūnichi Dragons baseball cap. One character who appears in both narratives, though, the lovely – if middle aged – Saeki, the "mother figure" with whom Kafka sleeps in fulfilment of his father's curse, goes beyond seriousness to sheer melodrama. She is a tortured soul who spends her days writing her memoirs only to hand them over to Nakata with a command that he burn them, after which she dies with dramatically impeccable timing. One can almost hear the strains of Verdi playing in the background when she enters the scene. So intense is her longing for her lost "Kafka by the shore" that the ghost of her 15-year-old self separates from her still living body. On whatever metaphorical level Kafka is able to bond with her, she helps to heal his endless (and rather whiny) longing for his mother and enables him to return to society with a new level of maturity.

Young Kafka

The popularity of *Kafka on the Shore* was evident not only in terms of sales but also in an outpouring of reader response when Shinchōsha established a web page to which readers could address email with the reasonable hope that they might receive answers from "Haruki-san" himself. Altogether 8,870 messages were received by the home page between 12 September and 20 December 2002, and Murakami wrote replies to 1,220 of them. This two-way correspondence then was committed to print, forming yet another – and particularly colourful – Murakami mountain in bookshops in June 2003. *Young Kafka* was a boldly conceived publication. Modelled after boys' cartoon magazines, it has the same kind of thick binding, and its cover is emblazoned with the same kind of wildly excited headlines that such magazines use. When a web page staff person expressed her amazement at the cover, editor Riki Suzuki replied, "This was Haruki-san's idea."[471] It is not hard to imagine how much fun Murakami, illustrator Mizumaru Anzai and the staff at Shinchōsha had putting it together. The cover proclaims its low ¥950 price in one corner and goes on to shout at potential readers:

Haruki Murakami, Editor-in-Chief

Young Kafka

Finally – the First (and Last) *Kafka on the Shore* Magazine
is in Print!
Gives You Ten Times the Reading Pleasure from
Kafka on the Shore!!!
Bare-Knuckle Brawl with Readers' Emails!
Murakami-san Answers a Surging Wave of 1220 Messages!!
496 Pages Eagerly Awaited by Haruki Murakami Fans!
Special Interview with Haruki Murakami
Book Factory Tour with Mizumaru Anzai
Complete Record of the *Kafka on the Shore* Home Page
A Must-Read for All *Kafka on the Shore* Fans!

Kafka on the Shore elicited many positive responses, but also some negative ones, and the balanced editing of *Young Kafka* reflects that. Mizumaru Anzai has applied cute little logos to many of the messages, including an erupting volcano to mark those expressing reader dissatisfaction. One reader, for example, took Murakami to task for "the thin characterization of [the "sister" figure] Sakura", adding, "The act of 'rape' felt unconvincing to me: it came out of nowhere . . . I wondered why the world had to be so full of meaningless sex and violence." Murakami's reply did not directly address the criticism of thinness of characterization, but to the objection regarding meaningless violence, he had this to say: "It seems to me that one of the first things we have to recognize is that meaningless violence is a fact; it's all around us."[472]

The vast majority of emails expressed how deeply moved readers were by the events or characters in the novel, how many times they had already read the book (three, five, ten times!), how devoted they were to Murakami's writing in general, how much strength the book gave them to deal with emotional and interpersonal difficulties in their own lives, and so on. Some readers complained about excessive echoes of earlier works, the number of plot questions left unresolved, the uneasiness they felt with the 15-year-old hero's sex with his "mother figure", Ōshima's sermonizing, or the presence of factual inconsistencies, but these negative remarks were often accompanied by apologies and assurances that the writer of the comment was a long-time fan who had enjoyed most or all of Murakami's earlier works.

Murakami's replies to these often took the form of assurances regarding natural discrepancies in literary taste. Some readers complained that the website itself was part of an overheated sales campaign, whereupon Murakami maintained that the site had nothing to do with sales: it was something that he himself had instituted to provide an unrestricted exchange of views, both positive and negative, between his readers and himself: "direct democracy".[473] Murakami commits himself to this Internet correspondence with his readers almost as energetically as he does to his fiction. He may have begun to develop into a kind of spiritual counsellor at this stage of his life, but he is still no authority figure: the communication always moves in two directions.

The Catcher in the Rye

The link between *Kafka on the Shore* and *Young Kafka* is obvious, but the translation of *The Catcher in the Rye* was also linked to Murakami's new novel in various ways, most notably in Murakami's handling of Salinger's narrative voice. This refers specifically to Murakami's decision to use the Japanese quasi-pronoun *"kimi"* (the same word used by "the boy named Crow" to address Kafka) for the English pronoun "you" as employed by the narrator/hero Holden Caulfield. We see this in the original from the opening sentence: "If you really want to hear about it, the first thing you'll probably want to know is where I was born, and what my lousy childhood was like . . ."[474] Murakami's handling of this feature of the style has been noted by Motoyuki Shibata, who remarks on the similarity of the 15-year-old dropout Kafka and the 16-year-old dropout Holden. Like other commentators, Shibata says, he, too, had assumed a direct influence of Salinger on Murakami, but was told by Murakami that the invitation to translate *The Catcher in the Rye* had only come from the publisher after he had completed the first draft of *Kafka on the Shore*.[475]

Of course, Murakami had been deeply immersed in – and hoping to translate – *The Catcher in the Rye* for many years, so the question of influence is not so easily dispensed with. Murakami himself suggests that Salinger might have had a subtler, less conscious influence on him than other writers such as Brautigan and Vonnegut, of whom he was more fond.[476] As Shibata's remarks suggest, however, the Murakami version of *The Catcher in the Rye* and *Kafka on the Shore* share qualities that make their appearance at this time in Murakami's career more than a matter of coincidence. The critic Masashi Miura had recently published a fascinating book-length study, in which he documented the gigantic impact that both Murakami and Shibata, as translators, were having on the shape of contemporary Japanese literature, and examined in great detail the subtle interplay between translation and original fiction in Murakami's case.[477]

The close relationship in Murakami between translation and the creation of original fiction could be almost physically perceived in bookshops after his *The Catcher in the Rye* appeared in April 2003 at a time when there was still a good deal of excitement over *Kafka on the Shore*. Many bookshops displayed piles of both books. The new

Murakami translation was often stacked alongside the still-available older translation and the Salinger original, inspiring readers to do some comparative reading.

Anyone genuinely interested in questions of "literary influence" between Japan and the US, however, would have to read David Mitchell, Richard Powers, Steven Millhauser, and others who have expressed admiration for – or a debt to – Murakami's work. Motoyuki Shibata has gone so far as to suggest that contemporary American writers are just beginning to "catch up with Murakami".[478] Though that remark in an interview seemed to embarrass Murakami some-what, he did offer an account of a recent experience that had brought home to him how much his work had penetrated markets abroad:

> A little while ago I went to Sakhalin. They have department stores there, but no supermarkets. Instead, all they have for shoppers is outdoor bazaars. They don't even have book-stores or CD shops. Nothing. You have to go to a bazaar for such things, too. Old women buy books in Siberia, swing a sack of them over their shoulder and haul them over on the ferry. They spread out their wares and sell them that way. It's all governed by market forces – and weight. There's no such thing as putting out good books that might not sell. Every little bookseller carries only books that will sell. And *all* of them have my books. I almost fell over when I saw that . . . Nobody had *A Wild Sheep Chase*, though. Somebody told me it's because they sell out of it right away.[479]

Birthday Stories

If *Kafka on the Shore* was a major addition to the work of Murakami as a novelist, the English edition of *Birthday Stories: Selected and*

Introduced by Haruki Murakami, published by Harvill Press on 12 January 2004 to coincide with Haruki's own fifty-fifth birthday, marked the emergence of a Japanese novelist as a world literary figure in a whole new way. Kenzaburō Ōe and Yukio Mishima both edited English-language publications of Japanese literature for a Western audience, but never had a Japanese writer been handed the literary authority to choose and comment upon works by Western writers for an English-speaking audience. The book contains a dozen stories, including one of Murakami's own, and others by William Trevor, Russell Banks, Paul Theroux, Raymond Carver, Denis Johnson, Ethan Canin, David Foster Wallace, Andrea Lee, Daniel Lyons, Lynda Sexson, and Claire Keegan. While the Japanese edition of the book was primarily a work of translation, with only Murakami's delightful and slightly disturbing "Birthday Girl" ("Bāsudei gāru") in the original Japanese, the English edition contains only one translated work, this same story of Murakami's. The rest of the stories are in the language from which Murakami's writing has derived so much nourishment. Murakami's introductory material, full of personal insights and perceptive comments on the anthologized writers, speaks with ease and assurance to a non-Japanese audience who accept his standing as an important literary voice whose nationality is almost irrelevant.

Indeed, the very *lack* of drama in the genesis of the English edition suggests how fully Murakami has come to be accepted abroad without the kind of exoticism that greeted Akutagawa, with his Heian-period costume dramas, or Kawabata, with his geisha and tea ceremonies, or Mishima, with his self-immolating modern samurai.

It all started from a conversation between Amanda Urban, Murakami's New York literary agent, and Christopher MacLehose, his British publisher. MacLehose expressed his interest in having something of Murakami's to publish in Britain while waiting for the translation of *Kafka on the Shore* to be completed. Urban would not ordinarily have known of the existence of the Japanese edition of *Birthday Stories*, which was strictly for a Japanese audience, but as agent for several of the American authors included in the anthology, her office had handled the permissions and so she knew that Murakami had done the book. She suggested an English version to MacLehose, and he liked the idea.

As Urban unceremoniously recounts it, "Haruki is certainly popular enough in the UK now to make plausible a collection edited by him, so it didn't seem like such a far stretch."[480] In other words, to her and to the British publisher it seemed like a perfectly natural idea. In terms of modern Japanese literary history, however, such a development was practically revolutionary.

As the translator of several Murakami works, I was frequently impressed by how little was known about Murakami's career – not only by his general foreign readership but by people in the publishing world who were actively engaged in promoting his works abroad. One of my central purposes in writing this book was to provide both general readers and literary professionals with factual information that was easily available to any Japanese reader: information about Murakami's life and the chronological development of his works, plus the broad range of American fiction he had translated.

The English-speaking audience first became aware of Murakami as the author of *A Wild Sheep Chase*, and they assumed that this was his first novel. After that, both early and late stories appeared in British and American magazines in no chronological order, and each new work was thought to be Murakami's latest. It seemed amazing to me that such sophisticated members of the British and American publishing elite as the editors of *The New Yorker*, *Granta*, The Harvill Press, and Alfred A. Knopf were almost wholly lacking basic factual information even as they committed the resources and reputations of their companies to publishing Murakami's writings. But while those people lacked any historical context within which to evaluate Murakami's work, what they possessed was impeccable literary taste. Amanda Urban and Christopher MacLehose may not realize what an unprecedented step they have taken in terms of Japanese literary history, but that in itself attests to the power of Murakami's writing to speak to readers far beyond the shores of Japan.

Far Beyond Cult Status

If *Birthday Stories* was a suggestion of broad interest in Murakami's writing in the English-speaking world early in 2004, several events over the next few years provided especially vivid illustrations of the writer's growing fame, both at home and abroad.

In Japan, several publications noted in 2004 that 25 years had gone by since Murakami's literary debut, and they attempted to account for his staying power. Japan's leading newspaper, the *Asahi Shimbun*, carried a full-page feature with revealing interviews. Psychologist Kayama Rika (b. 1960) felt that Murakami had seen through to the emptiness of her generation's mindless pursuit of sensual gratification in the early 80s and laid bare her own secret thoughts. The most common reaction among admirers both in Japan and abroad seems to be a sense of identification with his reassuringly muted voice. As filmmaker Tatsuya Mori (b. 1956) has noted, Murakami is disarmingly honest: "He doesn't pretend to understand what he doesn't understand." Reader and writer experience the mystery of life together.[481]

In March 2005 Shinchōsha published a special commemorative Japanese edition of Murakami's first English-language short story collection, *The Elephant Vanishes*, as a reflection at home of what the author had accomplished abroad. The book's cover proclaimed,

"Seventeen Early Murakami Short Stories Chosen by New York: Sent to You in the Same Format as the English Edition." In several ways, however, the contents of the book were not exactly the same as the English "original". For one thing, the version of "Lederhosen" was Murakami's Japanese re-translation of Alfred Birnbaum's edited English translation, which he found to be "a pretty good work in its own right. I hope my readers will enjoy it as a kind of game and not be too hard on it."[482] More importantly, the volume contained an introduction by Gary Fisketjon, the Knopf editor who assembled the volume in 1993, and a meditative introduction by Murakami himself entitled "Back Then: When *The Elephant Vanishes* was Published in America."

By nature, such a volume was necessarily retrospective, but Fisketjon pointed out that "like any truly extraordinary writer Haruki always looks to the challenges of the future instead of the accomplishments of the past . . . Viewed as a whole, these seventeen stories do exactly what I had hoped: they show that Haruki's versatile genius has a truly international reach, which has subsequently been demonstrated by the ten books of his we now have in print, the sales of each rising every year (the eleventh, *Kafka on the Shore,* will be published next month)."[483]

In his introduction to the Japanese edition of *The Elephant Vanishes*, Murakami recalls his joy and amazement upon hearing the news in 1990 that Alfred Birnbaum's translation of "TV People" had been accepted for publication by *The New Yorker*. "For me, the *New Yorker* had always been sacred territory, something close to legend or myth."[484] In 1993, he notes, he signed a contract giving the magazine the right of first refusal with all his translated stories. (Twelve pieces of Murakami's had appeared in the magazine by the time he wrote this introduction, a number that has already grown to at least sixteen.) Around this time, Murakami also contracted to publish his books with Knopf, the most prestigious publisher in America, thus setting his career abroad on the most favorable track a writer could hope for. The hardcover edition of *The Elephant Vanishes* sold poorly, but in paperback the book has never been out of print.

As a member of *The New Yorker* stable, Murakami was photographed in 1994 by the renowned photographer Richard Avedon with such luminaries as John Updike, Nicholson Baker, and Alice Munro. When the group went out for a drink afterward, Updike made a point of complimenting him on his work. Murakami remarks, "He was just being polite, of course, the veteran writer offering encouragement to a newcomer, but hearing this still made me very happy. I could recall how my chest had all but burst open when I read his beautiful novel *Centaur* at the age of 15. Now here I was, face-to-face with that very author, engaging in conversation with him as a fellow novelist. Suddenly I felt as if I were 15 again, kind of like the protagonist of my *Kafka on the Shore*. I felt strongly, too, that, whatever difficulties I might have had in writing over the years, I was glad I had kept at it and made it this far."[485]

In May 2005, Haruki and Yōko traveled back to Cambridge, Massachusetts for an extended stay: the call of those used record stores was irresistible. This time, Murakami was designated an Artist-in-Residence at the Reischauer Institute of Japanese Studies at Harvard University and given a spacious office in the Institute's newly-constructed building. If he was hoping to find the kind of anonymity he had enjoyed back in 1993–95, however, he was sadly mistaken. The minute word got out that he was at Harvard, requests started pouring in for him to talk at a variety of U.S. venues. Murakami himself helped to dash any hopes of anonymity by telling a *New York Times* interviewer about his new arrangement at Harvard, and he quickly found the office of use not only for writing but for interviews with the press and academics. One young scholar from New Zealand found his way there, as did journalists from Germany, England, and the U.S. People recognized him on the street and stopped him to chat. The contrast between this and his low-key stay of 1993–95 was dramatic. No longer was he just the darling of university Japanese literature programs: a broad new public now wanted a piece of him.

Things came to a head on Thursday, 6 October, when Murakami was scheduled to deliver a reading in the MIT Writers Series. This was a particularly prestigious invitation, coming as it did not from the university's Japan program but the MIT Program in Writing and Humanistic Studies, which numbered among its invitees such literary stars as Michael Ondaatje, Susan Sontag, Salman Rushdie, Ben Okri, Saul Bellow, Jonathan Lethem, Russell Banks, Jhumpa Lahiri, Barry Yourgrau, Paul Auster, and Cynthia Ozick. The organizers were shocked, however, when their largest venue, an auditorium that had always been roomy enough for admirers of even the best-known writers, proved disastrously inadequate. Not only were all 500 seats filled long before starting time, but the aisles were crammed with eager listeners, as was the entire stage area surrounding the speaker's podium. The crowd outside, which filled the long, broad corridor leading to the auditorium doors, was estimated by University police to amount to some 1,300. To make matters worse, the auditorium's air-conditioning system broke down, and the "lucky" ones inside were fanning themselves with books and magazines in a vain attempt to evaporate the sweat that clung to every brow.

Before the proceedings could begin, however, the University fire marshals looked in and declared that there could be no reading until all the aisles and floor space were emptied out, leaving "only" the 500 people actually occupying seats. A moan went through the crowd, and some disappointed fans were seen weeping as they reluctantly made their way out to join the late arrivals in the corridor. One woman ejected at this time had flown all the way from Cincinnati, Ohio after learning of the event on the Internet. One of those able to remain inside, a participant in the question-and-answer session afterward, said that she and a carload of friends had driven up from Virginia. The audience was overwhelmingly of college age and noticeably Asian, but there was a great variety in terms of age and nationality.

Murakami was allowed to enter the hall after the aisles were cleared. He quickly shed his sports coat when the body heat of 500 unventilated listeners hit him, and soon his dark green "Pickle" T-shirt was stained with sweat as he listened to the novelist Junot Diaz introduce him with the words: "Murakami reveals to us the world, not as we've never seen it before, but as we see it daily without knowing." After the applause died down, Murakami told a few humorous anecdotes about his experiences as a famous writer not always able to live anonymously in Tokyo. Then he read from the story "Super-Frog Saves Tokyo". His standard technique in doing readings for non-Japanese audiences is to read a few pages in Japanese to give some idea of the music of the original, then read the same passage in the English translation, and hand over the rest of the story to one of his hosts – in this case, the poet William Corbett, a writer-in-residence at MIT. For those people lucky enough to have been allowed to remain in the auditorium, it was a delightful (if sultry) evening.

Even some of the smaller-scale appearances Murakami made in the fall of 2005 partook of the fever. When he spoke at Bowdoin College in Brunswick, Maine on 14 October, Murakami requested that the event be kept more intimate, but the only way that could be accomplished even at this small college two hours from Boston was to limit attendance to 35 students of Japanese language, Japanese studies and literature. After Professors Tom Conlon and Vyjayanthi Selinger introduced Murakami, this select group got to ask him about his work for an hour and a half. Murakami enjoyed the small event itself, and got an unexpected bonus when he found a rare jazz record at a Brunswick record store.[486]

On 2 November Murakami made a sentimental return to Tufts University, where he had taught eleven years earlier. The event had been deliberately less well publicized, but still Tufts had to change the venue to a fair-sized auditorium in order to accommodate the demand. Professor Hosea Hirata, his old friend from Princeton, interviewed him and flashed English translations of selections from *The Spider Monkey Comes at Night* (*Yoru no kumozaru*, 1995) and other short pieces on a screen as Murakami did his readings entirely in Japanese.

Before his next public appearance, Murakami ran in the New York Marathon on 6 November. His official time was 4:10:17, which meant that 11,251 other runners finished before him, but only 340 of those had reached or surpassed his age of 56. His marathon times were growing longer with his advancing years, but he remained in remarkable shape, and would run again in the Boston Marathon on 17 April, 2006 (official time: 4:00:45).

The day after the New York Marathon, Murakami did a reading at Hofstra University in Hempstead, New York as part of the "Great Writers, Great Readings" series, another event that placed him on a roster of distinguished literary figures irrespective of nationality. Again the hall was filled to overflowing, and people arrived with armloads of books they wanted Murakami to sign.

Murakami fulfilled his obligation as an Artist-in-Residence of the Reischauer Institute by delivering a public lecture on 18 November, 2005. In a Reischauer talk at Harvard a decade earlier, he had spoken in Japanese to a roomful of perhaps 40 people, mostly Japanese students and members of the Japanese community of Boston. The organizers of this event, however, the Reischauer Institute and the Harvard Book Store, had witnessed the recent chaos at MIT and reserved the biggest venue available, a church near campus, and instituted a ticketing system to keep the numbers from getting out of hand. The main hall of the church held some 600 listeners, and closed-circuit television was fed into two adjoining rooms for a total close to 800. This still meant turning away over 1,000 people who entered the Harvard Book Store's ticket lottery or applied to the Reischauer Institute, but at least there were no threats from the fire marshals – and the lady from Cincinnati was finally able to secure a ticket and get a book signed by her favorite author.

Murakami did not disappoint his expectant audience. He put a lot of effort into this English-language lecture and delivered a talk that was both personal and broadly philosophical. Publicized far in advance with the title "Frogs, Earthquakes, and the Joys of Short Fiction", the talk finally came together as a general affirmation of the power of narrative in life and art. Aspiring writers in the audience came away inspired to trust the products of their own creativity, and fans were given fresh assurance that the dreams and images they enjoyed sharing with Murakami had come from someplace deep inside him.

He chose to speak about short stories that day, he said, because he had recently completed his five-story collection *Strange Tales from Tokyo* (*Tōkyō kitanshū*, September, 2005) and because the next book of his to be published in English (by Knopf in September 2006) was to be a collection of 24 short stories, *Blind Willow, Sleeping Woman*, containing such classics as "A Poor-Aunt Story", "The Year of Spaghetti," "New York Mining Disaster", and "Tony Takitani", plus all five stories of *Strange Tales from Tokyo*.[487] Murakami's Introduction to *Blind Willow, Sleeping Woman* echoes much of what he said in Cambridge that day: "I find writing novels a challenge, writing short stories a joy." In both the talk and the introduction, Murakami points out how liberating it is for him to write short fiction: it doesn't require the enormous commitment of time and physical energy of a novel, and allows him to experiment with materials that come to him spontaneously: "[Y]ou can create a story out of the smallest details – an idea that springs up in your mind, a word, an image, whatever. In most cases it's like jazz improvisation, with the story taking me where it wants to." In the talk, Murakami went so far as to outline the procedure whereby he made a list of phrases almost at random, chose three items from the list for each story, and built his five stories for *Strange Tales from Tokyo* around those 15 items. It was a kind of game, he said, but he insisted that it was not *merely* a game because the phrases came from inside him. He could conclude in the introduction, therefore: "Short stories are like guideposts to my heart, and it makes me happy as a writer to be able to share these intimate feelings with my readers."[488]

If there was any one message in the talk, it was that of trust. Writers should trust the wave of inspiration that flows through them and try to catch it at its peak. And both readers and writers should trust the ancient power of narrative. We may never be able to prove that storytelling has any innate value: any healing effect it might have might not become evident for years – perhaps "ten thousand years", to put it in terms of "A Poor-Aunt Story." Here, Murakami is echoing the early affirmation of faith in narrative he gave in *Hear the Wind Sing*: "And yet I find myself thinking that if everything goes well, sometime way ahead, years, maybe decades from now, I might discover myself saved. And then, at that time, the elephant will return to the plain, and I shall begin to tell the tale of the world in words more beautiful than these."

While Murakami was speaking about his own short fiction to his audience in Cambridge, touching upon both his newest stories and giving special mention to "Super-Frog Saves Tokyo" from *after the quake*, the Steppenwolf Theatre in Chicago was performing Frank Galati's stage adaptation of two stories from *after the quake*. The reviews were strong, and the production ran from 20 October, 2005 to 19 February, 2006, after which it moved to the Long Wharf Theatre in New Haven, Connecticut from 22 February to 19 March, 2006.

Galati's version of *after the quake* combines one of the most solidly down-to-earth stories with the most wildly fantastic one: "Honey Pie", about a short-story writer who longs for the woman he lost to his best friend, and "Super-Frog Saves Tokyo", in which a six-foot-tall, highly literate talking frog visits a bank employee to seek his help in fighting a monstrous subterranean worm that is threatening to destroy Tokyo with a massive earthquake. Galati's imaginative (fantasy)-story-within-a-(realistic)-story dramatic structure gives tangible – and often hilarious – representation to the internal stresses of Murakami's more earthbound characters. Just as Murakami presents his alternate worlds as matter-of-fact parts of everyday life, the fantastic side of the play is presented without special effects or stylization to distinguish it from the realistic side: the two blend seamlessly. The stage production captures Murakami's uncanny ability to treat the big questions in life – What's it all about? Where do human values of love and commitment fit in to the cosmic scheme of things? How do you keep a croaking giant frog from waking your neighbours? – without becoming ponderous or losing his sense of humour.

Neither Murakami nor a dedicated fan would find anything about the play that subverts the author's original intention. In fact, if there is a problem with the play, it's that the adaptation for the stage is almost too respectful. To a degree I have seen before only in Japan's medieval Nō drama, with its substantial narrative element, the production is a group reading of the text, with actors shifting smoothly from first-person dialogue to third-person narration as though such a thing were entirely natural. Whole pages are taken right out of the book even where, with a little cutting and pasting, there could be more showing and less telling. At the Steppenwolf, *after the quake* was performed in the upstairs experimental theatre rather than the main hall, and unless it is more fully dramatized in the future (and perhaps expanded by incorporating scenes from some of the other stories), it will probably remain confined to little

309

theatres rather than getting the wider audience it deserves.

This broad attention to Murakami was reflected in the rapid-fire magazine publication of his stories in English translation. *The New Yorker* carried three of the stories from *Strange Tales from Tokyo*: "Where I'm Likely to Find It" in May, "The Kidney-Shaped Stone That Moves Every Day" in September, and before "A Shinagawa Monkey" appeared in February 2006, the magazine also carried the old "The Year of Spaghetti" in November. "Chance Traveler" appeared in *Harper's* in July 2005. When the new year arrived, the *New York Times* put another feather in Murakami's cap by naming *Kafka on the Shore* one of the five best novels of 2005, and indeed put *Kafka* at the head of the list. Shortly afterward, a society called The Associates of the Boston Public Library took notice of Murakami's presence in the Boston area by inviting him to be named one of eleven "Literary Lights" at a formal black tie presentation on 30 April, 2006. This event honours "outstanding New England writers" and raises money for conservation at the Boston Public Library. In the past, writers such as poets Robert Pinsky, Seamus Heaney, and Rosanna Warren, critic Harold Bloom, historian John Dower, and novelists Nicholson Baker, Saul Bellow, Tim O'Brien, and John Updike had been among the honourees.

One other noteworthy indication of Murakami's stature arrived in the form of an invitation to write an introduction to a new Penguin Classic published in 2006: *Rashōmon and Seventeen Other Stories* by Ryūnosuke Akutagawa (1892–1927), translated by Jay Rubin. The suggestion that Murakami be asked to write an introduction was made by a Penguin editor, not the translator, who was thrilled that Murakami agreed immediately to take on the task. Clearly, the publishers felt that Akutagawa stood a better chance of attracting the attention of a broad audience with Murakami's name on the cover. Murakami could well have approached the work cynically by viewing this as a mere sales ploy, but he was too dedicated to literature in general, too respectful of Akutagawa in particular, and too aware of his role as a Japanese writer in the wider world to let himself do anything less than his best. He was asked to write 3,000 words, but the introduction he wrote came closer to 7,000 words, and the editors found it too valuable a contribution to cut.

Since Murakami tends to downplay his familiarity with the Japanese canon, it is refreshing to see him embracing it in his Akutagawa introduction. Sōseki and Tanizaki, he says, are his favourites among Japan's writers of national stature, with Akutagawa a somewhat distant third. He recounts for readers abroad how, as a typical Japanese schoolchild, he came to read some of Akutagawa's more popular works and then, as an independent reader, he went on to grapple with the darker, more challenging late works. He discusses Akutagawa's stylistic brilliance, drawing parallels to F. Scott Fitzgerald, and asks, "Has Akutagawa left behind a lesson for Japan's contemporary writers (including me)? Of course he has, both as a great pioneer and, in part, as a negative example." From Akutagawa, Japanese writers can learn that "It is possible to borrow the containers for our first stories, but sooner or later we have to transform the borrowed container into our own." Central to this issue is the question of a Japanese writer's encounter with Western culture:

The other lesson he has for us concerns the way we overlay the two cultures of the West and Japan. With great pain and suffering, the self-consciously "modern" Akutagawa groped for his identity as a writer and as an individual in the clash of the two cultures, and just at the point where he had begun to find what was, for him, a hint of a way to fuse the two, he unexpectedly ended his life. For those of us in the current age, this is by no means someone else's problem. Long after Akutagawa's time, we are still (with some differences) living

311

amid the clash of things Western and Japanese, only now we may call them things "global" and "domestic".[489]

Murakami's introduction, then, tells us a great deal about Akutagawa and about Murakami himself. His introduction to the 2009 Penguin edition of Sōseki's *Sanshirō*, would embrace that 1908 novel with special warmth, indicating parallels with his own *Norwegian Wood* and recalling his early married life as depicted in "Shaped More Like a Slice of Cheesecake Than Flat Broke".

International attention to Murakami received unusual recognition at home in the form of a major international symposium sponsored by The Japan Foundation. Titled "A Wild Haruki Chase: How the World is Reading and Translating Murakami", with a number of symposiums, workshops, and retreats, the event took place in Tokyo, Yamanashi, Kobe, and Sapporo from 25 to 29 March, 2006, and included Murakami translators, and scholars from France, Brazil, Canada, Germany, Hungary, Denmark, Indonesia, Czechoslovakia, Norway, South Korea, Russia, Taiwan, Hong Kong, China, Poland, and the United States. For the general public, attendance at the public events required an application by email or fax and was subject to a lottery system. Internet announcements of the event were careful to note: "Haruki Murakami himself is not expected to attend the symposium or workshops." Perhaps it would have been more honest to say, "While all you people are here getting yourselves worked up over Haruki Murakami, he will be in Cambridge, Massachusetts, running along the Charles River in training for the Boston Marathon."[490]

Strange Tales from Tokyo

Following the success of *Kafka on the Shore*, Murakami headed off in new directions, both in short and long fiction: *After Dark* of

September 2004 and *Strange Tales from Tokyo* of September 2005. For reasons explained below, they will be discussed in reverse chronological order here.

Murakami describes the creation of *Strange Tales from Tokyo* in his introduction to his 2006 collection of stories in English, *Blind Willow, Sleeping Woman* as follows:

> In 2005 . . . for the first time in a long time I was struck by a strong desire to write a series of short stories. A powerful urge took hold of me, you might say. So I sat down at my desk, wrote about a story a week, and finished five in not much more than a month. I frankly couldn't think of anything else but these stories, and I wrote them almost without stopping. These five stories (a series called *Strange Tales from Tokyo*) are collected at the end of this book. As the title indicates, all share the theme of being strange tales, and were brought out in a single volume. Though they share this theme, each story can be read independently, and they don't form a clear-cut, single unit as did the stories in *after the quake*. Come to think of it, however, everything I write is, more or less, a strange tale.[491]

If *Strange Tales from Tokyo* is reminiscent of any earlier Murakami work, it would be *Dead Heat on a Merry-Go-Round*. Like that earlier collection, this begins with an appearance by the author. The first story, "Chance Traveler", opens like this:

> The "I" here, you should know, means me, Haruki Murakami, the author of this story. Mostly this is a third-person narrative, but here at the beginning the narrator does make an appearance. Just as in an old-fashioned play where the narrator stands before the curtain, delivers a prologue, then bows out. I appreciate your patience, and promise I won't

313

keep you long.

The reason I've turned up here is that I thought it best to relate directly several so-called strange events that have happened to me. Actually, events of this kind occur quite often. Some of them are significant, and have affected my life in one way or another.

He goes on to recount a few odd coincidences that occurred while he was living in Cambridge, Massachusetts, insisting nevertheless that "I'm not the sort of person who's into occult phenomena . . . I'm not into paranormal powers, either . . . Still, a significant number of strange, out-of-the-blue kinds of things have colored my otherwise humdrum life."[492]

Having established that he is willing to accept the fact (without analysis) that strange things really do happen in life, he narrates a series of coincidental events supposedly told to him by "a friend of mine" much as the narrator of *Dead Heat on a Merry-Go-Round* did. Clearly the balance has shifted: that earlier work was determined to establish its credentials in reality, while this invites us to wonder if there might be supernatural forces at work in life. Here, those forces act as a metaphor for the characters' emotional needs and provide an opening for what these stories are really about, which is psychological healing.

Of the five stories, "Chance Traveller" remains the most firmly anchored in everyday life, telling the story of how a series of bizarre but utterly believable coincidences enable a gay man and his sister to reunite after a ten-year estrangement. It is one of Murakami's most emotional and healing tales, and it even verges on the religious as, at the end, the narrator ("I"=Murakami) utters something like a benediction for the cancer-stricken female character whose coincidental resemblance to the sister led to the siblings' reunion: "I don't care if it's the god of jazz, the god of gays, or some other species of

314

god, but I hope that, somewhere, unobtrusively, as if it were all coincidence, someone up there is watching over that woman. I hope this from the bottom of my heart. A very simple hope."[493]

"Hanalei Bay" is another powerful story of healing in which a mother deals with the grief of having lost her surfer-son to a shark. At one point, after she has been making annual pilgrimages for ten years to the beach where her son was killed, the son's ghost seems to make an appearance – though she herself is unable to see him. The story rambles somewhat as it recounts the mother's early career as a jazz pianist, and one tense scene goes so far as to reflect on U.S.–Japan relations, but the narration remains strictly in the third person, and so we never find out what, if anything, "I" (=Murakami) might think about ghosts. Angry that the ghost will not appear to her, the woman has an emotionally purging cry that enables her to confront the resentment she feels toward her son for having thrown his young life away but also to accept the unfair hand that life has dealt her. And then, "Sachi woke up the next morning as a healthy middle-aged woman."[494]

Far from carrying the emotional punch of the first two stories, "Where I'm Likely to Find It" is an oddball detective story, narrated not by "Boku" but "Watashi", an eccentric 45-year-old bachelor with an amateur interest in seemingly unexplainable disappearances. He is "hired" (for free!) by the wife of a stockbroker who mysteriously disappeared while climbing the stairs between the twenty-fourth and twenty-sixth floors of their high-rise apartment building. The stairway is spacious and clean, and is even outfitted with furniture, so that it attracts a certain small percentage of the building's inhabitants. The "detective" ends up learning about an unsuspected secret life that goes on inside the huge building, but he never finds the husband. The search is a metaphor for modern urban life, in which everyone is fruitlessly searching for "an umbrella, a door, or even a

315

doughnut" – an unnamable *something* that "I'm sure I'll recognize . . . when I see it. Like, 'Hey! This is it!'"[495] It is a typical inconclusive Murakami detective story (like *A Wild Sheep Chase*) except that this one does have a "realistic" ending when the husband is found by the police. The "detective's" search began long before the husband disappeared, and will continue long after he has been found.

"The Kidney-Shaped Stone That Moves Every Day" is a sequel – or rather more of a prequel – to *after the quake*'s "Honey Pie", featuring the short-story writer Junpei after he has lost his college sweetheart to his best friend but before the central events of the earlier story in which he is rejoined with her as his one true love. Here, he is still trying to interact with women in terms of the curse-like formula laid upon him in youth by his father: "Among the women a man meets in his life, there are only three that have real meaning for him. No more, no fewer . . . You will probably become involved with many women in the future . . . but you will be wasting your time if a woman is the wrong one for you. I want you to remember that."[496]

Wondering all the while if she is one of his "women who have real meaning", Junpei becomes involved with a mysterious woman who will not divulge her profession to him. He only learns after she has left him that she is a tightrope walker – a rather cool, detached personality who believes in the importance of balance in all things. She may be an unusual love object, but the truly "strange" element of this "strange story" occurs in a story that Junpei is writing while he carries on his affair with the tightrope walker. The protagonist of the story-within-the-story is a lady doctor reminiscent of Satsuki in "Thailand". Both lady doctors wrestle with dark emotions that take the form of dark stones that must be gotten rid of if they are to attain emotional health. The stone in this story seems to have a will of its own and is able to move every day. Junpei senses that his current love is somehow propelling the story as he writes it: "it was never his intention to write something so divorced from reality."[497] He and his fictional lady doctor achieve a level of healing around the same time. The interpenetration of the inner and outer worlds achieves perfect balance in this story – like the tightrope walker herself.

"A Shinagawa Monkey" also turns to the world of fantasy to deal with a real-world character's sense of psychological imbalance. The young married woman at the centre of this story, Mizuki, is reminiscent of "Watashi" of "Sleep". She insists that all is right with her marriage, and yet she can't seem to remember her married name when asked for it without warning. Forgetting her name is like forgetting who she is: her marriage has been robbing her of her identity. Rather than plunging into Tolstoy-like "Watashi", she seeks help from a psychologist, who effects a cure not by traditional analytical means but by dispatching her husband to capture a talking monkey that lives in the sewers of Shinagawa. The monkey had been in love with her boarding-school roommate, who left her name tag with Mizuki before committing suicide. When, years later, the monkey stole the roommate's name tag from Mizuki, he took Mizuki's tag along with it, thus causing her memory problems. Murakami stretches credibility beyond the breaking point for some readers here, especially when he gives the talking monkey the ability to diagnose Mizuki's problem as stemming from an absence of love. Mizuki's cure is a painful one, but at least she has regained her name and a clear sense of her identity.

After Dark

This startling short novel actually appeared a year before *Strange Tales from Tokyo*, in September 2004, but it did not appear in English until 2007 owing to Knopf's decision to publish Murakami's second

317

collection of short stories in 2006, continuing that company's pace of a book a year. For this reason it is being discussed here, somewhat out of order.

After Dark is unlike anything Murakami ever wrote before. Or perhaps it would be safer to say it is unlike anything he ever *published* before. In college, he wrote screenplays for a while, and *After Dark* is like a screenplay in many ways. For one thing, it is hyper-conscious of elapsed time, staying in the present tense throughout. Each numbered chapter begins with the image of a clock face, and we know exactly how much time each chapter (or "scene") takes to play itself out simply by looking at the clock. The first chapter opens at 11:56 p.m. and the last clock shown in the eighteenth and last chapter reads 6:52 a.m. (Murakami has provided graphic aids to some of his works before – a sketch of a T-shirt and "On" and "Off" switches in *Hear the Wind Sing*, a sketch of the Sheep Man in *A Wild Sheep Chase*, the map of the walled town in *Hard-Boiled Wonderland and the End of the World* – so the use of the clock faces should come as no great surprise.) The voice is also that of a scenario commentary, describing not only the setting of each scene but also the placement of the "camera" that views the action – and, in fact, often overtly referring to the point of view (*shiten*) as a camera. Especially startling in Japanese is the first-person-plural reference to the observing eye as "we" (*watashi-tachi*), something far more familiar in English – though less in novels than in scholarly discourse.[498] The book opens in movie-like fashion, with an aerial panorama of the city at night, after which the "camera" drops down, focusing in on increasingly specific objects and people:

1

Eyes mark the shape of the city.

Through the eyes of a high-flying night bird, we take in the scene from midair. In our broad sweep, the city looks like a single gigantic creature – or more like a single collective entity created by many intertwining organisms. . . Our line of sight chooses an area of concentrated brightness and, focusing there, silently descends to it – a sea of neon colors . . .

We are inside a Denny's . . .

After a quick survey of the interior, our eyes come to rest on a girl sitting by the front window. Why her? Why not someone else? Hard to say. But, for some reason, she attracts our attention – very naturally.[499]

Later the camera analogy becomes still more direct: "We allow ourselves to become a single point of view . . . Our viewpoint takes the form of a mid-air camera that can move freely about the room . . . Our angle changes at intervals as regular as the blinking of an eye . . . The camera draws back slowly to convey an image of the entire room. Then it begins observing details in search of clues . . . Our point of view, as an imaginary camera, picks up and lingers over things like this in the room. We are invisible, anonymous intruders. We look. We listen. We note odours. But we are not physically present in the place, and we leave behind no traces. We follow the same rules, so to speak, as orthodox time travellers. We observe but we do not intervene."[500]

"We" continue to observe the entire action of the novel, our presence made overt on nearly every page. Who are "we"? "We" are that mysterious melding of the mind of the author and the mind of the reader that occurs whenever we read literature – that miraculous state called "restorative influence" (*kangenteki kanka*) by Sōseki Natsume in which the distinction between reader and writer breaks down in an experience beyond time and space – [501], something that is usually left unstated, but here is brought to the surface by a writer who has always been highly conscious of the tools of his trade (from the opening sentence of his very first work: "There's no such thing as perfect writing"). After the operatic outpouring of *Kafka on the Shore*, the old Murakami is back: cool, detached, experimental. One wonders how readers swept up in the energy of *Kafka* will react to this stark, black-and-white exploration of technique.

The question is relevant to the contents of the novel as well. Where *Kafka* gave readers fish raining from the sky, and Johnnie Walker slaughtering cats, and Colonel Sanders pimping for a pony-tailed truck driver, and a young protagonist plunging through the woods of Shikoku into a dreamlike alternate reality peopled by the ghosts (?) of Second World War soldiers, *After Dark* is composed in large part of those characteristic super-minimalist Murakami moments where the protagonist makes a sandwich or cleans his ears or irons a shirt. Much of the book is absolutely focused on the minutiae of urban life after dark: the kinds of small events that occur in the city in the darkest hours of the night: people drinking coffee in an all-night Denny's, or feeding cats in a park, or twiddling a pencil in the fingers, or putting out the garbage, or just talking to each other (talk comprises a very large part of the book – another "screenplay" aspect of the text). In this low-key context, one of the most wonderful "action" scenes turns out to involve a salaryman named Shirakawa eating yogurt in the kitchen of his home:

> This is the kitchen of the Shirakawa house. Collar button open, necktie loosened, Shirakawa sits alone at the breakfast table, eating plain yogurt with a spoon. He scoops it directly from the plastic container to his mouth.
>
> He is watching the small TV they keep in the kitchen. The remote control sits next to the yogurt container. The screen is showing pictures of the sea bottom. Weird deep-sea creatures. Ugly ones, beautiful ones. Predators, prey. Miniature research submarine outfitted with high-tech equipment. Powerful floodlights, precision arm. The program is called *Creatures of the Deep*. The sound is muted. His face expressionless,

Shirakawa follows the movements on the screen while conveying spoonfuls of yogurt to his mouth.[502]

Part of what makes this wonderful is the sheer rightness of the observation of everyday life, its total lack of drama: the salaryman, still in his working clothes but with his tie loosened, is too tired to bother transferring the yogurt to a dish and, instead, spoons it directly to his mouth while staring at a typical late-night show, his mind an apparent blank. The next few lines tell us that, in fact, his mind is not a blank: he is thinking of other things – such abstract philosophical speculation as this: "Is action merely the incidental product of thought, or is thought the consequential product of action?"[503] As readers who have followed the action to this point late in the book, we know there is much more here than meets the eye. Shirakawa has, in fact, done a terrible thing in the course of his routine day. He has participated in the city's undercurrent of sex and violence. And while the TV programme he is watching seems like standard late-night fare, it has been chosen by no means at random by Murakami. The "creatures" here echo the observation in the opening paragraphs that "the city looks like a single gigantic creature", reminding us that an ordinary office worker like Shirakawa – and, indeed, any other human being – is simultaneously a unique individual responsible for his own actions and a nameless object in the grip of something far larger and more powerful than himself. Observing trainloads of commuters, the narrator comments: "Each of those under transport is a human being with a different face and mind, and at the same time each is a nameless part of the collective entity. Each is simultaneously a self-contained whole and a mere part. Handling this dualism of theirs skilfully and advantageously, they perform their morning rituals with deftness and precision: brushing teeth, shaving, tying neckties, applying lipstick."[504]

The "creature" motif reminds us of the jellyfish in *The Wind-Up*

Bird Chronicle that caused Tōru such emotional upheaval when he and Kumiko went to the aquarium on their first date: mysterious, brainless, nearly formless creatures that float through the ocean in the grip of great, indefinable forces – symbolic of the threat the universe holds out to all who prize their individuality. Here, the city itself is seen from above as a gigantic creature, perhaps like an octopus, that has no consciousness of the individuals who live in it:

> In our broad sweep, the city looks like a single gigantic creature – or more, like a single collective entity created by many intertwining organisms. Countless arteries stretch to the ends of its elusive body, circulating a continuous supply of fresh blood cells . . . To the rhythm of its pulsing, all parts of the body flicker and flare up and squirm.[505]

The character in *After Dark* who feels most threatened by "the creature" is the law student Takahashi. It is something he became aware of when he was attending trials as part of his course work:

> To my eyes, this system I was observing, this "trial" thing itself, began to take on the appearance of some special, weird creature . . . Like, say, an octopus. A giant octopus living way down deep at the bottom of the ocean. It has this tremendously powerful life force, a bunch of long, undulating legs, and it's heading somewhere, moving through the darkness of the ocean. I'm sitting there listening to these trials, and all I can see in my head is this *creature*. It takes on all kinds of different shapes – sometimes it's "the nation," and sometimes it's "the law," and sometimes it takes on shapes that are more difficult and dangerous than that. You can try cutting off its legs, but they just keep growing back. Nobody can kill it. It's too strong, and it lives too far down in the ocean. Nobody knows where its

heart is. What I felt then was a deep terror. And a kind of hopelessness, a feeling that I could never run away from this thing, no matter how far I went. And this creature, this *thing* doesn't give a damn that I'm me or you're you. In its presence, all human beings lose their names and their faces. We all turn into signs, into numbers.[506]

All the characters in the book feel the stress of living in the grip of the "gigantic creature", but some handle it better than others. Takahashi resolves to give up his passivity and indifference as a student and embark on a serious study of the law: he is going to grapple with the creature head-on. The 19-year-old student of Chinese, Mari Asai, feels estranged from her family (especially her elder sister Eri), and she escapes from this stress by reading a thick tome in an all-night Denny's. She is the "girl sitting by the front window" picked up by the camera in Chapter 1. Her study of Chinese and her plan to go off to Beijing as "a kind of exchange student"[507] are her method of coping with her unhappiness. As she and Takahashi spend long portions of the night together, we begin to hope that a relationship will blossom between these two attractive young people, both of whom have suffered from a shortage of love and could use some honest, emotional relating to people. If there is a central character in this ensemble piece of a novel, which is reminiscent of such films as *Short Cuts* or *Magnolia*, it is Mari: she has long, revealing conversations with Takahashi, with the blonde lady ex-wrestler/love hotel manager Kaoru, and with Kaoru's assistant at the love hotel "Alphaville" (named after the Godard movie and symbolic of the impersonal aspects of human exchange in the modern city).

The two most dramatic victims of urban stress are Mari's sister, Eri Asai, and the office worker ("salaryman") Shirakawa. A beautiful girl, Eri has been valued as a photographer's model since her teen years, more a commodity than an individual human being.

Shirakawa is of value to his company for the work he can do late at night, night after night, sacrificing his family life. Eri escapes by sleeping. We have seen how sleep – a little death – often seems to be the only way out for some earlier characters (most notably The Rat in *Pinball, 1973*), but Eri's sleep is reminiscent in its surreal scale of the extreme wakefulness in "Sleep": she has been sound asleep for nearly two months. Long passages of the book describe her near-oblivion. Shirakawa takes his stress out on others, by cheating on his wife at a love hotel and administering a violent beating to his Chinese prostitute when she announces to him the sudden onset of her period. (His status as a victim of the "creature" doesn't make his beating of the Chinese woman any less reprehensible: in fact, the very viciousness of the act only underscores the violence lying beneath the surface of everyday life.)

Both Eri and Shirakawa find themselves in abstract enclosures: he in the characterless office at a company called "VERITECH" where he spends so much of his life under the glare of fluorescent lights, she at first in her own characterless bedroom at home but then in a virtual space on the "other side" of her TV screen:

> We notice that the room resembles the office where Shirakawa was working late at night. It could well be the same room. Only, now it is perfectly vacant, stripped of all furniture, office equipment and decoration. The fluorescent lights on the ceiling are all that is left . . . Eventually she opens her eyes and picks something up that has fallen on the floor nearby. A pencil. With an eraser. Stamped with the name "VERITECH," it is the same kind of silver pencil that Shirakawa was using. The point is blunt.[508]

Eri doesn't recognize the room or the pencil or the name "VERITECH", but "we" know that this was the very pencil that Shirakawa was using at work late at night until the point wore down. Somehow, his "real" space and her "virtual" space are one and the same. What unites Shirakawa and Eri, who have never met and are unrelated in any way, is the way they have been used by the "gigantic creature" beyond the breaking point.

The tentacles of that "creature" reach everywhere, aided in large part by television. While Shirakawa is watching *Creatures of the Deep* in his kitchen and thinking about other things, Mari and her new friend Kōrogi are half-watching the programme in the love hotel where Kōrogi works as a maid, though they soon switch the set off and begin talking about Kōrogi's odd name ("Cricket"). As Takahashi said earlier, "this creature, this *thing* doesn't give a damn that I'm me or you're you. In its presence, all human beings lose their names and their faces. We all turn into signs, into numbers," and Kōrogi is one of those who has lost her name. Something terrible happened to her three years earlier, around the time of the Kobe earthquake (meaning the year of the novel's setting is around 1998–99), and she has been running away ever since, moving from town to town, working in the anonymous network of love hotels, where few questions are asked by employers and a nickname is all she needs. Kōrogi tells Mari the lesson she has learned from life in terms of the Kobe earthquake: "The ground we stand on looks solid enough, but if something happens it can drop right out from under you. And once that happens, you've had it: things'll never be the same. All you can do is go on living alone down there in the darkness."[509]

The earthquake is but another example of the vast, impersonal forces that rob people of their names – i.e., their individuality. These are forces from which it is impossible to escape, another related theme that surfaces repeatedly in the book. Eri tries to escape from the real world by sleeping. She wakes in the virtual world and tries fruitlessly to escape from the locked room while television signals distort her flesh. Shirakawa may think that he has escaped the consequences of his violent act, but we, at least, know from the voice of the Chinese pimp that keeps coming over the prostitute's cell phone, directed toward Shirakawa but applicable to all who hear it, including Takahashi and the clerk at the convenience store – and us – that "You will never get away. No matter how far you run, we're going to get you."[510]

If television is one tool of the "creature", cell phones appear to be another. It is through a cell phone (something that Mari doesn't like, just as she has doubts about the healthfulness of chicken meat) that the message of "you will never get away" goes out to all who hear it, anonymously. The way that Murakami sets this up is ingenious and amusing. Shirakawa keeps the phone he has stolen from the prostitute but decides to get rid of it when he is buying milk in the convenience store on his way home. He leaves it on the cheese shelf of the refrigerator case, and it rings when Takahashi is buying milk in the same store. Unnerved by the impersonal warning he hears (but which echoes his own earlier words about "the creature"), Takahashi puts the phone back, and the store clerk is the next one to pick it up and hear the voice of doom. There is low-key humour in this and in other "chance" events that make the lives of the characters overlap in unexpected ways, giving yet another sense of the interconnectedness of life governed by the "creature" (and another echo of *Short Cuts* and *Magnolia*). For example, the Chinese man is unaware that his motorcycle has pulled up alongside the taxicab holding Shirakawa, the very man he is warning "you will never get away". And although Mari actually met the Chinese man when he came to pick up the prostitute after Shirakawa beat her, she is unaware that his motorcycle has pulled up beside her and Takahashi when they are walking along the dark city street.

The Chinese man's use of "we" in his warning is worth noting. "'*We*,' Takahashi thinks. *Who could this 'We' possibly be?*"[511] Could Murakami be deliberately conflating the "we" who have been observing all the action – and even peering into people's minds – with the "we" of the Chinese gangsters who run the prostitution operation? Because then we lose the comfort of innocence. We cannot identify simply with the victims of the "gigantic creature" but are in fact part of it: we are like ubiquitous security cameras, watching everything and everyone. Just as Shirakawa is not merely a victim but a perpetrator, we all share some responsibility for the evils of the "creature".

Takahashi gives the most eloquent expression of this view, using familiar Murakami terminology of worlds and walls:

After I'd been to the court a few times, though, and observed a few cases, I started to become strangely interested in viewing the events that were being judged and the people who were involved in the events. Maybe I should say I found myself less and less able to see these as other people's problems. It was a very weird feeling. I mean, the ones on trial are not like me in any way: they're a different kind of human being. They live in a different world, they think different thoughts, and their actions are nothing like mine. Between the world they live in and the world I live in there's this thick, high wall. At least, that's how I saw it at first. I mean, there's no way I'm gonna commit those vicious crimes. I'm a pacifist, a good-natured guy, I've never laid a hand on anybody since I was a kid. Which is why I was able to view a trial from on high as a total spectator . . . As I sat in court, though, and listened to the testimonies of the witnesses and the speeches of the prosecutors and the arguments of the defense attorneys and the statements of the defendants, I became a lot less sure of myself. In other words, I started seeing it like this: that there really was no such thing as a wall separating their world from mine. Or if there was such a wall, it was probably a flimsy one made of papier-mâché. The second I leaned on it, I'd

327

probably fall right through and end up on the other side. Or maybe it's that the other side has already managed to sneak its way inside of us, and we just haven't noticed. That's how I started to feel.[512]

In the stark simplicity of this short novel, many of the familiar Murakami themes are given more straightforward expression than we have seen before. The walls that separate individuals from each other – and from their own inner worlds – are frustratingly high and thick and, at the same time, imaginary. Sometimes we find in them undeserved comfort, especially when denying what binds us with others who exhibit traits we do not wish to recognize in ourselves. Mari, however, is one for whom the walls are a source of anguish. She has stayed out all night because of the deep separation she feels between herself and her beautiful sister, Eri, and she thinks back nostalgically to a time when no such gap existed between them. Once, she says, when she was in kindergarten, they were trapped in an elevator together, and "during that whole time in the dark, Eri was holding me. And it wasn't just some ordinary hug. She squeezed me so hard our two bodies felt as if they were melting into one . . . The two of us became one: there were no gaps between us. We even shared a single heartbeat. Then suddenly the lights came on, and the elevator shook again and started to move . . . But that was the last time . . . After that, it seems, we grew farther and farther apart. We separated, and before long we were living in different worlds."[513]

Where the "other world" has occasionally seemed like an actual place as depicted in Murakami's fiction – a different dimension, another point in space to which people could actually go (as Sumire seems to have done in *Sputnik Sweetheart* and young Kafka in *Kafka on the Shore*), here it is more clearly a function of the separation between individuals and between parts of our inner selves. In that sense, it harks back to "The 1963/1982 Girl from Ipanema":

"Someday, too, I'm sure, I'll meet myself in a strange place in a far-off world . . . In that place, I am myself and myself is me. Subject is object and object is subject. All gaps gone. A perfect union."

After Dark is not entirely free of its gestures toward the supernatural, however. For one thing, its all-enveloping images of night and darkness are vivid and always suggestive of something mysterious and threatening. As young Takahashi says, "Historically speaking, it's quite a recent development that human beings have felt easy about going out after dark. It used to be after the sun set, people would just crawl into their caves and protect themselves."[514] But sometimes something more nearly occult is going on, occasionally involving mirrors. At one point, after Mari looks at herself in the mirror of a restaurant's restroom and goes out, "Our viewpoint camera lingers in here for a while, observing the restroom. Mari is no longer here . . . A closer look reveals that Mari's image is still reflected in the mirror over the sink. The Mari in the mirror is looking from her side into this side."[515]

In large parts of the book, television provides an inexplicable portal between this world and the other. In the bedroom of her home, where she has been sleeping for two months, Eri has a television set. Although it is *not plugged in* (like the switched-off cell phone in *Kafka*), it turns itself on and, after a painfully long struggle to produce a clear picture, it shows us the image of a man in a chair. The man wears an exceedingly thin, skin-tight translucent mask that obscures both his features and any hint of what might be in his mind but does not prevent us from seeing that he is somehow looking through the glass of the television screen into Mari's room. This "Man with No Face" is "looking from his side of the picture tube, through the glass, into *this side*. He is on the *other side*, looking straight into this room, where we are."[516] Perhaps he is meant to represent the anonymous mass audience out there that will pay to look at pictures of a beautiful girl like Eri on a magazine cover or in a

TV commercial and make her feel as if she has no defence against their prying eyes. Perhaps, as a middle-aged man (impeccably dressed but smeared with dust), he represents sexual abuse that she has suffered at home or through her work, or at least a kind of abuse by parents who have exploited her beauty for financial gain.

Before long (precisely 2 hours and 26 minutes later, at 3:03 a.m.), the two worlds have begun to interpenetrate: Mari has disappeared from her bed (which is neatly made, as though she had never been in it) and is now sleeping in a perfect duplicate of the bed in the room on the television screen. The "Man with No Face" is still there, but now instead of staring through the glass at her on *this* side, he is staring directly at her inside the space that he occupies – a stark, empty room with fluorescent lights (a hint, borne out later, that this is the room where Shirakawa had been working). When we return to the scene 22 minutes later, the man and his chair are gone from the image on the screen (never to be seen again), and Eri is beginning to show signs of wakefulness. "We" become impatient with viewing her from "this side" and "so we decide to transport ourselves to the other side of the screen. It's not that difficult once we make up our mind. All we have to do is separate from the flesh, leave all substance behind, and allow ourselves to become a conceptual point of view devoid of mass. With that accomplished, we can pass through any wall . . . We let ourselves become a pure single point and pass through the TV screen separating the two worlds . . ."[517] All it takes to go from one world to the other is an act of will – or, as the young Italian scholar of Murakami, Rebecca Suter, would put it, "the power of imagination" (*sōzōryoku*).[518]

Once we enter the bare, fluorescent-lighted space, Eri slowly continues her progress toward wakening, but when she does gain consciousness, she finds herself trapped inside an utterly unfamiliar space. She touches herself as if to ascertain her own reality. "Through her pajama top, she lays her hands on her breasts. She verifies that she is her usual self: a beautiful face and well-shaped breasts. *I'm a lump of flesh, a commercial asset*, her rambling thoughts tell her."[519] No windows or doors will open for her, and in despair she thinks, *"No one knows I'm here."* She is almost right about that, except:

> *We* know. But we are not qualified to become involved with her. We look down at her from above as she lies in bed. Gradually, as point of view, we begin to draw back. We break through the ceiling, moving steadily up and way from her. The higher we climb, the smaller grows our image of Eri Asai, until it is just a single point, and then it is gone. We increase our speed, moving backward through the stratosphere. The earth shrinks until it, too, finally disappears. Our point of view draws back through the vacuum of nothingness. The movement is beyond our control.
>
> The next thing we know, we are back in Eri Asai's room.[520]

"We" do not see Eri until another hour has gone by, at 4:25 a.m., when once again we are watching her image on the TV set in her room, still trapped in the virtual space with the fluorescent lights. Like the "Man with No Face," she seems able to see through the glass of the picture tube into this room, but she is unable to pass through it. But then, "Suddenly, the TV screen begins to lose its stability. The signal shudders. Eri Asai begins to blur and quiver slightly around the edges. She looks . . . at her wavering hands. She stares at them as their edges lose their clarity."[521] Her entire physical reality in the virtual space is composed of the electronic TV picture, and when the picture loses stability, she can see her own "flesh" disintegrating. She truly is nothing more than a commercially valuable television image, and when that image breaks up, she panics. She starts to flee, but the picture fades altogether.

At 5:09 a.m., after the deepest darkness of the night has passed, Eri is asleep at home in her room again, the television is dead, and

331

everything is back to normal – as normal as things can be for a young woman who has been asleep for two months. At 6:40 a.m., her sister Mari enters the room, driven by her memory of that one time in the elevator when she felt truly at one with her big sister. Mari undresses, joins her in bed, and weeps as if in penance for having drawn away from Eri over the years, for having contributed to the gulf between them: "she feels that she has committed some utterly inexcusable act, something she can never undo."[522] Feeling, too, a surge of hope that their estrangement can be overcome, Mari kisses her sleeping sister on the lips. "Mari feels almost as if she is kissing herself . . . Then, as if relieved, she curls up to sleep beside her big sister – to bond with her if possible, to share the warmth of their two bodies."[523]

Eri is still unconscious, and Mari's hopes for reconciliation with her might well be dashed, but for now, in her own heart, she has come to terms with herself and is ready to bond with her sister. Up to now, the Asai (literally, "shallow well") sisters have not done the necessary well-digging to relate on a deeper level, but with Mari so ready to take the initiative, perhaps it can begin to happen. "The night has begun to open up at last. There will be time until the next darkness arrives."[524] And so the book ends with more hope and healing than any Murakami novel has given us before – a tone that would continue into the following year's *Strange Tales from Tokyo*.

*

At the risk of closing this analysis of *After Dark* with a footnote, let me add some observations as the translator of the novel into English. Murakami's use of the camera viewpoint raises an interesting translation question that hinges on the subtle difference between two extremely close usages of the Japanese verb *naru* (to become), "X ni naru" and "X to naru," both meaning "to become X". The crucial difference is that "ni naru" implies actual, perceptible change in the real world while "to naru" implies only a change in the mind. Consider, for example, the difference between "Yuki ga tokete mizu ni naru" (The snow melts and becomes water) and "Yuki ga tokete kawa to naru" (The snow melts and becomes a river). In the first, the snow *actually becomes* water directly, physically. In the second, "river" is more of an idea than a phenomenon obeying the laws of physics: the snow "becomes" a river only because we can mentally conceive of the complex process involved. English has no such distinction, and I suspect that is true of most – perhaps all – other Western languages as well.

Conceptual becoming (to naru) is crucial to such passages as the following (in which *naru* appears in various inflected forms: *natte, nareba, nari*):

> "We [allow ourselves to] become a single point of view . . . Our viewpoint takes the form of (= becomes) a mid-air camera that can move freely about the room . . .(Watashi-tachi wa hitotsu no shiten to natte . . . Shiten wa chū ni ukanda kamera to natte, heya no naka o jizai-ni idō suru koto ga dekiru.)[525]

> "All we have to do is separate from the flesh, leave all substance behind, and [allow ourselves to] become a conceptual point of view devoid of mass . . . We [let ourselves] become a pure single point and pass through the TV screen separating the two worlds . . ." (Nikutai o hanare, jittai wo ato ni nokoshi, shitsuryō wo motanai kannenteki na shiten to nareba ii no da . . . Soshite jissai-ni, watashi-tachi wa junsui na hitotsu no ten to nari, futatsu no sekai wo hedateru terebi-gamen wo tōrinukeru.)[526]

> "[Allowing ourselves to] become pure point of view, we hang in midair over the city." (Watashi-tachi wa hitotsu no junsui na shiten to natte, machi no jōkū ni)."[527]

In none of these cases could Murakami have used "ni naru" instead of "to naru". If Murakami had written "We become a single point of view" using "ni naru" implying actual, real-world, physical change, he would have raised questions in the reader's mind: "What were 'we' *before* we *became* a 'point'? And *how* did 'we' make the change from whatever we were before into this so-called 'point'?" "Who are 'we'?" "What kind of a 'point'?" In other words, because "ni naru" is a statement about the real world, the use of "ni naru" would raise all kinds of questions about the validity of the statement in the real world.

Undoubtedly, Murakami never considered using "ni naru" because he was describing events that take place entirely within the imagination. As Frog said to Katagiri (here I am relying on Rebecca Suter's brilliant observation in the earlier-cited book), "The whole terrible fight occurred in the area of the imagination. That is the precise location of our battlefield."[528] "Watashi-tachi" is entirely "conceptual", "devoid of mass", lacking all "substance". As Murakami conceives it, the "power of imagination" is not merely an abstract "power" but has qualities of "place" so that he can use challenging phraseology such as "in the area of the imagination". or, more literally, "in the power of imagination". If that "place" is anywhere, of course, it is inside the human (or the frog) mind, which is physically located in the brain.

The problem for the translator is that while the Japanese can easily keep the discourse entirely within the realm of the imagination by using "to naru", thereby disarming any critical resistance the reader might have to the narrator's unsupported claim that "we" can "become" something so lacking in "substance" as a "point of view" or a conceptual "point" (*ten*), English offers no such ready-made tool. If the translator ignores the difference between "ni naru" and "to naru" and simply writes "We become a single point of view", he has in effect changed Murakami's "to naru" into "ni naru" and raised those annoying questions in the reader's mind. How, then, to render "We become a single point of view" ("Watashi-tachi wa hitotsu no shiten to natte") into English? We "mentally turn ourselves into"? "morph into"? "let ourselves become"? "allow ourselves to become"? "let ourselves turn into"? "will ourselves to become"? "imagine ourselves"? The bracketed phrases in the above examples indicate what I have added to the translation in a less-than-satisfactory attempt to deal with this problem.[529]

I tried at one point to skirt the problem by shifting the tense in English into the present perfect stative "Having become a single point of view, we observe . . .", but there really is no such time shift: it all happens *now*. The naru-ing happens as we say it: indeed, it happens *because* we say it – or *think* it. It is instantaneous, and entirely mental.

Finally, it behooves us to ask, if the linguistic tools to engage in imaginative discourse come so readily to hand in Japanese, why aren't all Japanese writers able to evoke the imaginative world with the ease and simplicity we see in Murakami? Perhaps the answer lies in that phrase "in the power of imagination", which tells us more about the individual Murakami mind than the Japanese mind in general. The creator of *Hard-Boiled Wonderland and the End of the World* is inordinately conscious of the human brain as the physical seat of all the world's magic. As colourful as Murakami's imaginative leaps may be, they are always firmly anchored in grey matter – in the physicality of the synapses. It is no doubt true, as he says, that "I'm not the sort of person who's into occult phenomena . . . I'm not into paranormal powers, either." He *is*, however, truly fascinated with the processes by which the brain produces such supernatural phenomena: the less demonstrable in reality, the better. Murakami's ability to communicate his sense of the physical reality of mystery is almost certainly the single greatest factor in his worldwide popularity. He is in touch with a sense of the moment-to-moment "meaning" of life that virtually all human beings share, regardless of nationality or degree of belief in the supernatural. No matter how many suicides or pointless deaths his works may contain on the level of plot, the ultimate thrust of those works is always positive because they convey this sense of life.

14

If You Believed in Me

Murakami shows no signs of slowing down. Within a few years of publishing the five *Strange Tales from Tokyo* in 2005, he managed to complete the translation into Japanese of such long-time favourites of his as *The Great Gatsby* (2006), Raymond Chandler's *The Long Goodbye* (2007), and Truman Capote's *Breakfast at Tiffany's* (2008), following these with at least six more translated volumes in the next four years.[530] He also wrote a remarkably personal book of essays on the relationship of physical health to creativity called *What I Talk About When I Talk About Running* (*Hashiru koto ni tsuite kataru toki ni boku no kataru koto*: 2007; tr. Philip Gabriel, 2008), in which we see him talking to his muscles – and hear what they say back to him. He let it be known, too, that, beginning in December 2006, he was working on a very long novel, and in 2008 he suggested to one interviewer that in the future he might be writing short stories in series (as in *after the quake* and *Strange Tales from Tokyo*) rather than singly as before: "I used to publish my stories in journals, first one here, then a while later another there, but I stopped. I just didn't like it. If I write them in a single flow, then I can feel how each story is related to the others – doing it any other way strikes me as pointless. If possible, I like to write five or six stories consecutively."[531]

International recognition of Murakami's work took the form of more literary prizes and honorary degrees. In 2006 he received the Frank O'Connor International Short Story Award presented in Cork,

Ireland on 24 September for *Blind Willow, Sleeping Woman*, and the Franz Kafka Award presented in Prague on 30 October for the Kafkaesque elements in Murakami's work in general, with special mention of *Kafka on the Shore*. Both prizes were awarded by international juries who chose Murakami over a cosmopolitan list of candidates, and the Kafka prize joined Murakami's name with such major earlier awardees as Philip Roth and Harold Pinter. By April 2008, Murakami's income from foreign sources had actually outpaced his domestic income. "I was very surprised to learn that situation," Murakami is reported to have said. "Two-thirds of the work done by people at my office is now about dealing with foreign publishers."[532]

In October 2008, Murakami became the inaugural recipient of the University of California's Berkeley Japan Prize, "a lifetime achievement award from the Center for Japanese Studies to an individual who has made significant contributions in furthering the understanding of Japan on the global stage." His Berkeley Una's Lecture back in 1992 had been well enough attended in a moderately large venue, but this time, he filled the university's enormous Zellerbach Hall to overflowing for the reading he gave, followed by an on-stage interview by the Japanese pop culture authority, Roland Kelts.[533]

In 2007, the University of Liège conferred an honorary doctorate on Murakami, to be followed in June 2008 and May 2012 by honorary doctorates from Princeton and the University of Hawaii. In December 2009, the Spanish government proclaimed Murakami an Excelentisimo Señor by conferring on him the Order of Arts and Letters. At Liège, he shared the honours with Paul Auster and four other authors of international renown. At Princeton, Murakami enjoyed chatting with fellow honouree, musical legend Quincy Jones.[534] The degree from Hawaii followed a public reading and talk on campus titled "What I Talk About When I Talk About Writing" (10 April). All 600 seats in the campus centre ballroom were filled, and 200 people listened standing.[535]

Not all of the honours were without controversy, however. Murakami faced a trial of conscience when, in November 2008, he was invited to accept the Jerusalem Prize that coming January. Earlier recipients of the biennial award included such luminaries as Bertrand Russell, Ignazio Silone, Jorge Luis Borges, Eugene Ionesco, Simone de Beauvoir, Octovio Paz, Graham Greene, V. S. Naipaul, Milan Kundera, Don DeLillo, Susan Sontag, and Arthur Miller. Murakami might have rationalized accepting the award by noting that it came *not* from the Israeli government but rather from the Jerusalem International Book Fair, and was given "to a writer whose work best expresses and promotes the idea of the 'freedom of the individual in society'", but he knew full well the potential symbolic power of accepting such an award, and his first thought was to reject it, especially after the Israeli bombing of the Gaza Palestinians commenced on 27 December 2008.

He decided in the end not to adopt the "negative" stance of rejecting the prize but rather to take the "positive" opportunity of directly addressing Israeli readers. He was surprised when one of those readers, Israeli President Shimon Peres, introduced himself before the talk on 15 January 2009 and declared that he liked Murakami's books, in particular *Norwegian Wood*, which he had read fourteen years earlier. Murakami recalled that Peres had indeed surprised him some ten years before by quoting from *Norwegian Wood* in a speech and the president was not just claiming to have read him out of politeness. This made it all the more awkward for Murakami to deliver his prepared talk, "Of Walls and Eggs", the central focus of which was precisely the trial of conscience he had been facing since November.[536]

Murakami opened by introducing himself as "a professional spinner of lies", someone whose job earns him more praise the more ingeniously he makes up his lies. With members of the Israeli leadership looking on, he pointed out that politicians, diplomats, and military men were also in the habit of lying. On this particular day, however, Murakami said, he would be telling only the truth, noting first of all that a good number of people in Japan had advised him not to travel to Jerusalem to accept the prize. Others had warned him they would instigate a boycott of his books if he did so. "The reason for this, of course, was the fierce battle that was raging in Gaza. The U.N. reported that more than a thousand people had lost their lives in the blockaded Gaza City, many of them unarmed citizens – children and old people." He did not wish his acceptance to create the impression that he "endorsed the policies of a nation that chose to unleash its overwhelming military power". He did not approve of war, he said, nor did he support one nation over another. Neither did he wish to see his books subjected to a boycott.

After much indecision, he continued, he decided to come to Jerusalem, to speak his mind rather than to say nothing, partly because, as a novelist, he tends to want to do precisely the opposite of what people tell him to do, and partly to see the situation for himself, as any novelist would want to do. Then, using characteristic Murakami imagery, he enunciated his operating principle: "Between a high, solid wall and an egg that breaks against it, I will always stand on the side of the egg," explaining, "Yes, no matter how right the wall may be and how wrong the egg, I will stand with the egg." Lest his metaphor prove too indirect, he explained further that "Bombers and tanks and rockets and white phosphorus shells are that high, solid wall. The eggs are the unarmed civilians who are crushed and burned and shot by them."

The intense criticism of Israel's slaughter of unarmed Palestinian civilians had focused in particular on those white phosphorus shells that had caused such horrific burns among the populace. By mentioning them, Murakami was making his critique as explicit as possible. He went on to relate the current situation to one of his most consistent themes. "Each of us is, more or less, an egg. Each of

340

us is a unique, irreplaceable soul enclosed in a fragile shell. This is true of me, and it is true of each of you. And each of us, to a greater or lesser degree, is confronting a high, solid wall. The wall has a name: it is 'The System'. The System is supposed to protect us, but sometimes it takes on a life of its own, and then it begins to kill us and cause us to kill others – coldly, efficiently, systematically."

It is the novelist's job, he said, to "keep a light trained on The System" in order to protect the fragile individuals that it wants to crush. He then took an unexpectedly personal turn, illuminating the relationship between The System and the people it sends to war:

My father died last year at the age of 90. He was a retired teacher and a part-time Buddhist priest. When he was in graduate school, he was drafted into the army and sent to fight in China. As a child born after the war, I used to see him every morning before breakfast offering up long, deeply felt prayers at the Buddhist altar in our house. One time I asked him why he did this, and he told me he was praying for the people who had died on the battlefield. He was praying for *all* the people who died, he said, both ally and enemy alike. Staring at his back as he knelt at the altar, I seemed to feel the shadow of death hovering about him.

My father died, and with him he took his memories, memories that I can never know. But the presence of death that lurked about him remains in my own memory. It is one of the few things I carry on from him, and one of the most important.

I have only one thing I hope to convey to you today. We are all human beings, individuals transcending nationality and race and religion, fragile eggs faced with a solid wall called The System. To all appearances, we have no hope of winning. The wall is too high, too strong – and too cold. If we have any hope of victory at all, it will have to come from our believing in the utter uniqueness and irreplaceability of our own and others' souls and from the warmth we gain by joining souls together.

Take a moment to think about this. Each of us possesses a tangible, living soul. The System has no such thing. We must not allow The System to exploit us. We must not allow The System to take on a life of its own. The System did not make us: we made The System.

That is all I have to say to you.

I am grateful to have been awarded the Jerusalem Prize. I am grateful that my books are being read by people in many parts of the world. I would like to express my gratitude to the readers in Israel. You are the biggest reason why I am here. I hope we are sharing something—something very meaningful. And I am glad to have had the opportunity to speak to you here today.[537]

Murakami said later that he was aware that both Susan Sontag and Arthur Miller had been critical of the Israeli government even as they accepted the award, but being Jews perhaps put them in a special category; as a Japanese, he felt, he had said as much as he could. The speech elicited energetic applause, he told an interviewer, but a lot of grim expressions, too, Shimon Peres's among them. It also stilled much of the criticism he had endured in Japan. He wondered, though, how many Japanese, himself included, would stand entirely with the egg in an actual situation. Doing so was not just a "feel-good" thing: you had to take responsibility to the end. This was something he felt strongly when observing the sarin gas trials. What those Aum Shinrikyō people had done was undeniably evil, but you had to see things from their perspective as well, a sense that he had written about in *Underground* and injected into his new novel, *1Q84*.[538]

Before Murakami could receive his next major award, Japan experienced one of the worst natural disasters in history, which in turn led to a man-made disaster of equally historic proportions. On 11 March 2011, the magnitude 9.0 earthquake off Japan's northeastern coast not only did major damage on its own but created a gigantic tsunami, in places over 100 feet high, that moved as far as 6 miles inland, killing over 15,000 people, injuring almost twice that number, and sweeping another 3,000 or more out to sea, never to be found. The world watched in horror as the black, roiling wave swept over the unprotected farmland and down city streets, carrying boats and cars and buses in its path, crushing houses, uprooting trees. Utterly unprepared for this onslaught were the nuclear power plants on the Fukushima coast, which led to meltdowns and explosions that eventually rendered a six-to-twelve mile radius area around the plants uninhabitable and caused the evacuation of hundreds of thousands of residents from what has become a dead zone comparable to Chernobyl.

Murakami himself was out of the country at the time, as horrified as anyone by the images of destruction on his television. The 19 March *The New Yorker* quickly reprinted his Kobe earthquake story, "UFO in Kushiro", with photographs of the unimaginable destruction left behind by the recent tsunami, but Murakami replied that the whole thing was simply "too big" for him to comment on when the many requests came in.

He waited until 9 June 2011, when speaking at the ceremony conferring upon him the International Catalunya Prize in Barcelona, to remark upon the terrible blow that Japan had suffered. He began by noting the enormity of the destruction and loss of life and went on to explain the spirit of resignation with which the Japanese have learned over the centuries to deal with the ceaseless changeability of the world (*mujō*) as conceptualized in Buddhist philosophy and experienced through the typhoons and earthquakes that visit the islands. He is not concerned, he says, about Japan's ability to rebuild and resume some semblance of a normal life in response to the physical

343

destruction. "What I want to touch on here is not buildings or roads, but rather . . . things like morality, or ethical standards . . . things that cannot be just put together if machinery is provided, materials supplied, and workers recruited." He is referring, he says, to the nuclear reactors in Fukushima, which continue to spew radiation into the environment, destroying the lives of thousands of people who may never be able to return to their homes.

The electric company, which failed to build for a disaster of this scale, of which it had been warned, and the government, which failed to enforce the necessary safety standards, were most obviously to blame. Their concern for profits above all was worthy of the people's outrage. As reluctant as the Japanese people may normally be to express anger, this time "the citizens of Japan will become really angry". But that is not the whole story because "we Japanese are the ones who allowed such a distorted system to operate until now. Maybe we will have to take ourselves to task for tacitly permitting such behavior".

Following the atomic bombing of Hiroshima and Nagasaki, this was "our second massive nuclear disaster. But this time no one dropped a bomb on us. We set the stage, we committed the crime with our own hands, we are destroying our own lands, and we are destroying our own lives", all in the name of efficiency. "The nuclear reactor is a highly efficient system for generating electricity according to the arguments of the electric power company. That is to say, it is a system efficient for increasing profits." So deeply entrenched has the nuclear industry become in Japan that "The label of 'unrealistic dreamer' has been slapped on anyone who expresses reservations about nuclear power." This represents a "failure of our morals and our ethical standards . . . While we are the victims, we are also the perpetrators. We must fix our eyes on this fact. If we fail to do so, we will inevitably repeat the same mistake again, somewhere else".

We Japanese should have continued to shout "no" to the atom.[539] That is my personal opinion. We should have combined all our technological expertise, massed all our wisdom and know-how, and invested all our social capital to develop effective energy sources to replace nuclear power, pursuing that effort at the national level. Even if the international community had mocked us, . . . we should have maintained, without compromise, our aversion for things nuclear that was planted in us by the experience of nuclear war. The development of non-nuclear energy sources should have been the primary direction for Japan in the post-war period.

Such a response should have been our way of taking collective responsibility for the many victims who perished at Hiroshima and Nagasaki. We needed a substantial moral foundation of just that kind, just such an ethical standard, precisely that sort of a social message. That could have been a tremendous opportunity for us truly to contribute, as Japanese, to the world. But as we rushed down the path of economic development, we were swayed by that simple standard of "efficiency". We lost sight of that important alternative course that lay before us. . .

We should not be afraid to dream dreams. We should not allow the dogs of misfortune named "efficiency" and "convenience" to overtake us. We must be "unrealistic dreamers" who step forward with a strong stride. A person must die one day and disappear from this earth. But humanity will remain. That humanity will continue on without end. We must first believe in the power of humanity.

Let me say in closing that I intend to donate the funds from this prize to help the victims of the earthquake and of the nuclear power plant accident. My deep thanks to the people of Catalonia and everyone at Generalitat de Cataluña for giving me such an opportunity. Finally, I would also like to express my deep condolences for the victims of the recent Lorca earthquake.[540]

Murakami may have been right about the welling anger of the Japanese people, and this powerful speech delivered on the world stage may have contributed to it. On 5 May 2012, the last of Japan's 50 functioning nuclear reactors was taken offline for routine maintenance, and as with the others before it, public demonstrations of distrust seemed likely to keep it from being restarted.[541]

1Q84

The controversy surrounding Murakami's decision to accept the Jerusalem Prize and the spectacle of his delivering a daring critique of the Israeli government on Israeli soil reawakened interest in the novelist beyond the bounds of his usual readership to a degree not seen since the fervour surrounding *Norwegian Wood*. This, combined with the Shinchōsha publisher's decision to keep details about Murakami's forthcoming first long novel in seven years strictly under wraps (partly in response to criticisms that it had revealed all too much about *Kafka on the Shore* before it reached the bookstores), served to ramp up the level of expectation for the oddly – but intriguingly – titled *1Q84* before its first two volumes were released on 30 May 2009. Pre-publication sales were explosive, prompting Shinchōsha to increase its first print run from 380,000 to 480,000, and readers who finally got their hands on the book were so eager to learn the fate of the heroine, left tantalizingly vague at the end of Book Two, that lines formed for midnight sales when Book Three was finally released on 16 April 2010. By the end of April 2012, Shinchōsha had printed well over a million sets of the three-volume novel in hardcover (3,865,000 volumes total) and had already printed 800,000 copies of the first paperback volume (the first half of Book One) as the more affordable edition began to appear.[542] *The New Yorker* printed an excerpt of the English translation, "Town of Cats", in its 5 September 2011 issue, but readers had to wait until 25 October for Knopf to bring out all three books at once (Harvill Secker released Books One and Two of the UK edition a week earlier, Book Three on 25 October), and midnight sales and giddy celebrations were not uncommon in this case, either.

Spoiler alert: *1Q84* is Murakami's longest novel, a central attraction of which is the gradual revelation of the information discussed in this chapter.

There cannot have been many novels as widely read as the English translation of *1Q84* with so much uncertainty regarding the pronunciation of its title. Some people, misreading the *1*, call it *IQ84* (pronounced "Eye-Q-eighty-four"), as though it were about a protagonist such as Forrest Gump with a low intelligence quotient. Investors might think it means "first quarter of 1984". Others, having learned of the book's references to Orwell, and possibly aware of the identical pronunciation of the Japanese number 9 and the English letter Q, pronounce it "One-Q-Eighty-Four" or "Nineteen Eighty-Four" just like Orwell's book. I have even heard "Q-Teen-Eighty-Four".

The author himself, however, supplied a Romanized gloss for the Japanese title, "*ichi-kew-hachi-yon*" (one-Q-eight-four), which is both reminiscent of Orwell and determinedly different.[543] The Japanese reader instantly gets the meaning of "9" from the "Q" but is more intrigued than enlightened by it because there is no indication that this is a reference to a year on the calendar. The Japanese title of Orwell's book is pronounced "*Sen-kyū-hyaku-hachi-jū-yo-nen*",[544] which is the standard way to write the year 1984, meaning exactly that: "The year one-thousand-nine-hundred-eighty-four". Murakami's title does not include the suffix for "year" (-nen), leaving the Japanese reader to question what relationship there could be between this odd group of four characters and the year 1984. As an English title, then, encountered before the reader has had a chance to open the novel, *1Q84* should be somewhat puzzling, as the original *"ichi-kew-hachi-yon"* is, and ought to be pronounced "One-Q-Eight-Four".

True, without access to the Q/9 pun, the reader in English will be slightly more puzzled than the Japanese reader, but that lasts only a little more than a hundred pages. At that point, the female protagonist, Aomame, convinces herself that she is no longer living in the normal world of 1984, that the world around her has changed or is on some kind of track parallel to 1984, and that she needs a name to distinguish this new mode of existence: *"1Q84 – that's what I'll call this new world,* Aomame decided . . . *Q is for 'question mark.' A world that bears a question . . . Like it or not, I'm here now, in the year 1Q84. The 1984 that I knew no longer exists."* From this point on in the Japanese text,[545] Murakami consistently adds the -nen suffix to his intriguing four-character title, writing it "1Q84-*nen*", for which the Japanese pronunciation would most likely be *"ichi-kew-hachi-yo-nen"*. Once this context of discussing year names is established, the pronunciation in English "One-Q-Eighty-Four" is all but inescapable. Many readers are likely to pronounce the title this way, though, strictly as a title, "One-Q-Eight-Four" is marginally more correct.

The unavailability of the Q/9 pun to readers in English raises the question of how best to translate the title. The "Q is for 'question mark'" idea might have been brought out by using an actual question mark: *1?84,* but that would have made the title even more unpronounceable, and it might have incorrectly suggested that the author was hinting at other centuries (1884, 1784, etc.). Finally, the *look* of "1Q84" with the capital Q boldly plunked among the numerals, is at least as important as the sound and is certainly more important than the Q/9 pun itself, which does not have a deep meaning. The pun simply makes Aomame's choice of the letter Q seem less arbitrary in Japanese than it does in English, but in a book with a million arbitrary-seeming decisions and story twists, Aomame's Q does not stand out.

Clearly, what Murakami was aiming for in his title was that it should be enigmatic, that it should be visually striking, and that it should have an Orwellian echo. Although the title evokes Orwell's *1984*, and both books begin on a chilly day in early April 1984, the novel *1Q84* cannot be called a homage to or a variation or commentary on Orwell. As a critique of the Soviet Union and totalitarianism in general, *1984* imagines one possible future. *1Q84* instead "looks back and imagines the past as it might have been", says Murakami, who points out that he is interested in examining the mentality of the era he lived through from a different perspective. Aomame and her beloved Tengo are five years younger than he was at the time. The student uprising that had been so decisive for Murakami was already a thing of the past when Tengo entered college.[546]

There are six direct references to *1984* in the entire novel.[547] Where the two books connect more broadly is in the theme of mind control. In both Orwell and Murakami, the rewriting and distortion of history come up for examination, but while the inhabitants of Orwell's futuristic totalitarian dystopia are subjected to invasive state-sponsored mind control in all aspects of their lives, Murakami looks back on a familiar 1984 in which the most overt users of techniques meant to control the thoughts of their adherents are religious cults. Commenting on an especially severe cult, the character called "Professor Ebisuno" echoes Murakami in *Underground* on the broad appeal of cult membership when he says:

> What Takashima is doing, if you ask me, is making mindless robots. They take the circuits out of people's brains that make it possible for them to think for themselves. Their world is like the one that George Orwell depicted in his novel. I'm sure you

realize that there are plenty of people who are looking for exactly that kind of brain death. It makes life a lot easier. You don't have to think about difficult things, just shut up and do what your superiors tell you to do.[548]

Aomame herself was raised to be an unquestioning adherent of a stern, ascetic Christian sect called the Society of Witnesses, which, like the Jehovah's Witnesses, forbids blood transfusions and preaches the coming of the End Times, but she abandoned the faith when she was eleven years old. Now, at age 29, it falls to her to assassinate the leader of another cult, the character in the novel who bears the closest resemblance to Orwell's Big Brother because he is physically big and his followers take his word as absolute. Called "Leader" (the word *Riidā* is used like a name in the Japanese text), he heads a faintly Buddhistic religious commune called "Sakigake," which means "Forerunner".[549] Granted official government recognition as a religion in 1979, the fictitious Sakigake can be seen as the "forerunner" of the all-too-real Aum Shinrikyō, the notorious Buddhist cult founded in 1984 that fomented the sarin gas attack against the Tokyo subway system in 1995.

Leader is said to have spent two years with a commune known as the "Takashima Academy", the cult decried by Professor Ebisuno as a maker of "mindless robots", where he gained the expertise to run his own commune. Likewise, before he founded Aum Shinrikyō in 1984, leader Asahara Shōkō spent the years 1980 to 1983 gaining organizational know-how from the Buddhist Agon Shū sect. It was around that time that Asahara is reported to have told a friend, "Do you know what the number one money-making business is? It's religion!"[550] Murakami has called it a "total coincidence" that *The Wind-Up Bird Chronicle* was also set in 1984,[551] but clearly he has an ongoing interest in the period's contrast between financial affluence and spiritual desolation and in Aum Shinrikyō's claims to possess the ultimate cure for such desolation.

Sakigake is as walled off and secretive and controlling as Aum Shinrikyō. It gives Leader sexual access to young girls in the manner of Aum leader Asahara and many other self-appointed religious leaders, and though this religion's Leader doesn't show himself levitating the way Asahara claimed he could,[552] he does demonstrate his powers to Aomame by levitating a heavy clock.[553] Levitation is also mentioned in *1984* as a technique that might be used by the Party if it wished to demonstrate its powers, which have rendered the laws of nature obsolete.[554]

Not only can Leader defy the laws of nature in this way, like the powerful Party member O'Brien, he can read minds and has knowledge far beyond that of ordinary mortals. He knows that Aomame has given the name "1Q84" to the parallel world she seems to have entered, though she has only done so mentally and never mentioned it to anyone.[555] He knows that she has felt strongly connected to a budding novelist named Tengo ever since she grasped his hand in an elementary-school classroom when they were both ten years old. He knows that they not only long for each other, but they picture each other whenever they masturbate. Further complicating matters, Leader knows that Aomame has been sent to assassinate him, and he welcomes the prospect of the painless death she offers him, promising to save Tengo's life in return (though his religious followers will surely pursue and destroy her). Only a god – or the author of a piece of fiction – could possibly be that omniscient.

The novelist Tengo, too, is physically large, suggesting that he rules over his created fictional world like a Big Brother, and Murakami draws several parallels between Tengo and Leader. At one point, on a fateful dark and stormy September night, Tengo even experiences the kind of paralytic seizure that Leader regularly endures, and, lying flat on his back in that passive state, he has "ambiguous" sex with one of Leader's pre-menstrual daughters, the seventeen-year-old Fuka-Eri, as a result of which Tengo sends his sperm through some "special kind of passageway" that opens up "for an instant", and, miles away, Aomame becomes pregnant with his child.[556] (Murakami leaves open the possibility that Aomame's massaging of Leader before she kills him might have involved something more: "Thirty minutes later, they were bathed in sweat, panting like lovers who have just had miraculously deep sex".)[557]

The year 1Q84 is presented not as an "actual" parallel universe, as if Murakami is a believer in multiverse theories, but rather as an entirely made-up world, in which anything can happen because the author says it happens: he writes it that way, and therefore it is true. Of course, Murakami never states it this overtly. Instead, he has Aomame and Leader discuss the nature of the 1Q84 world in enigmatic terms. When Leader says that he knows she has given her own entirely made-up label "1Q84" to the world in which she is living, this revelation is startling enough to serve as the cliffhanger at the end of the chapter. The next Aomame chapter (Book Two, Chapter 13) then picks up the discussion:

"1Q84," Aomame said. "Are you talking about the fact that I am living now in the year called 1Q84, not the *real* 1984?"

"What the real world is: that is a very difficult problem," the man called Leader said as he lay on his stomach. "What it is, is a metaphysical proposition. But *this* is the real world, there is no doubt about that. The pain one feels in this world is real pain. Deaths caused in this world are real deaths. Blood shed in this world is real blood. This is no imitation world, no imaginary world, no metaphysical world. I guarantee you that. But this is not the 1984 you know."

"Like a parallel world?"

The man's shoulders trembled with laughter. "You've been reading too much science fiction. No, this is no parallel world.

You don't have 1984 over there and 1Q84 branching off over here and the two worlds running along parallel tracks. The year 1984 no longer exists *anywhere*. For you and for me, the only time that exists anymore is this year of 1Q84.". . .

"And in this year of 1Q84, there are two moons in the sky, aren't there?"

"Correct: two moons. That is the *sign* that the track has been switched. That is how you can tell the two worlds apart. Not that all of the people here can see two moons. In fact, most people are not aware of it. In other words, the number of people who know that this is 1Q84 is quite limited."[558]

Of course, when a fictional character says "This is no imaginary world" and that "Blood shed in this world is real blood", what he is talking about is precisely the "imaginary world" created by the author, a "proposition" as "metaphysical" as the "metaphysical soles" of the Girl from Ipanema. Murakami is not saying that there are people in *this* world (the real 1984 or the real 2012) who are truly in touch with the divine, and who therefore deserve to be spiritual leaders with a god-given right to control the minds of their flock, but rather that, only in a world with two moons such as 1Q84, can a religious leader actually perform the "same old tricks" that religious leaders have used throughout the centuries to dupe their followers.[559] In the world of 1Q84, Leader exerts his psycho-kinetic energy and lifts the heavy clock without wires or pulleys. He could not have done that in plain, old 1984. Perhaps the one more-or-less "real" place where such a trick could work would be early twenty-first century America, where candidates for president argue about the difference between a "religion" and a "cult" and claim to see Satan working for their political enemies.

Leader's immense stature may be (at least verbally) reminiscent of Big Brother, but even he is in the grip of forces larger than himself.

Indeed, it is strongly implied that he is a captive of those who worship him. A charismatic former anthropology professor who used to have a "visceral disgust for religion", he is now prevented from communicating with anyone outside the walls of the Sakigake commune by his former students and other followers.[560] "There's no longer any place for a Big Brother in this real world of ours," says the wise Professor Ebisuno. "Instead, these so-called Little People have come on the scene. Interesting verbal contrast, don't you think?"[561]

Sparked perhaps by nothing more than this "verbal contrast" with *1984*'s Big Brother, Murakami creates a cartoon-like race of Little People, who enter this world mysteriously through a variety of passageways (the muzzle of a dead goat, the open mouths of both a sleeping girl and a dead detective) to "pluck white, translucent threads out of the air"[562] and weave them into five-foot-long, womb-like cocoons called "air chrysalises" that give birth to everything from alter egos to longed-for loves to a tangle of three angry snakes. For the most part, however, the Little People remain invisible in their other-worldly forest home,[563] causing the wild thunderstorm on that critical September night when their fury is aroused. Instead of the Big Brother that Orwell posited, it is the Little People who control the System inside of which all of us are trapped, that same oppressive machine of which Murakami spoke so eloquently in his Jerusalem Prize acceptance speech. The Little People might be seen as a metaphor for the faceless bureaucrats who run governmental agencies, corporations, and religious organizations. On a still more universal plane, they might stand for the human genes that "ride us into the ground like racehorses from generation to generation".[564] "*They* have been called by many different names, but in most cases have not been called anything at all. *They were simply there*. The expression 'Little People' is just an expedient," says the all-knowing Leader. "My daughter called them that when she was very young and brought them with her",[565] which perhaps explains why the Little People are like something out of a fairy tale (or a Disney version of a fairy tale).

One of *1Q84*'s most effective evocations of controlling forces at work in society is the figure of the NHK subscription fee collector, who shows up repeatedly outside people's doors, hounding them to let him in. The quasi-governmental broadcasting corporation NHK appeared powerfully in *The Wind-Up Bird Chronicle*, and here, too, it continues to exert its implied influence over the minds of its broadcast audience. Tengo's father was an NHK fee collector, and one of the most moving elements of the book is the story of how he exploited his little son by dragging him from door to door, like a trained monkey, to break down the resistance of citizens reluctant to pay their fee. As the father sinks into an Alzheimer's twilight and eventually dies, something like his disembodied spirit continues to pound on the doors of Aomame and other characters under threat.[566] Perhaps only Murakami could make something so mundane and even comical into something so spooky and unnerving. (He undercuts the mystery somewhat in Book Three by reporting that the comatose father would occasionally knock on his wooden bed frame.)[567]

Like Tengo, Aomame was exploited as a child, dragged from door to door by her mother in an attempt to spread the word of the Witnesses, and indoctrinated to pray loudly over her school lunches in a way that made her an object of ridicule among her classmates. Tengo observed her with puzzlement and pity when they were classmates for two years in the third and fourth grades. The two children also used to see each other on the streets on Sundays making rounds with their parents instead of playing with friends. This shared experience is partly what drew them to each other, though they never talked. Like Tengo, who refused to continue accompanying his father on his rounds once he entered the fifth grade, she rebelled that same year and went to live with a relative in another city.

The adult Tengo and Aomame have not seen each other for 20 years. They are profoundly lonely people who desperately want to believe in their love for each other as the only real thing in an otherwise empty world. The power of belief is suggested by the novel's epigraph from the song "It's Only a Paper Moon": "It's a Barnum and Bailey world, / just as phony as it can be, / But it wouldn't be make-believe / if you believed in me." To emphasize the authenticity of their love, both characters are shown participating in intense – but purely physical – sex with other partners, Aomame with a series of middle-aged, balding men reminiscent of Sean Connery who can satisfy her intense physical cravings but nothing more, and Tengo with a girlfriend whose full breasts are obviously far better than Aomame's small, lopsided ones but with whom he faces no threat of being forced into a committed relationship because she is married and intends to stay that way. Aomame's sexual escapades can be particularly ugly, as if to emphasize that none of this physical stuff matters: it's all in how deeply the two partners believe in each other.

If 1Q84 is a world in which religious leaders are capable of levitation, it is also a place where belief really works. As she waits to be reunited with her beloved Tengo, whom she firmly believes to be the father of the child inside her, Aomame realizes that she does believe in God after all, that to protect the *"little one . . .* it became necessary to somehow believe in God. Or to recognize the fact that she believed in God." This is not the harsh God that dominated her childhood but one more like "an elegant, middle-aged woman" driving a silver Mercedes coupe who offers a "beautiful spring coat to the naked Aomame" in a dream and later arranges for an empty taxi to pick up Aomame and Tengo on the backed-up expressway in "reality". "Pretty hard to believe, don't you think?" says the cab driver. "I can believe it," Aomame replies.[568]

Perhaps the greatest act of faith is exhibited by Tengo when Aomame tells him, "I'm carrying a child. I believe it's yours," adding that the child was conceived on that stormy September night when she killed Leader and he had every last drop of semen squeezed out of him by Leader's daughter, Fuka-Eri. When he hears about this immaculate (or, at least, long-distance) conception, Tengo, unlike Joseph, needs no special dream visitation from an angel of the Lord to be able to declare to Aomame that he believes "From the bottom of my heart" that he is the father of her child.[569]

As the two of them climb the emergency stairway in hopes of escaping from 1Q84 back to 1984, Aomame thinks, *"We have to get out of this world. To do that I have to believe, from the bottom of my heart, that these stairs will lead to the expressway. I believe,"* and she recalls the lyrics of the song – *"But it wouldn't be make-believe / If you believed in me."* And once again, with a liberal sprinkling of pixie dust from Tin Pan Alley, Aomame's faith works. The kind of faith seen in *1Q84* is more than a little reminiscent of the starry-eyed belief in Santa Claus seen in a children's book that Murakami translated back in 1987, Chris Van Allsburg's *The Polar Express*. Murakami is perfectly happy to create a fictional world in which God makes nice things happen from behind the wheel of her silver Mercedes and novels can have happy endings, but he would still almost certainly stand by the faith he expressed in the "human *system*" when he told an interviewer in 1985, "I don't believe in the existence of God, of course."[570]

As so often happens in a Murakami book, music provides a key to the workings of the novel. It is there in the opening sentences: "The taxi's radio was tuned to a classical FM broadcast. Janáček's *Sinfonietta* – probably not the ideal music to hear in a taxi caught in traffic".[571] Aomame instantly recognizes the piece and even thinks about the conditions in Bohemia when it was composed in 1926. Not a classical music fan, she wonders how she could have known so much about – and felt so deeply and personally affected by – a composition she cannot remember having heard before. "[T]he moment she heard the opening bars, all her knowledge of the piece came to her by reflex, like a flock of birds swooping through an open window. The music gave her an odd, wrenching kind of feeling . . . a sensation that all the elements of her body were being physically wrung out".[572]

The source of this flood of musical knowledge is never revealed. In fact, the mystery only deepens as we learn that it was not Aomame but Tengo who had a strong connection with Janáček's *Sinfonietta*. He played the timpani part in his second year of high school, but that occurred long after Aomame disappeared from his life in the fifth grade, so she would not have known about that, either. From the time she hears it in the cab, however, Aomame thinks, *"It makes me feel connected. It's as if that music is leading me to something. To what, though, I can't say"*.[573]

Obviously, the connection she feels is with Tengo, and the music is slowly leading her closer to him – *very* slowly, for these thoughts of hers occur in the second chapter of Book Three, 613 pages and six months after the opening taxi scene, by which time, although she has still not met him, she has become pregnant with Tengo's child.[574] If such an immaculate conception between deeply bound souls is possible in the world of 1Q84, then it would be no problem at all for her "knowledge" of Janáček's *Sinfonietta* to come to Aomame directly from Tengo's memory in that instant in the cab. In fact, it is precisely from that "wrenching" moment, "the moment I heard Janáček's *Sinfonietta* and climbed down the escape stairs from the traffic jam on the Metropolitan Expressway", that she has switched tracks from 1984 into 1Q84, "A strange world where anything can happen" – even the construction of a joint U.S./U.S.S.R. moon base.[575] In 1Q84, a man can "actually" impregnate a woman miles away from him at the exact moment he ejaculates into a pre-menstrual girl; his early musical memories can suddenly leap into the mind of the woman he continues to love though he has not seen her for 20 years; and long-separated lovers can meet almost entirely by chance, as they would not in the "real" world.

Murakami dramatized the near-impossibility of chance reunions in one of his earliest and most memorable stories, "On Seeing the 100% Perfect Girl One Beautiful April Morning" (1981). Occupying barely five pages in the translated collection *The Elephant Vanishes*, the story tells us how a perfectly-matched boy and girl, aged 18 and 16, tempt fate by separating in youth, convinced that they will find each other again if they are truly meant to be together. Tengo and Aomame, the boy and girl of *1Q84*, are even younger, only ten years old, and they have barely even spoken to each other when events separate them, but both become convinced, as the result of that one electric moment of hand-holding in a fourth-grade classroom, that they were each other's true loves, and both realize, at age 30, that the loneliness and emptiness of their subsequent lives are due entirely to each other's absence. At first, they don't want to do anything as practical as to actually *look* for each other. "What I want is for the two of us to meet somewhere by chance one day, like, passing on the street, or getting on the same bus," Aomame tells a friend.[576]

In the short story, the young couple's similar romantic notion is thwarted by a flu epidemic that nearly kills them and all but erases their memories of each other; when chance brings them together on a Tokyo street one April morning (yet another source for the April opening of *1Q84*), they feel only the faintest glimmer of recognition before they part forever.[577] The novel replaces the simple flu epidemic with a wildly elaborated series of events that turn the girl into a sexually adventurous vigilante killer and the boy into a passive lover and unfulfilled novelist involved in a literary fraud, but their memories from elementary school remain stunningly clear, and they grow determined to find each other.

The emotional core of the novel is to be found in Book Two, Chapter 4, when childhood memories begin flooding back to Tengo in a supermarket. Picking up a sprig of edamame (green soybeans on the branch), he is instantly reminded of Aomame ("green peas") and realizes how much she meant to him.[578] We have seen this kind of love before in Murakami's fiction, an attachment rooted in child-hood, and not just in "On Seeing the 100% Perfect Girl One Beautiful April Morning". In *South of the Border, West of the Sun*, Hajime and Shimamoto drew close at the age of twelve and had one memorable moment of holding hands. Their adult affair is a return to those inno-cent times. In *Norwegian Wood*, Tōru and Midori pledge their love amid the children's rides in a rooftop play area. When Aomame and Tengo finally reunite, it happens in a playground on top of a slide. That fourth-grade classroom was an emotional crucible for them, as hinted at when Aomame first enters the world of 1Q84, passing through a construction materials storage area that is "about the size of an elementary school classroom".[579] The stories of Aomame and Tengo's loveless childhoods are the most affecting parts of the novel, and Tengo's memories go even deeper, all the way to infancy.

Murakami himself has said that the tiny "On Seeing the 100% Perfect Girl One Beautiful April Morning" was the seed from which the three-volume novel grew,[580] but by planting that seed in 1Q84, he made it possible for the lovers to be reunited instead of parting forever. Leader tells Aomame she would never have even *thought* of searching for Tengo in the ordinary world of 1984.[581] There is only one Big Brother who controls the ultimately romantic world of 1Q84, and his name is Haruki Murakami. He steps out from behind the curtain, for example, when he lets the teenage author Fuka-Eri have just enough clairvoyance to tell Tengo that Aomame is hiding somewhere in the neighbourhood "like a wounded cat" without telling him the precise address, which might have brought the novel to a sudden close.[582] This is no more arbitrary than the short story's flu epidemic, but there the storyteller was in entertaining full view from beginning to end. (The practical-minded Murakami is also in evidence when, at the symphonic fulfillment of the lovers' desires beneath the moon, the narrator points out that the hotel clerk "gave them a special discount, too".)[583]

We see a writer in action in the character of Tengo, whose passageway into the anything-can-happen world of 1Q84 is not a physical one like Aomame's emergency stairway but the mental one of literary creativity. He is shocked to be seeing two moons in "reality" exactly like the ones he created, and he can only conclude that "*I have been drawn into the fictional world that I myself have written*".[584] His shock upon seeing a "real" air chrysalis, a glowing gossamer cocoon almost five feet long, complete with "the waist in the middle and the lovely [nipple-like] protuberances at either end," is even greater: "*This is the very air chrysalis I sketched and described,* Tengo thought . . . For some reason, every detail he had put into writing had now become a reality . . . He could no longer distinguish how much of this present world was reality and how much of it fiction."[585]

Aomame has her own difficulties distinguishing reality from fiction. At a couple of points, she wonders whether she might be a character in the novel that Tengo is writing.[586] This question is never answered definitively, but one thing is certain: both Aomame and Tengo are most definitely characters in the novel that Murakami has written. As he brings Aomame and Tengo ever closer to each other, he refers to her in literary terms as a *kyarakutā* (English "character") and a *jinbutsu* (the Japanese equivalent of "character") when the gay bodyguard Tamaru tells her "You're a rare sort of character, a type I've seldom come across before" and calls her coming reunion with Tengo beneath the moon (or moons) "Very romantic".[587] We can almost hear the narrator of the "100% Perfect Girl" story in Tengo's amazement: "Tengo could hardly believe it – that in this frantic, labyrinth-like world, two people's hearts – a boy's and a girl's – could be connected, unchanged, even though they hadn't seen each other for twenty years." He thinks, "the lines that constructed this story were complicated . . . But he had a faint sense that this chaos was, ever so slowly, heading toward a denouement."[588] Murakami started his career writing about writing ("There's no such thing as perfect writing," begins the narrator of *Hear the Wind Sing*), and he is still doing it in *1Q84*. He seems happy to blur the line between reality and fiction, whereas Orwell's Winston Smith reaches such a state of mind only when he has been sufficiently tortured by agents of the Party. Smith realizes "the fallacy" of perceiving levitation as a hallucination: "It presupposed that somewhere or other, outside oneself, there was a 'real' world where 'real' things happened."[589]

The character known as "Leader" embodies not only the theme of mind control shared with Orwell but also the novel's other major theme, that of male violence against women. Aomame has been sent to kill Leader in order to put a stop to his raping of his pre-menstrual daughters. She is motivated by the suicide of her dearest friend after two years of unrelenting abuse by a violent husband, and she has teamed up with a wealthy elderly woman whose pregnant daughter was also driven to suicide by similar domestic violence. The woman, "the dowager", devotes much of her riches to housing and rehabilitating victimized girls and women, but she also encourages Aomame to murder some of the more unregenerate offenders when the government fails to come to the women's defence. We know that Aomame has killed three men before her climactic murder of Leader,[590] but the morality of such vigilante justice is never seriously questioned. Aomame is presented as a physically and psychologically strong woman, a superbly trained athlete who teaches female health club members how best to defend themselves against male attackers. Sexually aggressive, she is known to the reader by her surname (the revelation of her given name in Book Three is all but irrelevant) in contrast to the passive, indecisive male protagonist, Tengo, who is identified primarily by his given name. The reversal of traditional roles is clearly deliberate and may be an echo of the aggressive Julia and timid Winston of *1984* (as well as the aggressive Shimamoto and more passive Hajime of *South of the Border, West of the Sun*).

From the moment we meet him, Tengo is identified as a man with a problem:

Tengo's first memory dated from the time he was one and a half. His mother had taken off her blouse and dropped the shoulder straps of her white slip to let a man who was not his father suck on her breasts. The infant in the crib nearby was probably Tengo himself. He was observing the scene as a third person . . . The infant was asleep, its eyes closed, its little breaths deep and regular . . . This vivid ten-second image would . . . envelop him like a soundless tsunami. By the time he noticed, it would be directly in front of him, and his arms and legs would be paralyzed. The flow of time stopped. The air grew thin, and he had trouble breathing. He lost all connection with the people and things around him. The tsunami's liquid wall swallowed him whole. And though it felt to him as if the world were being closed off in darkness, he experienced no loss of awareness. It was just a sense of having been switched to a new track. Parts of his mind were, if anything, sharpened by the change. He felt no terror, but he could not keep his eyes open. His eyelids were clamped shut. Sounds grew distant, and the familiar image was projected onto the screen of his consciousness again and again. Sweat gushed from every part of his body and the armpits of his undershirt grew damp. He trembled all over, and his heartbeat grew faster and louder.[591]

These brief "attacks" incapacitate Tengo at several points in the book, though they cease after he comes to terms with his origins and begins writing his own fiction.[592] While he recognizes the possibility that this "memory" from an impossibly early age may be a convenient fiction to explain his hatred for his father, Tengo does have an extreme breast fixation, perhaps from never having been suckled by

363

his mother (or merely from his having been created by Haruki Murakami, who rarely misses a chance to comment on the mammary endowments of his female characters).

The scene in which Aomame first punishes an abusive male is among the most startling and Murakamiesque in the entire novel, and as with all of Murakami's best writing, it is firmly anchored in mundane (and even historical) detail piled on just past the point of literal believability. It occurs in Chapter 13 of Book One, during Aomame's first year of college, when her best friend, Tamaki, has become a victim of date rape.

Aomame decided to take it upon herself to punish the man. She got his address from Tamaki and went to his apartment carrying a softball bat in a plastic blueprint tube. Tamaki was away for the day in Kanazawa, attending a relative's memorial service or some such thing, which was a perfect alibi. Aomame checked to be sure the man was not at home. She used a screwdriver and hammer to break the lock on his door. Then she wrapped a towel around the bat several times to dampen the noise and proceeded to smash everything in the apartment that was smashable – the television, the lamps, the clocks, the records, the toaster, the vases: she left nothing whole. She cut the telephone cord with a scissors, cracked the spines of all the books and scattered their pages, spread the entire contents of a toothpaste tube and shaving cream canister on the rug, poured Worcestershire sauce on the bed, took notebooks from a drawer and ripped them to pieces, broke every pen and pencil in two, shattered every light bulb, slashed all the curtains and cushions with a kitchen knife, took scissors to every shirt in the dresser, poured a bottle of ketchup into the underwear and sock drawers, pulled out the refrigerator fuse and threw it out a window, ripped the flapper out of the toilet tank and tore it apart, and crushed the bathtub's shower head. The destruction was utterly deliberate and complete. The room looked very much like the recent news photos she had seen of the streets of Beirut after the shelling.[593]

Who but Murakami could even think of such a thing? And who but Murakami could manipulate realistic detail to the point of leaving the reader simultaneously shocked and amused? Another passage that only Murakami could have written involves the self-defence training that Aomame gives to women at the health club.

The number of people who could deliver a kick to the balls with Aomame's mastery must have been few indeed. She had studied kick patterns with great diligence and never missed her daily practice. In kicking the balls, the most important thing was never to hesitate. One had to deliver a lightning attack to the adversary's weakest point and do so mercilessly and with the utmost ferocity – just as when Hitler easily brought down France by striking at the weak point of the Maginot Line. One must not hesitate. A moment of indecision could be fatal. . . .

As a woman, Aomame had no concrete idea how much it hurt to suffer a hard kick in the balls, though judging from the reactions and facial expressions of men she had kicked, she could at least imagine it. Not even the strongest or toughest man, it seemed, could bear the pain and the major loss of self-respect that accompanied it.

"It hurts so much you think the end of the world is coming *right now*. I don't know how else to put it. It's different from ordinary pain," said a man, after careful consideration, when Aomame asked him to explain it to her. . . .

Some time after that, Aomame happened to see the movie

On the Beach on late-night television. It was an American movie made around 1960. Total war broke out between the US and the USSR and a huge number of missiles were launched between the continents like schools of flying fish. The earth was annihilated, and humanity was wiped out in almost every part of the world. Thanks to the prevailing winds or something, however, the ashes of death still hadn't reached Australia in the Southern Hemisphere, though it was just a matter of time. . . .

Aomame was primarily in charge of classes in muscle training and martial arts. It was a well-known, exclusive club with high membership fees and dues, and many of its members were celebrities. Aomame established several classes in her best area, women's self-defense techniques. She made a large canvas dummy in the shape of a man, sewed a black work glove in the groin area to serve as testicles, and gave female club members thorough training in how to kick in that spot. In the interest of realism, she stuffed two squash balls into the glove. The women were to kick this target swiftly, mercilessly, and repeatedly. Many of them took special pleasure in this training, and their skill improved markedly, but other members (mostly men, of course) viewed the spectacle with a frown and complained to the club's management that she was going overboard. As a result, Aomame was called in and instructed to rein in the ball-kicking practice. . . .

In any case, Aomame had mastered at least ten separate techniques for kicking men in the balls. . . . If the need arose, she knew, she would never hesitate to apply her sophisticated techniques in actual combat. *If there's any guy crazy enough to attack me, I'm going to show him the end of the world – close up. I'm going to let him see the kingdom come with his own eyes. I'm going to send him straight to the Southern*

366

Hemisphere and let the ashes of death rain all over him and the kan-garoos and the wallabies.[594]

Here, Murakami has managed to weave in both historical and cinematic references to outrageous effect. That quirky brilliance of his is still there, and though the book is full of familiar Murakami tropes (a strangely philosophical cab driver like the one in *A Wild Sheep Chase*, a beautiful teenage girl with telepathic powers, a cartoonishly grotesque messenger/detective named Ushikawa like the one of the same name in *The Wind-Up Bird Chronicle*,[595] passages between worlds, the preparing and consuming of healthy "simple meals", detailed appreciations of both jazz and classical compositions, parallel narrative tracks that seem destined to intersect, and, yes, cats), it contains more surprises than a reader perhaps has the right to expect from a novelist heading into his middle sixties.[596] Indeed, more so than the attention paid to religious cults, which Murakami examined at length in the non-fiction *Underground*, the focus on the abuse of women can be counted as one of those surprises. Aomame combines the two – and the insistence on healthy eating – in one startling observation: "It was a simple meal, but ideal for preventing constipation. Constipation was one of the things she hated most in the world, on par with despicable men who commit domestic violence and narrow-minded religious fundamentalists".[597]

If the Tengo/Aomame love story serves as the strongest overall driver of the plot, and the story of Aomame's serial assassinations feeds into the two main themes of mind control and the victimization of women, the initial story of Tengo's participation in a literary fraud is less well integrated into the novel. Many pages are devoted to questioning the morality of his secretly polishing the prose of a first-time writer, the 17-year-old schoolgirl Fuka-Eri, so that her novella, *Air Chrysalis*, can win a magazine's fiction competition, and there is much hand-wringing over the threat posed to several lives if revelation of the truth should give rise to a scandal, especially if the work should win the still more prestigious Akutagawa Prize, but these questions fade to the point of irrelevancy as other more interesting events transpire. The young Fuka-Eri, with her uninflected way of speaking (asking questions without question marks) and her combination of non-existent pubic hair, delayed menstruation, and large, perfectly-formed breasts, is one of the more interesting of Murakami's many Lolita figures, but her function as a magical conduit between Aomame and Tengo is far more important than any role she might play in deceiving the reading public.

Had 1Q84 remained focused on the themes of mind control and domestic abuse, it would undoubtedly have been a much shorter novel. Instead, Murakami chose this point in his career to write a kind of novel that he had been talking about since completing *Kafka on the Shore* in 2002. In a long interview published in April 2003, he spoke of something he called a "comprehensive novel" (*sōgō shōsetsu*), a term he identified with one of the books he admired most, Tim O'Brien's *The Nuclear Age*, and also with Thomas Pynchon's *V*, which he called "a perfect" comprehensive novel.[598] The interviewer asked for an explanation of the term.

> What I've done so far is to see how much I could bring out the "drive" of the story, to put myself into it, to shove the story along and see how the characters move with it: that's been my proposition. It started with *A Wild Sheep Chase*, and I've written using a lot of different techniques – in *Hard-boiled Wonderland and the End of the World*, for example, I moved the story along conceptually; in *Norwegian Wood*, with pure realism – I've tried all kinds of methods. From here on out, I suspect the only thing left for me to do is to make the story

itself more complex. Just pushing things along that way in one story, I think I'm not going to be able to make everything fit in any more. The only thing for me to do, I think, is to create new work by piling one story on top of another in a multi-layered way – in other words, to make a "comprehensive novel" – something Dostoevskyan, nineteenth-century. I felt like that reading Dostoevsky's *The Devils*. That's a very strange story. You don't know who the protagonist is. They call it an "ensemble novel" or something, but that's not what it is, either, really. If you ask what the protagonist is, it's the "will of the story". You don't know which character to identify with at first. I feel a powerful attraction to a novel like that. For the first 20 or 30 pages you find yourself reading on and on about this ridiculous private tutor of literature and you think he might be the protagonist, but then it has nothing to do with the rest of the book.

What I have in mind now – and I don't know whether or not I can manage it or whether or not I'm even going to try – is this kind of complex story. A kind of microcosm. I definitely have the desire to write something like that. I'm not saying I've exhausted all the possibilities of pushing a single story along, but I do feel I'd like to go just one step higher. It could take a long time, though.[599]

He had never defined the term "comprehensive novel" more precisely than this, but it might be seen as a new elaboration of the "other worlds" theme that has been present in his work from the beginning, sometimes with seemingly supernatural overtones, sometimes with a hint of science fiction, sometimes as an exploration of the separate parts of the human brain, sometimes as a reflection of the impenetrable walls that separate human beings from each other, sometimes in tracing elements of chance that propel a person's life toward a new world of experience, sometimes as a place of retreat for wounded psyches. The theme yields rich humour in an early story such as "The Kangaroo Communiqué" (1981), as the narrator demonstrates the relationships between seemingly unrelated entities, tracing the "thirty-six intricate procedural steps, followed one by one in just the right order" that have led the narrator from seeing kangaroos in the zoo to "sending you this letter".[600] In fact, forging relationships among apparently unrelated worlds may well be the overall purpose of *1Q84*. Murakami himself said as much in a 2009 interview:

> [I]n my mind at least, [the term "comprehensive novel"] means a novel that's really long and very heavy (laughter). It features all kinds of characters, some normal and others highly peculiar, and combines various perspectives in a totally organic way ... As I conceive it, a comprehensive novel weaves together a number of stories that combine to create an anarchic mix of humour and seriousness; yet, while it deals with situations that are inherently chaotic, a clear and consistent worldview forms the backbone of the work. It operates as a kind of melting pot in which all these reciprocal factors can be combined.[601]

Murakami was still writing *1Q84* at the time of this interview, in which he also said that while the book might not in fact be a comprehensive novel, "it seems to be heading in that direction".[602] Clearly, Murakami recognizes the potential in such a book for chaos, but that very quality, paradoxically enough, might have contributed to the broad appeal of *1Q84*. The excitement generated by *Norwegian Wood* had been a source of stress for Murakami, who always felt that that novel, with its relatively conventional love story, was not in his normal creative mode, but he enjoyed the uproar over the surreal and truly Murakamiesque *1Q84*. The world's reaction to his novels had undergone a great change since the start of the twenty-first century, he said. There was something downright strange about a difficult novel like *1Q84* selling a million volumes in the first few weeks.[603]

He had expanded on this idea in an earlier interview while still writing the novel:

> The last few times I've visited the United States I've come away with the feeling that a certain kind of reality is rapidly disappearing from this world of ours. Think about it: a few terrorists hijacked two big jets and wiped out the World Trade Center . . . It's hard to swallow something like 9/11, to accept that it really happened . . . Had 9/11 never taken place, we would all be living in a different world. A saner, likely better world . . . To put it another way, the actual world today has less reality than made-up, fictional worlds. We are living, so to speak, in the wrong world. This is bound to have a huge impact on our spiritual selves.
>
> A lot of Americans are avidly reading my novels these days, especially young people . . . This makes me happy of course, but when I stop and ask myself what's changed, the only answer I can come up with is that, strange to say, people have grown used to this loss of reality and want to make it theirs by confronting it head-on . . . Wherever you look, competing forces are clashing, which breeds a certain kind of chaos, which in turn makes the sort of novels I write easier for people to appreciate.[604]

At this point, his interviewer, novelist Hideo Furukawa, remarks, "I think the sense of loss, of reality having been somehow diminished, arrived in Japan first," to which Murakami responds, "I agree completely. From that perspective, Japan may be the world's most developed society." Furukawa laughs and says, "Yes, we lead the way in spiritual disintegration! And it was the Aum gassings and the Kobe earthquake that pushed us to the forefront."[605] Murakami said much the same thing in an article he wrote for the *New York Times* in November 2010.[606]

Chaos is customarily reduced in novels by the presence of a plot – in this case, as noted above, an elaboration of the story "On Seeing the 100% Perfect Girl One Beautiful April Morning". Because it is so wide-ranging, *1Q84* presents not one tightly unified novel but a breathtaking compendium of stories-within-stories, some of which are tied to the main narrative in only the most tangential way. We find reflections on Japan's literary industry and the perpetration of a literary fraud, scenes depicting an exotic form of murder based on acupuncture, information on the history of the South Manchurian Railway Company and its role in Japan's pre-war empire, the hardships of pre-war Japanese settlers in Manchuria, the sufferings of ethnically Korean Japanese subjects at the end of the Second World War, the portrait of a young sculptor savant, the correct use and maintenance of automatic pistols, the best techniques for blowing one's brains out, the way to smoke hashish, the use and function of home pregnancy tests, reflections on the building of Tokyo's main east–west commuter line, extensive passages quoted directly from Chekhov's little-known book-length study of Sakhalin Island and the native Gilyak people, a fifty-eight line quotation from the classic chronicle of samurai battles in the twelfth century known as *The Tale of the Heike*, references to Proust as "a detailed report from a small planet light-years away",[607] a long passage from Isak Dinesen's *Out of Africa*, a comparison of three nurses to the three witches in *Macbeth*, a brief disquisition on Jung and God and death, reports on the Iran–Iraq war and Saddam Hussein's use of nerve gas, the assassination of Anwar Sadat, the marriage of Charles and Diana ("Charles looked less like a prince than a high school physics teacher with stomach trouble"),[608] the dangers of coal mining, the joys of mathematics, the 1969–70 student uprisings, the rise of the organic foods movement, reflections on bullying in schools, an explanation of dyslexia, quotations from American pop music lyrics and Bach (in the original German), a discussion of Frazer's *The Golden Bough* and its view of the king as intermediary between the human and divine worlds, biographical information on the composer Janáček, ruminations on the size and energy consumption of the human brain and its perception of time, and a long summary of a fantastic tale called "Town of Cats" made up by Murakami but presented as a German work from the inter-war period.

Murakami's ambitious scope here all but dictated that he would have to move decisively away from first-person into third-person narration. For the most part, he sticks with his two main protagonists, labelling every other chapter in Books One and Two either "Aomame" or "Tengo" in the familiar alternating pattern we have seen since *Hard-Boiled Wonderland and the End of the World*. He complicates this in Book Three by introducing the character Ushikawa's point of view so that the change in perspective rotates through three observers, all of whom are described in the third person, but all of whose thoughts are presented in lengthy sections of interior monologue, giving much of the book the familiar interiorized feel of a Murakami novel.

The love story moves things along through the first two books, but a large part of Book Three consists of the inherently static elements of retracing already-covered territory and depicting characters who do little but wait around for something to happen. By bringing Ushikawa into the foreground and letting him function as a detective trying to figure out the relationship of Aomame and Tengo, Murakami may well have written the world's first detective novel in which almost all the facts uncovered by the detective are already known to the reader. Aside from Aomame's discovery of her pregnancy and the ghostly NHK collector's pounding on locked doors,

373

nearly 200 pages go by before anything new occurs. Part of this has to do with Murakami's original intention of publishing Book Three almost a year after the appearance of Books One and Two, when constant reminders of the earlier action might feel less redundant. This seems like a strangely shortsighted way of putting a novel together since only readers of the first edition would experience the long wait between Books Two and Three. When Knopf insisted on publishing all three books of the English translation in a single massive volume, however, Murakami assented to the removal of many short passages that could only strike the reader as repetitious. Hence the notification in tiny type at the bottom of page iv of the U.S. hardcover edition, "Adapted for this single volume with the participation of the author".[609] The cutting was nowhere nearly as substantial as that of *The Wind-Up Bird Chronicle*, and in fact even after the discreet reshaping, many reviewers remarked on the book's slow pace and repetitiousness.

We have seen earlier Murakami characters killing time until something significant happens in their lives (the protagonist of *Dance Dance Dance* comes to mind), but here we see several characters with little to do – Aomame struggling to make headway through Proust as she evades reprisal for her killing of Leader, Tengo waiting by his dying father's bed in a sanatorium, Fuka-Eri hiding out in Tengo's apartment from members of the Sakigake cult, the editor Komatsu remaining incommunicado while in Sakigake captivity, and Ushikawa going through the boring routines of a stakeout. Finally, in Chapter 17, the pace begins to pick up as the author starts violating his point-of-view rules, allowing various heretofore isolated characters' paths to cross. For example, after having established the point of view as Ushikawa's, a disembodied narrative voice tells us (as only the author can) that "If Ushikawa had followed him that night, he would have found out that Tengo was on his way to meet with Komatsu at the bar in Yotsuya" as seen in an earlier chapter.[610]

Ultimately, near the end of Book Three, Ushikawa is killed by Tamaru, who promptly takes over his point-of-view duties even though Tamaru has only been viewed externally by Aomame so far.[611] In the final chapter bearing the "Ushikawa" label, two bodyguards are discussing how to dispose of Ushikawa's corpse, which lies there inert until, after the two men leave the room, six Little People pop out of his mouth and begin weaving an air chrysalis. Murakami is not quite ready to relinquish the dead Ushikawa's point of view, however. The narrator tells us that the corpse is lying in such a way that "the angle made it impossible for Ushikawa to see the moon. So he couldn't know if there was one moon, or two".[612]

The book's strong centrifugal force may also be explained in part by the circumstances of its composition. Murakami told an interviewer that he had originally planned to write a book called 1985 with Orwell in mind, but when he mentioned this to Michael Radford, who had directed the 1984 film version of 1984, Radford pointed out to him that Anthony Burgess had already published a novel called 1985. Mulling over other possibilities for a not-quite-1984 title, Murakami came up with 1Q84 containing the 9/Q pun and only then began wondering what kind of novel would go with such a title. The first thing he came up with were the names "Aomame" for the heroine and "Tengo" for the hero, at which point he felt certain that the novel would be a good one. It also occurred to him then to use Bach's *Well-Tempered Clavier* as a model for a two-book novel containing 24 chapters each, with Aomame and Tengo appearing in alternating chapters. "I like working within predefined limits," he said, but he realized sometime before Books One and Two were published that there would also have to be a Book Three.[613]

Until he actually started writing, however, he told his incredulous interviewer, he had no concept for the book and absolutely no idea what the two lead characters would be like. (Thinking that he had invented the name "Aomame", he was surprised to learn later that a family by that name actually made their existence known by an email to the publisher.) The one remaining problem was to come up with an opening scene. He had a vague memory of having heard a news report about someone who had climbed down an emergency stairway from the Shibuya-bound elevated expressway in a traffic jam, and he had often made a point of looking for such a stairway whenever he took that route. He decided that an escape stairs in the Sangenjaya area should be the entry to another world, one called 1Q84. Even after he started writing the first chapter, he had no idea why Aomame was in such a hurry or what her mission was.

Only when he started Chapter 2 did he begin thinking about character traits for his male protagonist. Tengo would have some kind of personal problem, and at some point his story would intersect with Aomame's. Maybe they had parted years before and were longing for each other as in "On Meeting the 100% Perfect Girl One Beautiful April Morning". Murakami had been inundated with requests from film school students all over the world for permission to make film versions of that story and had been told that the piece was being read in many college courses. What was it, he wondered, that stimulated people so? He had wondered, too, now and then, what kind of novel he could write by greatly expanding the story. With all these elements coming together, the novel began to move spontaneously.

The interviewer was finding it hard to believe that Murakami had still not come up with something like a Sakigake cult or its Leader at that point. Murakami admitted that he had copious notes from the Aum trial he had attended, but watching a living human being on trial had been "too heavy" to make into fiction. Some of the dark feelings he had at the time had coloured *After Dark*, and he suspected that they had influenced the structure of *1Q84* to some extent as well.[614]

Many questions remain at the end of *1Q84* despite the lovers' happy reunion. Will Sakigake continue to pursue Aomame and/or Tengo and perhaps lay claim to their child? Will Tamaru and the dowager continue to protect Aomame? Will the literary fraud ever have any repercussions? What happened to Tengo's married girl-friend, who seems to have become yet another victim of domestic violence? What will happen to Professor Ebisuno and Fuka-Eri? To what kind of child will Aomame give birth? She is sure it will be a daughter,[615] but will it be a normal human being? How many of the rules governing the world of 1Q84 will apply in the world to which they have escaped, where there is again only one moon? And is that world the original 1984, to which Leader said Aomame could never return, or yet another parallel track, as suggested by the seeming reversal of the tiger image on the Esso billboard?[616] Murakami him-self has said he "feels" that it is not the same old 1984, and has hinted that there might be a sequel or prequel in the works, but then how serviceable will the title *1Q84* be if the action is to continue past December?[617]

Given the tendency of the book to sprawl and to leave many ques-tions unanswered, Murakami preempts his critics by including commentary on *Air Chrysalis* that applies equally well to *1Q84* itself (if not to all of Murakami's works):

While the writing was deceptively simple, a closer read revealed that it was in fact calculated and arranged with great care . . . Figurative expressions were kept to a minimum, but the descriptions were still vivid and richly colored. Above all, the style had a wonderfully musical quality. Even without reading it aloud, the reader could recognize its deep sonority . . . It probably aroused some subconscious something, which was why readers were pulled in and kept turning pages . . . Her readers followed along, very naturally adopting [the protago-nist's] point of view, and before they knew it, they were in another world – a world that was *not this world*, a world in which the Little People made air chrysalises . . . To sane people, these things would seem like nothing more than the kinds of fabrications that appear in fiction, no more real than the Queen of Hearts or the white rabbit with the watch in *Alice in Wonderland* . . .

More than a few of the reviewers seemed perplexed by – or simply undecided about – the meaning of the air chrysalis and the Little People. One reviewer concluded his piece: "As a story, the work is put together in an exceptionally interesting way and it carries the reader along to the very end, but when it comes to the question of what *is* an air chrysalis, or who *are* the Little People, we are left in a pool of mysterious question marks. This may well be the author's intention, but many readers are likely to take this lack of clarification as a sign of 'authorial laziness.' While this may be fine for a debut work, if the author intends to have a long career as a writer, in the near future she may well need to explain her deliberately cryptic posture."

Tengo cocked his head in puzzlement. If an author succeeded in writing a story "put together in an exceptionally interesting way" that "carries the reader along to the very end," who could possibly call such a writer "lazy"? . . . As a story, *Air Chrysalis* was fascinating to many people. It had fascinated Tengo and Komatsu and Professor Ebisuno and an amazing number of readers. What more did it have to do?[618]

Murakami is all but declaring here that he intends to leave his readers puzzling over the meaning of the Little People and the air chrysalises they weave. The phrase *Air Chrysalis* appears countless times throughout the novel as the title of the bestselling novella, and the reader is shown an air chrysalis from several perspectives – as described in various summaries of the novella, as witnessed first-hand by Tengo, and as depicted "objectively" by the narrator independent of any character's point of view.[619] (The Little People and the two moons are also described by the "objective" narrator on occasion.) The use of the word "chrysalis" is doubly puzzling. As Tengo points out when discussing the rough first draft and its young author, "She even gets the title wrong: she's confusing 'chrysalis' and 'cocoon'",[620] and the confusion is noted at least twice more.[621] Woven from silken fibres, the objects clearly are enormous cocoons, not chrysalises, the hard pupal cases formed by butterflies, but Tengo chooses to keep the original title for his thorough rewrite, and Murakami seems to stress the deliberateness of the choice by depicting a hothouse full of rare butterflies on the wealthy dowager's property.[622] The butterflies are described as part of the timeless, womb-like enclosure where the dowager finds peace, and they re-emerge in a dream of Aomame's along with the little rubber plant that symbolizes vulnerable precious life to her,[623] but aside from generally resonating with images of wombs and fecundity (the air chrysalises themselves paramount in this regard), and perhaps providing a veiled reference to the lepidopterist Nabokov as the creator of the original Lolita, it is difficult to see exactly what the butterflies are there for, or why "'air chrysalis' was the only name by which Fuka-Eri (and Tengo himself) could possibly call" these cocoons.[624]

An air chrysalis is shown to have several different functions, most notably serving as a womb that gives birth to a woman's "*dohta*" (from English "daughter"), to whom the woman is related as a "*maza*" ("mother"). The *dohta* is defined as "the shadow of the *maza*'s heart and mind" (*kokoro no kage*),[625] which is reminiscent of the shadow cut away from the protagonist in the "End of the World" chapters of *Hard-Boiled Wonderland and the End of the World*. Separated from the *maza*, the *dohta* is able to function as a "Perceiver" (*pashiva*),[626] who conveys what she perceives to a "Receiver" (*reshiva*), thereby acting as a passageway for the Little People between their world and the "real" world of 1Q84. Like the shadow in the "End of the World", a *dohta* cannot long survive without the *maza*'s care, though the Little People refuse to explain what would happen to a *maza* who loses her *dohta*. (The impassive Fuka-Eri might be one such example.) When two moons appear in the sky, that is a sign that a *dohta* has awakened from her gestation.

All of this may be admirably complex and evocative of something, but it seems to have little impact on the lives of the characters or the working out of the story. When Aomame and Tengo see two moons in the sky, their first reaction is to doubt their own sanity and to feel incapable of mentioning the fact to anyone else, which emphasizes their loneliness and alienating sense of difference rather than anything supernatural or metaphysical. Loneliness lies at the heart of *1Q84* just as much as it did in the earlier and simpler "On Seeing the 100% Perfect Girl One Beautiful April Morning", but the novel has to go through so many contortions in order to bring its perfectly-matched lovers together that the complications paradoxically confirm the unchanging loneliness at the heart of Murakami's world.

When I'm Sixty-Four

Book Three of *1Q84* appeared in April 2010, to be followed that year and the next by some of the translations mentioned at the beginning of this chapter. In December 2011, Murakami came out with one of his most unusual and remarkable publications, a 375-page book of discussions of classical music with the conductor Seiji Ozawa called *Haruki Murakami and Seiji Ozawa Talk About Music* or, more literally, *I Talk with Seiji Ozawa About Music* (*Ozawa Seiji-san to, ongaku ni tsuite hanashi o suru*). The book consists of an introduction by Murakami, six lengthy conversations about various musical topics interspersed with four short dialogues that Murakami calls "interludes", a final essay by Murakami on Ozawa's annual music academy held in the Swiss town of Rolle, and an afterword by Ozawa.

Murakami notes that he had become acquainted with Ozawa through the conductor's daughter, the writer Seira Ozawa, but had never talked with him about music until recently, following Ozawa's surgery for esophageal cancer in December 2009. When Ozawa told him a fascinating story about Glenn Gould and Leonard Bernstein's 1962 performance of the Brahms First Piano Concerto, Murakami remarked that it would be a shame not to record such episodes, and he volunteered to be the one to do it. Inevitably, the impending loss of Ozawa to the world becomes the volume's ground bass as Murakami struggles against time to preserve Ozawa's rich experience for posterity.

Murakami conceived the project, did the recording and transcribing, and put the book together, and his deep admiration for Seiji Ozawa's great musicianship informs the whole. Murakami writes as a fellow artist impressed with Ozawa's total dedication to music even as the conductor's body is ravaged by cancer, but also as a music lover who is fortunate enough to have been in a position to observe Ozawa at work and to be able to ask the Maestro many of the questions that the other music lovers reading the book might have asked if they had had the chance.

Much of the conversation takes place as the two men listen to specific recordings of notable performances, with Ozawa recalling many important episodes in his career. Though Murakami is known as a jazz aficionado and insists on his "amateur" status in music, the depth of his knowledge of classical musicians and orchestras and composers quickly becomes evident; the two men speak as equals. The discussion never becomes technical but guides the reader through the works, pausing to remark on noteworthy passages. It is a miniature education in music appreciation presented with love and enthusiasm.

At the end of the project, Ozawa thrills Murakami by remarking,

"I've never talked about music like this before, in such a focused and deliberate way." Murakami is also pleased to find how much he and Ozawa have in common as artists: their ability to concentrate on their respective work, their continued youthful "hunger" for art, and their stubborn belief in the rightness of their own views. When the English translation eventually appears, established Murakami readers will be pleased to see new sides of the writer. And Ozawa fans will be fascinated to learn that, in those same early hours of the morning when Murakami is writing, Ozawa is reading scores with a similar intensity.

As energetic as his writings continue to be, the fact is that Murakami will be marking his sixty-fourth birthday on 12 January 2013, so he can hardly be blamed for looking back now and then. Retrospective collections of his interviews and miscellaneous talks and essays have appeared in print.[627] On 16 December 2008, while he was still writing *1Q84*, Murakami did a revealing survey of his whole career in the interview by the novelist Hideo Furukawa, cited earlier, which is available in English. A month after Shinchōsha published Book Three of *1Q84*, Murakami submitted to a three-day "long interview" (11–13 May 2010) by Masashi Matsuie, editor of the Shinchōsha-published intellectual journal *Kangaeru hito* (The Thinker), taking 80 pages in the magazine's summer issue to look back over his career to date.

Murakami begins the conversation with Matsuie by noting his change from first-person to third-person narration over the years. Especially after writing *The Wind-Up Bird Chronicle*, he felt strongly that he couldn't get by with first-person narration anymore. Seeing footage of Tran Anh Hung's film version of *Norwegian Wood* (which would be released a few months later in Japan), he says, he was shocked to realize that the book was primarily about the female characters even though the male narrator speaks in the first person. In effect, the movie had translated the book into a third-person narrative. Murakami also notes in passing that *Norwegian Wood* was the only novel he ever wrote that made him feel he never wanted to write another book like that: he had no desire to learn any more about those characters.[628]

Asked by Matsuie what he thinks about people looking for hidden meanings in his novels as if solving riddles, Murakami again asserts that there are no clear answers to the questions raised in his books. "This may sound irresponsible and arrogant, but I think it's pointless to go looking for answers to riddles. The point of a novel is not in its answers." In *1Q84* it took him three years of wrestling with a story to deal with stuff that couldn't be answered simply in a couple of pages. "Truly smart people don't write novels. They can't stand doing something so inefficient."[629]

The interview provides some new angles on Murakami's early life. Haruki's father, we learn, took him to hundreds of movies during his elementary school years – westerns (John Ford), war films (*The Bridges at Toko-Ri*), virtually the whole range of Hollywood offerings. Did the new prominence of fathers in his fiction (*Kafka on the Shore*, *1Q84*) mean that his writing had entered a new phase? Matsuie asked. Murakami replied that he believed he had been dealing with the father problem whenever he talked about The System, as in Jerusalem. He had always disliked authority figures—teachers and such—which, he insisted, had nothing to do with his actual father.[630] Unlike characters such as Aomame and Tengo, he said, he was not psychologically scarred in his youth. He had had an ordinary suburban upbringing that provided him with no drama, nothing worth putting into a novel (as noted in Chapter 2 here), but once he started writing, he realized he had not come through childhood and youth without wounds. Human beings, like other animals, hand their survival skills on to their offspring, but by doing so – especially in the case of humans with their complex social lives – parents can't help but close off certain circuits in their children. From the resulting pain and alienation inherent in growing up, your own inner story is born.

"The wounded characters in *1Q84* are greatly exaggerated reflections of myself."[631]

Murakami's desire for freedom and individuality was evident in his early years. He published a questionnaire in his high school paper asking students whether they were in favour of discontinuing the wearing of school uniforms, assuming that everyone would want to get rid of them as he did, but he was shocked to find that the overwhelming majority of his schoolmates preferred to remain in uniform. In his twenties, he saw a newspaper poll asking people to rank their values – peace, freedom, friendship, etc. Again he was shocked to see that where he would have ranked freedom first, the thousands of respondents ranked it no higher than seventh or eighth. "So, that's what the Japanese are like," he recalls feeling. "The Japanese people don't want freedom, I realized. I wanted to write about the difficulty of wanting to be free, wanting to be an individual in such a country. That was one of my themes in my thirties – to escape from the system imposed by Japanese society, to escape from the system imposed by Japanese literature, which were two sides of the same coin."[632]

A similar observation emerges when Matsuie asks him, "Why do you think you are so widely read here and abroad?" Murakami answers, "Abroad, they call me original, creating a world that no one else can, which makes me very happy, but as far as I know, no one says that here, whether they're praising me or damning me . . . But in fact, that's the thing I'm proudest of . . . I've begun to think that maybe originality is not very highly prized in Japan." Matsuie replies, "Maybe it's the effect of a culture that doesn't welcome difference – being the nail that sticks out."[633]

Reflecting on his background in Kansai, far from the Tokyo centre of modern culture, Murakami says he would probably not have become a writer had he stayed in Kansai with its own regional dialect. His high-school girlfriend went to a Kansai college, and he wanted to stay in the area and take it easy, but "unfortunately", he says with a laugh, it didn't work out that way. He had passed the entrance exam for Waseda University in Tokyo, but had no intention of going there. Then suddenly, for no clear reason, he changed his mind the evening before the tuition was due, and boarded the Shinkansen train to Tokyo the next day. (Murakami's introduction to the Penguin edition of Sōseki's novel *Sanshirō* tells about a girl he met on that train ride.) There, he experienced the shock of immersion in Tokyo standard speech and quickly became "bilingual". The mental bifurcation, he felt, the experience of existing in two separate worlds at once, was a necessary element in his development as a writer. Writing in the standard language of Tokyo was like Nabokov or Conrad writing in a foreign language, the move from Kansai dialect to Tokyo dialect to English enabling him to fashion his own style. At one point he toyed with the idea of translating *Franny and Zooey* into Kansai dialect, but the story "Landscape with Flatiron" may be his only work that made use of Kansai speech. [634]

The discussion of Murakami's work habits strikes a familiar note, emphasizing regularity and discipline. The deeper he gets into a novel, he says, the earlier he spontaneously wakes up. He never needs an alarm clock, is ready to start writing immediately. He writes ten Japanese manuscript pages a day (roughly 1,500–2,000 English words), neither more nor less, never stopping even when a natural break occurs on page eight, and never going beyond page ten, even if he thinks he wants to add a little. He loves working with galleys, does multiple rewrites at that stage. After the day's writing, he runs for an hour, covering ten kilometres. "Ten pages, ten kilometers, like an idiot." He does his translations after lunch. Since translation is a hobby and varies in difficulty, he has no set number of pages. Once he is through writing and running and translating, about two o'clock, "I do what I want – read, listen to music, stroll, buy used records, cook . . . I'm not stoic . . . I just put a little effort into doing things I like, that's all."[635]

Thinking of the future, Murakami can't help but reflect on his age. Dostoevsky died at 60, Fitzgerald in his mid-forties, Carver at 50. To Hideo Furukawa, he said of Carver's death:

> I was forty when I heard the news. To be honest, my immediate reaction was, Good for him, fifty is not that bad, and he managed to keep writing till the end; but when I reached that age myself I felt very differently. In fact, I was ashamed for having let myself think that way, even for a moment. Now I know how much he must have longed to live to write new and different kinds of works. How painful it must have been for him to watch death approach when there was still so much left to do. When I look at his life and the lives of others like him, I'm even more determined not to waste time.[636]

He has no role model for longevity, he says, but neither does he know of an author who continued running full marathons for 25 years. He is curious to see how far he can go with his healthy lifestyle and disciplined work schedule. Life is an experiment that you only get to try once, so, instead of doing nothing, he wants to keep collecting data, even if the experiment never yields a result. Motoyuki Shibata once told him that the Victorian novelist Anthony Trollope lived a very regular life, writing a fixed number of pages early each morning before going to work in the post office. He was wildly popular in the nineteenth century until people learned the secret of his productivity and stopped reading him. He wasn't living up to their romantic image of a novelist. People who wait for artistic inspiration, Murakami says, never write novels, citing Somerset Maugham and Raymond Chandler as novelists who know how to go to their desks and get their writing done. Chandler said that even when you didn't feel like writing, you had to spend at least an hour a day at your desk, thinking, not reading or doing crossword puzzles.[637]

Murakami has often joked in print about his "boring" lifestyle, but his readers never seem to let this detract from their admiration for his imaginative flights. Few commentators have been as cogent as Murakami himself in defining the special appeal his works have had for readers around the world. Looking to the future, he has said:

> If there is something in my style that draws people in, I think it is that even while my writing slips relentlessly downward towards a lonely isolation, it continues to discover in that very fact its own special kind of humour. That stance, at least, I will try not to lose no matter how old I get.[638]

Whatever form Murakami's work takes in the future, we can be sure that it will continue to be true to the spirit of inquiry that has informed both his fiction and his non-fiction. Now nearing 64, Murakami is considerably older than the wise bartender J in *Pinball, 1973* when he said:

> Me, I've seen 45 years, and I've only figured out one thing. That's this: if a person would just make the effort, there's something to be learned from everything. From even the most ordinary, commonplace things, there's always something you can learn. I read somewhere that they say there's even different philosophies in razors. Fact is, if it weren't for that, nobody'd survive.

APPENDIX A

Translating Murakami

(1) Translation and Globalization

Murakami's status as a world literary figure came in for some unusual attention in 2000, raising important questions about translation, re-translation, commercialism and the effect of globalization on literature. The story gives us a glimpse into the issues that confront a serious author with broad appeal, especially when his work crosses linguistic boundaries.[639]

Two of Murakami's novels, *South of the Border, West of the Sun* and *The Wind-up Bird Chronicle*, caused an uproar in Germany beginning on 30 June 2000 when *South of the Border, West of the Sun* was the subject of a popular book discussion programme on television (broadcast simultaneously in Germany, Austria, and Switzerland). The influential octogenarian critic Marcel Reich-Ranicki praised the book, but a critic from Austria, Sigrid Löffler, called it literary fast food unworthy of their attention. She regarded the sex scenes as pornographic and sexist, and accused Reich-Ranicki of being a dirty old man. He accused her of being a prude unable to deal with eroticism in literature. The debate grew heated and personal, and most people agree it was less about Murakami's novel than a long-standing personal hostility on both sides.

The German press picked up the spectacular quarrel, and suddenly the name Haruki Murakami was a household word. Six of his books were already available in German translation, but this televised debate raised his profile and people rushed out to buy *South of the Border, West of the*

Sun – the inevitable reaction when any work of literature is accused of being pornographic.

Soon a professor of Japanese Language and Culture from Hamburg named Dr Herbert Worm joined the fray, declaring that there were many problems with the German text owing to the fact that it was a re-translation from the English. He also pointed out that Murakami's German publisher, DuMont, had now issued two Murakami novels by re-translation from English: not only *South of the Border, West of the Sun*, but *The Wind-up Bird Chronicle*.

Dr Worm wrote to me asking for my views on the matter as the translator of *The Wind-up Bird Chronicle*. He noted that the English translation of *The Wind-up Bird Chronicle* was described as having been "translated and adapted from the Japanese by Jay Rubin with the participation of the author", while the German edition bore no such disclaimer. He wanted to know if "adapted" was a euphemism for "abridged", and he alluded to "the growing discontent with the quality of the German translation", as part of a larger issue:

> Gradually people have come to realize the fact that with the last two Murakami publications in Germany – treating your and Professor Gabriel's American versions as the "authentic original" – standards for translating belles lettres have been kind of ruined; we are actually back again to pre-romantic times, when Cervantes was translated from its awful elegant French version.

No one had ever consulted me about the re-translation of *The Wind-up Bird Chronicle* into other languages, so all this was news to me. I agreed with him that re-translation is an absurd procedure, and that I couldn't imagine why it was even considered in light of the fact that there were surely enough people qualified to translate Japanese literature into German. With regard to abridging the translation, I wrote to him that I would never have considered cutting it if the U.S. publisher, Knopf, had not stipulated in Murakami's contract that the book should not exceed a certain length. Concerned at what an editor might do to the text, I took the initiative to make cuts based on my knowledge of the novel, leaving in more than the specified number of words. Knopf accepted my edited version without a whimper (which suggested to me that I probably could have left more in).

In the end, I gave the U.S. publisher two versions, an entirely uncut translation and my edited version. Why did Knopf insist on having cuts in the first place? Murakami's U.S. editor, Gary Fisketjon, writing on Knopf's website, said simply: "My reaction was that it couldn't be published successfully at such length, which indeed would do harm to Haruki's cause in this country."

The cuts occur primarily at the end of Book Two and the beginning of Book Three. Books One and Two were published in Japanese as a single unit and were accepted as complete by many Japanese readers. Much of the end of Book Two, however, involving Tōru's indecisiveness about whether or not to go to Crete with Creta Kanō, was rendered almost irrelevant by Book Three, so I did not feel too bad about leaving that out. I still think the translation is tighter and cleaner than the original, but I suppose that very tightness can be viewed as a distortion of the original, an Americanization of a Japanese work of art. I had a great time doing it, though it turned out to be a *much* more complex process than I had imagined. Some of the footnotes in Chapter 11 of this book indicate specific differences between the original and the translation.

I did a lot of rearranging at the beginning of Book Three because I found several chronological inconsistencies which were not deliberately placed there by the author. I undoubtedly destroyed the chaotic, fragmented impression of the original Book Three, but I was not persuaded it was meant to be as chaotic as I had found it to be. I can be blamed for having rendered that section of the novel more conventional, but I'm not convinced that that was a great artistic loss. (If this sounds arrogant, you should have been inside my head just after I had finished the translation and I felt I knew every word of the book inside out – better than the author himself! This kind of megalomania is a form of temporary insanity.)

To further complicate the textual picture, Murakami contributed many minor cuts that have since been incorporated into the Japanese paperback edition of the novel (mostly in Book One). He read and approved my final edit, though he was admittedly uneasy that so much had been eliminated.

In an article on the debate raging in Germany, Professor Irmela Hijiya-Kirschnereit asks: "Where is the original?" She goes on to say:

> German readers and critics had absolutely no idea that the German translation, which was based *not* on the Japanese original but on the modified American version, was different from the Japanese original. Which version, then, should the reader now take to be the original? For there now exist two versions, Japanese and English, both of which have been authorized by the author.[640]

Actually, the textual situation is even more complicated. The more you look into it and into the question of revision, the more you realize there is no single authoritative version of *any* Murakami work: he reserves the right to tinker with everything long after it has found its way into print. I once heard that Willem de Kooning would occasionally follow a painting of his to the gallery and revise it on the wall. Murakami is the literary equivalent. There are many versions of *The Wind-up Bird Chronicle*: the serialized version of Book One; the published hardback editions of Books One, Two, and Three; my unpublished complete translation of that edition (with likely inconsistencies since I may have missed something in revising the version based on the serialized chapters); the American version; the British version from Harvill; and finally the paperback (*bunkobon*) version in Japanese, which incorporates some – but not all – of the cuts Murakami recommended for the American translation and possibly others he decided upon afterwards.

In her article, Professor Hijiya-Kirschnereit quotes a "joint declaration" by DuMont and Murakami on the DuMont website recognizing that the "ideal" in translation of his work would be for it to go directly from the Japanese to the German, but that in the interest of speed Murakami was willing to accept translation into other languages from the English. The emphasis here is on English as the starting point for the journey of his works around the world, for which reason Murakami takes special care with the English translations. DuMont insists that:

> In the case of the English edition of *The Wind-up Bird Chronicle*, which he participated in the completion of, with the cooperation of the publisher and the translator, a chronological leap between Books Two and Three was done away with, as a result of which an entirely new work was created.[641]

Professor Hijiya-Kirschnereit asks: "Is the *timing* of a translation more important to Murakami than accuracy and quality?" She also points out an entirely practical matter here: surely it would be faster to go straight from the Japanese to the German rather than waiting for the English translation. She continues:

> What status does the modified American version have vis-a-vis the Japanese? Is it indeed a new work? . . . If Murakami believes that the English version, which he helped to modify, is superior to the Japanese original, will this supposed 'new work' someday be translated back into Japanese (perhaps by Murakami himself)?[642]

DuMont's claims in favour of a "new work" are an overstatement. We are *not* talking about huge textual differences between the Japanese original and the English translation. For example, there is no reference to the "famous" illustrator Tony Takitani, the central character in the Murakami story of that title, in either the English translation or the Japanese paperback.[643] Murakami threw the name in as an injoke when he first wrote the book, then thought better of it during the process of revision for the edited translation, which he then carried over into the Japanese paperback. He did not, however, adopt the large cuts made for the English translation into the Japanese paperback. Another different text is the British edition from The Harvill Press, which has British spellings and idioms and a useful table of contents missing from the American version. The amount of "adapting" I did was small in the overall context. All the great scenes – especially those set in Mongolia and Manchuria – are uncut.

Regarding the question of translation into German by way of English, Professor Hijiya-Kirschnereit says:

> One would like to think that [Murakami], himself a translator, would not readily approve of re-translation. If this declaration [on the DuMont website] does accurately convey Murakami's intention, however, then by promoting the translation of the English version of his works into other languages, he himself comes to embody that English-language-centred cultural imperialism that we continue to deplore and resist. By taking American tastes as a model, what he is helping to bring about is nothing less than the globalization – indeed, the Hollywoodization – of his own works. The Japanese versions, in that case, are reduced to the status of mere regional editions.[644]

This is an excellent point. Translation is an interpretive art, which means that a re-translation is an interpretation of an interpretation. We would be rightly shocked to learn that a new pianist's performance of a Beethoven sonata was based on his hearing an older recording and that he had never looked at the score himself. I might point out here, too, that translations age in ways that original works do not. Translation is a form of close reading, an act of criticism, not creation, and the need for new interpretation becomes apparent when new ideas arise with the passage of time.

Murakami told me that he was not sufficiently consulted regarding the supposed "joint" statement from DuMont, but fortunately a new book of his on translation helps to clarify his position. *Hon'yaku yawa*, or *Night Talks on Translation* (basically, an "after-hours" chat on translating) features three forums, with audience participation, involving Murakami and his collaborator/consultant in American literary translation, Motoyuki Shibata, a Tokyo University professor specializing in American Literature. The book was published in October 2000, but here I would like to quote from Forum #2, which took place in Tokyo in November 1999, seven months before the broadcast that started the commotion in Germany.

Asked what he thought about re-translation of literary works into Japanese, which often results in drastic changes in meaning, Murakami replied:

> To tell you the truth, I kind of like re-translation. My tastes are a little weird anyway, but I'm interested in things like re-translations or novelizations of movies, so my views might be a little one-sided where this is concerned, but I think that with globalization and one thing or another, we're going to see a lot more of the kinds of problems you just mentioned. For example, four of my novels have been translated into Norwegian. Norway has a population of some 4,000,000, so there aren't many people who can translate from Japanese, and sales are small, which is why half the four have been translated from English.
>
> And let's face it: New York is the hub of the publishing world. Like it or not, the rest of the world revolves around New York. And English is the lingua franca of the industry, a tendency that is almost certain to increase . . .
>
> Properly speaking, of course, direct translation from the Japanese is the most accurate and desirable way to go, but I think there will be more and more instances in which it is impossible to demand the most proper, desirable thing.[645]

Joining the debate, Professor Shibata pointed out that translations between European languages are bound to produce fewer differences between texts than translations between European languages and Japanese. If you translated a text from English into French and then into Japanese, you would end up with far fewer differences than if you went from English to Japanese to French. Murakami then picked up on the idea of re-translation:

Given that my novels are being re-translated that way, what I think, as the one who wrote them, is "So what?" (*Laughter*). I'm *not* going so far as to say it's OK if there are a few translation errors or some of the factual connections are wrong, just that there are more important things to think about. I'm not so worried about the details at the level of linguistic expression; as long as the big things on the story level get through, that's pretty much going to do the job. If the work itself has power, it will get past a few mistakes. Rather than worrying about the details, I'm just happy to have my work translated.

(Murakami has said to me that this view applies more to a storyteller like himself than to a writer like 1968 Nobel prizewinner Yasunari Kawabata, whose works depend more for their effect on microscopically modulated poetic imagery.)[646]

"And then *speed* is important," continued Murakami on the forum.

Say I'm writing a book, and 15 years later it shows up translated into Norwegian, I would be glad for that, of course, but I would be *really* pleased if it came out just two or three years after I wrote it, even if the translation were a little off. This is important. Of course, accuracy is important, but speed is another thing you can't ignore.

He went on to say that Kurt Vonnegut's *Breakfast of Champions* was great when it first came out, but that by the time it appeared in Japan ten years later, it had lost much of its punch. "Novels have an impact in their own time," he explained. "There are works, I think, that have to be read in their own time." He cited John Irving's *A Prayer for Owen Meany* as another novel that suffered in Japan because ten years went by before it was translated.[647]

I knew that Murakami was already feeling frustrated by this kind of time-lag when he began working on *The Wind-up Bird Chronicle*, which is why he asked me to start translating it into English while Book One was still being serialized. Of course, as a scholar, it would have made sense for me to have waited to see how the book turned out, to judge whether it was an important part of Murakami's oeuvre, to decide whether Murakami was superior to his contemporaries, or if he was genuinely a spokesman for his time or his generation and the work was sure to enter the canon, but by then I'd be dead, and so would Murakami. You can't tell a 45-year-old author "This will be translated 60 years from now, and then you'll be famous in Hungary"; and you can't tell a translator who loves a work of literature "Wait a few decades to see if this work survives."

I make these points as a translator of contemporary literature, not as a scholar. Authors and publishers are not – and should not be – scholars. Publishers are thinking about sales, about deadlines, about "shaping" and "pacing" an author's career, about the timing and rhythm of releasing an author's work, about keeping the author in the public eye without flooding the market – about selling books. There are people in the industry who think about nothing but commercial matters, but there are also many people who want the books they produce to be important, and somewhere in the backs of their minds they are hoping they are promoting the career of the next Henry James or Hemingway. Nevertheless, in the end, they have to *sell* their books to keep the next Henry James or Hemingway fed so that he will keep writing and keep the publishing company in business. There are literary agents involved in the mix, too, and they have their own ideas about how best to manage their clients' careers. A lot of decisions have to be made to a deadline. Scholars have the luxury of time, and their most authoritative writings are concerned with authors who are safely dead and buried (or in the Japanese case, cremated).

I suppose I might be accused of having betrayed my responsibilities as a scholar by involving myself in "the industry", but it has been an adventure I'm glad I didn't miss. I never got to talk with Sōseki about his works (though I tried once), and I never went cross-country skiing or played squash with him either. I have been tremendously excited to find themes and patterns in Sōseki's works, but I never got to test any of my ideas out on him. It was a great kick to argue with Murakami in a Harvard classroom about the symbolic meaning of an undersea volcano in one of his stories, and to be told by him at the University of Washington, "You think too much."

As a translator and a scholar, I share Professor Hijiya-Kirschnereit's sense of outrage at an author's willingness to compromise on the quality of a translation in the interest of speed, but I also sympathize with Murakami's desire to witness the fate of his work in his lifetime. Books that last into succeeding generations will be translated again and again, and later translators will inevitably benefit from the long-range scholarly perspective.

When I translate the great Meiji novelist Sōseki Natsume, for example, I treat the text more as an untouchable artefact. If I find authorial inconsistencies, I remark on them in an appended commentary rather than attempt to fix them on the spot. When translating Haruki Murakami, however, I see myself as part of the ongoing global process of creation and dissemination (some might argue a cog in the machinery of the publishing industry). I am aware, too, of Japanese editorial practice, which is far less demanding than that of English-speaking countries, so if I find errors that Japanese editors have missed I usually fix them.

No one reads a book as closely as a translator, which is why the bracketed part of the following sentence was removed from the first page of the translation of Murakami's bestseller: "Once the plane was on the ground, [the NO SMOKING sign went out, and] soft music began to flow from the ceiling speakers: a sweet orchestral cover version of The Beatles' 'Norwegian Wood'." This may help prove Murakami's point that the details are less important than the story.

(2) Translators, Editors, and Publishers

At this point, there are three translators working in English on Haruki Murakami's major writings: Alfred Birnbaum, Philip Gabriel, and me. In the academic world of Japanese literary studies, Alfred was something of a mystery man when he translated *A Wild Sheep Chase* in 1989. He was a freelance translator and journalist who had no connections with the academic network, just a young guy who had grown up in Japan, knew the language, and could write English with a certain flair. The story of how he "discovered" Murakami and came to translate his work is discussed in Chapter 10.

Having translated all the long works up to *Dance Dance Dance*, Alfred was feeling justifiably burnt out by the time Murakami started writing *The Wind-up Bird Chronicle*. In the meantime, I had translated some of the short stories and was eager to do more when Haruki said he needed a translator for his next novel. The timing of Alfred's fatigue couldn't have been better for me. Alfred not only stopped translating Murakami for a while, he left Japan to live and work in Myanmar, marrying a Burmese woman.

Phil Gabriel was briefly a junior colleague of mine at the University of Washington, and is now a professor of Japanese Literature at the University of Arizona in Tucson. He did his academic work on post-war literature, particularly that of the writer Toshio Shimao, about whom he wrote a book entitled *Mad Wives and Island Dreams: Toshio Shimao and the Margins of Japanese Literature* (Honolulu: University of Hawai'i Press, 1999). He came across Murakami's works in a Nagasaki bookshop in 1986 and hurried to read all of the stories then available: "I was really bowled over by them," he said in a Knopf Internet roundtable discussion on translation. "I loved his light touch, his humour, his often quirky take on life, as well as the touch of nostalgia for the past that often appeared in these early works."

Phil's translation of "The Kangaroo Communiqué" was the first Murakami story published in the United States. It appeared in *ZYZZYVA*, a literary journal based in Berkeley, California, in autumn 1988. Since then he has translated *South of the Border, West of the Sun* and *Sputnik Sweetheart*, as well as the parts of *The Place That Was Promised: Underground 2* that became Part Two of the English translation *Underground: the Tokyo Gas Attack and the Japanese Psyche* (in 2001, this book won Alfred and Phil the Sasakawa Prize for Japanese Translation).

The importance of editors in the publication of literature cannot be overestimated. Without an editor who believes in a writer, there is no way for a publisher to promote that writer's career. The strategic role of Elmer Luke at Kodansha International has been outlined in Chapter 10.

When the US publishing industry began to take notice of Murakami, Robert Gottlieb and Linda Asher were his strongest editorial backers at *The New Yorker*. The magazine's receptivity to Murakami, their very first Japanese short story writer, has continued to this day under the regime of Bill Buford and Deborah Treisman, with eleven stories in print so far (including two excerpts from *The Wind-up Bird Chronicle*). This has to put Murakami among the most-published writers in *The New Yorker* of any nationality. The publication of this book, I think, demonstrates the devotion of Christopher MacLehose and Ian Pindar at The Harvill Press to Murakami's work.

Gary Fisketjon, who had been Raymond Carver's editor at Knopf, is the one who assembled the stories in *The Elephant Vanishes* for publication in 1993. Gary's interest in Japanese literature began with his reading of the so-called Big Three – Jun'ichirō Tanizaki, Yasunari Kawabata and Yukio Mishima – as an undergraduate at Williams College in the mid-1970s. The Kodansha International translations convinced him that Murakami "properly belongs next in that hugely distinguished line of writers", so when Murakami decided to make the move to Knopf, Gary was the most obvious choice as his editor.

As for me, my own work had been on writers who flourished in the early twentieth century, and I had little interest in contemporary Japanese writing. Whenever I sampled any, it seemed thin and immature in comparison with the early twentieth-century giant Sōseki Natsume, on whom I continue to work.

Then, in 1989, I read Haruki Murakami for the first time. I had only been vaguely aware of his existence – as some kind of pop writer, mounds of whose stuff were to be seen filling up the front counters in Tokyo bookstores – but I hadn't deigned to read what was sure to be silly fluff about teenagers getting drunk and bed-hopping. Some months before *A Wild Sheep Chase* came out in English, an American publisher asked me to read a Murakami novel to see if it was worth translating; they had been evaluating a translation but wanted an opinion on the original. I figured it wouldn't hurt me to discover what kind of junk was being read out there, so I took the job, but with some misgivings. The book was *Sekai no owari to hādoboirudo wandārando*, later translated as *Hard-boiled Wonderland and the End of the World*, and it absolutely blew me away – so much so that I hardly worked on anything besides Murakami for the next decade.

After years of concentrating on muted grey Japanese realism, I could hardly believe a Japanese writer could be so bold and wildly imaginative as I found Murakami to be. I can still see the colours of the dreams escaping into the atmosphere from the unicorn skulls near the end of the book. When I think back to that first reading of *Hard-boiled Wonderland and the End of the World*, I remember how much I regretted closing the last page and realizing that I couldn't live in Murakami's world any more. I told the publisher that they should by all means publish a translation and that if, by any chance, they were not satisfied with the translation they were considering, they should let *me* do it. They ignored my advice on both counts, and Alfred Birnbaum's translation came out a few years later from Kodansha International.

I think I would not have liked Murakami's writing so much if I had first read anything else, including *Norwegian Wood*. I've been able to enjoy almost everything of Murakami's knowing that he was the creator of that incredible mind trip *Hard-boiled Wonderland and the End of the World*, echoes of which are to be found in everything he has written since.

I hadn't responded to a writer so strongly since becoming obsessed by Dostoevsky as an undergraduate. I got everything of Murakami's I could lay my hands on and started reading him – and teaching him – to the exclusion of anyone else, as my students can attest. I especially loved the stories. I found Murakami's Tokyo address and wrote for permission to translate any of half a dozen stories I had in mind. His agent at the time got back to me from Tokyo saying I could go ahead. I sent her one of my favourites, "The Second Bakery Attack", and the next thing I knew Murakami himself was on the phone asking me if I minded publishing it in *Playboy*. Used to publishing my academic stuff for audiences of twelve, I leaped at the chance, whatever scruples I might have had regarding the so-called *Playboy* "philosophy". The illustration for that first story was a masterpiece: the McDonald's robbery scene done in the style of an eighteenth-century Japanese *ukiyo-e* woodblock print. *The New Yorker* took "The Elephant Vanishes" around the same time.

Murakami surprised me that first day on the phone when he said he was calling from Princeton. I was probably the only professor of modern Japanese literature in the country who didn't know he was there. In fact, he was going to be running in the 1991 Boston Marathon that April, and we met in Cambridge the day afterwards when he attended a class of Howard Hibbett's that was discussing my still-unpublished translation of "The Second Bakery Attack". Later we were neighbours in Cambridge and saw a lot of each other. I drove Murakami crazy more than a few times asking him to explain some obscure passages and finding inconsistencies that his Japanese editors had missed.

Let me turn to a few problems of translation from Japanese to English. As I point out in *Making Sense of Japanese* (Kodansha International, 1992/1998/2002; the original edition bore the title *Gone Fishin'*), the Japanese language is very different from English, but it is still just a language, and one should be on one's guard against the mystical nonsense that continues to cling to the image of Japanese both at home and abroad. The Japanese language is *so* different from English – even when used by a writer as Americanized as Murakami – that true literal translation is impossible, and the translator's subjective processing is inevitably going to play a large part. That processing is a *good thing*; it involves a continual critical questioning of the meaning of the text. The last thing you want is a translator who believes he or she is a totally passive medium for transferring one set of grammatical structures into another: then you're going to get mindless garbage, not literature.

Let me give a more concrete example of what I mean here. Take this unremarkable paragraph from "The 1963/1982 Girl from Ipanema":

When I think of my high school's corridor, I think of mixed salads: lettuce, tomatoes, cucumbers, green peppers, asparagus, onion rings, and pink Thousand Island dressing. Not that there was a salad shop at the end of the corridor. No, there was just a door, and beyond the door a drab 25-metre pool.

Now, here is the same paragraph in a style that might look familiar if you have read a lot of Japanese literature in translation:

When one says high school corridor, I recall mixed salads. Lettuce, tomatoes, cucumbers, green peppers, asparagus, onion rings, and pink Thousand Island dressing. Of course, it is not to say that at the end of the high school corridor there is a salad specialty shop. At the end of the high school corridor, there is a door, and outside the door there is only a 25-metre pool that is not very attractive.

Those without experience in translating literature will probably assume the second version is more "literal" or "faithful" simply because it is more awkward. In fact, the second one is no closer to the Japanese than the first; it is just closer to the usage found in language-learning textbooks, which gives it an *illusion* of literalness.

A great deal more would have to be done even to the "literal"-seeming paragraph before it began to approach the Japanese original. Japanese doesn't have any definite or indefinite articles – no equivalents to "the" or "a" – and no simple distinctions between singular and plural: *hako* means either "box" or "boxes" depending on the context. Subordinate clauses come before the nouns they modify, not after, and there are no relative pronouns. Instead of saying "the man who arrived yesterday", a Japanese will say "yesterday arrived man". Subjects and objects disappear from a Japanese sentence when they are clear from the context, so people routinely say "Went" (this is a complete sentence) rather than "I went", or "Ate" (again, a complete sentence) rather than "I ate it", and verbs come at the ends of sentences, with negative endings and tense markers coming last of all. "I didn't see *Monty Python* last night" would come out looking like "Last night *Monty Python* see-not-did".

If you *really* wanted a literal translation of that salad paragraph, it would have to look more like this, with English loan words in italics:

> High school's corridor say-if, I *mixed salad* think-up. *Lettuce* and *tomato* and cucumber and green pepper and *asparagus*, ring-cut bulb onion, and pink-colour's *Thousand Island dressing*. No argument high school corridor's hit-end in *salad* specialty shop exists meaning is-not. High school corridor's hit-end in, *door* existing, *door*'s outside in, too-much flash-do-not 25-*metre pool* exists only is.

Now, this is a simple paragraph written by a novelist whose writing has been heavily influenced by his reading of American literature. Murakami's style strikes the Japanese reader as fresh and new because it often reads like a translation from English. You would think that this sort of Japanese would be easy to translate. It should slip right back into its English skin with no strain. And to some extent that is true. But Japanese and English are so very different as languages that nothing is automatic.

Even in something so apparently straightforward as our example, much of which consists of a list of salad ingredients, there is no question of doing anything that could remotely be called a "literal" translation. Written in a special syllabary used for foreign words, some of the ingredients have a tantalizingly foreign sound and *look* in the Japanese text, but they inevitably lose this quality when they are translated "back" into English and are surrounded by other English words.

Translating Murakami into traditional clunky translationese might be one answer to the problem of accurately conveying his style, but his Japanese is not clunky. Its American flavour is subtle and feels both foreign and natural at the same time. This is largely due to the fact that Japanese readers are more tolerant of translationese than we are. A Japanese writer can bend his language more than a writer using English

403

can without being accused of stylistic clumsiness. Paradoxically, then, the *closeness* of Murakami's style to English can itself pose problems for a translator trying to translate it "back" into English: the single most important quality that makes his style fresh and enjoyable in Japanese is what is lost in translation.

I suspect that Alfred Birnbaum (and to a lesser extent Phil Gabriel) is trying to compensate for this loss by introducing a certain exaggerated hipness of expression into the English text. My own approach is to try to reproduce the clean rhythmicality that gives Murakami's style its propulsive force. Of course I prefer my own approach, but there is no doubt that Alfred's jazzy translation of *A Wild Sheep Chase* is what caught the attention of English-speaking readers.

Whether in Japanese or translation, Murakami has proven he has the power to attract a broad readership. Certainly his sense of humour is one of the most important elements that helps him leap national boundaries. But finally, I think that Murakami succeeds by getting inside your brain and doing weird things to it. I remember one Murakami moment I had after translating the passage in *The Wind-up Bird Chronicle* where little Nutmeg climbs on to her veterinarian father's lap and smells all the animal smells he brings home on his clothes from the zoo. Later in the day, all of a sudden, I found myself singing "Oh, My Papa, To Me He Was So Wonderful", a song I hadn't thought of in years.

Gary Fisketjon probably came as close as anyone to explaining Murakami's attraction when he characterized Murakami as "*the* breakthrough Japanese writer in the West . . . because he continues to grow and change and mystify, probably surprising himself as much as his readers en route".

APPENDIX B

A Murakami Bibliography

Notes

1 Murakami's works are listed under their Japanese titles in order of publication, with translated sources numbered in the left margin.
2 All Japanese names in citations of Japanese publications and of scholarly English-language publications are given in the Japanese order, surname first, and that includes the name "Murakami Haruki". In the body of this book, and in expository passages in the notes, all Japanese names have been given in the Western order.
3 All Japanese books cited have been published in Tokyo.
4 "Also" = Translations have been made into the languages of these additional countries, with year of initial publication. See *CD-ROM-ban Murakami Asahidō: Sumerujakofu tai Oda Nobunaga kashindan* (Asahi Shinbunsha, 2001); Japan Foundation, comp., *A Wild Haruki Chase* (Berkeley: Stone Bridge Press, 2008), pp.139–147; the Japan Foundation's online database of Japanese literature in translation under "Arts and Cultural Exchange"; publishers' websites; and information from the Curtis Brown Literary Agency, London.

WORKS BY MURAKAMI

Key to English Translations
Numbers in brackets refer to numbers in the margin below

> After Dark (25)
> *after the quake* (21)
> "Airplane: Or, How He Talked to Himself as If Writing Poetry"
>   (12/27)

Novels and short story collections

1 *Kaze no uta o kike*. Kōdansha, 1979. Trans. by Alfred Birnbaum as *Hear the Wind Sing*. Tokyo: Kodansha English Library [distribution limited to Japan], 1987. Also: Korea 1991 and 1996, Taiwan 1992, Hong Kong 1997, Russia 2003, Thailand 2003, Indonesia 2008.

2 *1973-nen no pinbōru*. Kōdansha, 1980. Trans. by Alfred Birnbaum as *Pinball, 1973*. Tokyo: Kodansha English Library [distribution limited to Japan], 1985. Also: Korea 1997, Taiwan 1992, Hong Kong 1997, Thailand 2003, Russia 2006.

3 *Hitsuji o meguru bōken*. Kōdansha, 1982. Trans. by Alfred Birnbaum as *A Wild Sheep Chase*. Tokyo: Kodansha International, 1989. Also: US 1993, UK (Hamish Hamilton, 1990; Penguin, 1991; Harvill 2000), France 1990, Germany 1991, Russia 1998, Italy 1992, Spain 1991, Holland 1991, Norway 1993, Finland 1992, Poland 1995, Greece 1991, Korea 1997, China 1997, Taiwan 1995, Hong Kong 1992,

Romania 2002, Lithuania 2003, Thailand 2003, Brazil 2001, Denmark 1996, Israel 2004, Latvia 2004, Slovakia 2004, Portugal 2007.

4 *Chūgoku-yuki no surō bōto*. Chūō Kōronsha, 1983. Partial contents trans. by Alfred Birnbaum as "A Slow Boat to China", "The Kangaroo Communiqué", and "The Last Lawn of the Afternoon" in *The Elephant Vanishes* (cited with bibliographic information below); by Philip Gabriel as "The Kangaroo Communiqué" in ZYZZYVA (Autumn 1988) and "The New York Mining Disaster" in *The New Yorker* (11 January 1999) and in *Blind Willow, Sleeping Woman*; and by Jay Rubin as "A Poor-Aunt Story" in *The New Yorker* (3 December 2001) and as "A 'Poor Aunt' Story" in *Blind Willow, Sleeping Woman*. Also: Korea 1991 and 1999, Taiwan 1998, Hong Kong 1995.

5 *Kangarū-biyori*. Heibonsha, 1983. Partial contents trans. by Jay Rubin as "On Seeing the 100% Perfect Girl One Beautiful April Morning", and "A Window" in *The Elephant Vanishes*; by Ted Goossen as "A Perfect Day for Kangaroos" in Alberto Manguel, ed., *Soho Square* (London: Bloomsbury Press, 1991) and as "In the Year of Spaghetti", in *Descant 76* (Summer 1992); by Philip Gabriel as "A Perfect Day for Kangaroos" in *Blind Willow, Sleeping Woman*; by Jay Rubin as "Dabchick" in *McSweeney's* Number 4 (Late Winter, 2000), ten-page "discreet booklet" in boxed issue and in *Blind Willow, Sleeping Woman*; and by Jay Rubin as "The Rise and Fall of Sharpie Cakes", read on BBC Radio 3 programme "The Verb" (4 October, 2003) and in *Blind Willow, Sleeping Woman*. Also: Taiwan 1992, Vietnam 2006, Germany 2006, Spain 2008, Italy 2010.

6 *Hotaru, Naya o yaku, sono-ta no tanpen*. Shinchōsha, 1984. Partial contents trans. by Alfred Birnbaum and Jay Rubin as "Barn Burning" and "The Dancing Dwarf" in *The Elephant Vanishes*; by Philip Gabriel as "Firefly" in *Blind Willow, Sleeping Woman*; and by Keith Leslie Johnson as "Three German Fantasies", in *The Review of Contemporary Fiction* 22:2 (Summer 2002). Also: Korea 2000, Taiwan 1999, Germany 1995, France 1998, Italy 2004.

7 *Sekai no owari to hādoboirudo wandārando*. Shinchōsha, 1985. Trans. by

Alfred Birnbaum as *Hard-boiled Wonderland and the End of the World*. Tokyo: Kodansha International, 1991. Also: US 1993, UK (Hamish Hamilton 1991, Penguin 1992), France 1992, Germany 1993, Holland 1993, Greece 1994, Korea 1997, China 1996, Taiwan 1994, Hong Kong 1994, Italy 2002, Russia 2002, Hungary 1998, Lithuania 2004, Norway 2001, Poland 1998, Romania 2004, Thailand 2004, Croatia 2005, Latvia 2007, Vietnam 2010.

8 *Kaiten mokuba no deddo hiito*. Kōdansha, 1985. Partial contents trans. by Alfred Birnbaum as "Lederhosen" in *The Elephant Vanishes*; by Jay Rubin as "Nausea 1979" in *Blind Willow, Sleeping Woman*; and by Philip Gabriel as "Hunting Knife" in *The New Yorker* (17 November, 2003) and *Blind Willow, Sleeping Woman*. Also: Korea 2000, Taiwan 1999.

9 *Pan'ya saishūgeki*. Bungei Shunjūsha, 1986. Partial contents trans. by Alfred Birnbaum and Jay Rubin as "The Fall of the Roman Empire, The 1881 Indian Uprising, Hitler's Invasion of Poland, and the Realm of the Raging Winds", "The Wind-up Bird and Tuesday's Women", "The Second Bakery Attack", "The Elephant Vanishes", and "Family Affair" in *The Elephant Vanishes*. "The Second Bakery Attack" was also anthologized in Alice K. Turner, ed., *Playboy Stories: The Best of Forty Years of Short Fiction* (Penguin/Dutton, 1994). Also: Israel no date, Korea 2000, Taiwan 1999.

10 *Noruwei no mori*. Kōdansha, 1987. Trans. by Alfred Birnbaum as *Norwegian Wood*. Tokyo: Kodansha English Library [distribution limited to Japan], 1989. Trans. by Jay Rubin as *Norwegian Wood*. London: Harvill Press, 2000, and New York: Vintage, 2000. Also: France 1994, Italy 1993, Norway 1999, Israel 2000, Korea 1989 and 1997, China 1996, Hong Kong 1991, Romania 2002, Czech Republic 2002, Latvia 2003, Sweden 2003, Brazil 2005, Bulgaria 2005, Indonesia 2005, Denmark 2005, Germany 2001, Lithuania 2005, Holland 2007, Poland 1995, Russia 2003, Slovenia 2005, Spain (Spanish and Catalan) 2005, Taiwan 2004, Thailand 2003, Lebanon 1990, Croatia 2004, Turkey 2004, Serbia 2007, Vietnam 2007, Hungary 2008.

11 *Dansu dansu dansu*. Kōdansha, 1988. Trans. by Alfred Birnbaum as *Dance*

Dance Dance. Tokyo: Kodansha International, 1994. Also: US 1994, UK Harvill, 2002, France 1995, Italy 1998, Norway 1995, Korea 1994, China 1996, Taiwan 1996, Hong Kong 1992, Germany 2002, Brazil 2005, Denmark 1996, Lithuania 2004, Romania 2004, Russia 2002, Serbia and Montenegro 2005, Slovakia 2006, Ukraine 2005, Thailand 2004, Poland 2005, Portugal 2007.

12 *TV Piipuru*. Bungei Shunjūsha, 1990. Partial contents trans. by Alfred Birnbaum and Jay Rubin as "TV People" and "Sleep" in *The Elephant Vanishes*; and by Jay Rubin as "Airplane" in *The New Yorker* (1 July 2002) and as "Airplane: Or, How He Talked to Himself as If Reciting Poetry" in *Blind Willow, Sleeping Woman*. "TV People" originally titled "Counterattack of the TV People" ("TV Piipuru no gyakushū"); and by Alfred Birnbaum as "The Folklore of Our Times" in *The New Yorker* (2 June 2003) and by Philip Gabriel as "A Folklore for my Generation: A Pre-History of Late-Stage Capitalism" in *Blind Willow, Sleeping Woman*. Also: Korea 1996, Taiwan 2000, Germany 1996, France 1998, Italy 2004, Vietnam 2007.

13 *Murakami Haruki zensakuhin 1979–89*. Eight volumes. Kōdansha, 1990–91. (Contains all above texts except "TV People", some significantly revised by the author.) Three stories initially published here have been translated into English: from Vol. 5, "Chinmoku", trans. by Alfred Birnbaum as "The Silence" in *The Elephant Vanishes*; from Vol. 8, "Hito-kui neko", trans. by Philip Gabriel as "Man-Eating Cats" in *The New Yorker* (4 December 2000) and in *Blind Willow, Sleeping Woman*; and the "long version" of "Tonii Takitani" trans. by Jay Rubin as "Tony Takitani" in *The New Yorker* (15 April, 2002) and in *Blind Willow, Sleeping Woman*.

14 *Kokkyō no minami, taiyō no nishi*. Kōdansha, 1992. Trans. by Philip Gabriel as *South of the Border, West of the Sun*. New York: Knopf, 1999. Also: UK Harvill 1999, Germany 2000, Italy 2000, Norway 2000, Israel 1999, Korea 1999, Taiwan 1993, Hong Kong 1997, Iceland 2002, France 2002, Romania 2002, Denmark 2003, Croatia 2003, Estonia 2003, Spain (Spanish and Catalan) 2003, Poland 2003, Russia 2003, China 2001, Czech Republic 2004, Holland 2001,

Slovenia 2005, Thailand 2003, Latvia 2004, Serbia 2006, Lebanon 2007, Lithuania 2007, Vietnam 2007, Turkey 2007, Portugal 2009.

15 "Losing Blue", initially unpublished in Japanese, trans. by Jay Rubin, in *Leonardo* (Seville Universal Exhibition, April 1992), pp.38–39.

16 *The Elephant Vanishes*. New York: Knopf, 1993. Anthology of 17 short stories compiled by Knopf editor Gary Fisketjon. For contents, see English key above. Also: UK Harvill 2001, France 1998, Germany 1996, Sweden 1996, Israel 1999, China 1997, Hong Kong 1995.

17 *Nejimakidori kuronikuru*. Three volumes. Shinchōsha, 1994–95. Trans. by Jay Rubin as *The Wind-up Bird Chronicle*. New York: Knopf, 1997. Two excerpts printed in *The New Yorker* as "The Zoo Attack" (31 July 1995) and "Another Way to Die" (20 January 1997). Also: UK Harvill 1998, Germany 1999, Italy 1999, Norway 1999, Korea 1994–95, China 1997, Taiwan 1995–97, Hong Kong 1995–96, Denmark 2000, France 2001, Greece 2005, Israel 2005, Holland 2003, Romania 2004, Russia 2001, Spain 2001, Poland 2004, Turkey 2005, Thailand 2006, Vietnam 2007, Sweden 2008, Lithuania 2008, Ukraine 2009.

18 *Yoru no kumozaru*. Heibonsha, 1995. Partial contents trans. by Jay Rubin as "Good News and Other Stories" in *Southword 11: New Writing from Ireland* (December 2006), pp.103–110, and in *Hayden's Ferry Review – Issue 50* (Spring/Summer 2012), pp.80–86. Also: Korea 1996, Taiwan 1996, Hong Kong 1996.

19 *Rekishinton no yūrei*. Bungei Shunjūsha, 1996. Partial contents trans. by Alfred Birnbaum and Jay Rubin as "The Silence" and "The Little Green Monster" in *The Elephant Vanishes*; by Jay Rubin as "The Seventh Man" in *Granta*, 61 (Spring 1998) and in *Blind Willow, Sleeping Woman*; by Jay Rubin as "Tony Takitani" in *Blind Willow Sleeping Woman*; by Philip Gabriel as "Blind Willow, Sleeping Woman" in *Blind Willow, Sleeping Woman*; by Richard L. Peterson as "Ice Man" in *The New Yorker* (10 February, 2003) and by Philip Gabriel as "The Ice Man" in *Blind Willow, Sleeping Woman*.

20 *Supūtoniku no koibito*. Kōdansha, 1999. Trans. by Philip Gabriel as *Sputnik Sweetheart* [Murakami's own English subtitle for the original] (Harvill, 2001; Knopf, 2001). Also: Korea 1999, Taiwan 1999,

Hong Kong 1999, Germany 2002, Spain (Spanish and Catalan) 2002, Croatia 2002, Poland 2002, France 2003, Brazil 2003, Finland 2003, Iceland 2003, Italy 2003, Bulgaria 2005, China 2001, Denmark 2004, Israel 2003, Holland 2005, Portugal 2005, Romania 2004, Russia 2004, Slovenia 2004, Thailand 2004, Lebanon 1990, Macedonia 2004, Serbia 2004, Vietnam 2008, Lithuania 2008, Norway 2010.

21 *Kami no kodomotachi wa mina odoru*. Shinchōsha, 2000. Trans. by Jay Rubin as *after the quake* (Harvill, 2002; Knopf, 2002). Also: Korea 2000, Taiwan 2000, Hong Kong 2000, Germany 2002, France 2002, China 2002, Norway 2002, Thailand 2003, Croatia 2003, Italy 2005, Iceland 2005, Romania 2006, Holland 2008, Denmark 2008.

22 *Murakami Haruki zensakuhin 1990–2000*. Seven volumes. Kōdansha, 2002–2003. Partial contents of Vol. 1 trans. by Jay Rubin as "Losing Blue" in Item 15 above.

23 *Umibe no Kafuka*, Two volumes. Shinchōsha, 2002. Trans. by Philip Gabriel as *Kafka on the Shore* (Harvill, January 2005; Knopf, January 2005). Also: Taiwan 2003, Korea 2003, China 2003, Hong Kong 2003, Germany 2004, France 2005, Holland 2006, Norway 2005, Russia 2004, Spain 2006, Czech Republic 2006, Romania 2006, Thailand 2006, Portugal 2006, Catalonia 2007, Lithuania 2007, Lebanon 2007, Italy 2007, Indonesia 2008, Denmark 2008.

24 "Crabs" ("Kani"), initially unpublished in Japanese, trans. by Philip Gabriel in bilingual English/Italian magazine, with accompanying interview and Italian translations, *Storie* (Fall, 2003) and in *Blind Willow, Sleeping Woman*: Japanese version first published in *Mekura-yanagi to nemuru onna* (2009).

25 *Afutādāku*. Shinchōsha, 2004. Trans. by Jay Rubin as *After Dark*. New York: Knopf, 2007. London: Harvill Secker, 2007. Also: Germany 2005, China 2005, Korea 2005, Taiwan 2005, Holland 2006, France 2007, Russia 2006, Norway 2007, Czech Republic 2007, Portugal 2008, Spain 2008, Italy 2008, Armenia 2010.

26 *Tōkyō Kitan Shū*. Shinchōsha, 2005. See *Blind Willow, Sleeping Woman*. *Zō no shōmetsu: tanpen senshū 1980–1991*. Shinchōsha. 2005. First Japanese release of *The Elephant Vanishes* (Knopf, 1993)

27 *Blind Willow, Sleeping Woman.* New York: Knopf, 2006. London: Harvill Secker, 2006. Anthology containing 24 short stories compiled by Knopf and Murakami, trans. by Philip Gabriel and Jay Rubin with Introduction by Murakami. Final five stories comprise complete contents of *Tōkyō Kitan Shū* (Strange Tales from Tokyo). For contents, see English key above.

28 *1Q84*, Three volumes. Shinchōsha, 2009 (Books 1 and 2), 2010 (Book 3). Books 1 and 2 trans. by Jay Rubin, Book 3 trans. by Philip Gabriel, as *1Q84*. New York: Knopf, 2011. London: Harvill Secker, 2011. US edition in one volume, UK edition in two volumes (Books 1 and 2 in first volume, Book 3 in second). Excerpt from Book 2, "Town of Cats", in *The New Yorker* (5 September 2011), pp.62–70. Also: (by the year of earliest volume): 2009: Korea, Taiwan; 2010: China, Germany, Holland, Poland, Denmark, Italy, France, Serbia, Ukraine; 2011: Thailand, Spain (Spanish, Galician, Catalan), Norway, Sweden, Russia, Romania, Czech Republic, Portugal, Lithuania, Hungary, Israel; 2012: Turkey, Greece, Bulgaria, Latvia, Slovenia, Brazil; 2013: Estonia.

Mekura-yanagi to nemuru onna. Shinchōsha, 2009. First Japanese release of *Blind Willow, Sleeping Woman (Knopf, 2006)*.

Essays, talks, interviews, travel writing, picture books, reportage

Uōku, donto ran, with Murakami Ryū. Kōdansha, 1981.

Yume de aimashō, with Itoi Shigesato. Tōjusha, 1981. Contains the original version of "The Bakery Attack" ("Pan'ya shūgeki"), under "Pan".

Zō-kōjō no happiiendo, with Anzai Mizumaru. CBS-Sony, 1983.

Nami no e, nami no hanashi, with Inakoshi Kōichi. Bungei shunjū, 1984.

Murakami Asahidō, with Anzai Mizumaru. Wakabayashi shuppan kikaku, 1984.

Hitsuji-otoko no kurisumasu, with Sasaki Maki. Kōdansha, 1985. Translation: Germany 1998.

Eiga o meguru bōken, with Kawamoto Saburō. Kōdansha, 1985.

Murakami Asahidō no gyakushū, with Anzai Mizumaru. Asahi Shinbunsha, 1986.

Rangeruhansu-tō no gogo, with Anzai Mizumaru. Kōbunsha, 1986.

'THE SCRAP' Natsukashi no 1980 nendai. Bungei Shunjū, 1987.

Hi-izuru kuni no kōjō, with Anzai Mizumaru. Heibonsha, 1987.

Za Sukotto Fittsujerarudo bukku. TBS Britannica, 1988.

Murakami Asahidō Hai hō! Bunka shuppan kyoku, 1989.

Tōi taiko, with Murakami Yōko. Kōdansha, 1990. Translations: Korea 1995, Taiwan 2000.

Uten enten, with Matsumura Eizō. Shinchōsha, 1990. Translation: Taiwan 2000.

Yagate kanashiki gaikokugo. Kōdansha, 1994. Translation: Korea 1993.

Murakami Asahidō jānaru: Uzumakineko no mitsukekata, with Murakami Yōko. Shinchōsha, 1996.

Murakami Haruki, Kawai Hayao ni ai ni iku, with Kawai Hayao. Iwanami shoten, 1996.

Murakami Asahidō wa ikanishite kitaerareta ka, with Anzai Mizumaru. Asahi Shinbunsha, 1997. Translation: Korea 1998.

29 *Andāguraundo*. Kōdansha, 1997. Partial contents trans. by Alfred Birnbaum as *Underground*. London: Harvill, 2000; New York: Knopf, 2000. Also: Korea 1998, Taiwan 1998, Germany 2002, Israel 2002, Italy 2003, Sweden 2005. See *Yakusoku-sareta basho de: underground 2* below.

Wakai dokusha no tame no tanpen shōsetsu annai. Bungei Shunjūsha, 1997.

Pōtoreito-in-jazu/Portrait in Jazz, with Wada Makoto. Shinchōsha, 1997. Translations: Korea 1998, Taiwan 1998.

Henkyō/Kinkyō. Shinchōsha, 1998. Translations: Korea 1999, Taiwan 1999.

Henkyō/Kinkyō shashin-hen, with Matsumura Eizō. Shinchōsha, 1998. Translation: Taiwan 1999.

30 *Yakusoku-sareta basho de: underground 2*. Bungei Shunjūsha, 1998. Partial contents trans. by Philip Gabriel as *Underground*. See *Andāguraundo* above.

Hon'yaku yawa, with Shibata Motoyuki. Bungei Shunjūsha: Bunshun shinsho 129, 2000.

CD-ROM-ban Murakami Asahidō: Yume no sāfushitii, with Anzai Mizumaru. Asahi Shinbunsha, 1998.

Moshi bokura no kotoba ga uisukii de atta nara, with Murakami Yōko. Heibonsha, 1999.

"Sō da, Murakami-san ni kiite miyō" to seken no hito-bito ga Murakami Haruki ni toriaezu buttsukeru 282 no dai-gimon ni hatashite Murakami-san wa chan-to kotaerareru no ka?, with Anzai Mizumaru. Asahi Shinbunsha, 2000.

CD-ROM-ban Murakami Asahidō: Sumerujakofu tai Oda Nobunaga kashin-dan, with Anzai Mizumaru. Asahi Shinbunsha, 2001.

Murakami rajio, with Ōhashi Ayumi. Magajin hausu, 2001.

Pōtoreito-in-jazu 2 / Portrait in Jazz 2, with Wada Makoto. Shinchōsha, 2001.

Hon'yaku yawa 2: Sarinjā senki, with Shibata Motoyuki. Bungei Shunjūsha: Bunshun shinsho 330, 2003.

Shōnen Kafuka. Shinchōsha, 2003.

31 *Hashiru koto ni tsuite kataru toki ni boku no kataru koto*. Bungei Shunjūsha, 2007. Trans. by Philip Gabriel as *What I Talk About When I Talk About Running*. New York: Knopf, 2008.

Ozawa Seiji-san to, ongaku ni tsuite hanashi o suru, with Ozawa Seiji. Shinchōsha, 2011.

32 "Of Walls and Eggs" (Jerusalem Prize speech), trans. Jay Rubin, *Bungei Shunjū* (April 2009), pp.165–169. Slightly abbreviated version on Salon.com (20 February 2009).

33 "Reality A and Reality B", trans. Jay Rubin, *The New York Times* (29 November 2010).

34 "Speaking as an Unrealistic Dreamer" (Catalunya Prize speech), trans. Emanuel Pastreich, *The Asia-Pacific Journal* 9:29:7 (18 July 2011).

TRANSLATIONS BY MURAKAMI

Adult fiction and non-fiction

Mai rosuto shitii [F. Scott Fitzgerald's "My Lost City" and other

416

stories]. Chūō Kōronsha, 1981.

Boku ga denwa o kakete iru basho [Raymond Carver's "Where I'm Calling From" and other stories]. Chūō Kōronsha, 1983.

Yoru ni naru to sake wa . . . [Raymond Carver's *At Night the Salmon Move*]. Chūō Kōronsha, 1985.

Kuma o hanatsu [John Irving's *Setting Free the Bears*]. Chūō Kōronsha, 1986.

Wāruzu endo [Paul Theroux's *World's End and Other Stories*]. Bungei Shunjūsha, 1987.

Idai-naru Desurifu [C. D. B. Bryan's *The Great Dethriffe*]. Shinchōsha, 1987.

Ojiisan no omoide [Truman Capote's *I Remember Grandpa*]. Bungei Shunjūsha, 1988.

Za Sukotto Fittsujerarudo bukku [F. Scott Fitzgerald miscellany]. TBS Britannica, 1988.

and Other Stories: totte oki no Amerika shōsetsu 12 hen [12 miscellaneous American stories]. Bungei shunjū, 1988. [*sic*]

Sasayaka da keredo, yaku ni tatsu koto [Raymond Carver's "A Small, Good Thing" and other stories]. Chūō Kōronsha, 1989.

Nyūkuria eiji [Tim O'Brien's *The Nuclear Age*]. Bungei Shunjū, 1989.

Aru kurisumasu [Truman Capote's *One Christmas*]. Bungei Shunjū, 1989.

Hontō no sensō no hanashi o shiyō [Tim O'Brien's *The Things They Carried*]. Bungei Shunjū, 1990.

Kurisumasu no omoide [Truman Capote's *A Christmas Memory*]. Bungei Shunjū, 1990.

Reimondo Kāvā zenshū [*Complete Works of Raymond Carver*]. Eight volumes. Chūō Kōronsha, 1990–97.

Sudden Fiction: chō-tanpen shōsetsu 70 [Robert Shepherd and James Thomas, eds., *Sudden Fiction*]. Bunshun bunko, 1994.

Carver's Dozen: Reimondo Kāvā kessakusen [A dozen of Raymond Carver's best stories]. Chūō Kōronsha, 1994.

Sayōnara, Bādorando [Bill Crow's *From Birdland to Broadway*]. Shinchōsha, 1995.

Babiron ni kaeru: za Sukotto Fittsujerarudo bukku 2 [F. Scott Fitzgerald's

"Babylon Revisited" and three other stories]. Chūō Kōronsha, 1996.

Shinzō o tsuranukarete [Mikal Gilmore's *Shot in the Heart*]. Bungei Shunjūsha, 1996.

Inu no jinsei [Mark Strand's *Mr and Mrs Baby*]. Chūō Kōronsha, 1998.

Saigo no shunkan no sugoku ōkina henka [Grace Paley's *Enormous Changes at the Last Minute*, 1974]. Bungei Shunjūsha, 1999.

Getsuyōbi wa saiaku da to minna wa iu keredo [Contemporary American essays: D. T. Max, Richard Ford, Tim O'Brien, John Paul Newport, Thom Jones, Denis Johnson]. Chūō Kōronsha, 2000.

Jazu anekudōtsu [Bill Crow's *Jazz Anecdotes*]. Shinchōsha, 2000.

Hitsuyō ni nattara denwa o kakete [Raymond Carver's *Call If You Need Me: The Uncollected Fiction and Other Prose*]. Chūō Kōronsha, 2000.

35 *Bāsudei-sutōriizu* [Ten British, Irish, and American short stories by various authors, plus Murakami's "Bāsudei-gāru", translated in *Blind Willow, Sleeping Woman*, in *Harpers* (June 2003) and in following item, by Jay Rubin as "Birthday Girl"]. Chūō Kōron Shinsha, 2002. Published in English, with one additional story, as *Birthday Stories: Selected and Introduced by Haruki Murakami* (Harvill Press, January 2004).

Jinsei no chotto-shita wazurai [Grace Paley's *The Little Disturbances of Man*]. Bungei Shunjūsha, 2005.

Kyatchā in za rai [J. D. Salinger's *The Catcher in the Rye*]. Hakusuisha, 2003.

Gurēto Gyattsubii [F. Scott Fitzgerald's *The Great Gatsby*]. Chūō Kōron Shinsha, 2006.

Rongo guddobai [Raymond Chandler's *The Long Goodbye*]. Hayakawa Shobō, 2007.

Tifanii de chōshoku o [Truman Capote's *Breakfast at Tiffany's*]. Shinchōsha, 2008.

Petto saunzu [Jim Fusilli's *Pet Sounds*]. Shinchōsha, 2008.

Sayonara, itoshii hito [Raymond Chandler's *Farewell, My Lovely*]. Hayakawa shobō, 2008.

Fuyu no yume [F. Scott Fitzgerald's *Winter Dreams*]. Chūō Kōron Shinsha, 2009.

Ritoru shisutā [Raymond Chandler's *The Little Sister*]. Hayakawa shobō, 2010.

Batto-byūtifuru [Geoff Dyer's *But Beautiful*]. Shinchōsha, 2011.

Kyokuhoku [Marcel Theroux's *Far North*]. Chūō Kōron shinsha, 2012.

Illustrated Books for Children

Seifū-gō no sōnan [Chris Van Allsburg's *The Wreck of the Zephyr*]. Kawade Shobō Shinsha, 1985.

Kyūkō Hokkyoku-gō [Chris Van Allsburg's *The Polar Express*]. Kawade Shobō Shinsha, 1987.

Namae no nai hito [Chris Van Allsburg's *The Stranger*]. Kawade Shobō Shinsha, 1989.

Harisu Bādikku no nazo [Chris Van Allsburg's *The Mysteries of Harris Burdick*]. Kawade Shobō Shinsha, 1990.

Hakuchōko [Mark Helprin and Chris Van Allsburg's *Swan Lake*]. Kawade Shobō Shinsha, 1991.

Sora-tobi neko [Ursula K. Le Guin's *Catwings*]. Kōdansha, 1992.

Mahō no hōki [Chris Van Allsburg's *The Widow's Broom*]. Kawade Shobō Shinsha, 1993.

Kaette kita sora-tobi neko [Ursula K. Le Guin's *Catwings Return*]. Kōdansha, 1993.

Masa-yume ichijiku [Chris Van Allsberg's *The Sweetest Fig*]. Kawade Shobō Shinsha, 1994.

Ben no mita yume [Chris Van Allsburg's *Ben's Dream*]. Kawade Shobō Shinsha, 1996.

Subarashii Arekisandā to, Sora tobu neko-tachi [Ursula K. Le Guin's *Wonderful Alexander and the Catwings*]. Kōdansha, 1997.

Imaimashii ishi [Chris Van Allsburg's *The Wretched Stone*]. Kawade Shobō Shinsha, 2003.

COMMENTARY ON MURAKAMI
IN ENGLISH

Sam Anderson, "Underground Man", *New York Times Magazine* (23 October 2011), pp.36–63.

Aoki Tamotsu, "Murakami Haruki and Contemporary Japan", eds. Philip Gabriel and Stephen Snyder, trans. by Matthew Strecher, in John Whittier Treat, ed., *Contemporary Japan and Popular Culture.* Honolulu: University of Hawai'i Press, 1996.

Lewis Beale, "The Cool, Cynical Voice of Young Japan", *Los Angeles Times Magazine* (8 December 1991), pp.36–83.

Ian Buruma, "Becoming Japanese", *The New Yorker* (23 & 30 December 1996), pp.60–71.

Matthew Richard Chozick, "De-Exoticizing Haruki Murakami's Reception", *Comparative Literature Studies* 45:1 (2008), pp.62–73.

Hideo Furukawa, "Pursuing 'Growth'", tr. Ted Goossen, *Monkey Business: New Writing from Japan* (Volume 01, 2011), pp.64–115, from "'Seichō' o mezashite, nashitsuzukete – Murakami Haruki intabyū,"*Monkiibijinesu* (2009 Spring Vol. 5), pp. 4–78.

Philip Gabriel, *Spirit Matters: The Transcendent in Modern Japanese Literature* (Honolulu: University of Hawaii Press, 2006).

Margaret Hillenbrand, "Murakami Haruki in Greater China: Creative Responses and the Quest for Cosmopolitanism", *Journal of Asian Studies* 68:3 (2009), pp.715–747.

Japan Foundation, comp., *A Wild Haruki Chase*. Berkeley: Stone Bridge Press, 2008.

Sumie Jones, "Vanishing Boundaries: Translation in a Multilingual World", *Yearbook of Comparative and General Literature* Volume 54 (2008), pp.121–134.

Jay McInerney and Haruki Murakami, "Roll Over Basho: Who Japan is Reading, and Why", in *The New York Times Book Review* (27 September 1992), pp.1–29.

Masao Miyoshi, *Off Center*. Cambridge: Harvard University Press, 1991.

Livia Monnet, "Televisual Retrofutures and the Body of Insomnia: Visuality and Virtual Realities in the Short Fiction of Murakami Haruki", in *Ga/Zoku Dynamics in Japanese Literature: PMAJLS*, Vol. 3 (Summer 1997), pp.340–80.

Susan Napier, *The Fantastic in Modern Japanese Literature: the Subversion of Modernity*. London and New York: Routledge, 1996.

Jay Rubin, "Deep Sheep Dip", *The World & I* (April 1990), pp.384–90.

———, "The Other World of Murakami Haruki", *Japan Quarterly* (October–December 1992), pp.490–500.

———, "Murakami Haruki's Two Poor Aunts," in Dennis Washburn and Alan Tansman, eds., *Studies in Modern Japanese Literature: Essays and Translations in Honor of Edwin McClellan* (Ann Arbor: University of Michigan Center for Japanese Studies, 1997), pp.307–19.

———, "Murakami Haruki's Two Poor Aunts Tell Everything They Know About Sheep, Wells, Unicorns, Proust, and Elephants", in *Ōe and Beyond: Fiction in Contemporary Japan*, ed. Philip Gabriel (Honolulu: University of Hawai'i Press, 1999), pp.177–98.

———, "Murakami Haruki", in Van Gessel, ed., *Dictionary of Literary Biography* No. 182 (Detroit: Bruccoli Clark Layman, 1997), pp.135–42.

———, "Murakami Haruki", in Jay Rubin, ed., *Modern Japanese Writers* (New York: Scribner's, 2001), pp.227–43.

Kathryn Schulz, "Escape Route" (Review of *1Q84*), *New York Times Book Review* (6 November 2011), pp.1–13.

Michael Seats, *Murakami Haruki: The Simulacrum in Comtemporary Japanese Culture*. Lanham, MD: Lexington Books, 2006.

Stephen Snyder, "Two Murakamis and Marcel Proust: Memory as Form in Japanese Fiction", in Xiaobing Tang and Stephen Snyder, eds., *In Pursuit of Contemporary East Asian Culture* (Boulder: Westview Press, 1996), pp.69–83.

Matthew Strecher, *Hidden Texts and Nostalgic Images: The Serious Social Critique of Murakami Haruki* (Ph.D. dissertation, University of Washington, 1995).

———, "Beyond 'Pure' Literature: Mimesis, Formula, and the

Postmodern in the Fiction of Murakami Haruki", *The Journal of Asian Studies* 57:2 (May 1998).

_____, "Murakami Haruki: Japan's Coolest Writer Heats Up", *Japan Quarterly* 45:1 (Jan.–Mar. 1998), pp.61–69.

_____, "Magical Realism and the Search for Identity in the Fiction of Murakami Haruki", *The Journal of Japanese Studies* 25:2 (Summer 1999).

_____, *Dances with Sheep: The Quest for Identity in the Fiction of Murakami Haruki* (*Michigan Monograph Series in Japanese Studies, No.37*) (Ann Arbor: University of Michigan Center for Japanese Studies, 2002).

_____, *Haruki Murakami's* The Wind-up Bird Chronicle: *A Reader's Guide* (*Continuum Contemporaries*) (London: Continuum Publishing Group, 2002).

Rebecca Suter, *The Japanization of Modernity: Murakami Haruki between Japan and the United States*. Cambridge: The Harvard University Asia Center, 2008.

Glynne Walley, "Two Murakamis and their American Influence", in *Japan Quarterly* 44:1 (Jan.–Mar. 1997), pp.41–50.

Philip Weiss, "Forget DeLillo and Pynchon – Murakami's the Guy for Me", *The New York Observer* (22 December 1997), pp.1, 18.

A SMALL SAMPLING OF STUDIES
OF MURAKAMI IN JAPANESE

Fujii Shōzō, *Murakami Haruki no naka no Chūgoku*. Asahi Shinbun-sha, 2007.

Fukami Haruka, Saitō Fumio, *Tanbō Murakami Haruki no sekai (Tokyo hen, 1968–97)*. Zesuto/Zest, 1998.

Hisai Tsubaki and Kuwa Masato, *Zō ga heigen ni kaetta hi*. Shinchōsha, 1991.

Imai Kiyoto, *Murakami Haruki – Off no kankaku*. Kokken shuppan, 1990.

Inoue Yoshio, *Murakami Haruki to Nihon no "kioku"*. Shinchōsha, 1999.

Katō Norihiro et. al., *Gunzō Nihon no sakka 26: Murakami Haruki*. Shōgakkan, 1997.

_____, *Murakami Haruki no tanpen o Eigo de yomu 1979-2011*. Kōdansha, 2011.

Kawamoto Saburō, "'Monogatari' no tame no bōken", *Bungakukai* (August 1985), pp.34–86.

Konishi Keita. *Murakami Haruki no ongaku zukan*. Japan Mix KK, 1998.

Kuritsubo Yoshiki and Tsuge Teruhiko, eds., *Murakami Haruki Sutadiizu*. Five vols. Wakakusa shobō, 1999. Too many Wakakusa shobō Murakami studies to list.

Kuroko Kazuo, *Murakami Haruki: za rosuto wārudo*. Rokkō shuppan, 1989; Daisan shokan, 1993.

Matsuie Masashi, "Murakami Haruki rongu intabyū", *Kangaeru hito* (Summer 2010), pp.13–101.

Miura Masashi, *Murakami Haruki to Shibata Motoyuki no mō hitotsu no Amerika*. Shinshokan, 2003.

_____, *Murakami Haruki to dōjidai no bungaku*. Kawai shuppan, 1990.

Murakami Ryū et. al., *Shiiku & fuaindo*. Seidōsha, 1986.

Shibata Motoyuki et. al., ed., *Sekai wa Murakami Haruki o dō yomuka*. Bungei Shunjū, 2006.

Shiohama Hisao, *Murakami Haruki wa dō goyaku-sarete iru ka*. Wakakusa shobō, 2007.

Ueno Chizuko, Ogura Chikako, and Tomioka Taeko, *Danryū bungaku ron* (Chikuma Shobō, 1992), pp.253–312.

Yasuhara Ken, "Murakami Haruki rongu intavyū", *Shōsetsu Shinchō* (Summer 1985), pp.12–35.

_____, *Hon nado yomu na, baka ni naru* (Tosho Shinbun, 1994).

SPECIAL MURAKAMI ISSUES OF
MAGAZINES IN JAPANESE

Brutus 433 (1 June 1999). "Murakami Haruki to kangaeru 'Nikutai no rinri': Nikutai ga kawareba, buntai mo kawaru!?.."
Bungakukai (April 1991). "Murakami Haruki bukku."
Kokubungaku (August 1988). "Murakami Haruki no gensō uchū."
Kokubungaku: Kaishaku to Kyōzai no Kenkyū 30, no. 3 (March 1985). "Nakagami Kenji to Murakami Haruki – toshi to han-toshi."
Kokubungaku: Kaishaku to Kyōzai no Kenkyū 40, no. 4 (March 1995). "Murakami Haruki: Yochi-suru bungaku."
Yuriika 21, no. 8 (June 1989). "Murakami Haruki no sekai."
Yuriika 32, no. 3 (March 2000). "Murakami Haruki o yomu."

FILMS

Ōmori Kazuki, director, "Kaze no uta o kike" [based on *Hear the Wind Sing*], feature film starring Kobayashi Kaoru as Boku, 1981.

Yamakawa Naruto, director, "Pan'ya shūgeki" [based on "The Bakery Attack"; not to be confused with "The Second Bakery Attack"], 16 minutes, 1982.

_____, "100% no onna no ko" [based on "On Seeing the 100% Perfect Girl One Beautiful April Morning"], 11 minutes, 1983. (Note English title: "A Girl, She is 100%").

Jun Ichikawa, director, "Tonii Takitani" [based on "Tony Takitani"], feature film, 2004.

Tran Anh Hung, director, "Noruwei no mori" [based on *Norwegian Wood*], feature film, 2010.

STAGE PRODUCTIONS

"Erefanto banisshu/The Elephant Vanishes", a dramatization of three Murakami stories, "The Elephant Vanishes", "Sleep", and "The Second Bakery Attack", by Setagaya Public Theatre, a co-production with Complicite, London, directed by Simon McBurney. Performed at the Setagaya Public Theatre, Tokyo (23 May–8 June 2003); Theatre Drama City, Osaka (13–15 June 2003), Barbican Theatre, London (26 June–6 July 2003). 2004 revivals in Tokyo, New York, London, Paris, and Ann Arbor.

"after the quake", adapted for the stage and directed by Frank Galati, based on the stories "Honey Pie" and "Super–Frog Saves Tokyo". Steppenwolf Theatre Company, Chicago, 20 October 2005–19 February 2006; Long Wharf Theatre, New Haven, Connecticut, 22 February–19 March 2006.

"Kafka on the Shore", adapted for the stage and directed by Frank Galati, Steppenwolf Theatre Company, 2008.

"The Wind-Up Bird Chronicle", adapted for the stage and directed by Stephen Earnhart. First performed as "sneak preview" at Ohio Theater, New York City, January 2010. Official "world premier" at Edinburgh International Festival, August 2011. Asian premier at Singapore Arts Festival, 25–26 May 2012.

Notes

Note: In source citations, a semicolon is used to separate the Japanese source from a published English translation. Translations cited without revision are indicated with **tr. p.** followed by the page number in the edition listed in the Bibliography (Appendix B). Translations that have been revised for interpretive purposes are indicated with **mod. tr. p.** In the few cases where it has been necessary to provide wholly new translations, the corresponding page in the published version is indicated by **cf. tr. p.** Where no published translation is cited, the translation in the text is mine.

1 For "Danny Boy" passages, see *Murakami Haruki zensakuhin 1979–89*, Eight volumes (Kōdansha, 1990–91) [cited below as MHZ] 4:17, 537, 542; tr. pp.3, 365, 368.

2 *Murakami Haruki bukku: Bungakukai* (April 1991), pp.103–14; Konishi Keita, *Murakami Haruki no ongaku zukan* (Japan Mix KK, 1998).

3 From Murakami's lecture, "The Sheep Man and the End of the World", delivered in English at Berkeley (17 November 1992). Thanks to Haruki Murakami for sharing with me the unpublished text of this lecture from the series called Una's Lectures in the Humanities, cited below as "Una's Lecture".

4 MHZ 6:190; tr. pp.129–30. The narrative of this day starts on MHZ 6:134; tr. p.90, UK tr. p.118.

5 *Kaiten mokuba no deddo hiito*, in MHZ 5:239–401, esp. pp.243–7. The confession can be found in "Jisaku o kataru: hosoku-suru monogatari-gun", MHZ 5: supplement, pp.9–12.

6 Murakami Haruki, *Nejimakidori kuronikuru*, Three volumes. (Shinchōsha, Vol. 1 and 2 1994, Vol. 3 1995) [Hereinafter, cited as NK, with chapter numbers separated from page numbers by period] 3:10.120; tr. p.410. To match page numbers in the Vintage Harvill paperback editions (1998), subtract 2 for Book Two and 4 for Book Three.

7 MHZ 1:123; cf. tr. pp.5–6.

8 Kawai Hayao and Murakami Haruki, *Murakami Haruki, Kawai Hayao ni ai ni iku* (Iwanami, 1996) [cited hereinafter as "Kawai and Murakami"], pp.51–5, 78,79.

9 Sōseki Natsume (1867–1916) is best known for *Kokoro* (1914; translated in 1957 as *Kokoro*). Fujii Shōzō, "Chikyū wa mawaru: Taiwan, Honkon", *Mainichi Shinbun* (6 November, 2000). Margaret Hillenbrand, "Murakami Haruki in Greater China: Creative Responses and the Quest for Cosmopolitanism", *Journal of Asian Studies* 68:3 (2009), p.718.

10 Kenzaburō Ōe (*b.*1935) is best known for *Kojinteki na taiken* (1964; translated by John Nathan as *A Personal Matter* in 1968).

11 Quoted in James Sterngold, "Japan Asks Why a Prophet Bothers", *The New York Times* (6 November 1994), p.5. Several decades ago, Keene was eager to introduce the world to Osamu Dazai, much of whose readership was of high school age.

12 Banana Yoshimoto (*b.*1964) is best known for *Kitchin* (1988; translated in 1993 as *Kitchen*).

13 Yukio Mishima (1925–70) is best known for *Kinkakuji* (1956; translated in 1959 as *The Temple of the Golden Pavilion*).

14 Masao Miyoshi, *Off Center* (Cambridge: Harvard University Press, 1991), p.234. "Kenzaburō Ōe: The Man Who Talks With the Trees", *Los Angeles Times* (19 October 1994), p.B7.

15 MHZ 3:81–8.

16 Biographical sources: Kuhara Rei, "Nenpu: 'Murakami Haruki ni yoru Murakami Haruki,'" in Murakami Ryū et al., *Shiiku & Fuaindo: Murakami Haruki* (Seidōsha, 1986), pp.243–51; Imai Kiyoto, "Nenpu", in Katō Norihiro et al., *Gunzō Nihon no sakka 26: Murakami Haruki* (Shōgakkan, 1997), pp.303–12; Imai Kiyoto, "Murakami Haruki nenpu", in Kuritsubo Yoshiki and Tsuge Teruhiko, eds., *Murakami Haruki Sutadiizu*, Five volumes. (Wakakusa shobō, 1999) 5:215–27; formal and informal interviews with Haruki and Yōko Murakami.

17 "The Man who Stank of Butter", BBC Radio 3, 45 minutes, Sunday 1 April 2001. Producer: Matt Thompson.

18 Kuhara, p.243.

19 Readers of my earlier "Murakami Haruki" in Jay Rubin, ed., *Modern Japanese Writers* (New York: Scribner's, 2001) may notice a shift to the left in my sketch of Murakami's parents, which is thanks to personal correspondence from Murakami of 12 January 2001.

20 Tanizaki is best known for *Kagi* (1956; translated in 1960 as *The Key*) and *Sasameyuki* (1943–48; translated in 1957 as *The Makioka Sisters*). Nakagami is best known in the West for "Misaki" ("The Cape", 1976) and other pieces of short fiction compiled in *The Cape and Other Stories from the Japanese Ghetto* (Berkeley: Stone Bridge Press, 1999).

21 "Taidan: shigoto no genba kara – Nakagami Kenji, Murakami Haruki", in *Kokubungaku* (March 1985)[cited hereinafter as "Nakagami/Murakami"], p.18.

22 Murakami Haruki, *Wakai dokusha no tame no tanpen shōsetsu annai* (Bungei Shunjūsha, 1997), p.10.

23 *Yagate kanashiki gaikokugo* [hereinafter, *Yagate*] (Kōdansha, 1994), pp.240, 241.

24 Nakagami/Murakami, p.25.

25 Kawamoto Saburō, "'Monogatari' no tame no bōken: Murakami Haruki", in *Bungakukai* (August 1985), p.40.

26 *Yagate*, pp.230–31. The movie, also known as *The Moving Target*, was a favourite of Murakami's because it was based on the very first hard-boiled fiction he ever read, at the age of 17, Ross MacDonald's *My Name is Archer*. See *Zō kōjō no happiiendo* (CBS-Sony, 1983), pp.82–5.

27 *Yagate*, p.244.

28 According to personal correspondence of 12 January, 2001.

29 See his "Amerika hijiki", translated by Jay Rubin as "American Hijiki", in Howard S. Hibbett, ed., *Contemporary Japanese Literature* (New York: Knopf, 1977), pp.344–53.

30 Nakagami/Murakami, pp.9, 15. Murakami Ryū is best known for *Kagirinaku tōmei ni chikai burū* (1976; translated as *Almost Transparent Blue*), which depicts Japanese youth amid the drug culture surrounding a US base.

31 Kawamoto, p.39.

32 Senda Akihiko, "Media no kao", in *Asahi Shinbun* (29 October 1989), p.4.

33 *Yagate*, p.244.

34 Ian Buruma, "Becoming Japanese", *The New Yorker* (23 & 30 December 1996), pp.60–71; quotation from p.71.

35 *Yagate*, pp.245–6.

36 *Murakami Haruki Bukku*, p.120. Also on Murakami's early reading, see Yasuhara Ken, "Murakami Haruki, rongu intavyū", *Shōsetsu Shinchō* (Summer 1985), pp.12–35.

37 Kuhara, p.245.

38 *Yagate*, p.242.

39 Murakami Haruki, *Murakami Asahidō*, with Anzai Mizumaru (Wakabayashi shuppan kikaku, 1984). Cited in Fukami Haruka, Saitō Fumio, *Tanbō Murakami Haruki no sekai (Tokyo hen, 1968–97)* (Zesuto/Zest, 1998), p.12. See this book for photos of the area – including the staircase.

40 Nakagami/Murakami, p.16.

41 Personal correspondence of 2 December 1997.

42 Kuhara, pp. 245–6.

43 "Jisaku o kataru: Daidokoro no tēburu kara umareta shōsetsu", MHZ 1: supplement, p.2.

44 Fukami and Saitō, pp.16–19.

45 Remarks at Berkeley seminar on his works, 20 November 1992.

46 Personal correspondence of 2 December 1997.

47 Fukami and Saitō, pp.21–5; Kuhara, p.245.

48 MHZ 6:87; tr. p.57 UK tr. p.74.

49 Kuhara, p.245.

50 MHZ 6:72; tr. p.47, UK tr. p.61.

51 Kuroko Kazuo, *Murakami Haruki: za rosuto wārudo* (Rokkō shuppan, 1989), traces the central position of the 1969–70 shift in Murakami's fiction.

52 Louis Menand, "Holden at Fifty: *The Catcher in the Rye* and What it Spawned", in *The New Yorker* (1 October 2001), p.82.

53 According to personal correspondence of 5 December 1997.

54 Interview with Yōko Murakami, Tokyo, 7 September 1997. *Kanashibari* will be discussed below with reference to Murakami's story "Sleep".

55 *Murakami Asahidō*, p.56; Kuhara, p.246.

56 According to personal correspondence and interview of 5 December 1997.

57 *Yagate*, p.153; personal correspondence of 27 November 2001.

58 From interview with Eizō Matsumura, 8 September 1997; Buruma p.67.

59 Buruma, p.67. Personal correspondence of 2 December 1997.

60 According to personal correspondence of 2 December 1997.

61 Nakagami/Murakami, p.8. The reference is to the later Peter Cat, which was located near the Kawade publishing company.

62 MHZ 5:142.

63 *Yagate*, p.153.

64 The trick is to cut them up so quickly the fumes don't reach your eyes. *Yagate*, p.214.

65 There was more luck connected with the event. Yakult won not only the game but the Japan series that year, the first championship in their 29-year history. Murakami was 29 at the time. He heard about their next championship in 1993, just as he was writing about the luck they had brought him 15 years earlier. See *Yagate*, p.221.

66 Una's Lecture.

67 "Jisaku o kataru: Daidokoro no tēburu kara umareta shōsetsu", p.3. See also *Murakami Haruki Bukku*, pp.36, 38; Kuhara, p.246.

68 *A Capote Reader* (New York: Random House, 1987), p.75.

69 *Murakami Haruki Bukku*, p.120.

70 Kawamoto, pp.38–9.

71 MHZ 1:71; tr. p.73.

72 MHZ 1:17; tr. p.17.

73 MHZ 1:13; mod. tr. pp.12–13.

74 MHZ 1:87; tr. p.91.

75 MHZ 1:24; tr. p.25.

76 MHZ 1:26; cf. tr. p.26.

77 MHZ 1:26; tr. p.27.

78 MHZ 1:86; cf. tr. p.90.

79 Kawamoto, p.50.

80 Una's Lecture.

81 Nakagami/Murakami, p.18.

82 Kuhara, pp.246–7. "Kono jūnen", *Murakami Haruki Bukku*, p.36.

83 On the absence of pronouns in Japanese, see my *Making Sense of Japanese* (Tokyo: Kodansha International, 1998), pp.25–31. See also Appendix A (2).

84 The passivity of *"Yare-yare"* has been noted in Ueno Chizuko, Ogura Chikako, and Tomioka Taeko, *Danryū bungaku ron* (Chikuma Shobō, 1992), pp.274–75.

85 Kuhara, p.247.

86 MHZ 1:11; tr. p.10.

87 Naoya Shiga (1883–1971) is best known for *An'ya Kōro* (1937; translated in 1976 as *A Dark Night's Passing*).

88 "Kono jūnen", p.37.

89 MHZ 1:7–11; mod. tr. pp.5–11.

90 "The Man who Stank of Butter"

91 Kawamoto, p.40.

92 *Yagate*, pp.278–9; Kawai and Murakami, pp.9–10.

93 "Kono jūnen", p.38. See also "Jisaku o kataru: Daidokoro no tēburu kara umareta shōsetsu", p.3.

94 Kuhara, p.248. Personal correspondence of 2 December 1997.

95 MHZ 1:200; mod. tr. p.108.

96 MHZ 1:236; mod. tr. pp.155, 156.

97 MHZ 7:135; cf. tr. p.87. The Sheep Man's remark, "This is reality", immediately follows his line, "Youandus, we'reliving. Breathing. Talking."

98 Translated by Philip Gabriel in *The New Yorker* (11 January 1999), pp.74–9.

99 MHZ 1:201–2. mod. tr. pp.109–10.

100 MHZ 1:190; tr. p.96.

101 MHZ 1:194–5; mod. tr. pp.101–2.

102 MHZ 1:200; tr. p.108.

103 MHZ 1:200; tr. p.108.

104 Yasunari Kawabata is best known for his novel *Yukiguni* (1937–48; translated in 1956 as *Snow Country*). He was awarded the Nobel Prize in 1968.

105 MHZ 1:254; cf. tr. p.179.

106 "The Izu Dancer", translated by Edward Seidensticker, in Theodore W. Goossen, ed., *The Oxford Book of Japanese Short Stories* (Oxford University Press, 1997), pp.129–48.

107 *Hear the Wind Sing* deals with such material indirectly. The translation and discussion use the revised version of the story, which clarifies several points made here. For a discussion of the differences between the original and later versions, see my "Haruki Murakami's Two Poor Aunts" in *Studies in Modern Japanese Literature: Essays and Translations in Honor of Edwin McClellan* (Ann Arbor: University of Michigan Center for Japanese Studies, 1997), pp.307–19, or the expanded version, "Murakami Haruki's Two Poor Aunts Tell Everything They Know About Sheep, Wells, Unicorns, Proust, and Elephants", in *Ōe and Beyond: Fiction in Contemporary Japan*, ed. Philip Gabriel (Honolulu: University of Hawai'i Press, 1999), pp.177–98.

108 "Jisaku o kataru: Tanpen shōsetsu e no kokoromi", MHZ 3:supplement, pp.4–6.

109 Charles Inouye's class at Tufts University on 1 December 1994.

110 Fukami and Saitō, pp.45, 79, makes the connection and provides photographs. The "Picture Gallery", an imposing domed building erected in 1926 and displaying scenes from the life of the Meiji Emperor (r. 1868–1912), is officially known as Meiji Jingū Gaien Seitoku Kinen Kaigakan.

111 MHZ 3:50; mod. tr. pp.86, 88.

112 MHZ 3:55; mod. tr. p.90. See also Murakami Haruki, *Chūgoku-yuki no surō bōto* (Chūkō Bunko, 1986), p.59. This version will also be cited below as "Bunkobon" to help trace the revisions introduced by Murakami into the new text.

113 MHZ 3:55; Bunkobon, p.59; mod. tr. p.89.

114 MHZ 3:60; Bunkobon, p.65; mod. tr. p.91.

115 MHZ 3:59; Bunkobon, pp.63–4; mod. tr. pp.90–1. Only the girlfriend's nod and the comment on it are new in the MHZ version.

116 MHZ 3:66; Bunkobon, p.72; mod. tr. p.93. The hunger is described in less gargantuan terms in the latter.

117 MHZ 3:67; Bunkobon, pp.72–3; mod. tr. p.93.

118 MHZ 3:64–5; mod. tr. p.92.

119 MHZ 1:253; tr. p.178. The phrase is *"moto no tokoro"* here.

120 MHZ 3:64–5; mod. tr. p.92.

121 MHZ 3:44–5; tr. p.86. Written after Murakami had become more conscious of his method, this line is in the revised version only.

122 "Jisaku o kataru: Tanpen shōsetsu e no kokoromi", MHZ 3: supplement, pp.3–4.

123 MHZ 3:114; tr. p.269.

124 Aoki Tamotsu, "Murakami Haruki and Contemporary Japan", trans. by Matthew Strecher, in John Whittier Treat, ed., *Contemporary Japan and Popular Culture* (Honolulu: University of Hawai'i Press, 1996), p.267. The article originally appeared as "60-nendai ni koshū-suru Murakami Haruki ga naze 80-nendai no wakamono ni shiji-sareru no darō" in *Chūō Kōron* (December 1983), pp.270–78. See page 271 for the quoted passage.

125 The one venue that was offbeat enough to publish an English translation was *McSweeney's*, which printed "Dabchick" in a ten-page "discreet booklet" of the boxed issue that appeared in Late Winter, 2000 (Number 4).

126 "Kaitsuburi", MHZ 5:155–65; tr. p.10.

127 MHZ 5:91; tr. p.188.

128 MHZ 5:99; tr. p.194.

129 MHZ 5:26; tr. p.69.

130 MHZ 5:129–36; tr. pp. 195–7.

131 Interview of 9 October 1993.

132 Buruma, p.62.

133 Senda Akihiko, "Media no kao", in *Asahi Shinbun* (29 October 1989), p.4.

134 "Senpyō" in *Gunzō* (June 1991), pp.92–7. The editor's remark was reported in "Shō e no sujigaki nijimu", in *Asahi Shinbun* Tokyo yūkan (22 June 1991), p.20.

135 Haruki Murakami, "A Literary Comrade", trans. by Tara Maja McGowan, in William L. Stull and Maureen P. Carroll, eds., *Remembering Ray: A Composite Biography of Raymond Carver* (Santa Barbara: Capra Press), pp.130–5.

136 Op. cit.

137 Op. cit.

138 Hashimoto Hiromi, "Raymond Carver to Murakami Haruki ni miru hon'yaku no sōgo sayō", in *Nanzan Eibungaku* 15 (January 1991), pp.15–35.

139 Edward Fowler, *The Rhetoric of Confession: Shishōsetsu in Early Twentieth-Century Japanese Fiction* (Berkeley: University of California Press, 1988).

140 This discussion is based squarely on Hashimoto's fine article. Her characterization of the Aoyama Minami translation as "objective" on pp.23–4 is itself perhaps evidence of the "naturalness" of the interiorizing tendency.

141 Translated by Stephen Snyder as *Coin Locker Babies* (Tokyo: Kodansha International, 1998).

142 "Jisaku o kataru: Atarashii shuppatsu", MHZ 2: supplement, pp.2–8. See also Kawai and Murakami, p.70.

143 MHZ 2:182; mod. tr. p.142.

144 MHZ 2:367; mod. tr. p.293.

145 Una's Lecture.

146 MHZ 2:61; tr. p.38.

147 Personal correspondence of 24 July 2001.

148 MHZ 2:282–3; cf. tr. p.225. The translation cuts the passage in which they go to bed without making love. To be restored in a new edition.

149 MHZ 2:333–34; tr. pp.265–6

150 MHZ 2:371; cf. tr. p.295.

151 MHZ 2:242; mod. tr. p.188.

152 MHZ 2:190; tr. p.149.

153 MHZ 2:39; mod. tr. pp.21–2.

154 MHZ 2:303; tr. p.241.

155 MHZ 2:313, 317; tr. pp.251, 253.

156 MHZ 2:327; cf. tr. p.260.

157 MHZ 2:330; tr. p.262.

158 MHZ 2:336; tr. p.267.

159 MHZ 2:337; cf. tr. p.268 ("everything came to pass").

160 MHZ 2:338; tr. p.269.

161 MHZ 2:345; tr. p.275.

162 MHZ 2:345; tr. p.276.

163 MHZ 2:359; tr. p.286.

164 MHZ 2:362; cf. tr. p.289. "Then I went and pissed so much I could hardly believe it myself."

165 MHZ 2:57; tr. p.35.

166 Kawamoto, pp.63, 64.

167 Una's Lecture.

168 MHZ 2:262–3; tr. p.208.

169 MHZ 2:83; mod. tr. p.57.

170 NHZ 2:154; tr. p.118.

171 MHZ 2:155–7; tr. pp.119–21.

172 MHZ 2:322, cf. tr. p.256.

173 "Nikutai ga kawareba, buntai mo kawaru!?" and related articles in Brutus (1 June 1999) [hereinafter, Brutus], pp.18–43. Here, see p.18 and "Boku no ima no buntai wa, hashiru koto ni yotte dekita to omou", p.25.

174 Personal correspondence of 12 January 2001.

175 Brutus, p.28. Murakami contrasts himself with Rimbaud, Osamu Dazai, and Ryūnosuke Akutagawa, noting that he has no such self-destructive tendencies, does not intend to die young or kill himself but will go on as a long-distance runner.

176 Brutus, pp.25, 27, 28.

177 MHZ 2: supplement, "Jisaku o kataru: Atarashii shuppatsu", pp.7–8.

178 *Brutus*, p.32.

179 *Brutus*, pp.20–3.

180 *Murakami rajio*, with Ōhashi Ayumi (Magajin hausu, 2001), pp.10–13.

181 Murakami Haruki, *Matatabi abita Tama* (Bungei Shunjūsha, 2000). In his post-script, Murakami denies that he is a workaholic.

182 The description of the meeting in Port Angeles and its aftermath is based largely on my telephone interview with Tess Gallagher on 24 July 2001.

183 "A Literary Comrade", p.133.

184 Raymond Carver, *All of Us: The Collected Poems* (Harvill, 1996), pp.146–8.

185 "A Literary Comrade", p.133.

186 Additional details from a telephone interview with Yōko Murakami on 14 August 2001. When the Murakamis sold the house, the furniture maker took the bed back to use the substantial materials in other projects. See also *Murakami Haruki Bukku*, p.127.

187 "Jon Āvingu-shi to Sentoraru Pāku o 6 mairu hashiru koto ni tsuite", *Marie Claire* (October 1984), pp.52–7.

188 Kawai and Murakami, p.41.

189 *Yagate*, pp.1–2.

190 Nakagami/Murakami, pp.17, 25.

191 Kuhara, p.249.

192 MHZ 6:234; tr. p.46, UK tr. p.60.

193 MHZ 3:237–59; tr. pp.131–49.

194 MHZ 3:302–05; tr. pp.243–5

195 MHZ 5:243–4.

196 "Jisaku o kataru: Hosoku-suru monogatari-gun", MHZ 5:supplement, pp.9–11.

197 According to personal correspondence of 24 July 2001.

198 Neither story appeared in the original serialization in a Kōdansha publicity booklet. "Lederhosen" was added when the collection first came out, and "The Silence" was added when the stories were reprinted in Volume 5 of the *Complete Works*. Ibid., pp.11–12.

199 MHZ 5:393; cf. tr. p.89.

200 "Atogaki", *Hotaru, Naya o yaku, sonota no tanpen* (Shinchō bunko, 1987), p.189.

201 "Kichōmen na bōkenka", *Chūō Kōron* (November 1985), p.585.

202 "A Novelist's Lament", *Japan Times* (23 November 1986).

203 "Jisaku o kataru: Hajimete no kaki-oroshi shōsetsu", MHZ 4:supplement, pp.5–6, 8–9.

204 The series title is: "Junbungaku kakioroshi shiriizu".

205 "Jisaku o kataru: Hajimete no kaki-oroshi shōsetsu", MHZ 4:supplement, p.5. The story can be found in the September 1980 issue of *Bungakukai*.

206 Susan Napier, *The Fantastic in Modern Japanese Literature: The Subversion of Modernity* (London and New York: Routledge, 1996), p.213.

207 Kawamoto, p.77.

208 Kawamoto, p.74.

209 MHZ 4:395; tr. pp.272–3.

210 MHZ 4:373–4; tr. p.256. The Professor's speech patterns are much closer to standard Japanese than one might suppose from the un-speakable dialect with which he is saddled in the translation.

211 MHZ 4:375; tr. p.257.

212 MHZ 4:25; tr. p.9.

213 MHZ 4:26; tr. p.9. Perhaps wisely, the translator makes up some resonant nonsense here (*"Truest? . . . Brew whist? . . . Blue is it?"*) rather than attempt anything more literal.

214 MHZ 4:26; tr. p.10.

215 Stephen Snyder, "Two Murakamis and Marcel Proust: Memory as Form in Japanese Fiction", in Xiaobing Tang and Stephen Snyder, eds., *In Pursuit of Contemporary East Asian Culture* (Boulder: Westview Press, 1996), p.82. Personal correspondence of 3 October 2001.

216 MHZ 4:15, 66; tr. pp.2, 43. Murakami often describes the visible "grains" or "powder" of light.

217 MHZ 4:32; tr. p.15. The wall is a bit higher in the translation than the original, in which it is described as being seven or eight metres (a little over 26 feet) high. See also MHZ 4:149; tr. p.108, where the number settles down to seven metres.

218 Yasuhara Ken, "Murakami Haruki rongu intavyū", *Shōsetsu Shinchō* (Summer 1985), pp.32–3.

219 Snyder, p.75.

220 MHZ 4:120–1; tr. pp.84–5. Birnbaum translates the last sentence: "By that age we already had had a lifetime together."

221 MHZ 4:198; tr. p.146.

222 MHZ 4:149–50; cf. tr. p.109: "You have to endure. If you endure, everything will be fine. No worry, no suffering. It all disappears. Forget about the shadow. This is the End of the World. This is where the world ends. Nowhere further to go."

223 MHZ 4:236; mod. tr. p.173. A few lines omitted from the translation have been restored here.

224 MHZ 4:325; tr. pp.226–7.

225 MHZ 4:423; tr. p.294. Birnbaum has improved on the original here.

226 MHZ 4:541–3; tr. pp.368–9.

227 MHZ 4:590; tr. p.399.

228 Kawamoto, pp.64–5. The word *"sokubutsuteki"* has been translated "physical" instead of "materialist" to avoid confusion.

229 Nakagami/Murakami, pp.27, 29, 30.

230 Una's Lecture.

231 MHZ 8:31–6, 276. Also in *Yume de aimashō* (1981).

232 MHZ 8:11–28; tr. pp.36–49.

233 Thanks to Charles Inouye for reminding me of this additional comment.

234 MHZ 8:39–61; tr. pp.308–27.

235 "Jisaku o kataru: Arata-naru taidō", p.3. The story appeared in the women's magazine *Lee*, and Murakami says he was writing with this audience in mind.

236 MHZ 8:69–104; tr. pp.158–86.

237 MHZ 8:131–8; tr. pp.112–18.

238 Personal correspondence of 24 July 2001.

239 Ishikura Michiko, "Arata-na sekaizō no kakutoku", in Kuritsubo Yoshiki and Tsuge Teruhiko, eds., *Murakami Haruki sutadiizu*, 5 vols. (Wakakusa Shobō, 1999), 4:119–51.

240 MHZ 8:141–77; tr. pp.4–33.

241 Personal correspondence of 24 July 2001.

242 Translated by Christiane von Wedel as *Schafsmanns Weihnachten* (Berlin: Mori-Ōgai-Gedenkstätte der Humboldt-Universität zu Berlin, 1998). See Klaus Kracht and Katsumi Tateno-Kracht, *Kurisumasu: Dō yatte Nihon ni teichaku-shita ka* (Kadokawa shoten, 1999). My thanks to Professor Kracht for this information.

243 This much romanized Japanese is way too long to keep on the page: *CD-ROM-ban Murakami Asahidō: Yume no sāfu shitii* (Asahi Shinbunsha, 1998); "*Sō da, Murakami-san ni kiite miyō*" *to seken no hito-bito ga Murakami Haruki ni toriaezu buttsukeru 282 no dai-gimon ni hatashite Murakami-san wa chan-to kotaerareru no ka?* (Asahi Shinbunsha, 2000); *CD-ROM-ban Murakami Asahidō: Sumerujakofu tai Oda Nobunaga kashindan* (Asahi Shinbunsha, 2001).

244 "*Sō da, Murakami-san ni kiite miyō*", pp.4, 12.

245 Kawamoto, pp.82–3.

246 Kawamoto, p.83.

247 "Jisaku o kataru: 100 pāsento rearizumu e no chōsen", MHZ 6:supplement, pp.2, 7.

248 *Tōi taiko*, pp.30, 36, 101.

249 "Mikonosu" and "Shishirii", in *Tōi taiko*, pp.137–41, 177–82.

250 The title could as well be translated "The Forests of Norway", "Norwegian Forests", etc. English song lyrics can be a problem in Japan. Many people seem to believe that the line "Ob-la-di ob-la-da, life goes on bra" in The Beatles' song "Ob-la-di ob-la-da" means "Life goes on flowing over the brassiere", a genuinely surreal sentiment. See Murakami's "Kashi no goyaku ni tsuite", in "*Sō da, Murakami-san ni kiite miyō*" pp.213–7.

251 MHZ 6:160; tr. p.109, UK tr. p.143.

252 "*Sōda, Murakami-san ni kiite miyō*", p.22.

253 Kawai, pp.166–7.

254 "Shishirii", in *Tōi taiko*, p.182.

255 Una's Lecture.

256 Kazumi Takahashi (1931–71) was a deeply political novelist and critic associated with the student movement whose works have not been translated into English. For an example of his critical prose, see Jay Rubin, *Making Sense of Japanese* (Kodansha International, 1998), p.108.

257 MHZ 6:46–7; tr. pp.29–30, UK tr. p.37.

258 MHZ 6:10–11, 17; tr. pp.5, 9–10, UK tr. p.4, 10.

259 Cited, in slightly different form, by Sumie Jones in her "*The Lower Depths*, Gorky,

Stanislavski, and Kurosawa", in Makoto Ueda, ed., *Explorations: Essays in Comparative Literature* (Lanham, Maryland: University Press of America, 1986),p.174.

260 Based in part on personal correspondence of 12 January 2001.

261 Ueno Chizuko, Ogura Chikako, and Tomioka Taeko, *Danryū bungaku ron*, pp. 265, 310; personal correspondence of 27 November 2001.

262 Personal correspondence of 24 July 2001.

263 MHZ 6:11–12; tr. pp.5–6, UK tr. pp.4–5.

264 MHZ 6:12; tr. p.6, UK tr. pp.5–6.

265 Thanks to Wenying Shi for her provocative contributions to class on 27 September 2001.

266 Una's Lecture.

267 MHZ 6:416; tr. p.292, UK tr. p.384. The figure is given twice in the original, though not in the translation.

268 Ueno Chizuko, Ogura Chikako, and Tomioka Taeko, *Danryū bungaku ron*, p.272.

269 "Norway zoku" in *Nikkei Ryūtsū Shinbun* (9 April 1988), p.1; "Jazu raibu no shinise 'DUG'", in *Yomiuri Shinbun* (3 June 1999); "Dokusho mo josei no jidai" in *Mainichi Shinbun* (27 October 1988); "Choko-sunakku tokushō kenkyū" in *Gekkan Ōpasu* (December 1989), pp.108–09; "'Noruwei no mori' binjō CD wa 'Noruwee no mori' datte" in *Shūkan Bunshun* (3 November 1988), p.35.

270 "Murakami Haruki wa futatabi 'Nihon-dasshutsu'-chū", in *Shūkan Bunshun* (22–29 December 1988), pp.160–1.

271 See "Jisaku o kataru: Arata-naru taidō", p.9. *Hear the Wind Sing* was filmed by director Kazuki Ōmori in 1981. Amateur director Naoto Yamakawa made short films of "On Seeing the 100% Perfect Girl One Beautiful April Morning" (1983, 11 min.) and "The Bakery Attack" ("Pan'ya shūgeki", 1981/film 1982, 16 min.), the story that preceded "The Second Bakery Attack". Both are little more than dramatized readings of Murakami's texts. As such, the former, a superior story, makes for a more effective film. The visual effects are also superior. A DVD containing both short films was released in Japan in November 2001, around which time rumours were circulating that *South of the Border, West of the Sun* would be filmed by Michael Radford, who directed *Il Postino*.

272 Precise figures as of 30 April 2012, according to the Murakami office: Volume 1: 2,415,800 hardcover, 3,419,00 paper (total 5,834,800); Volume 2: 2,132,100 hardcover, 3,150,000 paper (total 5,282,100). Total volumes: 11,116,900. Thanks to Yuki Katsura.

273 Una's Lecture.

274 "Gozen sanji gojippun no chiisana shi", in *Tōi taiko*, pp.211–18.

275 Personal correspondence of 8 September 2001.

276 Abe is best known for his novel *Woman in the Dunes*, which was later made into a brilliant film by Hiroshi Teshigahara. See Christopher Bolton's "Abe Kōbō", in Jay Rubin, ed., *Modern Japanese Writers* (New York: Scribner's, 2001), pp.1–18.

277 "Fuyu ga fukamaru", in *Tōi taiko*, pp.334–5.

278 "Jisaku o kataru: Hitsuji-otoko no monogatari o motomete", MHZ 7:supplement, pp.4–5.

279 MHZ 7:132; cf. tr. p.86. The published translation might be restored as follows: "Yougottadance. Aslongasthemusicplays. Yougottadance. Don't-eventhinkwhy. Youcan'tthinkaboutmeaning. There'sneverbeenanymeaning. Starttothink, yourfeetstop." The Sheep Man's speech has a few idiosyncracies in the original, but nothing quite as memorable as Birnbaum's rendering. For one thing, normal Japanese has no spacing between words.

280 Murakami confirmed this in answer to a letter dated 8 October 1998, from a reader on his website, under *Dokusha & Murakami Haruki Forum: Murakami sakuhin ni tsuite (1)*. Now that the website has been discontinued, this can be accessed using the CD-ROM contained in either Murakami Haruki and Anzai Mizumaru, *CD-ROM-ban Murakami Asahidō: Yume no sāfu shitii* (Asahi Shinbunsha, 1998) or Murakami Haruki and Anzai Mizumaru, *CD-ROM-ban Murakami Asahidō: Sumerujakofu tai Oda Nobunaga kashindan* (Asahi Shinbunsha, 2001) [cited below as *Sumerujakofu*].

281 MHZ 7:127; cf. tr. p.83: "Thisisyourplace. It'stheknot. It'stiedtoeverything . . . Thingsyoulost. Thingsyou'regonnalose."

282 Personal correspondence of 12 January 2001.

283 *Sumerujakofu* Forum No. 435 (13 October 1999, 0.24 p.m.).

284 "Fuyu ga fukamaru", in *Tōi taiko*, pp.334–8.

285 *Yagate*, p.132.

286 "Kanāri-san no apātomento", in *Tōi taiko*, pp.364–6.

287 Murakami Haruki, *Tōi taiko* (Kōdansha, 1990), pp.351–5. Additional details from telephone interview with Yōko Murakami, 14 August 2001. In "Yakusha atogaki", his postscript to the translation, Murakami says that, as he worked, he found himself cheering O'Brien on from the sidelines. Though full of irony, he says, the book was devoid of "intellectual sneering" and gave evidence of O'Brien's complete spiritual commitment to his work. Murakami says that he would like to call the book "a contemporary total novel" (*gendai no sōgō shōsetsu*). *Nyūkuria eiji* (Bungei Shunjū, 1989), pp.649–55.

288 In *Sumerujakofu* Forum No. 435 (13 October 1999, 0.24 p.m.), Murakami pairs "Sleep" with "TV People" as the first two products following his depression. He mentions "Sleep" as his first post-depression work in "Jisaku o kataru: Arata-naru taidō", MHZ 8: supplement, p.10.

289 *TV Piipuru*, pp.9–46; tr. pp.196–216. After appearing in *The New Yorker*, the English translation of "TV People" was chosen for inclusion in *The Year's Best Fantasy and Horror* for 1991. See Ellen Datlow and Terri Windling, eds., *The Year's Best Fantasy and Horror: Fourth Annual Collection* (St. Martin's Press, 1991).

290 See *Garasudo no uchi* 38, in *Sōseki zenshū*, 29 vols. (Iwanami Shoten, 1994) 12:613.

291 In *Sumerujakofu* Forum No. 289 (27 April 1999, 7.29 p.m.) Murakami says that he has never experienced *kanashibari*, but once introduced the concept to American students when he assigned the story to his class; the Japanese members of the class could not believe that the Americans had never heard of the phenomenon and had no word for it.

437

292 MHZ 8:181–223; tr. pp.74–109.

293 *Murakami Haruki, Kawai Hayao ni ai ni iku*, pp.158, 159–60, 163. "Land of the dead" here is *yomi no kuni*, the Shintō idea of a subterranean afterworld rather than any Buddhist abstraction or transcendence.

294 MHZ 8:227–48.

295 MHZ 8:232.

296 MHZ 8:251–75; "Man-Eating Cats", tr. pp.84–94.

297 Murakami Haruki, *Rekishinton no yūrei* (Bungei Shunjūsha, 1996), pp.43–52; tr. pp.152–6.

298 Interview 22 October 1994. See the introduction to Murakami's book on his European travels, *Tōi taiko* (Kōdansha, 1990). *Yagate kanashiki gaikokugo* is another book in which the thought crops up repeatedly.

299 Interview 22 October 1994.

300 Kuhara, p.250. In personal correspondence of 27 November 2001, Murakami re-confirmed his lack of regret regarding the choices that he and Yōko had made, but pointed out, too, that the few brief public comments he has offered pertaining to this most personal of matters have been minimal responses to intrusive questioning.

301 "Karupatosu", in *Tōi taiko*, pp.401–2.

302 *Yagate*, p.133.

303 Murakami, *Andāguraundo* (Kōdansha, 1997), p.693; tr. p.198.

304 Buruma, p.67.

305 Buruma, p.68.

306 According to personal correspondence of 2 December 1997.

307 Interview with Murakami, 9 October 1993. The example of the small publisher's cringing approach is: "Uchi-nanka-ni kaite itadakenai deshōga . . ."

308 Personal correspondence, 27 November 2001.

309 *Yagate*, pp.10–14, 21–4, 37, 42; supplemented by information from Murakami and an interview with Elmer Luke on 4 August 1997.

310 *Yagate*, pp.272–3.

311 According to personal correspondence of 2 December 1997.

312 Interview with Alfred Birnbaum, 7 September 1997.

313 The title was in no way inspired by *A Wild Sheep Chase: Notes of a Little Philosophic Journey in Corsica*, translated [anonymously] from the French of Emile Bergerat (New York: Macmillan and Co., 1894). The Corsica connection must seem a great coincidence to readers of *The Wind-up Bird Chronicle*, though the title of the current French translation of *A Wild Sheep Chase* can hardly be a coincidence.

314 Personal correspondence of 8 September 2001.

315 Lewis Beale, "The Cool, Cynical Voice of Young Japan", *Los Angeles Times Magazine* (8 December 1991), p.38. *Yagate*, pp.227–8 on fashions.

316 *Yagate*, pp.118, 211–12.

317 *Yagate*, pp.232–3.

318 Murakami Haruki, *Wakai dokusha no tame no tanpen shōsetsu annai* (Bungei Shunjūsha, 1997), pp.19–20, 22, 241.

319 Buruma, p.70.

320 *Yagate*, p.14.

321 Murakami Haruki, *Kokkyō no minami, taiyō no nishi* (Kōdansha, 1992) [hereinafter, *Kokkyō no minami*], p.96; tr. p.72, UK tr. p.63.

322 *Kokkyō no minami*, pp.257, 268; cf. tr. pp.187, UK tr. p.165 ("But that reality was like nothing I'd ever seen before . . .), 196, UK tr. p.172 ("I would never see her again, except in memory").

323 *Kokkyō no minami*, pp.274, 275; tr. pp.200–1, UK tr. p.176.

324 *Kokkyō no minami*, p.262; tr. p.192, UK tr. p.169.

325 MHZ 2:215; tr. p. 167.

326 *Kokkyō no minami*, p.210; tr. p.155, UK tr. p.136.

327 *Kokkyō no minami*, pp.258, 279, 280; tr. pp.189, 203, 204, UK tr. pp.166, 178, 179.

328 MHZ 8:327; tr. p.327.

329 *Kokkyō no minami*, pp.270, 269; tr. pp.197, 196, UK tr. pp.173, 172.

330 *Kokkyō no minami*, p.282; tr. p.205, UK tr. p.180

331 The publishing date for Books One and Two was set on a Tuesday to commemorate the title of the original story, but the "Friday" was added to the date of Book Three with no special meaning, purely for consistency's sake.

332 *Sumerujakofu*, pp.148–9.

333 Kawai and Murakami, pp.12–13, 69–70, 74, 75.

334 Murakami has said that the marriage depicted in Sōseki Natsume's *Mon* (1910) was in the back of his mind when he was writing *The Wind-up Bird Chronicle*. Kawai and Murakami, p.84.

335 The Japanese is *"kichin-to"*. For *A Wild Sheep Chase*, see MHZ 2:215; tr. pp.167–8.

336 NK 2:6.99; tr. p.225. Cf. note 6 above for numbering discrepancies in paperback editions of the translation.

337 NK 2:18.331; tr. p.340.

338 NK 2:18.345; tr. p.327.

339 Kawai and Murakami, pp.196, 197, 81.

340 NK 2:9.153–4; tr. p.256.

341 Laura Miller, "The Outsider: The Salon Interview: Haruki Murakami", www.salonmagazine.com/books/int/1997/12/cov_si_16int3.html. Kobe reading observed by the author on 9 September 1995. See also "'Murakami Haruki ga suki' genshō no nazo", in *SPA!* (4 October 1995), p.22. Here, rather than saying he would be "too scared", Murakami said he would like to try it someday. I have added "visibly excited" from direct observation of the event.

342 The character is used on NK 1:3.63.

343 NK 1:2.43, 56, 57; tr. pp.24, 30, 30–1.

344 Once they have finished creating the land through sexual union, the male and female deities Izanagi and Izanami set to work bearing the deities that will live there. Giving birth to fire proves fatal for Izanami, however. Heartsick, Izanagi pursues his dead mate to the dark underworld, where she forbids him to look upon her. When he does look, however, he finds her infested with

maggots. He flees in horror and disgust, and as soon as he returns to the world he washes the corruption of death from his body. See *Kojiki*, tr. Donald L. Philippi (Tokyo: Univ. of Tokyo Press, 1968) for this founding myth of Japan.

345 NK 3:23.259; tr. pp.492–3.

346 NK 3:35.432; tr. p.577.

347 Kawai and Murakami, p.86.

348 Kawai and Murakami, pp.82–4.

349 Buruma, p.70.

350 While much attention was paid to designating the day of the week on which the volumes of the novel were published, by an incredible oversight, the dating of the action on the back of the title page was omitted from Book Three.

351 NK 1:1.23; tr. p.14.

352 MHZ 2:269; mod. tr. p.213.

353 Kawai and Murakami, p.59.

354 MHZ 3:13; tr. p.220.

355 MHZ 3:38–9; tr. pp.238–9.

356 Richard Lloyd Parry, "The Conversation: Haruki Murakami", in *Tokyo Journal* (August 1994), p.20.

357 NK 1:5.113; tr. p.62.

358 NK 3:33.397–8; tr. p.558.

359 NK 3:33.398; tr. p.558.

360 These are the chapter numbers in the published translation. Add two in each case for the numbers in the original.

361 NK 3:8.94; tr. p.389.

362 NK 3:10.117–18; tr. p.408.

363 NK 3:29.329–33; tr. pp.528–9.

364 MHZ 6:301, 304; tr. pp.208, 210, UK tr. pp.274, 277.

365 "Kusahara no naka no, tetsu no hakaba" in *Marco Polo* (September, October, November 1994): September, p.48. Cf. revised text in *Henkyō/Kinkyō* (Shinchōsha, 1998), pp.135–90. Alvin D. Coox, *Nomonhan: Japan Against Russia, 1939*, 2 vols. (Stanford: Stanford University Press, 1985).

366 *Marco Polo* (September 1994), p.48.

367 *Marco Polo* (October 1994), p.63; (November 1994), p.73.

368 *Marco Polo* (November 1994), p.79.

369 Buruma, p.70.

370 Kawai and Murakami, pp.155–65.

371 From interview with Eizō Matsumura, Tokyo, 8 September 1997.

372 Interview, 26 February 1994.

373 "The Man who Stank of Butter".

374 *"Sō da, Murakami-san ni kiite miyō"*, p.60.

375 Buruma, p.61.

376 See Murakami Haruki, "Waza-waza konna isogashii nenmatsu ni kuruma o nusumanakutatte ii darō ni", in *Uzumaki neko no mitsukekata* (Tokyo: Shinchōsha, 1996) pp.119–32.

377 Strecher produced an exceptionally lucid and readable study of Murakami, "Hidden Texts and Nostalgic Images: The Serious Social Critique of Murakami Haruki" (University of Washington, 1995). See the Bibliography for Strecher's subsequent insightful publications on Murakami, many of which contain revealing quotations from this wide-ranging interview.

378 Interview, 22 October 1994.

379 Interview, 10 September 1997.

380 *Yagate*, pp.278–9.

381 *Sumerujakofu*, Forum No. 357 (24 July 1999, 8.30 a.m.).

382 NK 2:62–9; tr. pp.208–11.

383 Thanks to Kenzaburō Ōe for having shared his speech manuscript with me. Another early critic of Murakami who may have relented somewhat is Donald Keene, the American scholar cited in Chapter 1. Professor Keene and his colleagues at the Donald Keene Center of Japanese Culture, Columbia University, awarded the 1999 Japan-United States Friendship Commission Prize to the translation of *The Wind-up Bird Chronicle*. The novel was also one of the eight finalists that year for the International IMPAC Dublin Literary Award, and has been made the subject of a one-volume guide for readers. See the Bibliography for Matthew Strecher's brilliant analysis of the book, its narrative structure, and reception.

384 Murakami Haruki, *Andāguraundo* (Kōdansha, 1997), pp.710–11, 714–15; mod. tr., pp.204–6.

385 *Andāguraundo*, p.686; tr. p.195.

386 According to personal correspondence of 24 July 2001. The Ashiya Public Library also makes a brief appearance in *Hear the Wind Sing*.

387 *Yakusoku-sareta basho de*, pp.262–68; tr. pp.306–9. The title derives from a phrase in Mark Strand's poem, "An Old Man Awake in his Own Death."

388 *Andāguraundo*, p.722; mod. tr. p.208.

389 *Andāguraundo*, pp.715, 716; tr. p.206.

390 *Andāguraundo*, p.720; tr. p.207.

391 *Yakusoku-sareta basho de*, pp.16–17; tr. p.215.

392 *Andāguraundo*, pp.701–4; tr. pp.201–2.

393 Howard W. French, "Seeing a Clash of Social Networks: A Japanese Writer Analyzes Terrorists and Their Victims", in *The New York Times* (15 October 2001), pp.E1, E5.

394 *Andāguraundo*, pp.704–5; tr. p.202–3.

395 Sakaguchi Ango, "Darakuron" ("On Decadence", 1946).

396 As beautifully parodied in Scene 19 of the 1979 film, *Monty Python's Life of Brian* when the hapless "messiah" shouts to the worshipping hordes, "You don't need to follow *me*. You don't *need* to follow *anybody*."

397 *Andāguraundo*, pp.693–705; tr. pp.198–203.

398 *Yakusoku-sareta basho de*, p.262; tr. p.306.

399 *Andāguraundo*, p.721; cf. tr. p.208.

400 *Sumerujakofu*, Forum No. 116, (12 July 1998).

401 *Rekishinton no yūrei* (Bungei Shunjūsha, 1996), p.9.

402 Personal correspondence of 25 August 2001.

403 *Rekishinton no yūrei*, pp.163–4; *Granta*, 61 (Spring 1998), p.229. See the complete translation on pp.229–42.

404 *Sumerujakofu*, pp.148–9.

405 Private correspondence of 12 January 2001.

406 *Supūtoniku no koibito* (Kōdansha, 1999), p.231; tr. p.172.

407 *Supūtoniku no koibito*, p.243; tr. p.181.

408 *Supūtoniku no koibito*, pp.141, 245, 182, 64, 102–11; tr. pp.106, 183, 137, 47, 75–82.

409 *Supūtoniku no koibito*, pp.55, 191, 194; tr. pp.41, 144, 146.

410 The question was sent at 11.21 a.m. on 7 June 1999 by a 25-year-old wife and mother. It can be found in "Dokusha & Murakami Haruki Forum No. 314", and abridged in "Murakami sakuhin ni tsuite 20". The latter is printed in the book section of *Sumerujakofu*, pp.152–3.

411 The immediate source of the title of the story "All God's Children Can Dance" is the jazz album *All God's Chillun Got Rhythm*, which itself is derived from the spiritual "I Got Shoes", with its line "All God's children got shoes". The literal meaning of the Japanese title is "All God's Children Dance". "Can" has been added for rhythm.

412 *Andāguraundo*, pp.99–100; tr. p.44.

413 *Kami no kodomotachi wa mina odoru* (Shinchōsha, 2000) [hereinafter abbreviated as *Kami no kodomotachi*], pp.34–7; tr. pp.18–19.

414 *Kami no kodomotachi*, p.45; UK tr. p.26.

415 *Kami no kodomotachi*, p.89; UK tr. p.56.

416 *Kami no kodomotachi*, pp.92–3; UK tr. p.59.

417 *Kami no kodomotachi*, p.121; tr. p.77.

418 According to personal correspondence of 24 July 2001.

419 The girlfriend in "All God's Children Can Dance" calls Yoshiya "*Kaeru-kun*", simply "Frog" plus "*-kun*", the untranslatable suffix conveying familiarity which we noted in *South of the Border, West of the Sun*. If that story had not been paired with the one on the giant frog, the nickname "Froggy" might have sufficed. In the later story, however, the great running gag of having the frog correct Katagiri each time he calls him "Mr Frog" ("*Kaeru-san*") required a less conspicuous translation for "*Kaeru-kun*". In the context of the story, a simple capitalized "Frog" quickly turns into a name in English, but the title of the story needed more. Attentive readers may notice that "Super-Frog" appears only in the title, but the term seemed the perfect link with the earlier story, which is how Yoshiya got his nickname in English.

420 *Kami no kodomotachi*, pp.139, 144–5; UK tr. pp.89, 93.

421 *Kami no kodomotachi*, p.154; UK tr. p.99.

422 *Kami no kodomotachi*, p.201; UK tr. p.132.

423 "The Man who Stank of Butter".

424 *Kami no kodomotachi*, pp.178, 177; UK tr. pp.116, 115.

425 Personal correspondence of 24 July 2001.

426 This is on the *obi*, or belt, wrapped around the base of the volume over the dust jacket of Murakami Haruki and Ōhashi Ayumi, *Murakami rajio*, a title taken from the web page, though the contents of the book were all originally serialized in a magazine (Magajin hausu, 2001).

427 The full title of this 1996 book of light essays on the Murakamis' life in Cambridge, Massachusetts, *How to Find a Twistercat* (*Uzumakineko no mitsukekata*), contains a comical variation on the sound of the expression "wind-up bird". See the Bibliography.

428 *"Sōda, Murakami-san ni kiite miyō"*, pp.22–3.

429 *"Sōda, Murakami-san ni kiite miyō"*, p.21.

430 Big Question No. 73, *"Sōda, Murakami-san ni kiite miyō"*, pp.60–1.

431 Murakami Haruki, *Sydney!* (20 January 2001, Bungei Shunjū Sha).

432 Personal correspondence of 8 September 2001.

433 Yukawa Yutaka and Koyama Tetsurō, "Murakami Haruki rongu intabyū: *Umibe no Kafuka* o kataru", *Bungakukai* (April 2003) [abbreviated hereinafter as RI], p. 12.

434 If the character Nakata was 9 in 1944 and is now "past 60" (1:86; tr. p.48), the present should be well past 1995; 19 May fell on a Monday in 1997 and not again until 2003.

435 Murakami Haruki, *Umibe no Kafuka* [abbreviated hereinafter as UK], Two volumes (Shinchōsha, 2002), 1:341–2; tr. p.209–10.

436 Ibid., 1:396; tr. p.243.

437 RI, pp.32, 33. For the remark on *Hard-boiled Wonderland and the End of the World*, see p.116 above. For the reference to "In The Penal Colony" in the novel, see UK 1:97; tr. p.57.

438 UK 2:155; tr. p.461.

439 UK 1:3; tr. p.vii.

440 Thanks to Kathy Lu for this excellent insight in her paper, "The Memory of Prophecy: Coming of Age in *Umibe no Kafka*" (22 January, 2003).

441 RI, p.35.

442 UK 2:429; tr. p.501.

443 UK 1:76; tr. p.43.

444 UK 2: 423; tr. p.498.

445 UK 1:132; tr. p.79.

446 UK 1:128; tr. p.76.

447 UK 1:137; tr. p.81.

448 UK 1:138; tr. p.82.

449 UK 1:141; tr. p.84.

450 UK 1:209; tr. p.126.

451 *Bartlett's Familiar Quotations* (Boston: Little, Brown and Company, 1992), p.684.

452 The rooms are described in very general terms. Cf. UK 1:6, 214–19; tr. p.viii, 129–32.

453 UK 1:216; tr. p.131.

454 UK 1:245–6; tr. 149.

455 UK 1:247; tr. p.150.

456 UK 1:254, 256; tr. p.155.

457 UK 2:192; tr. p.359. This speech of Colonel Sanders' is based on "Wealth and Poverty" ("Hinpuku-ron"), a story in Ueda Akinari's *Ugetsu monogatari*, translated by Leon Zolbrod as *Ugetsu Monogatari: Tales of Moonlight and Rain* (Vancouver: University of British Columbia Press, 1974), pp.194–203. RI, pp.11–12.

458 RI, p.30.

459 UK 2:293; tr. p.419.

460 UK 2:288; tr. p.417.

461 RI, p.21.

462 UK 2:181, 185; tr. p.354.

463 UK 1:373; 1:365–72.

464 UK 1:362.

465 RI, p.31.

466 Kawai Hayao and Murakami Haruki, "Kyōto de no taiwa: Part 1", in *Foresight* (October 2003), p.53.

467 Murakami Haruki, *Shōnen Kafuka* [abbreviated hereinafter as SK] (Shinchōsha, 2003), pp.479–82.

468 UK 1:309: tr. p.189.

469 SK, pp.198–9.

470 RI, p.36.

471 SK, p.496

472 Mail no. 006.

473 Mail no. 117.

474 J. D. Salinger, *The Catcher in the Rye* (New York: Bantam, 1964), p.1.

475 Shibata Motoyuki, "Osutā, Murakami Haruki, Sarinjā", *Shinchō* (October 2002), pp.312–15, esp.p.315.

476 Shibata Motoyuki, *Nine Interviews* (ALC, 2004). 11 July 2003 interview with Murakami, pp.258–91; see p.287.

477 Miura Masashi, *Murakami Haruki to Shibata Motoyuki no mō hitotsu no Amerika* (Shinshokan, 2003).

478 Shibata Motoyuki, *Nine Interviews*, p.259.

479 Ibid., pp.259, 263–4.

480 Personal correspondence of 12 August 2003.

481 "Sansha sanron: Murakami Haruki 25-nen," *Asahi Shinbun* (12 November 2004), p.13.

482 *Zō no shōmetsu* (Shinchōsha, 2005), p.24.

483 *Zō no shōmetsu*, pp.10, 11. Thanks to Gary Fisketjon for sharing his English original with me.

484 *Zō no shōmetsu*, p.13.

485 *Zō no shōmetsu*, pp.24–25.

486 Thanks to Professor Conlon for this report.

487 "The 1963/1982 Girl from Ipanema" was supposed to have been included in the

collection, but a problem with rights to the lyrics kept it out of both the Knopf and Harvill editions. See earlier editions of this book for a complete translation.

488 *Blind Willow, Sleeping Woman* (Knopf, 2006), pp.vii, viii–ix.

489 Ryūnosuke Akutagawa, *Rashōmon and Seventeen Other Stories*, tr. Jay Rubin (London and New York, 2006), pp.xxxiii–xxxiv.

490 See Shibata Motoyuki et. al., eds., *Sekai wa Murakami Haruki o dō yomu ka* (Bungei Shunjū, 2006).

491 *Blind Willow, Sleeping Woman*, pp.ix–x.

492 *Tōkyō kitan shū* (Shinchōsha, 2005), pp.9, 15-16; tr. p.p.235, 238.

493 *Tōkyō kitan shū*, p.42; tr. p.252.

494 *Tōkyō kitan shū*, p.76; tr. p.269.

495 *Tōkyō kitan shū*, pp.114, 115; tr. p.288.

496 *Tōkyō kitan shū*, p.123; tr. p.291.

497 *Tōkyō kitan shū*, p.147; tr. p.303.

498 Paul Auster's *Travels in the Scriptorium* (New York: Henry Holt, 2006), which appeared a few months before the English translation of *After Dark*, uses startlingly similar narrative tools.

499 *Afutādāku* (Kōdansha, 2004), pp.3–5; translated by Jay Rubin as *After Dark* (New York: Knopf, 2007), pp.3–4.

500 Ibid., pp.35, 36, 37, 38–39; tr. pp.24, 25, 26. Murakami does not follow his own "rules" scrupulously. For example, when describing Mari's reading of a thick book in Denny's, the narrator is careful to point out, "A bookstore wrapper hides the title from us" (p.6; tr. p.5), but in many subsequent passages, the same narrator is able to describe the thoughts and feelings of several different characters – things far beyond the scope of any camera, which can be said of "We note odors" (p.38; tr. p.26) as well.

501 Natsume Sōseki, "Bungei no tetsugakuteki kiso" (1907), in *Sōseki zenshū* (Iwanami shoten, 1995) 16:131, 132.

502 *Afutādāku*, pp.220–21; tr. p.146.

503 Ibid., p.221; tr. p.146.

504 Ibid., p.284; tr. p.188.

505 Ibid., pp.3–4; tr. p.3.

506 Ibid., pp.138–39; tr. p.92.

507 Ibid., p.269; tr. p.177.

508 Ibid., p.160; tr. pp.107–08.

509 Ibid., p.227; tr. p.151.

510 Ibid., p.256; tr. p.169.

511 Ibid., pp.261–2; tr. p.172.

512 Ibid., pp.137–38; tr. pp.91–92.

513 Ibid., pp.273–74; tr. pp.180–81.

514 Ibid., pp.265–66; tr. p.175.

515 Ibid., p.94; tr. p.63.

516 Ibid., p.72; tr. p.49.

517 Ibid., p.153; tr. pp.102–03.

518 Rebecca Suter, *The Japanization of Modernity: Murakami Haruki between Japan and the United States*. (Cambridge: The Harvard University Asia Center, 2008), pp.176–77, 179.

519 Ibid., p.162; tr. p.109.

520 Ibid., p.164; tr. p.110.

521 Ibid., p.219; tr. p.145.

522 Ibid., p.279; tr. p.184.

523 Ibid., p.280; tr. p.185.

524 Ibid., p.288; tr. p.191.

525 Ibid., p.35; tr. p.24.

526 Ibid., p.153; tr. pp.102–3.

527 Ibid., p.283; tr. p.188.

528 *Kami no kodomotachi wa mina odoru*, p.152; tr. p.135.

529 Interestingly, the German translation simply omits the difficult *shiten to naru* phrasing in the first and last instances, and in the middle case, it in effect goes with "ni naru": "Wir können uns aus unserem Körper lösen, ihn zurücklassen und zu einem ideellen *Blickpunkt* ohne Materie werden."

530 See Bibliography

531 Furukawa Hideo, "'Seichō' o mezashite, nashitsuzukete – Murakami Haruki intabyū," *Monkiibijinesu* (2009 Spring Vol. 5), pp.56–7. Translated by Ted Goossen as "Pursuing 'Growth'", in *Monkey Business: New Writing from Japan* (Volume 01, 2011), p.104. References below indicate only the English version.

532 Tetsuro Koyama, "Storyteller Murakami plumbs depth of the soul", interview in the online *Japan Times* for 16 April 2008.

533 Roland Kelts, *Japanamerica: How Japanese Pop Culture Has Invaded the U.S.* (New York: Palgrave Macmillan, 2006), quotes Murakami on the "stoicism" with which his lonely protagonists "survive a meaningless life strictly on [their] tastes in things, [their] styles" (p.158).

534 Furukawa, p.74.

535 "Novelist Murakami: Imagination leads to 'special room that lies within us'", *The Asahi Shimbun Asia & Japan Watch* (17 April 2012).

536 "Boku wa naze Erusaremu ni itta no ka," *Bungei Shunjū* (April 2009), pp.156–69, contains an interview on his acceptance of the prize and the text of the speech in both Murakami's Japanese and the "official" English translation. Other journals had rushed their own Japanese translations into print based on the English text Murakami delivered at the ceremony.

537 "The Novelist in Wartime", Salon.com (20 February 2009). See also "Boku wa naze Erusaremu ni itta no ka", pp.165-9 for the final paragraph, which is missing from the Salon text.

538 Matsuie Masashi, "Murakami Haruki rongu intabyū," *Kangaeru hito* (Summer 2010), p.97a–98b. "Boku wa naze Erusaremu ni itta no ka", p.160.

539 Translator's note: The phrase "Kaku ni tai suru" here suggests both nuclear power and nuclear weapons. The standard term for "nuclear" employed in the case of nuclear power is "genshi", Murakami intentionally employs the term

"kaku" more commonly associated with nuclear weapons here to suggest a link between the two technologies.

540 Murakami Haruki, tr. Emanuel Pastreich, "Speaking as an Unrealistic Dreamer", *The Asia-Pacific Journal* Vol 9, Issue 29 No 7, 18 July 2011.

541 As reported in the *New York Times* for 5 May 2012: "Last Reactor of 50 in Japan is Shut Down".

542 2012 figures according to the Murakami office, thanks to Yuki Katsura.

543 *"Kew"* is normally written *"kyū"*.

544 The title's *yon* changes to *yo* before *-nen*.

545 1:9.202; tr. p.110/1:124. References to the text take the form: Japanese book number:chapter number.page number; US translation first edition page number/ UK first edition volume number:page number. See bibliography for *1Q84* publication information.

546 Matsuie, pp.57a–58b.

547 1:10.222, 18.421–2, 20.458–60, 23.521, 2:6.141, 23.473; tr. pp.121–2, 236, 257, 291, 389, 575/1:136, 252–3, 274–5, 311, 413, 606.

548 1:10.222; tr. pp.121–2/1:136. See pp.245–6 above for the passage from *Underground*.

549 10.225; tr. p.123/1:138.

550 Japan Wikipedia, "Asahara Shōkō."

551 Matsuie, p.30c.

552 Shoko Asahara, *Supreme Initiation: An Empirical Spiritual Science for the Supreme Truth* (New York: AUM USA Co., Ltd., 1988), p.iv.

553 2:11.243–4; tr. pp.446–7/1:472.

554 George Orwell, *1984* (New York: A New American Library Signet Classic, 1949/1981), p.218.

555 2:11.249–50; tr. pp.449–50/1:475.

556 2:13.277, 3:11.219; tr. pp.465, 712/1:491, 2:135.

557 2:11.233; tr. p.440/1:466.

558 2:13.271–2; tr. pp.462–3/1:488–9.

559 1:19.437; tr. p.244/1:260.

560 1:12.264; tr. p.147/1:162.

561 1:18.422; tr. p.236/1:253.

562 1:18.447; tr. p.250/1:266.

563 The novel suggests at several points that the Little People live in the forest (2:2.59, 12.267, 3:9.181; tr. pp.341, 459, 690/1:362, 485, 2:111), but in an interview, Murakami visualized them as crawling up from underground, equating them with the Inklings of *Hard-Boiled Wonderland and the End of the World* and the central figure of the story, "The Little Green Monster". See Matsuie, p.45a.

564 1:17.385; tr. p.215/1:231.

565 2:11.242; tr. p.445/1:471.

566 Murakami has called this an *ikiryō* (living spirit) as seen in *Kafka on the Shore*. Matsuie, p.62a.

567 3:21.452; tr. pp.842–3/2:276.

568 3:14.270–2, 31.595–7; tr. pp.742–3, 921–2/2:168–9, 360–1.

569 3:30.576–8; tr. pp.910–11/2:348–9.

570 Cited in Chapter 6 above.

571 1:1.11; tr. p.3/1:11.

572 1:1.16; tr. p.6/1:14.

573 3:2.50; tr. p.617/2:35.

574 The possibility of her pregnancy is not raised until 3:8.156; tr. p.676/2:98.

575 1:5.120, 9.189, 3:11.219; tr. pp.62–3, 103, 712/1:74, 116, 2:135.

576 1:15.340; tr. p.190/1:207.

577 1Q84 has an in-joke reference to the flu epidemic on 2:16.349; tr. p.505/1:534.

578 2:4.91; tr. p.361/1:383.

579 1:3.62; tr. p.32/1:42.

580 Sam Anderson, "The Underground Man", *The New York Times Magazine* (23 October 2011), p.39. As we have seen, Murakami has derived plot material for some of his novels from his own stories – *Norwegian Wood* from "Firefly", *The Wind-Up Bird Chronicle* from "The Wind-Up Bird and Tuesday's Women", and *Hard-Boiled Wonderland and the End of the World* from "The Town and Its Uncertain Walls".

581 2:13.288; tr. p.471/1:498.

582 2:18.379–80; tr. p.521/1:552.

583 31.601; tr. p.924/2:363.

584 2:24.485; tr. p.582/1:614.

585 2:24.495; tr. pp.587–88/1:620.

586 2:19.421–2, 3:23.476; tr. pp.545, 855–6/1:577, 2:290–1.

587 3:26.533, 534; tr. pp.885, 886/2:322, 323.

588 3:27.542–3; tr. pp.890–1/2:328.

589 Orwell, p.229.

590 1:15.348; tr. p.194/1:211.

591 1:2.30–2; tr. pp.13–14/1:22–3.

592 2:10.206–7, 20.428; tr. pp.426, 549/1:452, 580.

593 1:13.295–6; tr. pp.164–5/1:180.

594 1:11.232–6; tr. pp.128–30/1:142–5.

595 Cf. the description of *1Q84*'s Ushikawa on page 330–1/1:350–1 (2:2.40) with that of *The Wind-Up Bird Chronicle*'s Ushikawa on p.427 of the paperback edition (3:14.153).

596 The following "Breakdown of a Murakami Novel", complete with pie chart, appeared on Facebook on 26 January 2012: "Bizarre dream sequences 16.67%, Ears 4.17%, Preparing food 12.50%, Cats 25.00%, Classical music 8.33%, Dissociative females 25.00%, Jazz music 8.33%."

597 1:9.203–4; tr. p.111/1:125.

598 Furukawa, p.104.

599 RI, p.41.

600 *The Elephant Vanishes*, p.53.

601 Furukawa, p.100.

602 Furukawa, p.102.

603 Matsuie, pp.69c, 76c.

604 Furukawa, pp.94–5 (slightly modified).

605 Furukawa, p.95.

606 "Reality A and Reality B," tr. Jay Rubin, *New York Times* (29 November 2010).

607 3:17.329; tr. p.775/2:204.

608 1:9.189; tr. p.102/1:115.

609 The notice appears, with slightly different wording, on the copyright page of the Harvill Secker British edition but not at all in the U.S. three-volume boxed paperback edition of 2012.

610 3:22.455; tr. p.844/2:278.

611 3:25.507–8; tr. p.872/2:308.

612 3:28.565; tr. p.904/2:341.

613 Matsuie, p.40a.

614 Matsuie, pp.30c–33b.

615 3:30.580; tr. p.912/2:350. The term here is *dohta*, defined below.

616 3:31.591–2; tr. p.919/2:358.

617 Matsuie, p.42b, 48c, 56ab.

618 2:19.396, 397, 418, 420, 6.123, 124–5; tr. pp.531–2, 543, 545, 380, 381/1:563, 575, 576, 403, 404.

619 For example, 1:19.446–7; tr. pp.249–50/1:266–7.

620 1:2.35; tr. p.16/1:25.

621 1:4.93, 2:24.494; tr. pp.48, 587/1:59, 620.

622 1:7.143–56; tr. pp.76–83/1:88–96.

623 3:17.341–2; tr. pp.781–2/2:211.

624 2:24.494–5; tr. p.587/1:620.

625 2:19.411; tr. p.539/1:570–1.

626 2:19.411–2; tr. p.540/1:571.

627 *Yume o miru tame ni maiasa boku wa mezameru no desu: Murakami Haruki intabyū–shū 1997–2009* (Bungei Shunjū-sha, 2010); *Murakami Haruki zatsubun-shū* (Shinchō sha, 2011).

628 Matsuie, pp.21c–22ab. Cited earlier in this chapter and in bibliography.

629 Matsuie, pp.46c–47b.

630 Matsuie, pp.75a, 61ab.

631 Matsuie, pp.36b, 36c, 37a.

632 Matsuie, pp.67c–68a.

633 Matsuie, pp.68c–69a.

634 Matsuie, pp.63c, 64a, 64c, 65a.

635 Matsuie, pp.78c–80c.

636 Furukawa, pp.98–9.

637 Matsuie, p.99a–c.

638 Personal correspondence of 13 August 2001.

639 This section of Appendix A is based on a talk I gave at the Deutsches Insitut für Japanstudien, Tokyo, on 30 January 2001: "How to Carve a Wind-up Bird:

Murakami Haruki in English". Both the talk and this chapter have benefited greatly from Irmela Hijiya-Kirschnereit, "Murakami Haruki o meguru bōken" ("A Wild Murakami Chase"), *Sekai* (January 2001), pp.193–9 and from e-mail correspondence with Ulrike Haak.

640 Hijiya-Kirschnereit, p.197.

641 Hijiya-Kirschnereit, pp.197–8. This passage is itself a re-translation of the German original via Hijiya-Kirschnereit's Japanese.

642 Hijiya-Kirschnereit, p.198.

643 NK 1:29; Bunkobon, 1:34; tr. p.17.

644 Hijiya-Kirschnereit, p.198.

645 Murakami Haruki and Shibata Motoyuki, *Hon'yaku yawa* (Bungei Shujūsha: Bunshun shinsho 129, 2000), pp.82–3. Murakami said virtually the same thing to me on the telephone on 30 January 2001.

646 Phone call, 30 January 2001.

647 *Hon'yaku yawa*, pp.84–5.

Index

461